The Grand Lodge Committee on Masonic Education
Grand Lodge of F. & A. M. of Pennsylvania
presents this Book to

Brother   RALPH SCOTT HALLMAN

For being raised to the
Sublime Degree of a Master Mason

R.W. Grand Master

THE MASTER BUILDERS

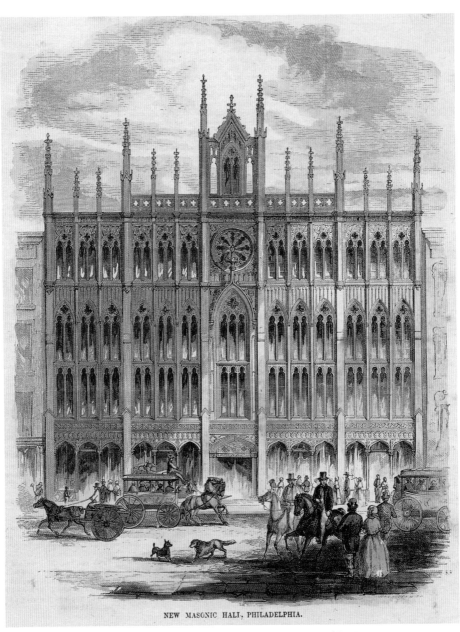

NEW MASONIC HALL, PHILADELPHIA.

The New Masonic Hall on Chestnut Street (1855-1873). From
Ballou's Pictorial Newspaper (Boston) October 13, 1855 (Grand Lodge
of Pennsylvania).

THE MASTER BUILDERS:

A History of the Grand Lodge of Free and Accepted Masons of Pennsylvania

Volume I: 1731–1873

Wayne A. Huss

PHILADELPHIA
GRAND LODGE F. & A.M. OF PENNSYLVANIA

Contents

Illustrations

Preface

It is with considerable pleasure and pride that I introduce *The Master Builders: A History of the Grand Lodge of Free and Accepted Masons of Pennsylvania*. The first volume covers the period from the origins of the Fraternity in 1731 to the dedication of the present Masonic Temple in Philadelphia in 1873. Volume II, to be published next year, will cover the period from 1874 to 1986. A third volume, consisting of portraits and biographies of all Past Grand Masters, will appear in 1988. These volumes are a unique and appropriate way of commemorating the two-hundredth anniversary of the independence of the Grand Lodge.

This history is the first comprehensive study of the Fraternity in Pennsylvania. The author, Wayne A. Huss, is a professional historian and a non-Mason. He earned his B.A. from Ursinus College in 1971, an M.A. from Villanova University in 1973, and a Ph.D. from Temple University in 1984. Dr. Huss also took extensive graduate work at the University of Virginia and is currently teaching American and European history at Villanova. The subject of Dr. Huss' dissertation was Pennsylvania Freemasonry, in which he analyzed the intellectual and social aspects of the Fraternity in the period before the outbreak of the Antimasonic era.

While he was researching his dissertation, the Grand Lodge became acquainted with Dr. Huss and observed the seriousness of purpose with which he pursued his topic. The result was impressive; and with the anniversary celebration approaching we decided to commission him to write the history. In choosing Dr. Huss as the author, we were motivated by a desire to have an objective, nonbiased and professional work, which would take a broad view of the Fraternity by placing it within the historical context in which it functioned. The finished product gives us complete satisfaction. Although scholarly and soundly based upon careful research, the history takes a narrative approach and is written in a readable style. The membership statistics that appear in the Appendices are a particularly valuable contribution to our knowledge. Buried in masses of dusty manuscripts and bulky ledger books, these statistics have never been compiled or studied before.

I congratulate Dr. Huss on his notable achievement and eagerly await the appearance of the next two volumes. I trust that the Fraternity as a whole, as well as the academic community and the general public, will greet this work with the attention it deserves and with the same enthusiasm that I feel.

Carl W. Stenberg, Jr.
R. W. Grand Master
September 26, 1986

Acknowledgments

In researching and writing this book, I have benefited from the cooperation and assistance of a number of people, and I wish to express my gratitude to some of them individually: to Carl W. Stenberg, Jr., R. W. Grand Master, for providing me with the opportunity and the financial assistance to continue my study of a fascinating subject; to Melvin S. Mundie, Assistant to the Grand Master, for permitting me complete access to all documents and records of the Grand Lodge and for providing me with the necessary computer technology, without which this work would not have been possible; to Frank W. Bobb, Librarian and Curator, for his absolute faith in my ability from the beginning and for his constant encouragement throughout the project; to Whitfield J. Bell, Jr., retired executive officer of the American Philosophical Society, for his careful reading of the several versions of the manuscript; to John H. Platt, Associate Librarian and Curator for coordinating the printing of the volume; to the members of the Grand Lodge History Committee for their support and guidance; and to my research assistants, Sarah J. Parker and Maureen Beary, for their diligent counting of members, Margo Szabunia, for working with Sarah and Maureen and for ferreting out all sorts of miscellaneous information to round out the study, and Norma Gourley and Patty Anderson, for their competent computer entry of membership data.

Wayne A. Huss
September, 1986

CHAPTER 1:

English Historical Background

The origins of Freemasonry cannot be determined with any degree of certainty. The historiography of the Craft contains many legends and unverifiable traditions which make it difficult to determine what is authentic. Older Masonic authors uncritically accepted many stories that more recent scholars consider questionable and unsupportable by the tests of modern scholarship. It is now believed, for example, that although modern Freemasonry shares many ideas with various institutions of the ancient world, this does not necessarily indicate any connection between them.[1]

Current scholarly opinion takes the position that the most likely antecedents of Freemasonry were the craft guilds of the British Isles, particularly of England, during the late Middle Ages. Associations of operative stonemasons are known to have existed in the last quarter of the fourteenth century, if not before. These organizations not only provided for the better regulation of their members and ensured the perpetuation of a high degree of technical skill, but also offered a sense of comradeship and mutual support. Trade secrets were passed on among the most highly skilled members; because of the general illiteracy of the time, this was done by word of mouth. Since masons were highly mobile, special signs of recognition were devised to enable a craftsman to gain acceptance among masons of other geographical areas and to obtain employment. Special information passed on by verbal instruction and secret signs of recognition are features that have been preserved in modern Freemasonry.[2]

In the late medieval period a number of other traditions were established and were later adopted by the Freemasons. For example, stonemasons worked out of, and stored their tools in, temporary structures on the work site, known as "lodges," which were clearly differentiated from the masons' living quarters. This designation was used by later Freemasons to identify their local organizations. Master masons were permitted the use of an individually registered "signature" or "Master's Mark," which they placed on their own work. One of the higher degrees in

1

contemporary York Rite Freemasonry, the "Mark Master," follows this practice.

The operative guilds also recognized the various levels of skill and acceptance within their profession by the terms "Apprentice," "Fellow," "Master" and "Warden." The term "cowan" was used to designate a worker of less skill who either was not a full member of the guild or did not possess the "Mason's Word," or secret occupational information. Such a worker thus did not enjoy complete recognition. This term had stronger negative meaning in later Freemasonry, indicating an outsider or uninitiated person who was to be avoided.

Of even greater interest is the derivation of the term "Freemason," which first began to be used about 1376. Masonic authorities do not agree on its real meaning, but several theories have been advocated. It may have derived from the more general term "Freeman," which was used in the late Middle Ages to designate a person who possessed certain degrees of personal liberty such as someone who was not a slave or a serf, or who was exempt from restrictive laws, taxes or guild regulations. Another view is that the word is a corruption of an original French term "frère maçon" (brother mason) in use among that country's medieval stonemasons' guilds.

The most generally accepted explanation, however, is based upon purely operative conditions. A "Freemason" was one who worked with a better-quality material known as freestone, a finely grained sandstone or limestone that was particularly suitable for carving and sculpturing. It served a decorative function and was used for door and window frames, vaulting and capitals. At first these particular workmen were called "Masons of Free Stone," then "Free Stone Masons" and finally "Freemasons." Therefore, a Freemason came to be known as an individual with special abilities that elevated him above the workers in rough stone, who were known as "hard hewers." The more numerous common workers were generally excluded from the special secrets and passwords of their more highly skilled associates.[3]

The earliest written record originating from the stonemasons' guilds dates from about 1390. It is the so-called Regius Manuscript and was the constitution of the Masons' Company of London, which had been formed about 1356. The tone of this document was moralistic and Trinitarian Christian. It was composed of six basic sections: (1) the legendary history of geometry, as masonry was called; (2) working rules for craftsmen; (3) ordinances regulating the annual assembly of English masons; (4) the legend of the four crowned martyrs, the patron saints of masons, executed by the emperor Diocletian; (5) duties to God and religion; and (6) rules of general etiquette.[4]

The Regius Manuscript became the model for more than a hundred other such documents pertaining to operative masonry in the late medieval and early modern periods. Known as the "Gothic Constitutions" or "Old Charges," these manuscripts were used in all parts of the British Isles, but with the heaviest concentration in northern England. They followed an established pattern although with individual variations.[5]

The Gothic Constitutions usually began with an invocation to the three elements of the Trinity, related the history of the development of the arts and sciences from Old Testament times to the supposed convocation of all English masons at York (circa 926), gave extensive rules of behavior for masons and provided for an oath of compliance, with a stress on secrecy. The same legends were repeated in these manuscripts, with the later ones being more elaborate than the earlier. They claimed that many illustrious historical personages had been patrons of masonry, such as Abraham, Nimrod, Moses, King David, Solomon, Nebuchadnezzar, Euclid, Augustus Caesar, St. Alban, Charles Martel, St. Dunstan and the Anglo-Saxon King Athelstan, among others. The authors of these documents hoped that an emphasis upon scriptural authority, mathematical and scientific exactitude and royal patronage would lend a greater air of respectability to the medieval stonemasons' guilds. These Old Charges reflected idealized contemporary religious, moral and ethical precepts, and they advocated a brotherhood of mutual helpfulness that would benefit the patron or owner of the structure being built as well as the craftsmen involved with it.

Unfortunately, additional information regarding the history of the English masonic guilds throughout the remainder of the medieval period is fragmentary. Such organizations probably either temporarily died out as the great age of cathedral building passed or were severely limited in their activities by unfavorable legislation. Two English statutes, one dating from 1360 and the other from 1425, specifically forbade the organization of masons in any form. The aim of this legislation, however, was the limiting of combinations of workers designed to force wages higher at a time of labor shortage rather than the specific extermination of the masonic societies. The Masons' Company of London may have revived briefly in the 1480s.

The record on English Freemasonry is silent thereafter until about the middle of the seventeenth century, when scattered references began to reappear. For example, Elias Ashmole (1617-1692), a prominent antiquarian and Fellow of the Royal Society, noted in his diary that he became a member of a lodge in Lancashire in 1646 and attended meetings of Freemasons in London in 1682. He also named other non-operative masons associated with the Society. In 1686 two histories of local English counties, Staffordshire and Wiltshire, included sections on the Fraternity and its practices. These works, the first by Dr. Robert Plot and the second by John Aubrey, praised the manners and morals of the Freemasons, offered a brief history of the organization, and mentioned ways in which persons could become members. The notable architect, Sir Christopher Wren (1632-1723), also may have been associated with the Freemasons in some way, although this connection is not certain.

By the end of the century English Freemasonry had become successful enough to arouse jealousy and suspicion. A leaflet appearing in London in 1698 condemned the organization as a "devilish sect of men," "anti-Christ," "evildoers," and "corrupt people." It warned "all godly people in the citie [sic] of London" against the "Mischiefs and Evil practiced in the sight of GOD by those called Freed [sic] Masons." The Society was also mentioned in a familiar tone in two issues of Richard Steele's *Tatler* in 1709 and 1710. Two operative masonic lodges are known to have been in existence in Northumberland and Yorkshire in approximately the same period.[6]

At least two dozen different documents pertaining to Masonic ritual from the late seventeenth and early eighteenth centuries have survived. These include catechisms, exposés, attacks and defenses, and dialogues. The documents were composed in an era of basic reorganization within Freemasonry, when it was being transformed from a society of working stonemasons ("operatives") to one composed primarily of men from other trades and professions ("accepted" Masons). At this time a substantive change in the direction of greater interest in history, symbolism and architecture occurred within Freemasonry.[7]

Some caution must be exercised when dealing with the earliest of these Masonic catechisms, especially those printed and sold for profit. Most claimed to be confessions of renegade Masons or compilations drawn from the papers of deceased Brethren. No authenticated ritual survives from this period since "officially" all such ritual was conducted verbally, and there is no way now to determine the extent of use of any particular form of the ritual. A careful comparison of the manuscript versions of these works with the printed ones yields a remarkable uniformity in basic format, and gives the impression that they all developed from some original text, now lost.

Insight into Masonic practices of this period can be gained from a survey of the contents of the earliest dozen or so of these catechisms.[8] Through a series of questions and answers, current members of a lodge determined whether a candidate for admission was already a Mason, how he was known to be one and where he was made one; also determined were the various signs and symbols of Freemasonry, the definition of a lodge, the functions of the officers, the Mason's Word and how it was given, and the text and form of the oath of secrecy. In addition, the proper physical postures and manner of greeting the appropriate officials were indicated. Only after the candidate had passed the test was he accepted by the use of the special Masonic handshake. This ritual presumed that the candidate had received some previous instruction in the Craft and that he held at least two of the three degrees. These early documents do not seem to be concerned with the novice's first exposure to Freemasonry.

These sources also offered lists of signs of recognition of the Freemasons. Some of these signs were simple, such as removing the hat with the thumb underneath and only two forefingers above the brim or making two soft knocks and one loud knock on a door before coming into a room, but others required considerable dexterity and could not have been performed with any degree of subtlety.[9]

Of special significance to Masonic ritual were lights, which symbolized knowledge or instruction, jewels worn around the officers' necks, which represented moral conduct, and King Solomon's Temple, which became the physical model for all lodges. The two pillars that upheld the porch of the building, called Jachin and Boaz, were symbolic of the permanence of truth, since they could not be destroyed by either fire or water. The Seven Liberal Sciences, which corresponded to the medieval academic trivium and quadrivium, supposedly were inscribed upon them.[10]

The oath of secrecy was especially serious. The candidate pledged upon the Bible and his immortal soul not to reveal any of the secrets he learned within a lodge to any living person, except a fellow Mason, or even to any inanimate object. He could not speak, write, or trace in sand or snow, or in any manner communicate what he knew, but had to keep Masonic secrets in a bone box locked by ivory keys; that is, in a firmly shut mouth. If a Mason violated his oath, he was subject to having his throat cut from ear to ear, his tongue ripped out, and being buried where no man could find his body. Needless to say, such threatened penalties evoked criticism and alarm among the uninitiated when they became widely known. They probably had only ceremonial significance, however; no record of ritualistic murders exists even though Masonic secrets began to be revealed almost as soon as they were devised.

The most important era in the history of English Freemasonry was from 1717 to 1723, when several dedicated individuals reorganized the Society, opened up membership more fully to non-operatives and infused the Fraternity with new motivation and character. This "revival" of Freemasonry, as it was called, occurred at a time when England was achieving stability after suffering political and religious disruptions in the seventeenth century. Political reorganization, however, was accompanied by widespread disintegration of morals. This was the age of the infamous "Hell-Fire Clubs," which ridiculed accepted religious beliefs and encouraged licentious personal behavior, especially among the aristocracy. To the founders of revived Freemasonry the familiar institutions of government, nobility and Church had failed notably to provide effective leadership in the re-establishment of traditional values. The Masons therefore sought to create a fundamentally new organization dedicated to stability, solidarity and, above all, moral regeneration.

The two chief founders of modern English Freemasonry were Drs. James Anderson (1684-1739) and John Theophilus Desaguliers (1683-1743). Both were influential Presbyterian clergymen and members of the Royal Society. As such they were in close touch with the scientific revolution and adhered to emerging Enlightenment ideas. In several published sermons Anderson espoused the cause of Protestant dissenters, but he is chiefly remembered for his compilations of royal genealogies. Desaguliers was a personal friend of Sir Isaac Newton and made notable contributions in various fields of natural philosophy. He lectured extensively throughout England and Holland and wrote numerous scientific papers and over a dozen books. Anderson wrote the first official treatise of the Society, called *The Constitutions of the Freemasons*, with the close cooperation of Desaguliers. In addition to spelling out the rules, regulations, procedures and doctrines of the new society, this work also contained a compilation of the various Old Charges of the medieval stonemasons and perpetuated the mythological history of the Craft, tracing its origins as far back as Adam.[11]

These men took advantage of the contemporary practice of joining voluntary associations and developed a system that combined convivial pleasures and good fellowship with seriousness of purpose. They saw in the old stonemasons' guilds potential for a society that could become an instrument for secular, scientific and social education. The existing lodges of operative masons could put forward a legitimate claim to a long and solid history going back to the days of medieval cathedral building, yet they remained socially acceptable institutions in their own day, having already admitted men from other professions.

Anderson and Desaguliers skillfully blended current scientific and rational religious ideas with the rhetoric of the building trade to explain effectively the Newtonian universe, which operated according to mathematically verifiable natural laws. This combination was strengthened by the infusion of traditional Christian morality and a large measure of mysticism. According to Masonic legend, the chief architect of King Solomon's Temple, Hiram Abiff of Tyre, was murdered by three cowans because he would not reveal to them the Master's Word. Later he was raised from the grave by associates who possessed secret knowledge concerning life and death. For the early Freemasons, the physical resurrection of Hiram Abiff represented the spiritual resurrection experienced by each individual Mason as he proceeded along the path to moral improvement and character development through three progressive stages of knowledge. The result of this process was the Mason's achievement of a well-ordered personal life, which reflected the regularity of the universe around him.[12]

Revived Freemasonry quickly became popular; it seemed to offer something for everyone. Intellectuals were attracted by rationalistic opinions, ecclesiastics and religious laymen approved of the preservation of traditional morality, and the nobility joined because they were looking for something new and exciting. Freemasonry offered mysterious and brilliant ceremonies, initiations and processions that inspired the imagination of participants, and promised them special knowledge and recognition.

The organization of revived Freemasonry centered around a newly created supervisory body called the "grand lodge." In late 1716 the four extant Masonic lodges in London and Westminster met together and set up the framework for unity by agreeing to reconvene officially on June 24, 1717, the feast of St. John the Baptist, to elect a Grand Master and other officers. In due course the Grand Lodge of England was established; it became known within the Fraternity as the "Premier" Grand Lodge. Membership in this body consisted of officers of subordinate lodges, who were required to meet four times a year in "quarterly communications."[13]

Among the four "original" lodges that founded the Grand Lodge, only No. 1 appears to have been composed primarily of actual stonemasons. It was mostly likely founded in the late seventeenth century in connection with the rebuilding of St. Paul's Cathedral after the disastrous fire of 1666. Although this lodge had only twenty-two members by 1723, it provided several Grand Lodge officers. The most important founding lodge, however, was No. 4, which was clearly aristocratic in composition. Of its seventy-one members in 1724, ten were titled noblemen, three were sons of peers, four were baronets and two were general officers. The majority of the remainder were listed as esquires, and there was a smattering of clerics and other intellectuals, including Anderson and Desaguliers. At the time of the establishment of the Grand Lodge of England, therefore, the majority of Freemasons were "accepted" rather than "operative."[14]

The first four Grand Masters, in office from 1717 to 1721, were also non-operatives. Little is known about the first, Anthony Sayer, except that he was listed as a "gentleman." George Paine, an antiquarian and a high-ranking official in the London Tax Office, was both the second and the fourth Grand Master; J. T. Desaguliers became the third Grand Master in 1719 as his influence began to be felt more strongly.

The desire of the Freemasons for social respectability can be seen in the election of the first Grand Master, who was only chosen until ". . .

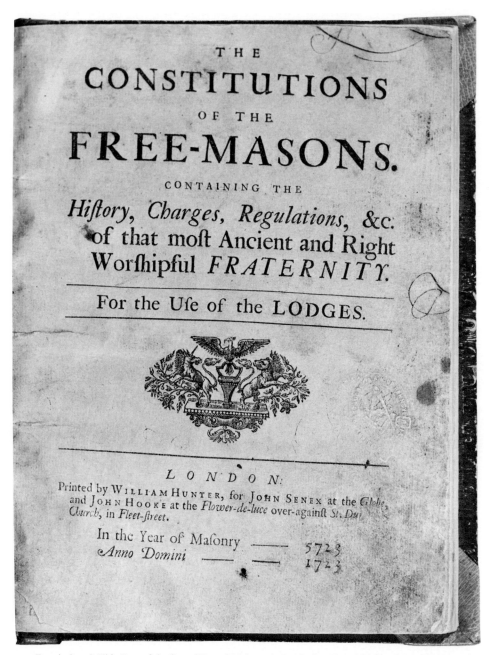

THE

CONSTITUTIONS

OF THE

FREE-MASONS.

CONTAINING THE

Hiſtory, Charges, Regulations, &c.
of that moſt Ancient and Right
Worſhipful *FRATERNITY.*

For the Uſe of the LODGES.

LONDON:
Printed by WILLIAM HUNTER, for JOHN SENEX at the *Globe,*
and JOHN HOOKE at the *Flower-de-luce* over-againſt *St. Dun*
Church, in *Fleet-ſtreet.*

In the Year of Maſonry ———— 5723
Anno Domini ———— ———— 1723

Frontispiece & Title Page of the first edition of Anderson's *Constitutions* (Grand Lodge of Pennsylvania).

they [the Masons] would have the Honour of a Noble Brother at their Head." Not until 1721 was a peer, John, Duke of Montague (1688?-1749), elected Grand Master, thus establishing a precedent that has been carried down to the present. English Freemasonry, therefore, gained the backing of the aristocracy, whose wealth, authority and connections helped to make the Society more secure.[15]

Not all Masons, however, wholly approved of the election of the Duke of Montague. A schism developed between two separate factions: convivial clubmen, only interested in having a good time, led by Philip, Duke of Wharton (1698-1731), and more intellectually oriented social architects, led by Montague. After a brief period when each faction elected its own Grand Master, the Masons worked out a compromise in 1722 whereby Wharton became Grand Master, with Desaguliers as Deputy Grand Master and Anderson as Grand Warden, the last two being members of the scientific camp. Wharton, who lasted in office less than a year, proved to be an unsatisfactory Freemason, and by his libertine behavior contributed to the fall of his faction. Thereafter, the reins of government passed out of the hands of the clubmen; neither did any operative mason ever again hold high Grand Lodge office.[16]

Masonic reorganization was strengthened by the publication of Anderson's *Constitutions* in 1723, and these two events set the stage for an impressive growth of "speculative" (philosophical and scientific) Freemasonry. Within two years, sixty-four subordinate lodges were established within the British Isles under the jurisdiction of the Grand Lodge of England; by 1732 the number had risen to more than a hundred. The English organization also spread to foreign countries through merchants, ship captains and military officers. By 1740 lodges were located in such far-flung regions as France, Spain, India, Bengal, Philadelphia, Boston, Savannah, Hamburg, Holland, Portugal, Italy, Sweden, New Hampshire, Switzerland, the West Indies, New York, Nova Scotia, Turkey, Poland and Russia. Separate grand lodges on the English model were also established in Ireland (1725), in Pennsylvania (1731), in Massachusetts (1733) and in Scotland (1736).[17]

As English Freemasonry grew in popularity, it came under increased public scrutiny and suspicion. Rival societies, such as the "Ancient and Noble Order of the Gormogons," "The Musical Society," the "Order of the Gregorians," the "Noble Order of Bucks" and the "Scald Miserable Masons," sprang up; these groups appropriated Masonic ritual and mocked Masonic ceremonies. Although these organizations ceased operations within a few years, they contributed to a lessening of public esteem of the Fraternity. Several prints by the famed satirist, William Hogarth, also expressed disapproval of Freemasonry.[18] In addition, some legitimate Masonic bodies refused to recognize the authority of the Grand Lodge of England and formed their own supervisory bodies. The most notable example was the Grand Lodge of York (1725-1740), which claimed control over Freemasonry in the north of England.

An exposé of Masonic secrets, the most extensive yet published, appeared in 1730. It was Samuel Prichard's *Masonry Dissected*. This work was so popular that it ran through three printings in eleven days and was reprinted at least thirty-five more times throughout the remainder of the eighteenth century. It contained a brief history of the legends of the Fraternity, the text of the ritual for all three degrees and a list of sixty-seven lodges working under the jurisdiction of the Grand Lodge of England. Prichard's exposé was so accurate that it caused considerable consternation among Masons. As a result, over the next decade the Grand Lodge restricted the rights of visiting Masons, tightened membership requirements and changed certain aspects of the ritual as well as the passwords.[19]

In 1738 the first in a series of papal bulls was issued condemning Freemasonry and forbidding Roman Catholics to become members on pain of excommunication. The Pope condemned the Fraternity because it accepted men from a variety of religions and sects under the pretense of natural religion, which was damaging to the purity of the doctrines of Roman Catholicism, a denomination that claimed to represent the only true faith. He also condemned the Society for its secrecy, which he thought was designed to protect it from legitimate investigation by civil and ecclesiastical authorities.[20]

Conflict between Freemasonry and the Roman Catholic Church remained one-sided throughout the subsequent history of the Fraternity. Masonic ritual and belief contained nothing in any way restrictive toward Roman Catholic membership or compromising to the religious ideas of individual believers. Many Roman Catholics did, in fact, join, and one, a wealthy Englishman by the name of Thomas Mayhew, even became Grand Master in 1767.

Papal disapproval carried little weight in the primarily Protestant country of England and her American colonies, but the continued development of Freemasonry in such countries as Spain, France and Italy attests to the widespread disregard of papal directives on this issue. Nonetheless, anti-Masonic activity took place in Holland, Portugal, France, Poland, Austria and in British North America in the eighteenth century.[21]

By the mid-1740s the central administration of English Freemasonry was faltering. Individual lodges increasingly followed their own versions of the ritual and refused to abide by the decisions of the Grand Lodge. From 1742 to 1752 forty-five English lodges, or one-third of the total, were dropped from the rolls because of insubordination. Grand Masters in this period were negligent and indifferent, and they tolerated frequent "irregular making" of Masons. The situation was serious enough to provoke a disparaging comment from the non-Masonic social commentator, Horace Walpole: "The Freemasons are in so low repute now in England. I believe nothing but a persecution could bring them into vogue again."[22]

Persecution from the outside did not revive the Fraternity, but internal disputes did. Beginning in 1751, for more than sixty years English Freemasonry was split into two rival camps: those supporting what they believed to be a more authentic ritual, who called themselves the "Ancients," and those who adhered to the current practices, known as the "Moderns." The conflict overflowed the boundaries of Great Britain and particularly affected the workings of Freemasonry in Pennsylvania and in other colonies.[23]

The leading protagonist of the "Ancient" reform was Laurence Dermott (1720-1791), an Irish Mason who had arrived in England in 1748. Although only a journeyman painter at the time, Dermott had managed to obtain an education above his station, and he ended his life as a successful wine merchant. He associated with other Irish Masons then residing in London, who, being essentially tradesmen and shopkeepers, grew dissatisfied with the Grand Lodge of England, which was dominated by aristocrats. Although the schism may well have had an underlying class bias, as well as a nationalistic one, the chief complaint of the dissenting Masons dealt with ritual.[24]

In July 1751 the representatives of six London lodges met in a Soho tavern to organize a rival grand lodge based upon ritual more in accordance with the "ancient usages." By February 1752 the number of rebel lodges had grown to nine. At that time Dermott was elected Grand Secretary, a post he held until 1771, when he became Deputy Grand Master. As an administrator, he displayed ability and energy, and he contributed greatly to the success of the "Ancients."[25]

Not until December 1753 did the "Ancients" choose a Grand Master. He was Robert Turner, Master of one of the subordinate lodges; his occupation is unknown. By that time the "Ancient" Grand Lodge had completed its organization: it had enacted various financial and governing resolutions, established a charity fund, worked out the process of warranting new lodges and established the proper ritual. Like the founders of the Premier Grand Lodge, Dermott quickly realized the need to obtain social recognition of the new organization. Toward that end he arranged to have the Earl of Blessington elected Grand Master in 1756. Thereafter the "Ancient" Grand Lodge, although originally founded by men of the working classes, was also graced with leaders from the aristocracy or the gentry. Evidence suggests, however, that the real power and daily operations resided among the lesser officers of more common background.

Laurence Dermott wrote the official textbook for the "Ancient" Grand

Lodge, which appeared in 1756 under the name of *Ahiman Rezon*. This Hebrew title caused considerable confusion among contemporary Masons, as well as among later Masonic scholars, but the meaning generally agreed upon is "a help to a brother." With regard to the general codes of conduct of Masons and basic membership requirements, the work closely followed previous Masonic constitutions produced by the "Moderns," although it defined these requirements more rigorously. The work also reflected a desire to restore more accurate ritualistic and administrative practices according to the Old Charges.[26]

Unfortunately, the *Ahiman Rezon* was marred by a discursive and cumbersome style. Dermott engaged in frequent, seemingly childish and often hyberbolic diatribes against his rivals, the "Moderns," for following what he considered unacceptable innovations in Masonic practice. Dermott hoped that ultimately reconciliation could be effected, but he died before the reunion of the two factions was accomplished.

The "Ancients" objected to many practices then in use by the original Grand Lodge, but none of these dealt with the essential matters of Freemasonry: the intellectual and moral tenets and the desire to remake society by ordering the lives of individual men. The principal distinctions between the two Grand Lodges can be summed up as follows:

1. Changes in the wording of the ritual and in the modes of recognition. In light of the published exposés, the original Grand Lodge changed the wording of the ritual for the three degrees as well as the passwords as a means of forestalling impostors. The "Ancients" believed that it was not in the power of any man or even of the Grand Lodge to change the wording that had been handed down from "time immemorial" as one of the "universal landmarks" of the Fraternity.

2. Observance of the feast days of St. John the Baptist (June 24) and St. John the Evangelist (December 27). The "Moderns" came to neglect these days when special celebrations were to be held and officers installed. Between 1730 and 1753 not one "Modern" Grand Master was installed on these days; instead, the "Moderns" met to suit the convenience of their leaders. The "Ancients" found this to be unacceptable.

3. The installation ceremony. For the "Ancients" the installation of officers was both formal and secret and it had to be observed properly and to the letter. Some "Moderns" did without it or treated it with only limited respect.

4. Recognition of the Royal Arch Degree. This additional degree, developed before 1750, was usually appended to the third degree. The "Ancients" considered it an essential completion of a Mason's education and devised a special ritual to present it. The "Moderns" officially refused to sanction the degree but did not object when it was, in fact, conferred.

5. Neglect of catechisms attached to each degree. The "Ancients"

insisted that a specific statement of belief be associated with each degree to better educate the candidate. The "Moderns" often dispensed with this in their haste to initiate as many Masons as possible.[27]

In addition, the "Ancients" and "Moderns" disagreed upon the time of stated meetings (the "Ancients" were more strict); the use of the Grand Lodge seal (the "Ancients" gave it more importance); the issuance of a Grand Lodge Certificate to Masons in good standing on leaving their present jurisidiction (the "Ancients" wished to issue them, the "Moderns" did not); the keeping of a register of members' names (the "Moderns" neglected to do this); the compiling of more complete and accurate records (favored by the "Ancients"); the right of Past Masters to sit in Grand Lodge (the "Moderns" did not permit this); the functions and privileges of minor Grand Lodge officers such as Deacons and Stewards; and the placing of certain lodge paraphernalia while the lodge was in session. These points of dispute were considerable and had developed over the course of time. In essence, the "Ancients," although technically rebels, were stricter in their observance and more conservative in their practices. They wished to restore the ancient purity of the Society to offset what they believed to be the indifference and laziness of the "Moderns," who accepted many variations and innovations.

The "Ancients" also offered their members more thorough instruction in the ways and meanings of the Craft than did their "Modern" counterparts. According to Dermott, his followers were in possession of more Masonic knowledge than his competitors since "Ancients" knew enough to follow the "Modern" ritual, but not the other way around.

Although it enjoyed healthy growth, "Ancient" Freemasonry initially proved to be only moderately successful compared to the advances made by its "Modern" rival. By 1771, for example, the "Ancient" Grand Lodge had warranted seventy-four lodges in London, eighty-three country lodges and forty-three overseas lodges, whereas the "Moderns" had under their jurisdiction one hundred fifty seven lodges in London, one hundred sixty-four lodges in the country and one hundred overseas lodges. The "Ancient" system was more prevalent in the North American colonies, however, where forty-nine military lodges were warranted during the French and Indian War. The "Ancient" Grand Lodge gained considerable prestige by receiving official recognition by the Grand Lodges of Ireland and Scotland, which preferred it to the Premier Grand Lodge of England.[28]

Despite occasional bitterness caused by members of one society attempting to visit a lodge meeting of the other, relations between the opposing grand lodges remained essentially cordial and they improved throughout the remainder of the eighteenth century. Members of both jurisdictions often walked together in public processions and attended joint church services during Masonic festivals in London.

By the turn of the nineteenth century a new generation of Masons in both camps began to make serious moves toward reconciliation, although the initiative came from the "Ancients." By that time the dispute had become technical and remained a matter for experts. The majority of Masons agreed on the basic principles of the Fraternity; they did not fully understand, or care to understand, the original reason for the division.

Reunion was facilitated because royal brothers, sons of George III, were at the same time leaders of the two factions. Edward, Duke of Kent, was the Grand Master of the "Ancients," while Augustus, Duke of Sussex, headed the "Moderns." After negotiations lasting several years, a final agreement was officially approved by both sides and was signed and sealed on November 25, 1813.

The agreement consisted of seventeen articles and represented a clear victory for the "Ancients." At least six major points of contention were resolved in their favor: (1) the "Modern" Grand Lodge acknowledged that it had deviated from the old forms and agreed to return to them; (2) oaths of obligation, the ritual and the ceremonies as practiced by the "Ancients" were, in essence, adopted; (3) the "Ancient" practice of admitting Past Masters to seats in the Grand Lodge was adopted with only slight modifications; (4) the Royal Arch Degree was accepted as a legitimate completion of the third degree; (5) all past officers of the "Ancients" were accorded equal seniority to those of the "Moderns;" and (6) the name adopted by the new organization, "The United Grand Lodge of Ancient Freemasons of England," contained the appellation "Ancient." In addition, the first "Ancient" lodge was placed first on the roll of the new Grand Lodge when the subordinate lodges of both camps had drawn lots to determine precedence. All former "Ancient" lodges then received odd numbers and the "Moderns" even ones. In exchange, the "Ancients" agreed to abandon their book of constitutions, the *Ahiman Rezon,* and to accept as Grand Master the Duke of Sussex, with the Duke of Kent as Deputy Grand Master.[29]

At the time of reunion the United Grand Lodge of England had on its rolls six hundred forty-seven subordinate lodges. For a variety of reasons it had to strike off two hundred sixty-one others that were warranted in the period of division, including thirty-seven that had come under the jurisdiction of American grand lodges. Thereafter, the history of English Freemasonry was untroubled by any serious internal disputes, and the Fraternity flourished in an atmosphere of public acceptance and royal patronage.

CHAPTER 2:

"Modern" Freemasonry in Pennsylvania, 1727–1761

Pennsylvania was one of the three British North American colonies in which Freemasonry was first "officially" established. On June 5, 1730, the Grand Lodge of England under the leadership of the Duke of Norfolk issued a deputation to Daniel Coxe, a prominent West Jersey proprietor, appointing him Provincial Grand Master of the provinces of New York, New Jersey and Pennsylvania. This document gave Coxe the power to select a Deputy Grand Master and Grand Wardens and to warrant subordinate lodges for a space of two years beginning the next St. John's Day (June 24). It also authorized the "regular making" of Masons according to procedures outlined in *The Book of Constitutions* and specified a number of regulations pertaining to the operation of a provincial grand lodge. The deputation required that a Provincial Grand Master be elected every two years, that returns of members' names be made on a regular basis, that a charity fund be established and that the feast days of Freemasonry, St. John the Baptist's Day and St. John the Evangelist's Day, be celebrated annually.[1]

Colonel Daniel Coxe (1673-1739) was the son of Dr. Daniel Coxe, a Fellow of the Royal Society and personal physician to Charles II and Queen Anne. The younger Coxe arrived in America in 1702 as an aide to Lord Cornbury, governor of New York. He became a leading spokesman of the Anti-Proprietary (Anti-Quaker) Party of West Jersey and held numerous high political offices throughout his career. A devout Anglican, Coxe was a founder of St. Mary's Episcopal Church in Burlington (1709), where his own estate was located. In 1716 Coxe was elected to the New Jersey Assembly and became its speaker. His position on the West Jersey Council of Proprietors (1723) was enhanced by his promotion, eleven years later, to justice of the Supreme Court. At the time of his death, Coxe was the third-largest landowner in West Jersey.

The several references in the Coxe Deputation to "the Brethren now residing" in the stated provinces indicate that one or more lodges were already meeting and were in need of official recognition. Although these bodies, about which next to nothing is known, probably met according to Masonic custom as "time immemorial" lodges, they must have been recognized as "regular" by the Grand Lodge of England; otherwise, the petition of their members would not have been honored by the issuing of the deputation. One Philadelphia lodge, St. John's, is known to have been in operation as early as 1727, the date of its surviving constitution. At this time the *Pennsylvania Gazette* frequently carried news of Masonic events in England; this seems to indicate the presence of Masons in Pennsylvania who were interested in such news.[2]

The most important early published reference to Pennsylvania Freemasonry appeared in the *Pennsylvania Gazette* of December 8, 1730, in which the editor, Benjamin Franklin, wrote:

> As there are several Lodges of FREE-MASONS erected in this Province, and People have lately been much amus'd with Conjectures concerning them; we think the following Account of Free-Masonry from London will not be unacceptable to our Readers.[3]

This is the earliest concrete evidence of actual working lodges in Pennsylvania or, indeed, in any of the colonies.

In the same issue Franklin published the first American exposé of the ritual of the Fraternity. Quoting London authorities, which used the familiar technique of asserting that they had discovered the account of Masonic secrets among the private papers of a deceased Brother, Franklin poked fun at the Society by saying that its great secret was that there was no secret at all and that members, once initiated, had to keep up the jest. The whole ritual struck this critic as "childish and ridiculous." Whether the published London account was authentic, Franklin referred the reader to the future conduct of the Brotherhood: ". . . if they ridicule it, or look very grave upon it, or if they are very angry and endeavor to decry it, he may be satisfied it is the real Truth."[4]

Given Franklin's character and his inquiring nature, his publication of this exposé may not have been merely the objective reporting of foreign news. If his purpose had been to gain the attention of the Fraternity, as was probable, it certainly worked. A few months later, in February of 1730/31, Franklin himself became a Freemason, and he quickly rose to a position of leadership within the organization.[5] Thereafter, references to the activities of the Fraternity in the *Pennsylvania Gazette* were official and respectful. A case in point was Franklin's reprinting of a positive description of the Society from Chambers' *Dictionary* in May 1731. This described Masons as men of high character and some social standing and praised the organization as "truly good and laudable, as it tends to promote Friendship, Society, mutual Assistance, and Good Fellowship." From 1732 to 1738, and once in 1741, notices of the elections of Grand Lodge officers appeared in Franklin's paper, as well as much news of European Freemasonry.[6]

Within a year of the Coxe Deputation Masonic activity was well under way in Pennsylvania, although no solid evidence indicates that Coxe himself was responsible for it. Whereas several modern Masonic historians discount Coxe's role in the execution of his commission, the leading student of the period, Henry S. Borneman, argues that the organization of Pennsylvania Freemasonry did, in fact, meet with Coxe's approval, if not his personal involvement.[7]

Although Coxe was honored at special ceremonies held by the Grand Lodge of England on January 29, 1730/31, no mention was then made of what, if anything, he had done to encourage Freemasonry in the colonies. On that occasion Coxe was referred to as the "Provincial Grand Master for North America," a title suggesting that his authority had been extended from its original limits of New York, New Jersey and Pennsylvania. It seems unlikely that special attention would have been paid to an individual who had not made valuable contributions to the Fraternity. Coxe returned to Burlington later in 1731 and remained active in provincial affairs until his death eight years later, but no further evidence of his connection with Freemasonry exists. Although Coxe was a member of Lodge No. 8, Devil's Tavern, London, he is not known to have been affiliated with any American lodge. His death notice in the *Pennsylvania Gazette* did not mention that he was a Mason, but this omission may be explained by the low profile maintained by Pennsylvania Freemasons at that time because of recently generated anti-Masonic feeling.[8]

Evidence indicates that the Grand Lodge of Pennsylvania was meeting in Philadelphia as early as June 24, 1731, with William Allen, a prominent merchant and attorney, as Grand Master. No one is certain, however, how this body was established. If Coxe authorized it, it should more properly be referred to as a "Provincial" Grand Lodge, but if organized without the specific approval of the representative of the Grand Lodge of England, which is also possible, it should be termed an "Independent" Grand Lodge.[9]

Under the terms of his deputation Daniel Coxe was empowered to act only from June 24, 1730 to June 24, 1732. After that date it was not necessary for Pennsylvania Masons to petition for another Provincial Grand Master because the document specifically gave them the authority to act on their own:

> . . . after which time It is Our Will and Pleasure and We Do hereby ordain that [Masons] in all or any of the said Provinces, Shall and they are hereby

Impowered every other year on the feast of St. John the Baptist to elect a
Provincial Grand Master who shall have the power of nominating and
appointing his Deputy Grand Master and Grand Wardens and We do
hereby Impower our said [officers] . . . for Us and in our place & Stead to
Constitute the Brethren . . . into one or more regular Lodge or Lodges as
they shall think fit, and as occasion shall require.[10]

No other deputation issued by the Grand Lodge of England to an
American provincial grand lodge conferred such a large measure of
authority. In Pennsylvania, Grand Lodge officers could be chosen by the
members without the specific prior approval of the English Grand Lodge.
Accordingly, on June 24, 1732, when Coxe's term of office had expired,
William Allen was elected (re-elected?) as Provincial Grand Master of
Pennsylvania. Whether he was appointed by Coxe or elected by the
Brethren one year earlier is of little significance. Either way, the authority
of the Grand Lodge of Pennsylvania to act rested on a secure foundation.

St. John's Lodge and the Grand Lodge that issued from it antedated
by at least two years any other lodge on record in the American colonies.
These organizations were established within the first Masonic district,
comprising New York, New Jersey and Pennsylvania, as officially recognized by the Grand Lodge of England. The Grand Lodge of Pennsylvania was thus the third oldest Masonic supervisory body in the world,
antedated only by the Grand Lodges of England (1717) and Ireland
(1725).[11]

The authority of the Pennsylvania Grand Lodge was a source of
uncertainty among contemporary Masons, however. In April 1733 the
Grand Lodge of England issued another deputation, this time to Henry
Price, a Boston merchant; the document named Price Provincial Grand
Master of New England.[12] Unlike Coxe, who may or may not have
warranted subordinate lodges, Price acted quickly, establishing the first
Boston lodge by the end of July of the same year. Subsequently he played
a prominent role in New England Freemasonry and served as Provincial
Grand Master a total of four terms.

Although Price's deputation limited his authority to New England,
some American Masons came to believe that it had been extended by the
Grand Master, the Earl of Crawford, to include all of North America.[13]
If such indeed had been true, it would have been necessary for the
Pennsylvania Grand Lodge to apply to the Massachusetts Grand Lodge
for a charter to reaffirm its status, because the former would then have
been subordinate to the latter. Accordingly, on November 28, 1734, Benjamin Franklin, then the Grand Master of Pennsylvania, wrote officially
to Henry Price concerning this matter. Franklin explained that he had
read in various newspaper accounts that Price's authority had been ex-

tended. After congratulating Price on what he hoped to be true, Franklin inquired why the Grand Lodge of Pennsylvania had not been properly notified of this important development. He went on to request a charter "in order to promote and strengthen the interest of Masonry in this Province which seems to want the sanction of some authority derived from home, to give the proceedings and determination of our Lodge their due weight." This statement hinted at some difficulty within Pennsylvania Freemasonry that added prestige would remedy.

Although showing due regard to one who might be his superior, Franklin made it clear that he wished the authority of his Grand Lodge to remain supreme within Pennsylvania, with the Grand Master ". . . only yielding his chair when the Grand Master of All America shall be in his place." He wanted Price to reconfirm the privileges of the Brethren, who now had the right to hold a Grand Lodge, to choose their officers and to "manage all affairs . . . here with full power and authority." It seems that Franklin remained uncertain of Price's authority because he requested official copies of both the original deputation and its augmentation.[14]

In a personal letter to Price of the same date, Franklin spelled out more clearly the specific problem in Pennsylvania:

> I beg leave . . . to inform you that some false and rebel brethren, who are foreigners, being about to set up a distinct Lodge in opposition to the old and true Brethren here, pretending to make Masons for a bowl of punch, and the Craft is like to come into disesteem among us unless the true Brethren are countenanced and distinguised by some such special authority being desired.[15]

The irregular proceedings complained of by Franklin were a common problem in eighteenth-century Freemasonry. Renegade Masons would hold a special dinner and "make" Masons unofficially for a fee, which they then pocketed. They had little concern for the character of the men they "initiated," and this factor contributed to a negative public reaction to the Fraternity. The tone of Franklin's letters was urgent and expressed his desire to make regular the Masonic system in America.

The newspaper accounts to which Franklin referred in his first letter have not been identified, but another one, printed in the *American Weekly Mercury* in March 1735, referred to a meeting of the Grand Lodge of Massachusetts in which Henry Price appointed the appropriate Masonic officials for Massachusetts and also confirmed Franklin's appointment as Provincial Grand Master for Pennsylvania. No surviving evidence indicates that Franklin received proof of Price's extended authority or that he accepted his appointment by Price; therefore one cannot be certain whether either event occurred. In any case, unless notified to the contrary

by the Grand Lodge of England, the Pennsylvania Grand Lodge constituted a separate and independent jurisdiction; its authority needed no
confirmation by the Massachusetts Grand Lodge, which was only its equal,
not its superior. Franklin had been duly elected to his position by the
Pennsylvania Brethren according to the provisions of the Coxe Deputation and he should have felt secure in holding it.[16]

The Grand Master of England did not appoint a (another?) Provincial Grand Master for North America until September 23, 1743. He was
Thomas Oxnard, a prosperous Boston merchant, who was given full
authority over Freemasonry in the colonies. On July 10, 1749, Oxnard
appointed, or, more correctly, reconfirmed, Franklin as Provincial Grand
Master of Pennsylvania.

Evidently William Allen, former Provincial Grand Master of Pennsylvania, was dissatisfied with Franklin's leadership, and he questioned
the extent of Thomas Oxnard's jurisdiction. Allen believed the Grand
Lodge of Pennsylvania was an independent organization, answerable only
to England. Marshaling his considerable legal skills, Allen appealed over
the head of Oxnard directly to the Grand Master of England, Lord
Byron, who on March 13, 1749/50 reappointed Allen to his former position. Franklin accepted the subordinate position of Deputy Grand Master, and the other Grand Officers were reconfirmed. Thereafter, William
Allen remained Provincial Grand Master of Pennsylvania until the dis-
solution of the "Modern" Grand Lodge sometime after 1761. This action
on the part of the Grand Lodge of England indicated that it accepted
Pennsylvania's claims to self-government and supremacy as legitimate.
The original source of this authority could only be the Coxe Deputation
of 1730. Members of the Grand Lodge of Massachusetts protested this
restriction of Oxnard's jurisdiction, but the English Grand Lodge took
no action on their "Humble Remonstrance," and allowed Allen's appointment to stand.[17]

In its monthly operations the Pennsylvania Grand Lodge was apparently self-regulating until 1734, when Benjamin Franklin issued a reprint
of Anderson's *Constitutions*. This edition had official approval from England as its title page indicates: "Reprinted by special Order [of the
English Grand Lodge], for the Use of the Brethren in North America."
It was advertised in the *Pennsylvania Gazette* on May 9, 1734. This work
superseded an earlier constitution, known as the Thomas Carmick Manuscript, which had been used by St. John's lodge since at least 1727.
Although presenting the legendary history of Freemasonry and containing membership requirements, codes of conduct for Masons and the
layout of a lodge room, the Carmick Manuscript did not offer rules and
regulations for the operations of a grand lodge, which were needed if
the Pennsylvania body was to be properly governed.[18]

Anderson's work filled this need. It spelled out thirty-four regulations concerning the Grand Lodge and its functioning. They dealt with such matters as the composition of the Grand Lodge, membership qualifications, duties and elections of officers, procedures for forming new lodges, precedence at official functions, filling of positions pro tempore, keeping of records, provisions for the annual feast, and guidelines for the handling of charity funds. In addition, it included a comprehensive, but largely imaginary, history of the Society from Old Testament times to the present, rules of behavior for Masons, and several Masonic songs.[19]

The membership of the Grand Lodge was composed of the Masters and Wardens of all subordinate lodges, each of whom had one vote. All Masonic matters were to be decided in democratic fashion by majority vote. The Grand Lodge was required to meet four times a year, the most important of these meetings being the annual feast held on St. John the Baptist's Day (June 24), primarily to hold elections and to pass new legislation.

To qualify for Grand Lodge office an individual had to work his way up through the ranks by serving first as a Warden and then as a Master of a subordinate lodge. He could then serve as a Grand Warden and finally as Grand Master. In addition to experience, Anderson noted other desirable traits of a Grand Master:

> [He] . . . is also to be nobly born, or a Gentleman of the best Fashion, or some eminent Scholar, or some curious Architect, or other Artist, descended of honest Parents, and who is of singular great Merit in the Opinion of the Lodges.[20]

This statement would seem to give weight to the later charge of the "Ancients" that the Premier English Grand Lodge and its American offspring were aristocratic and elitist in orientation.

The Grand Master was the most important officer. He nominated the other officers, presided over the functions of all lodges whenever he was present, granted dispensations for the formation of new lodges, heard appeals from individual Brethren, called emergency lodges at his discretion, and visited each subordinate lodge at least once during his term of office. He had two votes in all the business of the Grand Lodge. He could be approached only through his deputy, who worked closely with him and with the Grand Wardens on any business of the Fraternity. In the interest of efficiency, the Grand Lodge could grant the Grand Master the right to rule without holding a vote. No provisions were made for the removal of a Grand Master because none to date had abused his office.

Although seemingly comprehensive, Anderson's *Constitutions* did permit the Fraternity to adjust to changing conditions. The Grand Lodge had the unlimited right to make new regulations from time to time or to alter existing ones as it saw fit. The only limitation was that such changes were to be "for the real Benefit of this Ancient Fraternity: Provided always that the old LANDMARKS be carefully preserv'd." In the absence of minutes of the Pennsylvania Grand Lodge from this period, it cannot be determined which of these regulations were followed and which altered. Given the official nature of Franklin's reprint, however, it is probable that most of them were adhered to closely.[21]

*   *   *   *   *   *   *   *

Within a few years of its debut, Pennsylvania Freemasonry suffered serious attacks from outsiders. In June 1737 an outburst of anti-Masonic sentiment, the first in the Colonies, occurred in Philadelphia. An apothecary by the name of Evan Jones, along with two accomplices, perpetrated a hoax mocking the Society that resulted in the death of Dr. Jones' apprentice, David Rees. A coroner's inquest acquitted the participants of murder, but it recommended indictments on charges of manslaughter.

Dr. Jones and his associates were tried in January 1737/8, at which time the full details of the incident became known. Rees had expressed a desire to be initiated into the mysteries of Freemasonry and looked to his master, Dr. Jones, for answers. Not being a Mason himself, Jones concocted an absurd ritual that had nothing to do with authentic Masonic practices. After harmlessly passing Rees through the first two "degrees," Jones submitted him to more intimidating ceremonies for a "higher" rank. He made his apprentice believe it was necessary to raise the Devil, which he proceeded to do by the use of blasphemous invocations, acknowledging the power of, and expressing faithful allegiance to, Satan. After forcing Rees to drink a powerful purgative, which weakened him, Jones conducted him blindfolded into his cellar where he lit a "pan of spiritous liquors" to persuade the boy that the fires of Hell were before him. When Rees expressed no fear of the flames after the blindfold was taken off, Jones tossed the burning liquid on him in a final attempt to scare him. Rees died three days later of severe burns.

The jury returned a verdict of guilty against Dr. Jones, who was punished by branding in the hand. Of Jones' two accomplices, who were arraigned at the same time, one was found guilty but pardoned, and the other was acquitted.

The Jones-Rees incident caused a furor in colonial Philadelphia and all sorts of accusations were leveled against the Fraternity. Andrew Bradford, editor of the *American Weekly Mercury*, took the lead in the anti-Masonic agitation. He accused his professional rival, Franklin, of complicity in the affair and claimed to have proof. This prompted Franklin to print a defense in his *Pennsylvania Gazette*. Bradford countered with additional charges, but Franklin did not respond since his name had been cleared. Bradford also charged that a band of Negro thieves, then operating in Philadelphia, was actually a lodge of Freemasons.[22] News of these events reached Boston and caused concern among Franklin's relatives there. In a letter to his parents, dated April 13, 1738, Franklin assured them of his innocence and praised his fellow Freemasons: "They are in general a very harmless sort of People; and have no principles or Practices that are inconsistent with Religion or good Manners."[23]

Because of the numerous rumors in circulation concerning the Fraternity, the Grand Lodge of Pennsylvania felt obliged to publicly disavow all connection with the Jones-Rees incident. In Franklin's *Gazette* the Grand Lodge officers expressed their abhorence of the "horrid and diabolical rites" that caused the death of the "unsuspecting youth" by the use of "Purging, Vomiting, Burning and Terror." The guilty parties were definitely not Masons or in any way connected with the Society. The Pennsylvania Masons hoped that future incidents of this sort would be avoided and that the good name of the Fraternity would be restored.[24]

Probably in an attempt to draw public attention away from the Fraternity, no further notice of local Masonic activities appeared in the *Pennsylvania Gazette* after 1738, although some news of foreign Freemasonry continued to be reported. Except for a brief report of an election in June of 1741, the paper made no further references to Freemasonry in Pennsylvania until 1755.[25]

*   *   *   *   *   *   *   *

Throughout its early years Pennsylvania Freemasonry had no permanent meeting place; its members met in local taverns as was the custom in England. Taverns played an important part in the social intercourse of colonial Philadelphia, and the Masons took advantage of the convivial atmosphere and the private rooms available there. In 1731 and 1732 the Grand Lodge of Pennsylvania convened at the Sun Tavern on Water Street owned by John Hobart, a member of St. John's Lodge. For the next two years it met at the Tun Tavern, also known as Peggy Mullen's Beefsteak House, on the southeast corner of Water Street and Tun Alley. Thomas Mullen, the proprietor, was a member of the third "Modern" lodge, which also held meetings there. In 1735 the Grand Lodge moved

Tun Tavern. Masonic meeting place (1733-1734, 1749-1755). Early nineteenth century print (Free Library of Philadelphia).

Indian King Tavern. Masonic meeting place (1735-1748). Drawing by Frank H. Taylor (Free Library of Philadelphia).

to the Indian King Tavern on the southwest corner of High (Market) Street and Biddle Alley, where it continued until 1748. It then relocated to the Royal Standard Tavern on the northeast corner of High Street and Strawberry Alley west of Second Street. Both these inns were owned by members of St. John's Lodge, the first by Owen Owen and the second by Henry Pratt, who was also a Grand Lodge officer. These establishments appear to have been better than most of the city's taverns.[26]

Having achieved a certain prosperity by midcentury, the Pennsylvania Grand Lodge embarked upon the ambitious project of building a permanent meeting house. Two subscriptions for that purpose were conducted, one in March of 1752, which raised £695, and another two years later, which produced £435. It is not known what portion of the total costs these amounts represented.[27]

The new Freemason's Lodge, as it was called, was located on the south side of Lodge Alley, west of Second and north of Walnut Streets. Situated on a lot measuring sixty feet in depth and forty-two feet in width, this two-story brick structure contained "rooms [which were] very large and commodious, the floors supported by strong and substantial joices, and there being dry and deep cellars under the whole building, with a chimney to suit a kitchen." It appears that special windows were constructed on the east side to allow an abundance of light to enter the upper rooms. This feature was undoubtedly related to Masonic symbolism.[28]

Freemason's Lodge in Lodge Alley (1755-1763, 1779-1785). Water Color by Phares F. Goist (Grand Lodge of Pennsylvania).

The Freemason's Lodge was the first building erected in America for strictly Masonic purposes. At its dedication on the anniversary of St. John the Baptist, June 24, 1755, Grand Master Allen and Deputy Grand Master Franklin presided over elaborate ceremonies, which included a procession with Masons in full regalia, the pealing of bells, cannon fire and music. One hundred twenty-seven members were in attendance including Robert Hunter Morris, deputy governor, and James Hamilton, lieutenant governor of Pennsylvania, respectively. In his capacity as Grand Chaplain of the Grand Lodge of Pennsylvania, the Rev. William Smith, provost of the College and Academy of Philadelphia, preached a dedicatory sermon at Christ Church. Ostensibly intended to praise the ideals of Freemasonry, the sermon also offered opinions on many topics of contemporary interest, including the truths of rational religion, the evils of Roman Catholicism, the values of democratic government, loyalty to the Crown, the right of a people to resist oppression, and the fearful challenge to the American colonies represented by France. The essence of Smith's sermon was exemplified by his text: "Love the brotherhood; fear God; honour the king." Following the religious service, the members of the Masonic Fraternity held a festive banquet in their new hall.

According to a newspaper account of the affair:

> The whole Ceremony was conducted with the utmost Decorum and Solemnity, and . . . afforded great Satisfaction to the Inhabitants in general. The greatest Order and Regularity was observed, Cheerfulness, Harmony and good Fellowship abounded . . . .[29]

By the late 1750s Pennsylvania Freemasonry suffered the same internal divisions as did its counterpart in England in the same period. The conflict over proper ritual and procedures so weakened the Fraternity that eventually the original Grand Lodge, retrospectively called the "Moderns," was soon overshadowed by the newer and more vigorous organization, the "Ancients." Many members and some leaders of the "Moderns" switched their allegiance to the "Ancients." Examples include William Ball, William Shute and William Smith, all officers of subordinate "Modern" lodges who became Grand Lodge officers of the "Ancients." William Allen, however, remained loyal to the "Moderns," but he ceased to have much influence within the Fraternity.

Although apparently inactive after the establishment of the "Ancient" Grand Lodge in 1761, remnants of the "Modern" Masons persisted until the early 1780s.[30] Their meeting hall was used for a variety of purposes during the Revolutionary War years: as a hospital by both armies, as a meeting place for the "Ancient" Grand Lodge, and as a temporary prison for Pennsylvania Quaker loyalists. On October 1, 1785, the building was sold at public sale, the "Ancients" not having raised sufficient funds to purchase it. The proceeds from the sale, $1,533.57, were placed in trust until July 23, 1793, when they were used to establish a fund to purchase fuel for the poor. Following the sale, the hall was temporarily used as a dancing school by a French immigrant, Louis D'Orsiére, and in 1786, as a church by the Universal Baptists. Freemason's Lodge was demolished in 1801 when the Second Bank of Pennsylvania was built on the site.[31]

The last reference to "Modern" Pennsylvania Freemasonry occurred in a letter from the "Ancient" Grand Lodge of Pennsylvania to the "Modern" Grand Lodge in London. Dated November 18, 1791, it indicated the fate of the "Moderns" in Pennsylvania:

[The] Provincial Warrant from your Grand Lodge . . . has longe [sic] ceased to Operate in Pennsylvania, and the Body that obtained it has been many years entirely extinct.[32]

*   *   *   *   *   *   *   *

The Grand Lodge of Pennsylvania, formed in 1731, was in existence for at least thirty years. During that period it warranted four subordinate lodges, all located in Philadelphia: No. 1 or St. John's, No. 2, No. 3 or Tun Tavern, and No. 4. With the exception of No. 4, warranted in 1757, it is not known exactly when any of these lodges was founded. St. John's was already meeting as a "time immemorial" lodge by the early 1730s, and Nos. 2 and 3 were in operation by the late 1740s.[33]

Fragmentary evidence suggests that other "Modern" Pennsylvania lodges may also have been in existence. In 1734 Franklin sent nine copies of the *Book of Constitutions* to Brethren residing in Lancaster County; this would seem to indicate that these Masons met together in some sort of fraternal way, especially since only five were required to form a lodge. They may have been connected to James Hamilton, the Senior Grand Warden at that time, who was a resident of the town of Lancaster which had been laid out four years previously on property owned by his father, Andrew Hamilton.[34]

It is possible to reconstruct the leadership of "Modern" Pennsylvania Freemasonry although surviving information is far from complete (see Appendix C). That all known officers of the Provincial Grand Lodge, with only two exceptions, were also members of St. John's Lodge seems to indicate that the subordinate lodge also served in the capacity of a grand lodge. Officers in this period were elected for one-year terms, despite a provision of the Coxe Deputation that called for biennial elections.

Eight men held the office of Grand Master. Four of these were lawyers or judges (William Allen, James Hamilton, Thomas Hopkinson, William Plumstead), one each was a distiller (Humphrey Murray), a printer (Benjamin Franklin), a merchant (Joseph Shippen), and a silversmith (Philip Syng). These men were relatively young at the time of their elections; their average age was twenty-nine years, with a range between twenty-five and thirty-eight years. All but two of them were of the Episcopal faith.

William Allen (1704-1780) was the wealthiest and most prominent "Modern" Mason. He possessed inherited wealth, which he augmented by astute business deals and speculations. Allen lived like an English country gentleman on his estate of Mt. Airy, near Germantown; he was one of three persons in the city in 1761 who owned a carriage, and he owned extensive acreage in Pennsylvania and New Jersey. Allen held more political office than any other member of the Fraternity. From 1727, when he became a member of the Philadelphia Council, he extended his influence throughout the province. He subsequently served as a member of the Pennsylvania Assembly (1731-1739), mayor of Philadelphia (1735-1736), recorder of the city (1741-1750), justice of the lower courts (1737-1750), and finally chief justice of Pennsylvania (17501774). Allen also generously supported a number of humanitarian causes and cultural institutions, such as the Pennsylvania Hospital, the College of Philadelphia and the American Philosophical Society. William Allen held the position of Provincial Grand Master for at least seventeen one-year terms; he shared power only briefly in a thirty-year period. Allen was the most dramatic example of concentration of power in all of Pennsylvania Masonic history.

Even though it ultimately disappeared, "Modern" Pennsylvania Freemasonry proved to be popular. In the span of three decades the "Modern" lodges initiated over seven hundred persons into membership (see Appendix D). With the exception of the period between 1739 and 1748, for which no records are extant, new members joined the Fraternity in each year. Membership increased in the early 1750s when the Fraternity undertook fund-raising for a new lodge hall. Undoubtedly, new men were attracted by renewed Masonic activity after the period of quiet caused by anti-Masonic feeling.

These statistics are rather surprising because the Society adhered to rigorous membership requirements; not everyone who expressed an interest in joining was permitted to do so. A prospective Mason had to be free-born and of good parentage; he had to be steadily employed in some respectable trade or occupation, and he had to be free of debts. He could not be an indentured servant, nor have any physical deformity. Ideologically, he had to believe in a Supreme Being; otherwise his particular religious beliefs remained personal. In addition, the candidate had to be of a "mature and discrete age" in order to understand the special learning that was about to be conferred on him. "Modern" Pennsylvania Masons routinely interpreted this requirement to mean the age of twenty-five years, although younger men of superior capacities were occasionally admitted by special permission.

Even when these preliminary qualifications were met, the Masonic candidate still had to submit to a thorough investigation into his background and character; if found acceptable, he might then apply for membership. At this point the current members of the lodge had to vote unanimously to accept him. Then the new Mason had to pay various initiation fees and make a contribution to the charity fund of the lodge. These expenses were considerable. For example, both St. John's Lodge in the 1730s and Tun Tavern Lodge twenty years later charged an admission fee of £5, which included all three Masonic degrees and miscellaneous expenses. In addition, the member had to pay his share of the cost of food and drink on lodge nights and to make periodic contributions to the charity fund. This sum of £5 represented approximately thirty days' wages and over half the estimated annual food budget of an unskilled Philadelphia laborer in the mid-eighteenth century.[35]

A sampling of occupations of the members of "Modern" Pennsylvania Masons reveals a wide diversity of backgrounds (see Appendix D). Information is available for over ninety percent of the members of St. John's Lodge and for over two-thirds of those of Tun Tavern Lodge. A significant number of members of the first lodge were professionals, mostly lawyers and physicians; these men represented nearly thirty percent of the total, but they were outnumbered by the artisans and retailers, who composed about thirty-five percent of the total. The members of Tun Tavern Lodge showed a greater diversity than those of St. John's (thirty versus twenty-three separate occupations). Whereas artisans and retailers comprised the dominant element in the earlier lodge, the majority in Tun Tavern were individuals who worked in trade and commerce, specifically in connection with the sea. Over fifty percent of the men whose occupations are traceable were in this category. Whereas the single most numerous group in St. John's Lodge was composed of lawyers, sea captains were most numerous in Tun Tavern. Artisans and retailers, at sixteen percent, were the second most numerous group. Taking both lodges together, men engaged in trade and commerce ranked first (38.9%), artisans and retailers second (22.4%) and professionals third (15.4%).[36]

Under the auspices of Freemasonry, large numbers of men from many backgrounds were able to put aside their everyday differences and come together in a community of purpose. Despite exacting membership requirements and costly fees, mid-eighteenth-century Pennsylvania Freemasonry enjoyed substantial growth and material prosperity. Not even public scandal and internal conflict weakened its broad appeal. No other voluntary association in colonial Philadelphia could boast such success.[37]

CHAPTER 3:

"Ancient" Pennsylvania Freemasonry: The Early Years, 1758–1785

The genesis of "Ancient" Pennsylvania Freemasonry can be found in the circumstances surrounding the operation of the fourth and final "Modern" lodge, which was warranted in June 1757 by Grand Master Allen. The majority of the original petitioners appear to have been British immigrants, including soldiers then stationed in Philadelphia, who had been made Masons according to the "Ancient" manner, a fact of which the "Modern" Pennsylvania Grand Lodge was initially unaware.[1]

Almost immediately, Lodge No. 4 ("Moderns") began to admit as members other "Ancient" British Masons and adopted the "Ancient" manner in initiating new men. By the middle of August 1757 the Pennsylvania Grand Lodge was receiving reports of these "irregularities;" it responded by sending four members of Lodge No. 1 to investigate. Lodge No. 4 did not welcome these investigators in any amicable, fraternal spirit; the minutes expressed its members' attitude succinctly: "All [the visitors] behaved as spies from an enemy's camp." Although summoned before a Grand Lodge committee on September 21, the officers of No. 4 remained firm in their resolve to continue to work in the "Ancient" way, regardless of the consequences, because they believed the "Ancient" forms were more authentic than those currently in use by the Pennsylvania Grand Lodge. As a result, the warrant of Lodge No. 4 was recalled less than six months after it had been issued.

For the remainder of 1757 and into 1758, however, Lodge No. 4 continued to operate as an "Ancient" body but without any proper authorization or official standing. The members, regarding themselves as "Sheep without a Shepherd" and "determined never to forsake the good old way," resolved to petition the "Ancient" Grand Lodge in London for a new warrant. The petition reached London in late spring; it was acted upon favorably, and an "Ancient" warrant was issued on June 7, 1758. It was received in Philadelphia in January 1759. The lodge was listed as No. 1, Pennsylvania, and No. 69, England, on the official register.[2]

Although its membership had doubled in less than two years—from twenty to forty—the "Ancient" Pennsylvania lodge still did not feel itself to be secure. The relationship with the three "Modern" lodges continued to be marred by lack of cooperation and absence of fraternal feelings. One "Modern" Philadelphia Mason, for example, going to London on other business, refused to carry the "Ancient" lodge's payments of its fees to the "Ancient" Grand Lodge. This refusal necessitated extra effort, expense and delays on the lodge's part. The Master of the subordinate "Ancient" lodge, John Blackwood, wrote in a letter to London: "The Moderns are at prest a verry powerfull Body . . . thay dont Chuse to Countenance us in the least . . . we have many Enemies that are powerfull and watching an oppertunity [sic] [to destroy the lodge]." Feeling the need for greater supervision from abroad, Blackwood, acting on behalf of the lodge as a whole, requested the "Ancient" Grand Lodge of England to appoint "some proper person . . . to precide [sic] over us as deputy Grand Master of Antients [sic] in Pennsylvania ." This move was to give the lodge even more official recognition and to strengthen its position vis-à-vis the "Modern" Philadelphia Grand Lodge.[3]

This appeal went unanswered for many months and the lodge remained uncertain as to what course of action to take. Then, in February 1760 the members of Lodge No. 1 took matters into their own hands: they elected one of their number, William Ball, as Grand Master and then petitioned the "Ancient" English Grand Lodge to issue a warrant to establish a Provincial Grand Lodge of Pennsylvania. They also wrote to the members of London Lodge No. 2, with which they enjoyed close personal ties, for their intercession in obtaining the desired document. In April of the same year the Philadelphia lodge divided into two sections, with separate officers, in anticipation of the formation of a grand lodge.[4]

These actions eventually received the full approval of the "Ancient" Grand Lodge of England, which granted a Provincial Grand Warrant for Pennsylvania on July 15, 1761. This document confirmed the election of the Provincial Grand Lodge officers and gave them full power to establish and constitute subordinate lodges, to make or admit Freemasons according to the "Ancient" method, to hear and determine all matters relating to the Craft within their jurisdiction and to nominate, choose and install their successors. The Grand Lodge Warrant was intended to supersede any previous grants of authority or power pertaining to Freemasonry in any part of the colonies, even those of the "Modern" Grand Lodge.[5] The new Pennsylvania Grand Lodge was registered as No. 89, England, and No. 1, Pennsylvania; the former subordinate Lodge No. 1 became Lodge No. 2. The warrant was lost when the ship carrying it was

Original Warrant of the Provincial Grand Lodge of Pennsylvania, July 15, 1761 (Grand Lodge of Pennsylvania).

captured by a French vessel; another was issued on December 30, 1763, but this too was lost. Finally, a third warrant was drawn up on June 20, 1764, and the Philadelphia Masons received it in early 1765.[6] The last of these documents, however, stated that the authority of the Pennsylvania body to operate as a grand lodge dated from 1761 even though that particular warrant was never received. Thus the Pennsylvania "Ancient" Grand Lodge was the first such Masonic supervisory body in the American colonies, preceding that of Massachusetts by eight years.

While waiting for the official warrant, Lodge No. 2 (formerly No. 1) received on December 30, 1763, a letter from Laurence Dermott, the Grand Secretary of the "Ancients" in London, informing it of the London Grand Lodge's approval of a Provincial Grand Lodge of Pennsylvania. Upon the authority of this letter, the Pennsylvania "Ancients" officially inaugurated their Grand Master on February 2, 1764, in a simple ceremony. Fifteen individuals, all holding some official position, marched around the lodge room three times, after which the Grand Lodge officers were installed according to the "Ancient" manner. William Ball, a goldsmith, served as the "Right Worshipful Provincial Grand Master of Ancient York Masons in the Province of Pennsylvania." The other Grand Lodge officers were: Blaithwaite Jones, a ship captain, as Deputy Grand Master; Franklin's partner David Hall as Senior Grand Warden and Hugh Lennox, merchant, as Junior Grand Warden.[7]

William Ball (1729-1810), as the most important "Ancient" Mason, occupied a position of prominence much like William Allen's among the "Moderns." First elected at the age of thirty-one, he held the office of Grand Master for at least fifteen one-year terms during a twenty-year period, and once again in 1795. A man of substantial wealth, Ball inherited his father's extensive estate of "Hope Farm," which comprised some seven hundred sixty-seven acres in the Shackamaxon section of Philadelphia (now the Richmond and Kensington districts), and he owned hundreds of acres of land in other parts of Pennsylvania and in Delaware. He became a leading member of his trade; Ball belonged to the London goldsmiths' guild and headed the goldsmiths, silversmiths and jewellers in the Grand Federal Procession on July 4, 1788. Originally entered as a "Modern" Mason in 1750, Ball withdrew from membership and applied to the "Ancients" a decade later.

The first official act of Grand Master Ball was to authorize the establishment of a second subordinate lodge, No. 3, Philadelphia, which had been meeting unofficially for about ten days. This new lodge was created from a division of No. 2, whose numbers were probably too large for convenient operation. The separation was amicable; the members of the new lodge were given the option of taking jewels and other paraphernalia or a cash settlement of £45.[8]

During its early years the membership in the Pennsylvania Grand
Lodge and Lodge No. 2 was coextensive; because surviving records do
not indicate which minutes apply to which lodge, it is often difficult to
determine the particular role of the members. The same men served as
officers of both bodies until 1772, when two members of No. 3 were
elected to Grand Lodge office (see Appendix C). It appears that the
Grand Lodge officers did not monopolize power since, with the exception
of William Ball, most of them held office for only a few terms. The
pattern of office-holding of the "Ancients" was therefore similar to that
of the "Moderns."

The first important St. John the Evangelist's Day celebration for the
"Ancients" was observed in 1772 with a festive dinner at the Sign of Sir
John Falstaff, at the corner of Sixth and Carpenter Streets, at which a
Masonic ode especially composed for the occasion was sung. The next
year members of the Grand Lodge and the two subordinate lodges celebrated at an inn located at the Upper Ferry of the Schuylkill, just outside
the city limits. In June 1774 they celebrated again at this inn, where they
were joined by members of No. 4. In December 1774 members of the
Fraternity participated in a public procession to St. Paul's Episcopal Church
on Third Street between Walnut and Spruce Streets, where a special
Masonic service was held.[9]

From its beginning the "Ancient" Pennsylvania Grand Lodge operated in accordance with the *Ahiman Rezon*, written by Laurence Dermott,
the Grand Secretary of the "Ancient" English Grand Lodge. "Ancient"
Pennsylvania Masons acquired several copies of this important work within
two years of its publication in London in 1756, and they continued to
place orders for additional copies throughout the 1760s.[10]

In its aims and organization, Dermott's *Ahiman Rezon* made a clear
break with Anderson's *Constitutions*, used by "Modern" Pennsylvania Freemasons. It deliberately eschewed the colorful, but largely legendary, history of Freemasonry, which was a prominent feature of the earlier work,
and concentrated upon the proper functioning of the Fraternity in its
own day. Dermott's purpose in producing a new version of the Masonic
constitutions was at least twofold: to point out to outsiders "their Folly in
ridiculing a Society founded upon Religion, Morality, Brotherly-Love,
and good fellowship" and to exhibit to Masons the superiority of the
"Ancient" way over the "Modern" one.[11]

Dermott's work was helpful in differentiating between the two vari-
eties of Freemasonry. It carefully compared the regulations that governed the two bodies in such specific matters as precedence and authority
of high-ranking Masonic officials, wearing of regalia and special clothing,
procedures for admitting new members, membership requirements, formation of new lodges, measures to guard against "clandestine" Masons,

appropriate Masonic behavior and rules of order. Dermott included eleven specific regulations for the running of Grand Lodge meetings, not found in Anderson's *Constitutions,* and he also provided regulations for the Grand Lodge charity fund. These guidelines, which were based upon Irish, not English, models, stressed the need for care in selecting objects of charity and cautioned against a too-liberal disbursing of funds.

In most particulars, no significant procedural difference existed between the rival Grand Lodges, but those of the "Ancients" had a more authoritative tone. Dermott's rules were stricter and the penalties for violating them more severe. Dermott did not so much throw out the old regulations as to modify, clarify and amplify them and to emphasize uniformity and propriety.

The early leaders of "Ancient" Pennsylvania Freemasonry were quick to advance the interests of the Fraternity and to extend the influence of the Grand Lodge. Unlike the "Moderns," who had established only four lodges, all in Philadelphia, the "Ancients" warranted lodges with greater zeal and over a wider area. Within the first decade of its existence, for example, the Grand Lodge founded seventeen subordinate lodges: five in Philadelphia; four in Maryland; two each in Bucks County and Delaware; and one each in Chester and Lancaster Counties, New Jersey and Virginia (see Table 1).

Despite comfortable growth in the 1760s and 1770s, the "Ancient" Philadelphia lodges could not afford to purchase their own meeting hall and therefore rented rooms in various local taverns owned by members. They also met periodically in a small building in Videll's Alley (Lodge Alley) west of Second between Chestnut Street and Carter's Alley (Ionic Street).[12]

*   *   *   *   *   *   *   *

The first years of the Revolutionary War were a time of turmoil for Pennsylvania Freemasonry, as for most organizations. The meetings of over a dozen subordinate lodges, as well as those of the Grand Lodge, were disrupted or suspended, their records were lost or destroyed and their memberships were dispersed. The premier "Ancient" lodge, No. 2, for example, did not meet regularly for several years until late 1778; its members were "extremely unhappy that the present contest (though in favor of liberty) hath rendered it impossible for them to give that attendance which they would willingly have given [otherwise]."[13]

The Grand Lodge of Pennsylvania held no meetings in the four years following St John the Baptist's Day 1774 and issued no warrants for new lodges from August 1775 until May 1779. Not until July 1779 were normal operations resumed and regular minutes once again kept. The former records of the Grand Lodge were, to its officers' dismay, "either mislaid or carried away by some Enemies to the Royal Art, during the Confusions of the present War." When the Grand Lodge was beginning to recover, it issued a circular letter to all lodges under its jurisdiction and asked for cooperation in reconstructing the Fraternity and in restoring its financial basis. It directed them to produce evidence of proper authority to operate, but allowed them to pay back dues and contributions to the charity fund as they saw fit. Despite the recent political, social and economic turmoils, Pennsylvania Masons responded generously to the last of these requests by raising £790 for a permanent charity fund for future disbursement to distressed persons of the city. This sum was sufficient to provide for the basic economic needs of seven to ten laboring families of four persons each for a period of one year.[14]

Officially apolitical at the beginning of the war, the Grand Lodge issued no statements and took no public stand on the disputes; it preferred to allow members to make up their own minds. Although certainly a necessary and proper stance on the part of an organization which owed

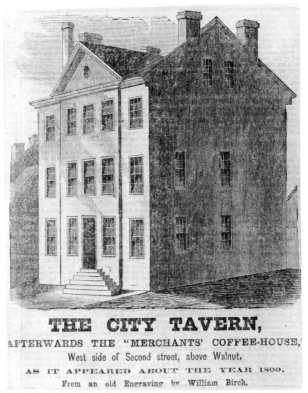

THE CITY TAVERN,
AFTERWARDS THE "MERCHANTS' COFFEE-HOUSE,"
West side of Second street, above Walnut.
AS IT APPEARED ABOUT THE YEAR 1800.
From an old Engraving by William Birch.

Masonic meeting place, Lodge No. 3 (1775-1777). Unidentified newspaper clipping (Free Library of Philadelphia).

allegiance to a supervisory body in England and whose members were not unanimous on the issues of the day, it nonetheless left the subordinate lodges without direction at a critical time.

Several subordinate lodges, however, were not so cautious. For example, members of No. 3 participated in military exercises as early as June 1775 and offered thirteen toasts in tribute to the thirteen united colonies in their St. John's Day (June 24) celebrations of 1776 and 1777, in the first instance just two weeks before the Second Continental Congress accepted the Declaration of Independence. At the beginning of 1777 Lodge No. 18 also took a firm stand against Great Britain:

> . . . the Unnatural and cruel War, in which this Continent is now engaged, with the Despotic King of England, who is endeavoring to deprive the Inhabitants of this Land of their inestimable and just Rights and Privileges, have [sic] necessarily called away many of the Members of this Body, from their respective Habitations, And also the . . . officers of this Lodge, to oppose the force of our Enemy.[15]

Many Masons played active roles in the armed forces of the United States. Lodge Nos. 2, 3 and 4 (all Philadelphia), No. 5 (New Castle County, Delaware), No. 8 (Chester County) and No. 18 (Kent County, Delaware) together provided a total of over two hundred fifty Continental Army officers. The most striking example of patriotism came from Lodge No. 3 whose membership roll contained the names of eighty-five of these individuals. Many other American officers attended the meetings of these lodges during the war but did not become members themselves. During their occupation of Philadelphia in 1777 and 1778, British soldiers, describing Lodge No. 2 as a "nest of rebels," broke into its meeting room and stole its jewels, books and paraphernalia in reprisal.[16]

Lodge No. 18, the majority of whose members also served in the American forces, feared the same treatment:

> Whereas from the near situation of our Enemy the British Troops, Together with their daily advance and depredations on the Borders of this Town [Dover] . . . And from the scattered Situation of our Members, it was found Necessary to remove the Jewels and Implements to a place of Safety.[17]

Even the so-called "patriotic" lodges had some loyalists, however. One member of No. 8, for example, became a prominent Tory, as did two members of No. 2 who were later tried and convicted of treason. Lodge Nos. 3 and 4, Philadelphia, appear to have been taken over by the British since they continued meeting throughout the occupation, during which time they initiated ten British officers and five Tories. Eight additional British officers appear in the records as visitors to these lodges. Through the intercession of Lodge No. 3 the stolen possessions of No. 2 were eventually returned. Lodge No. 3 also held the warrant of the Grand Lodge, whose members had fled the city. Under that authority, it formed itself into a Grand Lodge — an irregular proceeding — and warranted a military lodge in a British army regiment.[18]

In the Seventeenth Regiment of Foot, which had served in North America since 1757, an "Ancient" military lodge had been held under a warrant from the Grand Lodge of Ireland, where the regiment had formerly served. This document was subsequently lost and a new warrant was issued by the Grand Lodge of Scotland in 1771. The regiment fought on Long Island and at the battles of Trenton, Princeton, Brandywine and Germantown and was quartered in Philadelphia beginning in September 1777. While in Philadelphia, the regiment applied to the Grand Lodge of Pennsylvania for another warrant to replace the Scottish one which was lost at Princeton, and this was granted sometime in early 1778.[19]

At the battle of Stony Point in July 1779 the Seventeenth Regiment's Pennsylvania warrant was captured along with prisoners and its baggage train. The warrant eventually fell into the hands of a Connecticut officer, General Samuel H. Parsons, also a Mason, who graciously returned it to the regiment with a fraternal message: "however our political sentiments may impel us in the public dispute, we are still Brethren, and (our professional duty apart) ought to promote the happiness and advance the weal of each other." This incident, occurring amid hostilities between the United States and Great Britain, was remarkable evidence of the pervasiveness of the Masonic spirit in the eighteenth century. Although Masons served their respective countries, they remained loyal to the higher values of universal brotherhood and bore no personal ill will toward each other.[20]

The Seventeenth Regiment of Foot continued to operate under the Pennsylvania warrant throughout the war and afterwards. In March 1786, three years after American independence had been achieved, the officers of the lodge wrote to the Grand Lodge of Pennsylvania to inquire as to the status of its warrant, which they feared had been canceled. They expressed their wish to continue Masonic affiliation with the Grand Lodge and offered to pay all back dues. The Grand Lodge replied that it wished the same result, allowed the regiment to determine its own dues as all records pertaining to it had been misplaced or lost, and promised to search for the missing warrant. It extended its best wishes for the welfare and prosperity of the military lodge. These communications were curiously devoid of any of the bitterness or hostile feeling that one might expect to find between former enemies.[21]

The departure of the British from Philadelphia in June 1778 occasioned thanksgiving on the part of Pennsylvania Masons. In succeeding months the Grand Lodge organized a great Masonic celebration to be held on St. John's Day, December 28. Notices were published in Philadelphia newspapers inviting all Masons under the jurisdiction of the Grand Lodge of Pennsylvania to attend.[22]

The celebration was a great success. Nearly three hundred Masons took part, including General George Washington, who had arrived in Philadelphia only a few days before. This was the first public Masonic function in which Washington was actively involved.[23] A grand procession assembled at the College and Academy of Philadelphia on the west side of Fourth Street below Arch and then proceeded to Christ Church. The religious services were conducted by two of the city's most prominent clergymen, the Rev. Dr. William White, later the first bishop of Pennsylvania, who gave the prayer, and the Rev. Dr. William Smith, now an "Ancient" Mason, who delivered the sermon, dedicated to General Washington. Smith's sermon had no single theme, but covered a wide area of concern to Masons, Christians and patriots alike. Smith extolled such Masonic virtues as wisdom, beauty, strength, temperance and charity; he re-emphasized traditional Christian beliefs; and he hailed the fledgling United States in its quest for liberty.

At the conclusion of Smith's sermon, a collection taken for the relief of the poor raised a total of £400, a substantial amount at that time, and an elaborate program of instrumental and choral music was performed. Amid the pealing of church bells and the strains of Masonic and patriotic tunes played by a military band, the Brethren withdrew from the church and retired to their respective lodges to dine. The largest public gathering of Masons to date, this celebration increased the prestige of the Fraternity, associated it with the name of Washington and the cause of the United States and enhanced its reputation for support of charitable endeavors.[24]

As a result of the success of these festivities, some members of the Grand Lodge of Pennsylvania began to suggest that George Washington be elected Grand Master for all the American states, a position to be created specifically for him. The movement gathered momentum until January 13, 1780, when the Grand Lodge unanimously passed a resolution to that effect. The Grand Lodge no longer considered it possible to work under the jurisdiction of the Grand Lodge of England, owing to the present state of hostilities and the declaration of American independence. It also believed that a new supervisory body would give much-needed direction to the Fraternity in America. A circular letter was accordingly drafted and sent to the other Masonic jurisdictions of the United States.[25]

This proposal was seconded one month later by a committee drawn from American army lodges then in winter quarters in Morristown, New

Jersey. Complaining of the "disputes, and the many irregularities and improprieties committed by weak or wicked brethren, which too manifestly show the present dissipated and almost abandoned condition of our lodges in general, as well as the relaxation of virtue amongst individuals," the American military Masons regarded the establishment of a general grand lodge to be the "means most eligible for preventing impositions, correcting abuses and for re-establishing the generous principles of Masonry." They set forth these opinions in a circular address to the Provincial Grand Masters of the United States. This document represented the sentiments of a cross section of American soldiers; it was signed by members of seven state regiments, two military lodges and the general staff of the Continental Army.[26]

In October 1780 the Grand Lodge of Pennsylvania received a reply from the Grand Lodge of Massachusetts, whose support was crucial to the success of the proposal. Joseph Webb, its Grand Master, foresaw no objection on the part of his membership to Washington's being named General Grand Master, but he was concerned about his prerogatives and whether they would infringe upon those currently enjoyed within the Fraternity. He was certain that Massachusetts Masons would never give up the right to elect their own Grand Lodge officers. Webb was not aware of any support for the proposal among other American provincial grand lodges. Nonetheless, he promised to place the issue before the next meeting of the Massachusetts Grand Lodge.

Wishing to reinforce its position, the Grand Lodge of Pennsylvania sent another, more detailed, communication to the Grand Lodge of Massachusetts. It stated that the idea of a general grand lodge was not new and mentioned a precedent in Sweden, where a General Grand Master for all lodges in that country, as well as for several on the Continent, had recently been installed. The Pennsylvania Grand Lodge had never intended that a General Grand Master should assume the powers of the existing grand lodges, but rather that he should warrant new lodges in areas outside their control. The Pennsylvania institution had already over-reached its legal bounds by warranting lodges outside the state's borders; a larger supervisory body, formed according to federalist principles, was therefore needed. What the other powers of the General Grand Master might be was left to a meeting of delegates at some future convention of American Masons.[27]

Despite these assurances, the Grand Lodge of Massachusetts ultimately rejected the proposal, stating that it was impossible to deal adequately with the issue until the opinions of the other grand lodges had been heard and after a general peace with Great Britain had been concluded. With that, the matter died. Thereafter, the leaders of Pennsylvania Freemasonry eventually changed their opinions and declined to support the measure of a general grand lodge when it again arose, on the grounds advanced by Massachusetts, namely, its challenge to the authority of existing grand lodges.[28]

During the remainder of the Revolutionary War, involvement of the Grand Lodge of Pennsylvania in politics increased substantially. By the fall of 1782 seven additional military warrants had been issued to regiments from Pennsylvania (Nos. 19, 28, 29), Maryland (No. 27), North Carolina (No. 20), New Jersey (No. 36) and Delaware (No. 30). These lodges initiated or admitted over a hundred American officers. By definition, however, these warrants were only temporary and were called in shortly after the end of the war.[29]

Following the example of American politics, Pennsylvania Freemasons began to take preliminary steps toward complete independence from the jurisdiction of the English Grand Lodge. The Pennsylvania Grand Lodge now discarded the British edition of the "Ancient" *Book of Constitutions,* which it had used since its inception, and produced its own version. In December 1779 it commissioned the Rev. Dr. Smith to head a committee "to revise and Prepare the Constitution . . . leaving out what may be superfluous." The draft was read and approved by the Grand Lodge two years later and was ordered to be printed. The Fraternity maintained its advantageous association with Washington's name by including a laudatory dedication to him. Printed by Hall and Sellers, the first American edition of the *Ahiman Rezon* was ready for distribution by St. John's Day, June 24, 1783. Two thousand copies were offered for sale at a modest price.[30]

Compared with Dermott's edition of 1756, Smith's work was more succinct. It was about forty pages shorter, used updated and simplfied language, and was organized more rationally. In his description of membership requirements, codes of behavior of Masons and characteristics of subordinate lodges, however, Smith closely followed Dermott; any changes were of degree and form rather than of substance. Smith restored a general summary of Masonic history, which Dermott had omitted, but he concentrated upon the developments in "Ancient York Masonry," after which the Grand Lodge of Pennsylvania styled itself. This designation was based upon a popular Masonic legend that the earliest convocation of operative masons was held in 926 in York, England. It was supposedly called by Prince Edwin, believed to be the son of Anglo-Saxon King Athelstan, who held the masons in high regard. By identifying with this event, although apocryphal, the "Ancient" Masons claimed a heritage that was older and therefore "purer" than that of the "Moderns."[31]

What made Smith's edition distinctive was its inclusion of detailed regulations pertaining to the composition, aims and functioning of the

Benj Morris

AHIMAN REZON

ABRIDGED AND DIGESTED:

AS A

Help to all that are, or would be

Free and Accepted MASONS.

TO WHICH IS ADDED,

A SERMON,

PREACHED IN CHRIST-CHURCH, PHILADELPHIA,

AT A GENERAL COMMUNICATION,

CELEBRATED, AGREEABLE TO THE CONSTITUTIONS, ON MONDAY, DECEMBER 28, 1778, AS THE ANNIVERSARY OF ST. JOHN THE EVANGELIST.

PUBLISHED BY ORDER OF

The GRAND LODGE of PENNSYLVANIA,

By WILLIAM SMITH, D. D.

PHILADELPHIA:

PRINTED BY HALL AND SELLERS,

M,DCC,LXXXIII.

Frontispiece and Title Page of the first edition of the *Ahiman Rezon* (Grand Lodge of Pennsylvania).

Pennsylvania Grand Lodge. It was the most complete of the eighteenth-century Masonic constitutions that dealt with this subject.

According to Smith, the Grand Lodge was composed of the Masters and Wardens of all regular lodges and, by courtesy, all Past Grand Lodge officers and all Past Masters, each of whom had one vote in any decision. Other Master Masons were permitted to attend Grand Lodge meetings but they did not have the right to vote. A quorum consisted of at least one current Grand Lodge officer along with the representatives of at least five subordinate lodges. All members had to appear at each meeting in proper clothing with regalia appropriate to their ranks.

The Grand Lodge was required to meet at least four times a year, with special ceremonies on St. John the Evangelist's Day (December 27), although other meetings could be called "monthly or otherwise, as business may require." The Grand Lodge was to discuss and consider all matters relating to the prosperity of the Fraternity in general or to particular lodges or single Brethren in particular. It also served as a court of appeal to settle differences among aggrieved members.

Grand Lodge officers were selected either by appointment or by election. With the approval of the Grand Lodge, the Deputy Grand Master was to ask the current Grand Master to continue in office for another year. If he agreed, he was reappointed by acclamation. If he declined, an election was held. The Grand Master then had the right to nominate the Deputy Grand Master and the Grand Secretary, choices subject to majority approval. The Grand Wardens and the Grand Treasurer were to be nominated and elected by majority vote, whereas previously they also had been appointees of the Grand Master. The process of choosing officers was to be completed at least one month before their installation on St. John's Day to ensure a smooth transition of power between the two administrations.

The "Ancients" set no special qualifications for the position of Grand Master, unlike the "Moderns," who preferred someone with education, wealth and social position. Although Smith's version regarded these as desirable traits, it was more important that selection be "founded upon real worth and personal merit, and not upon mere seniority or any other particular rank or quality." The Grand Master presided over all lodge meetings, whether Grand or subordinate, when present; he could make Masons at sight or by dispensation, and he had two votes in all decisions. He could also rule by fiat if necessary. The Grand Master's only other real duty was his annual visitation of all subordinate lodges, although this could be accomplished by his appointing a representative.

What comes out clearly in the native Pennsylvania edition of the *Ahiman Rezon* is a stress upon the sovereignty of the Grand Lodge. It was an "absolute and independent body, with legislative authority" to regulate

Freemasonry within its area of jurisdiction. This strong statement indicated that Pennsylvania Masons were anticipating the break with the Grand Lodge of England at least three years before it was made. They also may have reconsidered the legal position of the Grand Lodge of Pennsylvania as a result of communications with the Grand Lodge of Massachusetts, three years earlier, concerning the abortive plan for an American Grand Lodge.

The rules and regulations of the Grand Lodge, as summarized above, formed the bulk of Smith's version of the Masonic *Constitutions*. He concluded his presentation with detailed rules on parliamentary procedure, the operation of the charity fund, prayers for the opening and closing of lodges, charges to be read at the completion of each of the three degrees, Masonic songs, a letter from the philosopher John Locke, reputedly a student of Freemasonry, and a series of clarifications offered by Dermott on subjects not clearly addressed in his edition. Smith also added an account of the grand Masonic procession of 1778, as well as his sermon on that occasion and a prayer offered a year later.[32]

In the mid-1780s Pennsylvania Freemasons increasingly opened themselves to public exposure by conducting more processions and ceremonies than ever before. In December 1783 they marched in procession from the Freemason's Lodge to St. Paul's Episcopal Church on Third Street below Walnut, to hear a Masonic sermon delivered by the Rev. Dr. Samuel Magaw, the rector, who was also vice-provost of the University of Pennsylvania and a Mason. Magaw took as his main theme the values of benevolence. Quoting appropriate scriptural passages, he took the position that all mankind was interconnected through nature and through the fatherhood of God. Charitable work, although directed at one specific individual or group of individuals, nonetheless benefited all of society because it generated attitudes of generosity and sympathy for the condition of one's fellow man. Although specifically extolling Masonic virtues, among which charity had a major role, Magaw also expressed patriotic sentiments. Following the sermon, a collection was taken to be distributed equally among needy Masons, the city's poor and debtors in jail. This ceremony also included anthems and instrumental music composed for the occasion.[33] One year later Pennsylvania Masons participated in another public procession, this time to Christ Church to hear a sermon on the character of St. John the Evangelist, one of the patron saints of Freemasonry, delivered by Dr. White. Since one of the purposes of this event was to raise money for the poor, White concentrated upon the importance of charity.[34]

The most impressive procession of this period did not occur on the usual Masonic feast days of the SS. John, however, but in a special ceremony held in September 1785 to dedicate a new lodge room located in

Black Horse Alley, below Market Street and east of Second, for the use of a "Sublime" Lodge to confer higher degrees than those offered in the "Blue" lodge. Accompanied by "an elegant oration" and a "beautiful ode set to music," the festivities elicited favorable public comment in a local newspaper: "There has been no instance of a Masonic procession which exhibited a more respectable appearance, and the solemnities used in consecrating the lodge were very striking." In the afternoon, the Brethren dined together at the City Tavern "and spent the day in the greatest harmony."[35]

Also in this period the Pennsylvania Grand Lodge began to take measures to obtain a more secure meeting place. Since late 1778 it had been using the old Freemason's Lodge in Lodge Alley, which was still owned by some "Modern" Masons to whom the "Ancient" Philadelphia lodges paid rent. This arrangement proved unsatisfactory because several disputes arose over use of the building and proper rental charges. In late 1782, after conducting an inquiry into the matter, the Grand Lodge resolved to raise money by subscription, either to purchase the building from the remaining "Moderns" or to find a suitable lot on which to construct a new hall. Over the next few years, some money was raised, but it fell far short of the amount needed for either purpose. In October 1785 the Freemason's Lodge was sold at public auction. Forced to relocate, the Grand Lodge moved to the building in Videll's Alley it had used prior to the Revolutionary War.[36]

In December of the same year the Fraternity received a gift of a plot of ground, seventy by one hundred twenty-four feet, located at Twelfth and Walnut Streets, from a wealthy member of Lodge No. 2, Joseph Dean, a merchant. The Grand Lodge agreed to pay Dean the small sum of 10s. with an annual rent of one acorn for full rights to the property. The only condition Dean imposed was that a permanent meeting place for the use of Philadelphia lodges had to be built upon it within three years. Already calling the future building the "Grand Lodge House of Pennsylvania," the Fraternity optimistically embarked upon another program of fund raising.[37]

*   *   *   *   *   *   *   *

As measured by the number of its subordinate lodges, the "Ancient" Pennsylvania Grand Lodge was much more successful than the Grand Lodge of the "Moderns." During its first twenty-four years of operation, the "Ancients" warranted a total of fifty-two lodges (Table 1). Twenty-four, or nearly half, of these were located outside Pennsylvania: nine in

Maryland, five in Delaware; three each in New Jersey, Virginia and South Carolina, and one in Georgia. Those within Pennsylvania were established in the counties of Allegheny (1), Berks (1), Bucks (3), Chester (2), Cumberland (1), Lancaster (3), Montgomery (1), Northumberland (1), and Philadelphia (6) (Table 2, Figure 1). An additional nine lodges operated under temporary authority as traveling or military warrants.

The greatest years of expansion for Pennsylvania Freemasonry, between 1780 and 1785, coincided with the final stages of the Revolutionary War and with official British recognition of the independence of the United States. Almost as many lodges were warranted in these five years as in the previous eighteen years combined. This indicates that the Grand Lodge benefited from its firm commitment, made in late 1778, to the American cause.

The majority (thirty-five or 67.3%) of the early "Ancient" lodges were still functioning at the end of 1785. Although seventeen lodges had ceased to exist, most of them (eleven or 65.7%) either were located outside Pennsylvania, and thus naturally gravitated toward the grand lodges of their respective states, or were by definition temporary. This record is rather strong considering the politically and socially turbulent era in which these lodges were warranted. It also speaks well for the influence and ability of the leaders of an organization originally established within the unfriendly atmosphere of "Modern" Freemasonry, which had previously prevailed in Philadelphia.

Membership statistics are extant for thirty-seven (71.2%) of the early "Ancient" lodges (see Appendix E). Through 1785 more than nineteen hundred men were either initiated or admitted into Freemasonry under the auspices of the "Ancient" Grand Lodge of Pennsylvania. Since surviving records are fragmentary, one cannot know what percentage of the actual total this figure represents. In any case, at least two and a half times as many individuals became "Ancient" Freemasons as "Moderns" in a similar span of time. It is not possible to determine the net or cumulative membership for any one year, but literary evidence indicates that in August 1778 the Grand Lodge had under its jurisdiction thirty-one regular lodges "containing on the whole more than one thousand brethren." The Masons maintained the largest membership of any voluntary society in Philadelphia at that time.[38]

After an initial surge of new members at the time of the establishment of the "Ancient" Grand Lodge came five years of more limited activity. Thereafter, with few exceptions, growth was steady and consistent throughout the period with peaks in 1779 (245 members) and 1780 (351 members). Many individuals probably became interested in the Fraternity and desired to join it as a result of the elaborate celebration of St. John's Day, December 28, 1778. The public processions and ceremonies held in

TABLE 1
"Ancient" Pennsylvania Lodges, 1758-1785

Years	Number of new lodges (lodge numbers)		Number of ceased lodges (lodge numbers)
1758-1774	17	(2-12, 12a, 13-17)	1 (12)
1775-1785	32	(9a, 11a, 13a, 18, 18a, 19, 21-30, 31a, 32-45, 47)	10 (9, 11, 13, 19, 26, 27, 28, 29, 30, 36)
Unknown, but before 1786	3	(20, 29a, 31)	6 (16, 20, 24, 31, 39, 47)
Totals	52	Net: +35	17 (32.7%)

Twenty-four of the new lodges were located outside Pennsylvania, as follows: Delaware (5, 14, 18, 33, 44); Georgia (42); Maryland (6, 7, 15, 16, 17, 29a, 34, 35, 37); New Jersey (10, 23, 32); South Carolina (38, 40, 47); Virginia (12a, 39, 41). In addition, nine warrants were granted to military or traveling lodges (18a, 19, 20, 27, 28, 29, 30, 31, 36).

Eleven of the ceased lodges were located outside Pennsylvania, as follows: Maryland (16); Virginia (39); South Carolina (47); military or traveling (19, 20, 27, 28, 29, 30, 31, 36).

By definition, military or traveling lodges were only temporary.

A number with an "a" appended indicates that more than one lodge was assigned the same number. This system provides a more accurate accounting of the actual number of separate lodges.

The origins of new lodges are based on their warrant dates.

Lodges "ceased" in basically two ways: by voluntary surrender of the warrant by the members or by order of the Grand Lodge. Various terms were used to describe such warrants: "surrendered," "returned," "vacated," or "ceased."

Sources: Julius F. Sachse, *Old Masonic Lodges of Pennsylvania, "Moderns" and "Ancients,"* Vol. I *1730-1777,* and Vol. II, *1779-1800* (Phila., 1912, 1913); Charles E. Meyer, *Masonic Lodges in Pennsylvania from 1730 to 1880, "Moderns" and "Ancients"* (Phila., n.d.); "Information Pertaining to Early Freemasonry in the Western Hemisphere , Including the Warrant and Constitution Dates of the Subordinate Lodges under the Provincial and Present Grand Lodge of F. and A.M. of Pennsylvania" (unpublished list, n.d.); Register of Members, Vol. 1, 1789-1823.

TABLE 2
Geographical Distribution of Pennsylvania Lodges, 1758-1785

County	Number of new lodges (lodge numbers)	(%)	Number of ceased lodges (lodge numbers)	(%)
Allegheny	1 (45)	5.3		
Berks	1 (24)	5.3	1 (24)	16.7
Bucks	3 (11, 12, 25)	15.8	2 (11, 12)	33.3
Chester	2 (8, 11a)	10.5		
Cumberland	1 (26)	5.3	1 (26)	16.7
Lancaster	3 (9, 21, 43)	15.8	1 (9)	16.7
Montgomery	1 (31a)	5.3		
Northumberland	1 (22)	5.3		
Philadelphia	6 (2, 3, 4, 9a, 13, 13a)	31.6	1 (13)	16.7
Totals	19	100.0	6	100.0

Sources: Julius F. Sachse, *Old Masonic Lodges of Pennsylvania, "Moderns" and "Ancients,"* Vol. I, *1730-1777,* and Vol. II, *1779-1800* (Phila., 1912, 1913); Charles E. Meyer, *Masonic Lodges in Pennsylvania from 1730 to 1880, "Moderns" and "Ancients,"* (Phila., n.d.); "Information Pertaining to Early Freemasonry in the Western Hemisphere, Including the Warrant and Constitution Dates of the Subordinate Lodges under the Provincial and Present Grand Lodge of F. and A.M. of Pennsylvania" (unpublished list, n.d.); Register of Members, Vol. 1, 1789-1823.

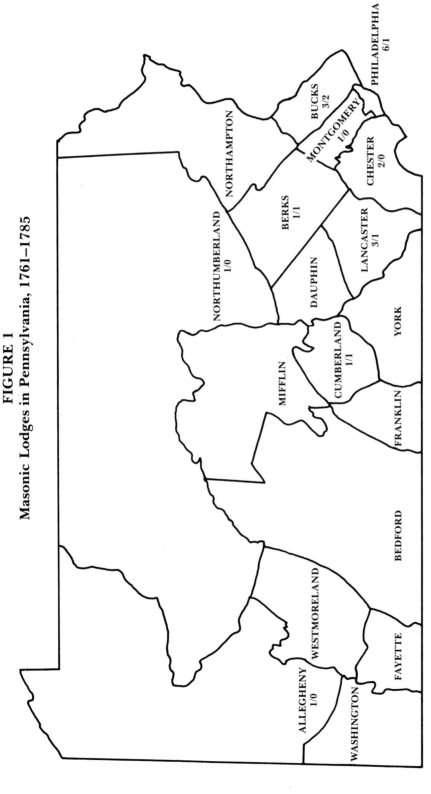

FIGURE 1

Masonic Lodges in Pennsylvania, 1761–1785

PENNSYLVANIA IN 1785 (18 counties)

Key: new/ceased lodges
Totals: 19/6   Net: +13

Sources: Julius F. Sachse, *Old Masonic Lodges of Pennsylvania, "Moderns" and "Ancients,"* Vol. I, *1730-1777,* and Vol. II, *1779-1800* (Phila., 1912, 1913); Charles E. Meyer, *Masonic Lodges in Pennsylvania from 1730 to 1880,* "*Moderns" and "Ancients"* (Phila., n.d.); "Information Pertaining to Early Freemasonry in the Western Hemisphere, Including the Warrant and Constitution Dates of the Subordinate Lodges under the Provincial and Present Grand Lodge of F. and A.M. of Pennsylvania" (unpublished list, n.d.); Register of Members, Vol. 1, 1789-1823.

the ensuing years, however, do not appear to have had the same effect, although an appreciable number of men did become new members shortly thereafter. Most of the men who became "Ancient" Masons in this period lived in Philadelphia, at least long enough to obtain their Masonic degrees. With nine hundred eighty nine men, the Philadelphia lodges had the most initiates. The country lodges had one hundred forty, the non-Pennsylvania lodges had five hundred seventy eight, and the military and traveling lodges had two hundred three.

No record exists of the specific occupational or social backgrounds of the men who became "Ancient" Masons in this period. Judging from membership fees charged by the lodges and by frequent appeals for charitable contributions, however, these men probably came from the middle to upper ranks of society. For example, in the 1760s Lodge No. 2 charged 2s. 6d. for the application fee, 20s. for each of the three degrees, and 15s. for the charity fund. Full membership in the lodge, therefore, entailed a total initial cost of £.3. 17s. 6d. In addition, a member had to pay for the food and drink consumed on stated lodge nights, usually not exceeding 1s. 6d., and had to make a contribution of 1s. per month to the charity fund. Fines for non-attendance at meetings and for minor infractions of the rules and regulations also went into the charity fund. These fees appear to have remained consistent over the next twenty years, except for a brief period of inflation during the Revolutionary War; Lodge No. 3, for example, charged essentially the same amounts in the 1780s.

The cost of membership in an "Ancient" Pennsylvania Masonic lodge, £3. 17s. 6d., was equivalent to approximately twenty days' wages of a common laborer in the 1760s and about sixteen days' wages in the 1780's. Although such an individual conceivably could belong, it is unlikely, since this membership fee also amounted to more than one-third of his estimated yearly food budget in the 1760's and about one-quarter of the same in the 1780s. Among other lower socio-economic groups, mariners earned somewhat less and cordwainers (shoemakers) and tailors slightly more than laborers. By contrast, skilled craftsmen and artisans usually earned twice the wages of these groups and thus could more easily afford Masonic membership.[39]

Financial security alone did not ensure an individual's acceptance. As evidenced by both "Ancient" Constitutions used by Pennsylvania Masons in this period, a candidate also had to fulfill a number of other membership requirements. Not only did he have to meet the usual "external" qualifications, such as free-born status, maturity, physical perfection, and steady employment, but he also had to possess certain "internal" qualities, such as irreproachable character and native intelligence. By his personal religious and philosophical attitudes, he had to be predisposed to the Fraternity's teachings. Both Dermott and Smith emphasized the need for a thorough investigation into the backgrounds of candidates before they could be seriously considered. In light of these qualifications, which were similiar to, but more stringent than, those for "Modern" membership, the great number of "Ancient" Masons becomes even more surprising.[40]

The success of "Ancient" Pennsylvania Freemasonry was greater than that of "Modern" Freemasonry that preceded it. The leaders of the Grand Lodge were especially vigorous in propagating the ideals of Freemasonry and in extending their organization's jurisdiction. They associated themselves with the American revolutionary struggle, sponsored a scheme for the establishment of an American Grand Lodge, published an updated version of the "Ancient" constitutions, increasingly opened their activities to public view and undertook plans for the building of a permanent lodge house—all to the greater benefit and reputation of the Fraternity. In its first twenty-four years of existence, the Grand Lodge of Pennsylvania provided a solid foundation upon which future Masonic leaders could build. An era of even greater expansion was to follow.

CHAPTER 4:

The Independent Grand Lodge,
1786–1811

By the mid-1780s the Masonic Fraternity in Pennsylvania enjoyed favorable public opinion, increased membership, and a stable institutional structure. Its leaders therefore felt sufficiently secure to take the final steps in severing administrative ties with its parent body, the Grand Lodge of England. They based this decision, in part, upon favorable responses to an inquiry on this subject which they had circulated among other American grand lodges two years previously. The Pennsylvania Grand Lodge considered independence for at least four reasons: (1) the changed political situation that "renders it improper to continue any acknowledgement of dependency . . . [upon any] . . . kind of foreign jurisdiction;" (2) the example of other independent American grand lodges; (3) the desire of some of its own subordinate lodges to form grand lodges outside Pennsylvania; and (4) its desire to extend its influence abroad, which was restricted by too close a connection with the Grand Lodge of England. The Grand Lodge also hoped that national Masonic conventions might be held annually to discuss general matters of interest to the Craft. This motive was similar to Pennsylvania's encouragement, a few years earlier, of a general grand lodge for the United States, but neither measure received the necessary support.[1]

In early February 1786 the Grand Lodge considered deleting from future warrants words that indicated its subordination to the Grand Lodge of England, but definitive action on this measure was postponed. Such a move would have been nearly a declaration of independence. Masonic leaders preferred to wait for a resolution of uncertainties. In its next regularly scheduled meeting, in March, the Grand Lodge by circular letter summoned all subordinate lodges to the September quarterly communication to discuss the important issue of independence from England.[2]

At that meeting, the representatives of twelve lodges unanimously approved, without discussion, the following resolution:

That this Grand Lodge is, and ought to be, a Grand Lodge, Independent of Great Britain or any other Authority whatever, and that they are not under any ties to any other Grand Lodge except those of Brotherly Love and Affection, which they will always be happy to cultivate and preserve with all Lodges throughout the Globe.[3]

Although only about one-third of all functioning lodges participated in this action, it nonetheless generated much interest, since normally only between five and seven lodges were represented at quarterly communications of the Grand Lodge in this period. The measure of independence was supported by Masons from a wide geographical area. Of the twelve lodges represented, only three were from Philadelphia (Nos. 2, 3, 9). The others were from Sunbury in Northumberland County (No. 22) and from Pittsburgh in Allegheny County (No. 45); five were located in Delaware (Nos. 5, 14, 18, 33, 44), one in Virginia (No. 12) and one in South Carolina (No. 38).

Immediately after passage of this important resolution, the Provincial Grand Lodge of Pennsylvania "Ancients", which had operated under warrant from the Grand Lodge of England "Ancients" since 1761, was closed forever. The next day, September 26, the representatives of a thirteenth lodge, No. 25, Bristol, joined with the others in forming a "Grand Convention." Proceedings then began under the new designation: "The Grand Lodge of Pennsylvania, and Masonic Jurisdiction thereunto belonging." The last phrase was added to signify that the Grand Lodge had under its jurisdiction lodges located outside the boundaries of Pennsylvania. The membership, officers and rules and regulations of the new supervisory body remained the same as before.[4]

The Pennsylvania organization was the fourth-oldest independent grand lodge in the United States, preceded only by those of Massachusetts and Virginia in 1778 and South Carolina in 1783. Before the end of the year, independent grand lodges were established in Georgia and New Jersey, and in 1787 in Maryland, New York and North Carolina.[5]

Within three days of declaring independence, the Grand Lodge formed a Committee of Correspondence to officially inform the Grand Lodge of England of the break. By mid-October the Committee had prepared a document, which met with unanimous approval from the Pennsylvania body. The letter contained expressions of fraternal affection and respect for the older Grand Lodge: ". . . we shall look up to you as venerable Masters and Instructors in the Royal Art whenever we find ourselves lacking in Knowledge." Nonetheless, the Grand Lodge justified its move on the grounds of the recent political separation of the two countries. It did not wish to alienate the American government or to encourage the Fraternity's detractors by maintaining allegiance to a foreign jurisdiction, especially in Great Britain, although it avowed its purposes to be apolitical. The Grand Lodge also enclosed copies of its recent proceedings, no doubt to establish the legitimacy of its actions.[6]

For some reason, this communication failed to reach England and a duplicate had to be drawn up two years later. To ensure delivery, a member of Lodge No. 2, Solomon Bush, was given the task of personally carrying it to London, with additional instructions to inform other European grand lodges of the independence of the Pennsylvania body. This action complicated matters since, evidently ignorant of the Masonic dispute still going on in England, Bush unwittingly delivered the letter to the "Modern," rather than the "Ancient," English Grand Lodge. This error provoked the resentment of the Premier Grand Lodge, which believed the Pennsylvania organization to be the Provincial Grand Lodge that it had warranted in 1749 with William Allen as Grand Master.[7]

The "Modern" English Grand Lodge disapproved the vote for independence. It considered it to be unjustified, and that the two countries had separated was irrelevant:

> Masonry [is] an universal and beautiful System of Philanthropy unconnected with the politicks [sic] of States or modes of Religion with with the maxims of the Craft wisely forbids us to meddle lest dissentions might ensue.

According to "Modern" English Masons, the institution of Freemasonry was indivisible and the jurisdiction of the "Modern" Grand Lodge was superior. Instead of separating, the subordinate lodges were to unite into:

> . . . one great extensive and respectable Body concentr'd under one common Head for their general welfare, and which Head can surely be no where more properly placed than in the Grand Lodge from whence they all derive . . . .

Such an attitude on the part of the Premier Grand Lodge may have served to lengthen the dispute between the two Masonic rivals in England.[8]

The misunderstanding between Pennsylvania and England was cleared up, or at least explained, by a subsequent letter from the Pennsylvania Grand Lodge to the "Moderns." Although fraternal, it firmly stated the Grand Lodge's commitment to its present course. The Pennsylvania Brethren held to a different conception of the expansion of the Masonic system and were more liberal in their application of its modes of government than their "Modern" English counterparts. They believed that each jurisdiction ought to govern its own geographical area but also that the enlightened principles of Freemasonry nonetheless served to unify them

Philadelphia Sept 26. 1756

At a Grand Convention of 13 different Lodges working by Virtue of Warrants from the late Grand Lodge of Pennsylvania with full power from their Constituents to decide upon the Question, whether the Grand Lodge of Pennsylvania should establish themselves as a Grand Lodge independent of Great Britain or any other Authority and with the concurrence of other Lodges signified by Letter. It was unanimously Resolved That the Lodges under the Jurisdiction of the Grand Lodge of Pennsylvania lately held under the authority of the Grand Lodge of England will and now do form themselves into a Grand Lodge to be called the Grand Lodge of Pennsylvania and Masonic Jurisdiction thereunto belonging to be held in Philadelphia and that the late Grand officers continue to be the Grand officers of Pennsylvania invested with all the Powers Jurisdictions preeminence and Authority thereunto belonging, til the usual time of the next election, and that the Grand Lodge and the particular Lodges govern themselves by the Rules & Regulations heretofore established, 'til other Rules and Regulations shall be adopted —

Jos. Fox   Will Adcock
Jas. Whitehead   B. Smith
Chas. Young   Alexr. Rutherford
                         Thomas Duncan Smith
Wm. Delany   Praise Wadman
John. Stafford   Jos. Dean

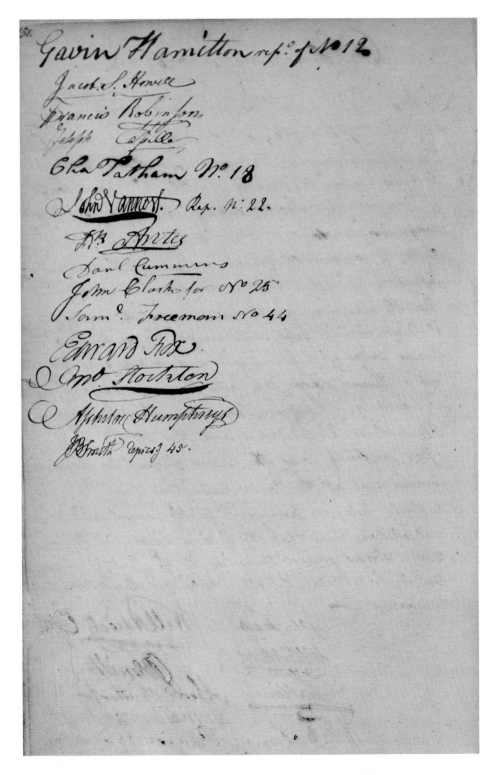

Original Grand Lodge Minutes, September 26, 1786 (Grand Lodge of Pennsylvania).

"like the Orbs of Heaven revolving around the Sun . . . bound in one splendid system." They expressed sincere warmth and affection for their English Brothers and even offered to continue official correspondence, which accident had initiated. No record exists of any response by the "Modern" Grand Lodge to these overtures. At the same time the Pennsylvania Grand Lodge sent communications to the "Ancients" as well. These were carried by another member of Lodge No. 2, Eleazer Oswald, and reached their proper destination safely.[9]

Not until early December 1792, six years after declaring its independence, did the Pennsylvania Grand Lodge finally receive a reply from the "Ancient" English Grand Lodge. In contrast to the "Moderns," the "Ancients" heartily congratulated the Pennsylvania Masons on their new status as "highly satisfactory to the Masonic world at large." They expressed approval of the Grand Lodge's *Book of Constitutions,* which they had received, and applauded its adherence to the "Ancient Landmarks of the Craft." The "Ancient" English Masons shared the views of their Pennsylvania Brothers regarding the overall structure of Freemasonry:

> All Grand Lodges in Masonry [are] necessarily Free, Independent, and Equipollent within their respective jurisdictions, which consquently excludes the ideas of subjection to a foreign authority or the establishment of an Imperium in Imperio.[10]

Meanwhile, confident of its own legitimacy, the Grand Lodge of Pennsylvania conducted business as usual: the warranting of lodges, the hearing of appeals, the raising of funds and the relief of indigent persons. Two of its most important actions were preparing a new form of Grand Lodge warrant and notifying its subordinate lodges of the Fraternity's new status. Both actions were accomplished within a month of the declaration of independence. Over the course of the next few years, the subordinate lodges turned in their old warrants, issued by the Provincial Grand Lodge, and received new ones. This was purely a formal matter and was conducted without cost.[11]

In addition to breaking with England, the Grand Lodge also sponsored two public ceremonies in 1786, on each St. John's Day. The June event included an "Ode on Masonry" for grand chorus, especially composed for the occasion.[12] The December celebration appears to have been one of the most impressive of the period. There was a grand procession to St. Paul's Church, where participants heard a Masonic prayer by the Rev. Dr. Samuel Magaw and a charity sermon by the Rev. Joseph Pilmore, rector of several Episcopal parishes in Montgomery County. Pilmore's main theme was that Masons could best show their appreciation for the blessings God had given them by contributing to the relief of suffering of their fellow creatures. Understandably, these clergymen offered traditional Christian viewpoints, but they also expressed a number of deistic concepts as well, more in keeping with the Fraternity's rationalistic ideology. Masonic music accompanied the services, and such money collected on this occasion was distributed to distressed Masons as well as to prisoners in local jails.[13]

*   *   *   *   *   *   *   *

Shortly after declaring independence from England, the Grand Lodge of Pennsylvania undertook a revision of its rules and regulations to better govern the Fraternity. In December 1789 it adopted a comprehensive set of provisions consisting of twenty-eight separate articles. They were designed to augment, rather than replace, the *Ahiman Rezon* of 1783. These rules were written in more straightforward language than the rhetorical style of the earlier version. They also dealt with new matters not previously covered, however, and they showed greater concern for regularity and propriety.[14]

The Rules and Regulations of 1789 spelled out the composition of the Grand Lodge, the procedures for election and installation of officers, the process of forming and disbanding subordinate lodges, the rules of order to be observed during meetings, proper attire for members and officers, the process of hearing appeals from individuals, and various fees for certificates, warrants and dispensations. Most of these provisions clarified ones found in the *Ahiman Rezon*. Some new rules dealt with the Deputy Grand Secretary, a new position, as well as an annual audit of the Grand Treasurer's accounts, public processions, the Correspondence Committee, the returns of members of the subordinate lodges and the appointment of proxies.

Also included were provisions for the establishment of a standing Charity Committee, whose function was to meet monthly to assess the needs of, and grant relief to, deserving Brothers and their widows and orphans. To provide the necessary funds, each Pennsylvania Mason was required to pay 5s. ($.65) per year to the Grand Lodge Charity Fund, in addition to 1s. ($.13) quarterly to his own lodge for its own charitable work. Before this reorganization, the disbursement of relief to distressed persons had been handled more casually. Other than holding periodic collections of money during special Masonic gatherings, such as at St. John's Day celebrations, and relying upon the largesse of the subordinate lodges, the Grand Lodge had had no more organized method of fulfilling this important Masonic obligation.

After 1789 the Grand Lodge Charity Committee was able to disburse at least some money each year, but small sums were expended, and relatively few persons were aided. Surviving data for the years 1792 to 1809 indicate that just over a hundred persons received charity from this fund, of which the average grant per person was $12 (Table 1). This was equal to about twelve days wages for a common Philadelphia laborer and about six for a skilled artisan. It appears that the Fraternity as a whole was much more generous, however. In the years 1798, 1799 and 1800, for example, the total disbursements of all Pennsylvania Masonic lodges (both Grand and subordinate) amounted to approximately $3,000, $1,500 and $1,800 respectively. These figures exceeded the median annual expenditures of other private Philadelphia charities in operation at this time. The Grand Lodge also purchased shares in the Philadelphia Dispensary, a special facility established in 1786 to provide free medical care to worthy poor persons.[15]

In April 1790 Benjamin Franklin died. Although he was a prominent Pennsylvania Freemason, the Grand Lodge granted him no official recognition. It passed no resolutions, performed no Masonic funeral service and observed no period of mourning. As an organization the Fraternity did not appear at his burial, although no doubt some members did so as individuals. In contrast, a number of other societies with which Franklin was associated were represented, such as the American Philosophical Society, the College of Physicians, and the Society of Cincinnati, as well as all manner of public officials. This event would have been a good opportunity for the Masons to continue to polish their public image, with which they seemed very much concerned, but they did not take advantage of it.[16]

This reticence on the part of the Fraternity to recognize Franklin officially may be explained by two factors. First, it seems that at least a portion of the leadership did not approve of public processions. Only a few months before, in December 1789, the Grand Lodge decided, against its usual practice, not to hold a public procession on St. John's Day. The rules and regulations of the same date also restricted public processions by requiring not just a plurality of votes for approval, but a full two-thirds majority. They also stated that a funeral service should not be conducted unless the Master of the deceased Brother's lodge requested it. The approval of at least five Master Masons was necessary for a public funeral of an individual who was not a member of a Pennsylvania lodge.[17] Despite these restrictions, however, one would think that Franklin was of sufficient prominence to warrant some special consideration.

The second reason probably carried even more weight. There is no evidence that Franklin ever changed his allegiance from the "Moderns" to the "Ancients." Although a Past Grand Master and an active participant in Masonic affairs, both at home and abroad, Franklin had little connection with, and thus earned no official consideration from, the Grand Lodge of Pennsylvania, which had long since become "Ancient."

TABLE 1
Charitable Disbursements of the Grand Lodge of Pennsylvania, 1786–1811

Year	Amount ($)	Number of Persons	Average Grant ($)
1786	—	—	—
1787	8	—	—
1788	—	—	—
1789	—	—	—
1790	—	—	—
1791	—	—	—
1792	57	9	6
1793	26	4	7
1794	30	1	30
1795	125	9	14
1796	144	11	13
1797	—	—	—
1798	2,998*	—	—
1799	1,492*	—	—
1800	1,791*	—	—
1801	100	7	14
1802	80	7	11
1803	64	7	9
1804	60	5	12
1805	155	13	12
1806	103	8	13
1807	150	14	11
1808	100	9	11
1809	50	5	10
1810	—	—	—
1811	—	—	—

Dashes indicate that no information is available for the given year.

*The amounts given for the years 1798, 1799 and 1800 represent the disbursements not only of the Grand Lodge Charity Fund, but also of all the subordinate lodges, which were reported together.

Information pertaining to the period before 1792 is fragmentary.

Subordinate lodges had their own charity funds separate from the above. Information on the amounts disbursed is not generally available.

All figures have been rounded off to the nearest dollar.

Amounts originally given in Pennsylvania pounds have been converted to dollars at the rate of £1 = $2.67 or $1 = 7s. 5d.

Sources: Joshua L. Lyte, comp., *Reprint of the Minutes of the Grand Lodge of Pennsylvania* (Phila., 1895-1907), Vol. I, *1779-1801*, 112, 135f., 182, 201, 203f., 210f., 219f., 243, 256, 259, 341, 385, 456, 475; December 27, 1787, March 5, 1792, June 3 & 24, 1793, June 2, 1794, December 31, 1795, March 7, June 6, September 5, 1796, December 27, 1798, December 27, 1799, December 27, 1800, June 15, 1801; Vol. II, *1801-1810*, 12, 18, 31, 32, 37, 75, 93, 111, 117, 145, 160, 171, 185, 196, 205, 261, 269, 296, 310f., 338, 344, 368, 391, 407, 438; September 7, December 7, 31, 1801, March 1, June 7, 1802, March 7, September 5, 1803, March 5, June 4, 1804, March 4, November 4, December 2, 1805, March 3, 1806, June 2, September 1, 1806, April 6, June 1, December 7, 1807, March 7, June 6, September 5, November 6, 1808, June 5, September 4, December 1809. For conversion rates and a discussion of wages and prices, see: Donald R. Adams, "Wage Rates in the Early National Period, Philadelphia, 1785-1830," *Journal of Economic History*, XXVIII (1968), 404-426; Billy Smith, "Material Lives of Laboring Philadelphians, 1750-1800," *William And Mary Quarterly*, 3rd Series, XXXVII, no. 2 (Apr. 1981), 163-202.

Lest this attitude seem unusually narrow for a Society that prided itself on principles of universalism and brotherhood, it should be noted that the "Ancients" at least respected Franklin. The Rev. Joseph Pilmore dedicated his sermon of 1786 to him, not only as a leading citizen, a "most sublime philosopher," the "Friend of his Country" and a "great and successful Asserter of Liberty," but also as "An Illustrious Brother, whose distinguished Merit among Masons entitles him to their highest Veneration."[18] Pilmore was not a Mason and may not have been familiar with the differences between "Moderns" and "Ancients." Even so, the sermon was specifically commissioned by the Grand Lodge and received its official approval before publication. It is unlikely that the Grand Lodge harbored bitterness toward the "Moderns," who had long since dissolved, especially in light of the "Ancients'" fraternal letter to the "Modern" English Grand Lodge of the same period.

In contrast, the Grand Lodge declared a special period of mourning two years later upon the death of Laurence Dermott, the founder of the "Ancients." Members were requested to wear "Aprons bordered with Black or other Marks of Mourning" in the procession on the next St. John's Day. The same signs of respect were offered on the occasion of the death of the Senior Grand Warden, Joseph Dean, which occurred that same year.[19]

If the Fraternity had any doubts as to the propriety of exposing itself to public view, it overcame them in the 1790s when the Grand Lodge, hoping to gain additional reputation, renewed its earlier association with George Washington. This policy was especially noticeable after he became President of the United States and the capital of the country was moved to Philadelphia. The Grand Lodge sponsored another public procession and feast on St. John's Day, 1791, which included a Masonic oration, "suitable to the Grand Day," delivered by Dr. William Smith in the morning in the lodge room and a banquet in the afternoon at an unspecified nearby hotel. Presumably, this oration, which has not survived, dealt with Washington since Smith was chosen on that occasion to head a special committee of Grand Lodge officers to prepare a congratulatory address which was presented personally to the President on January 3, 1792. The address expressed patriotic and Masonic themes in a laudatory and rhetorical style. Pennsylvania Masons hailed Washington as "the Great Master Builder (under the Supreme Architect) by whose Labours the Temple of Liberty hath been reared in the West, exhibiting to the Nations of the Earth a Model of Beauty, Order and Harmony worthy of their imitation and Praise." Washington acknowledged these sentiments in a simpler and less florid style, with expressions of gratitude for his association with the Craft.[20]

Despite this successful episode, there was still considerable debate among Grand Lodge members on the issue of processions. In December 1792 a member proposed that the requirement of a two-thirds vote for approval be amended back to a simple majority. A final decision on this measure was postponed for more than a year, when a tie vote was broken by the Grand Master's intervention. Although records are not clear, presumably he was in favor of the resolution since processions were conducted frequently over the next few years.[21]

The yellow fever epidemic of 1793 forced the Grand Lodge to suspend operations throughout the summer and fall, as did most of the subordinate lodges in Philadelphia. Although the Fraternity as a whole did not respond to the crisis, individual Masons did so, for example, Israel Israel from Lodge No. 3 and Stephen Girard, both of whom belonged to the voluntary Citizen's Committee.[22]

The Masonic celebration on St. John's Day, 1793, was accompanied by the usual pomp and circumstance, but was particulary notable for two reasons. In the first place, it was dedicated to the relief of suffering caused by the recent epidemic. Masons were encouraged to contribute to the charity fund; by way of example, the Grand Lodge gave up its customary annual feast so that monies thereby saved could also go to the poor. Second, George Washington was present for the first time since 1778; he reportedly made a "generous Donation to the Poor." Religious services were held at St. Paul's Episcopal Church, where Brother Samuel Magaw once again gave the prayer and charity sermon. He vividly portrayed the desolation in the city and urged Masons to follow the example of Jesus Christ, whom he depicted essentially as a doer of good works.[23]

In 1795 the Fraternity suffered a potentially damaging division over the establishment of a Grand Royal Arch Chapter in Philadelphia. The Royal Arch was a fourth degree, reflecting a higher level of Masonic knowledge, which the "Ancients" had developed during the previous forty years. This degree was a point of contention between them and the "Moderns," who refused to recognize it. The conferring of this degree had been sanctioned in Pennsylvania by the warrant of Lodge No. 3 in 1764. The same right was contained in all subsequent warrants, which permitted each lodge to set up governing bodies, known as "chapters."

Upon petition by members of Lodge Nos. 19, 52 and 67, the Grand Lodge investigated the actions of James Molan, an individual of unknown Masonic membership, who had claimed to have exclusive knowledge of the correct procedures for the granting of the degree. Upon his own initiative, Molan had set up a Grand Royal Arch Chapter in Philadelphia, claiming authority from the warrants of the three foregoing lodges. Molan's new organization denied admission to other Royal Arch Masons, who were offended and confused. The Grand Lodge condemned the actions of Molan and considered them "irregular and disorderly, and tending to destroy the Harmony of the Brethren in this State." At the same time it exonerated Master Masons who unwittingly had been taken in by this scheme and restored the warrants of the three affected lodges suspended at the beginning of the controversy. To regularize matters for the future, the Grand Lodge sanctioned the establishment of the Grand Royal Arch Chapter in February 1798 with full authority to regulate all matters pertaining to this degree and to preside over the local chapters. This organization, separate from, but subordinate to, the Grand Lodge, was to meet on the day before St. John the Evangelist's Day. This was the first grand chapter established in the United States. This incident is indicative of both the expansion of the Fraternity and the desire of the Grand Lodge to control the actions of all Pennsylvania Masons.[24]

Pennsylvania Masons participated in another public procession in June 1795. It appears to have been among the most well attended of the period: there were thirty-two officially designated positions of honor for Grand Lodge members. Religious services were held at St. Peter's Episcopal Church at Third and Pine Streets, where Dr. William Smith gave his last Masonic sermon. This discourse was influenced by Masonic ideology and contemporary scientific knowledge and was among the least Christian of all late eighteenth-century Masonic sermons. Christ's role as Redeemer and Savior of man was mentioned almost gratuitously; Smith emphasized His role as a great moral teacher and exemplifier of Masonic truths, along with other notable historical figures such as King Solomon.[25]

The keynote of the celebration of St. John's Day in 1796 was the adoption of another address to George Washington, this time on his retirement from public office. Regarding him as "a Friend, a Benefactor and a Father," the Grand Lodge praised him for his many years of devoted service to his country and for his continual advancement of Masonic principles. The Pennsylvania Masons prayed that after a long and fruitful life on earth he "may be received by the Great Master Builder of this World and of Worlds unnumbered into the ample felicity of that Celestial Lodge, in which alone distinguished virtues and distiguished labors can be eternally rewarded." The next day seventeen members of the Grand Lodge presented the address to Washington, who received it "with all the feelings of Brotherly Affection mingled with those Sentiments for the Society which it was calculated to excite."[26]

During the next three years the Grand Lodge once again revised its rules and regulations. Several committees met regularly and members engaged in frequent debates on existing practices. The final product of this effort was adopted in March 1799, but it was not substanitally different from the version of ten years earlier. For the most part, changes of wording, refecting a somewhat stricter interpretation of the Masonic constitution, were all that was new. Two significant changes did take place, however. The first concerned the issue of Past Masters by dispensation. Officially, only men who had actually served at least six months as Masters of their lodges could sit in Grand Lodge, but some Master Masons had obtained this privilege through dispensation from the Grand Master although they had not held lodge office. By the Rules and Regulations of 1799 this practice was forbidden. Moreover, the provision requiring a two-thirds majority in holding processions was restored. The new rules also established slightly higher fees for various Masonic documents. At the turn of the nineteenth century it appears that the leaders of Pennsylvania Freemasonry were becoming more conservative, trying to restore what they believed to be the "ancient usages" of their Society.[27]

The Grand Lodge participated in yet another procession in the eighteenth century but one not essentially Masonic in character. In recognition of the death of George Washington, twelve days earlier, the United States Congress invited civic groups, including the Masons, to participate in an official memorial service at Zion Evangelical Lutheran Church on December 26, 1799. After hearing the Grand Master's solemn oration on the virtues of Washington and his dedication to Freemasonry, the Grand Lodge passed a resolution of bereavement and closed; then, dressed in full regalia with aprons trimmed in black, its members joined the general procession, which formed at Congress Hall to escort a bier meant to represent Washington's. At the church, musicians performed specially-composed pieces including an anthem, a monody and a dirge. Bishop White conducted the memorial service, and General Henry Lee of Virginia, a member of the House of Representatives, delivered the eulogy in which he apostrophized Washington as "first in war, first in peace, and first in the hearts of his countrymen."[28]

At its own St. John's Day ceremonies the next day, the Grand Lodge resolved that the lodge room be draped in black and that all Grand Lodge officers wear black arm bands and black emblems on their aprons for six months. Members of the subordinate lodges were encouraged to do the same.[29]

On January 1, 1800, Lodge No. 73, composed primarily of French immigrants, held a memorial service in its own lodge room, in Taylor's Alley (Ionic Street) between Second and Front Streets, to which it invited the officers of the Grand Lodge. Decorated completely in black, the lodge was adorned with Masonic symbols of death, including a bier on a platform, thick drapery with attached emblems, urns and three hundred lights. The Grand Master, Jonathan B. Smith, was much impressed by the solemnity of the atmosphere: "the interior of the Lodge exhibited a display of superior taste, elegance and splendor truly appropriate to the interesting occasion." One member of No. 73, Simon Chaudron, delivered an oration on the Masonic virtues of Brother Washington and his unselfish dedication to his country. Attending Grand Officers found the address "irresistably impressive, critically Judicious and Sublime . . . ." The oration was later published, in both English and French editions, and was widely circulated among the Fraternity, not only within Pennsylvania but among other Masonic jurisdictions as well. Copies were also sent to high-ranking officials of the American government and to foreign ministers and consuls.[30]

A few weeks later the Grand Lodge debated whether to hold a public procession of its own on February 22 in memory of George Washington. This was in response to a recommendation by Congress to commemorate the anniversary of Washington's birth by appropriate public expressions of grief. The vote was seventeen to fourteen, not enough for passage according to the two-thirds provision of the most recent version of the rules and regulations. The supporters of the measure, however, evaded this restriction by declaring it to be a funeral procession, which the Grand Master alone had sufficient authority to authorize and which he did. The difficulty of passing this measure even for so important a reason as to memorialize "one of the great lights" of the Craft, indicates that opposition to public exposure was growing within the Fraternity.

Philadelphia Masons assembled at their lodge room in the Pennsylvania State House at eleven o'clock in the morning on the appointed day. Dressed in full Masonic regalia augmented by black arm bands, members of ten subordinate lodges and the Grand Lodge participated. A place of honor was accorded Lodge No. 59, which had been named for Washington at the time of its founding (1793). This lodge carried a bier covered in black cloth, upon which was placed a four-foot high gilt urn on a marble base of three steps. Surmounting the urn was a drooping American eagle in whose beak was a shield bearing the commemorative inscription: "Washington Lodge, Honored by the Name, let us emulate his Virtues, whose loss we deplore." Consisting of three to four hundred Masons, the procession marched to the Zion Lutheran Church on Fourth Street above Arch, where the Rev. Dr. Samuel Magaw gave an effusive oration on the "Virtues and Greatness of General George Washington." Solemn funeral odes with chorus and orchestra accompanied the service. The leaders of the Fraternity were proud of the public appearance of the members: "The whole was arranged and conducted with that Order, simplicity and dignity, which was suitable to the impressive occasion, and which the Masons of Pennsylvania have always endeavored to cultivate."[31]

*   *   *   *   *   *   *   *

A major concern of the Masonic Fraternity in the late eighteenth and early nineteenth centuries was the establishment of a permanent meeting place for the Grand Lodge and the subordinate lodges. Since declaring its independence in 1786, the Grand Lodge had had to move every few years. Between 1786 and 1790 it occupied the building in Videll's Alley where it had previously met from 1769 to 1777. This building was unsuitable, probably because of its size, and the Grand Lodge had to find "a more convenient place to meet." Committees were formed to investigate the possibilities, but without immediate success.

One option was to build upon the lot of ground at Twelfth and Walnut Streets, which had been donated by Joseph Dean at the end of 1785. Attempts to raise money by subscription and by investing in lotteries failed. Without sufficient funds to construct a building, which was the condition of the gift, the Grand Lodge had to relinquish the lot in 1791. A year later Joseph Dean became bankrupt and his creditors put the lot up for sale. Still intending to build on it, but at some future date, the Grand Lodge purchased it. In 1795 after the death of Dean, the Grand Lodge offered to give the income from the property to his widow; but she refused it. Eventually the Grand Lodge, realizing that the lot was too far away for the convenience of its members, decided to sell it and donate the proceeds, which amounted to $2,000, to charity. This was not done until February 1809, however.[32]

In August 1790 the Grand Lodge decided to rent rooms in the Free Quaker's Meeting House at Fifth and Arch Streets and subsequently signed a nine-year lease. The annual rent of £75, as well as the expenses of moving and furnishing the rooms, was to be borne by the contributions of the subordinate lodges. At the end of nine years, the Quakers declined to renew the lease, and the Grand Lodge once again had to search for a suitable meeting place.

To buy or erect a building specifically for the Fraternity's use, the Grand Lodge developed ambitious schemes for raising revenue. In May 1796 the Finance Committee drew up a plan for a Masonic loan to sell four thousand shares at $10 each, in what was called the "Pennsylvania Free Mason Hall Association." Shareholders were permitted the right to vote based upon the amount of shares they held. It was hoped that the interest from the Association's investments would be sufficient to avoid burdening subordinate lodges. Money came in slowly, so the Grand Lodge devised a new plan to raise the more modest sum of $6,000 by a lottery. Shares were $5 apiece, with the option of buying half shares. This plan eventually proved more successful, providing the Grand Lodge with enough for its needs. Another means the Grand Lodge used to raise money in this period was by participating in lotteries in the states of Pennsylvania, Massachusetts and Delaware, but these efforts produced no additional income.[33]

Until a permanent building could be obtained the Grand Lodge searched for temporary quarters. In November 1799 its officers petitioned Governor Thomas Mifflin for permission to use vacant rooms in the Pennsylvania State House. The Grand Lodge apologized for not having sufficient funds to purchase a meeting place of its own and explained that this was due to the Masons' extraordinary charitable contribution of about $3,000 to sufferers in the yellow fever epidemic of 1798. This plea was an obvious attempt to impress the governor with the benefits the Fraternity had brought to Philadelphia, and it worked. He granted use of the secretary's chamber in the State House on condition that it be vacated upon demand.[34]

This arrangement lasted only two years, from 1800 to 1802, when the Pennsylvania Assembly granted Charles Willson Peale the use of the State House for his natural history museum. Peale moved in early in 1802 and made considerable internal changes. He complained to both the Grand Lodge and the Pennsylvania authorities that Masonic meetings lasted late into the evening and were disruptive of museum activities specifically and of the neighborhood generally. After the work of Freemasonry was finished, members usually attended the so-called "festive board," and some of them, having had too much to drink, made boisterous processions to their homes. At first the two tenants tried to work out an accommodation, but by late spring the Grand Lodge was asked to leave. From May until December 1802 the Masonic lodges met at a dancing academy, located at 90 North Eighth Street, owned by a member of Lodge No. 51. This member, an actor named William Francis, offered his rooms without charge in atonement for his unauthorized use of Masonic regalia in one of his productions, which the Grand Lodge had considered to be "degrading to the Dignity of the Craft [which] has a manifest tendency to render it trifling and ridiculous in the Eyes of the public and of all sensible men . . . ." In recognition of his generosity, Francis was made Past Master by dispensation, entitled to all honors and regalia associated with that position.[35]

During 1801 and 1802 the Grand Lodge was under increasing pressure to find a permanent meeting house. It considered purchasing a spacious lot and building on the corner of Ninth and Arch Streets, but its funds were insufficient because the subordinate lodges were in arrears of dues. In any case, a number of members judged the location inconvenient. Motivated by "the extreme anxiety of some Brethren" to have a permanent building, the Grand Lodge held an extra communication in September to form a special committee for the purpose, composed of representatives of each subordinate Philadelphia lodge. This extra impetus was effective, and at the end of May 1802 the committee purchased from a coachmaker named William Hunter a lot with a three-story brick building, thirty-six feet wide by thirty-three feet deep, on the south side of Filbert Street, between Eighth and Ninth, The lot was seventy-five feet deep and included an alley nine-feet wide, and a courtyard of thirty square feet to which it led. The cost was only $3,000, which was well within the Grand Lodge's means, but another $5,850 were ultimately required to renovate the structure and to refurbish and furnish the rooms for Masonic purposes. This work was supervised by two members of the Fraternity, Robert Jackson, a carpenter, and Joseph Campbell, a bricklayer.

As a means of raising additional revenue to cover these expenses, the Grand Lodge approved fund-raising ventures such as selling subscriptions to the Masonic loan to lodges and to private individuals, expropriating a portion of all initiation fees, raising fees for warrants, certificates and dispensations, charging rent to subordinate lodges and chapters, establishing a private school that charged tuition, and renting rooms to other organizations and individuals. It also put pressure upon delinquent lodges to pay their dues or face loss of their warrants. Calling the new building "the Pennsylvania Free Mason's Hall," the Grand Lodge commissioned a commemorative copper plaque and unanimously resolved to hold a procession at special dedication ceremonies on the next St. John's Day, December 27, 1802.[36]

Pennsylvania Free Mason's Hall, Filbert Street (1802-1810, 1819-1820). Photograph by F. Gutekunst shortly before it was demolished in January 1880 (Grand Lodge of Pennsylvania).

On the appointed day members of the Grand Lodge and twenty-four subordinate lodges met at the Universalist Church on Lombard Street, between Fourth and Fifth, for morning religious services conducted by the Rev. George Richards, a Mason and later Grand Chaplain. Then they proceeded to the new hall on Filbert Street. It is not known how many persons marched but there were thirty-eight places of honor for Grand Lodge members, in addition to a band. Representatives from the Grand Lodge of New Jersey also participated.

The elaborate dedication ceremony held deep symbolic meaning. Opened by prayers from Brothers William Smith and John Andrews, both leading Episcopal clergymen, and accompanied by music, members of the Grand Lodge marched around the large central meeting hall three times. On the first circuit the Grand Master spread corn over the lodge, symbolizing plenty, opportunity and work and dedicated it to "Masonry." The second time he used wine, representing health, spirituality and peace, with a dedication to "Virtue and Silence." Finally he poured oil over the lodge, representing joy, happiness and gladness, with a dedication to "Universal Charity and Benevolence." Corn, wine and oil, known in Freemasonry as the "Wages of a Fellowcraft," are used to represent the "rewards of a good life," one of the major aims of Masonic teaching. Following this, musicians performed an anthem written by Philadelphia composer, Alexander Reinagle, a member of Lodge No. 51, as well as other orchestral and choral music. To conclude the ceremony, Grand Master Jonathan Bayard Smith delivered "an Affectionate Address which was received by the Brethren with the most lively tokens of Gratitude and Acknowledgement."[37]

The Grand Lodge did not hold another public procession until May 31, 1810, when it conducted a funeral service for William Ball, the first Grand Master of the "Ancients" in Pennsylvania. Members of fourteen subordinate lodges and the Grand Lodge, three clergymen and a band of musicians participated. Members congregated at the Filbert Street hall and proceeded to Ball's former residence on Market Street, whence they accompanied the body to the burial ground of the First Baptist Church. Ball was buried with full Masonic honors according to the custom of the Fraternity. In contrast to previous processions, Masons did not debate the propriety of this means of showing respect to a noteworthy Pennsylvania Freemason. In succeeding years the Grand Lodge engaged in similar forms of recognition to its most prominent deceased officials.[38]

The Pennsylvania Free Mason's Hall, dedicated in 1802, proved to be inadequate within only a few years. The membership of the Fraternity had grown so rapidly that the building no longer could accommodate all the lodges wishing to use it. In April 1807 the Grand Lodge entertained a motion to sell the hall and to purchase a new plot of ground upon which "an elegant Masonic Hall, suitable to the Dignity of the Grand Lodge," could be built. In the next few months the Grand Lodge gradually came to realize the merit of this proposal and various committees were established to implement it. At first the Masons had hoped to purchase a lot adjoining the hall, but because this did not happen, they were forced to look elsewhere. Despite this initial disappointment, they quickly progressed toward their goal. By the end of 1807 the Grand Lodge had purchased a vacant lot on the north side of Chestnut Street between Seventh and Eighth, had studied plans for a building, and had devised means for obtaining necessary funds to finance it.[39]

Not being professional architects, the members of the Building Committee held a public competition for designs, which was advertised in local newspapers. About a half-dozen entries were submitted. The winning design was by twenty-year-old William Strickland, who was on the threshold of his notable career. Despite the soundness of his plan, the Grand Lodge did not accept it completely until November 1808, after more than a year's debate. Contracts with artisans and laborers were drawn up in December, but actual work did not begin until the following spring when the weather cleared. The cornerstone was laid with appropriate Masonic ceremonies on April 17, 1809, by Grand Master James Milnor. The block of marble was placed in the northeast corner of the foundation because, for Masons, that location represents the halfway point between the darkness of the north and the brilliance of the east, thus symbolizing a new beginning or the start of a new project. Building progressed steadily but slowly over the next two years, owing in part to the committee's frequent changes of details, but also because of constantly rising costs. The project was supervised by a master builder, John Darragh, also a member of the Fraternity.

The completed structure was Neo-Gothic in style, eighty-two feet wide and sixty-nine feet deep, on a large lot measuring one hundred one by one hundred seventy-eight feet. Mostly wooden, the new Masonic Hall was faced in marble and brick, with a slate roof for protection against fire. Four large arched windows flanked a heavily buttressed entrance portal and five more were placed in the second story. Marble steps and a small rose window at the entrance also contributed Gothic elements. The edifice was surmounted by a wooden steeple one hundred eighty feet high.

Originally the Grand Lodge had planned to set the hall at the rear of the property, to allow the sale of two large lots in the front, but this plan was altered to enhance a view of the building. It was placed fifty feet behind a low retaining wall along Chestnut Street topped by marble capping on which was set an iron fence. The wall was intersected by two gates, which were supported at either end by marble piers. A six-foot-wide brick walkway led from the street to the main entrance and various plants and shrubbery decorated the interior courtyard. Along the rear of the property a small passageway, subsequently called Lodge Alley, was built and connected Seventh and Eighth Streets. A eight-foot brick wall ran along the sides of the building and another, nine feet high, with three gates, enclosed the back.

The interior consisted of two and a half stories of greater height than other contemporary structures. The four main rooms on the second floor were to be used strictly for lodge meetings, whereas a spacious banquet hall, described as an "elegant ball room," on the first floor was reserved for larger Masonic functions. This room measured seventy-eight by thirty-six feet with a twenty-two-foot high ceiling. The Masons frequently advertised its availability to other societies when it was not in use. They also solicited tenants for three smaller rooms and a kitchen on the first floor. In addition, there were three cellars for storage, two of which the Masons were willing to rent out. Rooms were furnished lavishly with chandeliers, candelabras, oil lamp fixtures, hand-carved mahogany furniture and pedestals, upholstered chairs, benches and settees, and draperies and curtains made from several types of woolen fabric, all red. Various means of heating and lighting were used: mostly coal and sperm oil for the upper floor and wood and candles below. A full-time building superintendent, Samuel Blanchard, was hired to guard the property, to perform routine maintenance and to keep "every part of the Premises and Furniture clean."[40]

Even before the hall was completely finished, Masons held their annual communication of December 27, 1810 there. In the next few months the Fraternity planned elaborate dedication ceremonies for June 24, including the largest Masonic procession ever held. Criticizing the more liberal policy of their predecessors, the leaders of the Grand Lodge said that they had deliberately refrained from engaging in public spectacles in recent years, except on truly momentous occasions (only three since 1800), in the belief that the infrequency of the processions would make those that were held more interesting and impressive. For the ceremonies for the Chestnut Street hall, however, the Grand Lodge recommended a full display: "This event will form an Epoch in the Annals of Masonry to which Brethren of future Ages will, we trust, look back with feelings of exultation and delight." Pennsylvania Masons were obviously proud of their new meeting place, considering it "a Temple unparalleled in this Country for its elegance and convenience."

In preparation for the dedication ceremonies, the Grand Lodge issued strict dress regulations and expected all Masons to carry themselves with proper deportment and personal dignity, to avoid "those irregularities which would bring discredit upon the Society." Masonic leaders were justifiably concerned about the Fraternity's public image because certain members did not always act appropriately. Grand Master James Milnor, who served from 1806 to 1813, in particular, stressed the importance of moral conduct and propriety among Masons in their general behavior and especially urged moderation while participating in Masonic functions. Milnor was very much concerned with preserving the reputation of the Society and removing any evidence its detractors could publicize.[41]

By any standard, the festivities connected with the official opening of the Chestnut Street hall were impressive. The program lasted all day and included a morning procession and church service, an afternoon dedication ceremony, and an evening banquet. Approximately seven hundred and fifty brethren met at the Old College Hall on Fourth Street near Arch and proceeded to St. John's Lutheran Church on Race Street east of Sixth. Members of twenty-one lodges, two military bands, visitors from the Grand Lodges of Maryland and New Jersey, and twenty-seven positions of honor for the Grand Lodge, comprised the procession, the largest yet assembled. The Masons marched in the proscribed order of six feet between ranks. Each lodge was led by a member who served as marshal; he walked on the lodge's flank and carried a blue silver-tipped wand. Two grand marshals on horseback, carrying gold-tipped wands, presided over the whole procession, which filled many city blocks.

At their destination, the Masons halted, turned inward and opened ranks to allow Grand Lodge members led by the Grand Master, who had marched at the rear, to pass into the church. The service consisted of an organ voluntary, a grand chorus, two prayers, two Masonic hymns, an "Oration on Masonry" delivered by Grand Master James Milnor, and a benediction. Invited guests included the attorney general of Pennsylvania, judges of several Pennsylvania courts, city officials, the clergy of various denominations, and the directors of the Academy of Fine Arts, "together with many other respectable Characters and a brilliant assemblage of Ladies."

Following the service, the procession reassembled and marched on to the new hall in the same manner as before. The members of the Grand Lodge made a grand entrance into the large banquet room on the first floor, where the project supervisor, John Darragh, ceremoniously turned over his work implements. The hall was dedicated in the usual three-part Masonic manner, with separate invocations to the "Grand Architect of the Universe," "Virtue and Science" and "Universal Charity and Benevolence." Three prayers were offered. In the evening, about two hundred Brethren attended a three-and-one-half-hour banquet during which numerous patriotic, religious and Masonic toasts were offered.[42]

The dedication ceremonies were conducted with great solemnity and participants behaved in an appropriate manner. The procession, about

The Masonic Hall on Chestnut Street (1811-1819). Drawing by William Strickland (Grand Lodge of Pennsylvania).

which Masonic authorities had felt some initial hesitancy, "far excelled in Beauty and Order any former exhibition of a similar kind." The Chestnut Street hall greatly enhanced the prestige of the Fraternity in the public eye and elicited the admiration of members and non-members alike. A local newspaper, for example, described it as "one of the most splendid Ornaments to our City."

Within a year of the dedication ceremonies the Grand Lodge was formally referring to itself as "The Grand Lodge of [the] Most Ancient and Honourable Fraternity of Free and Accepted Masons, of Pennsylvania and Masonic Jurisdiction, Thereunto Belonging according to the old institutions." This more impressive designation was probably adopted to match the name of the organization to the splendor of its meeting place.[43]

At the time of the dedication of its new hall the Grand Lodge had already spent nearly $55,000, including ground, materials, labor and interior decoration, an amount far exceeding original estimates. In addition, the Building Committee estimated that it would take at least another $17,000 to finish the building properly, entailing a debt of over $4,000. The Grand Lodge proceeded to raise money by a number of expedients: soliciting private subscriptions; increasing the price of warrants, dispensations and certificates; taking out loans; selling property; holding public lotteries; calling for special contributions by individual lodges; selling tickets to Masonic affairs; and renting rooms in the new hall to other Masonic as well as to non-Masonic organizations. The Grand Lodge also established a sinking fund to pay off at interest money which it had borrowed from a variety of sources. Redeeming the debt was a matter of great concern for the organization for the next few years.[44]

Not until April 1813 was the Chestnut Street hall finished to the satisfaction of the Grand Lodge. By then, total costs had risen to nearly $90,000: $14,167 for extinguishing the ground rent; $67,851 for the New Hall and appurtenances; $4,963 for furniture for the upper rooms and lodge paraphernalia; and $2,525 for furnishing the lower rooms. Despite this large expense, the operating budget actually showed a surplus of $972. The Building Committee completed its work and was discharged. On retiring, it recommended that any surplus be used to purchase lamp fixtures for the steps at the main entrance and for three statues for the facade, as was done.

Because of the enormous debt assumed for this project, the Grand Lodge redoubled its fund-raising efforts. It was especially insistent upon prompt collection of fees and dues, which were raised again. The Grand Lodge Charity Fund was temporarily suspended; the Fraternity relied upon the generosity of subordinate lodges to take up the slack. The Grand Lodge also tried to gain tax-exempt status for its new hall from both the Pennsylvania legislature and the Philadelphia city government, but was unsuccessful.[45]

The new Masonic Hall soon proved to be of benefit to the Fraternity, financially, fraternally and otherwise. The building quickly attracted popular attention and acclaim, and the Masons experienced no difficulty in renting rooms. The first tenants included such cultural and social organizations as the Harmonic Society, the Amateur Concert Society and the Philadelphia Dancing Assembly, beneficial associations such as the Welsh Society, and private individuals such as Victor Guillou, a French emigré who ran a dancing academy. These and other sponsors held frequent concerts, recitals, balls, banquets, art exhibitions and recitations. These affairs soon became so frequent that in March 1816 the Grand Lodge had to take out special liability insurance to protect itself against unforeseen accidents. An unusual series of concerts was performed in the winter and spring of 1812 by a musician named John Pardi, a self-acknowledged master of a new instrument known as the "Panharmonicon." Invented by the Viennese musical entrepreneur and Barnum-like showman, Johann Nepomuk Maelzel, this mechanical device imitated most of the sounds of a full orchestra through the use of air pressure. It had a short but distinguished history; even Beethoven was coaxed into writing for it.[46]

*   *   *   *   *   *   *   *

Growth of the Masonic Fraternity in Pennsylvania increased more in the twenty-five years after independence than in any previous period. By the end of 1811 eighty-nine new lodges had been founded (Table 2). They were dispersed throughout twenty-five Pennsylvania counties as well as nine other states or territories (Table 3, Figure 1). Although nearly sixty percent of the lodges in operation at this time ceased, this should not necessarily be considered evidence of failure; most of these lodges were located outside Pennsylvania, and they quite naturally changed their allegiances to geographically more convenient jursidictions. For example, eleven lodges went over to the Provincial Grand Lodge of Santo Domingo when it was formed in 1802, and six others joined the Grand Lodge of Delaware in 1806. Two of the lodges that ceased were in the army and were by definition only temporary. Fifteen Pennsylvania lodges were dissolved in this period after they had failed to pay their dues, despite numerous extensions.[47]

TABLE 2
Lodges Warranted by the Grand Lodge of Pennsylvania, 1786-1811

Years	Number of new lodges (lodge numbers)		Number of ceased lodges (lodge numbers)
1786-1799	37	(19a, 27a, 46, 47a, 47c, 47d, 48, 50-78, 80)	25 (4, 6, 7, 8, 10, 13a, 15, 17, 23, 27a, 29a, 32, 34, 37, 40, 42, 47a, 47d, 53, 58, [18, 18a, 35, 38, 44,]*)
1800-1811	52	(79, 81-85, 87-98, 98a, 99-131)	27 (12a, 14, 25, 31a, 33, 41, 47c, 48, 55, 56, 57, 63, 65, 74, 76, 78, 80, 87, 88, 89, 90, 95, 96, 97, 98, 98a, 99)
Totals	89	Net: +37	52 (58.4%)

*Not known when ceased, but probably before 1800.

No lodges were warranted in the first nine months of 1786.

Twenty-eight of the new lodges were warranted outside Pennsylvania, as follows: Cuba (103); Delaware (63, 96); Indian Territory (107); Louisiana Territory (90, 93, 109, 111, 112, 117, 118, 122, 129); Northwest Territory (78); Ohio (105); Santo Domingo (47a, 47c, 87, 88, 89, 95, 97, 98, 98a, 99); South Carolina (27a); Trinidad (77); and military (58).

Thirty-seven of the ceased lodges were located outside Pennsylvania, as follows: Delaware (14, 18, 33, 44, 63, 96); Georgia (42); Maryland (6, 7, 15, 17, 29a, 34, 35, 37); New Jersey (10, 23, 32); Northwest Territory (78); Santo Domingo (47a, 47c, 87, 88, 89, 90, 95, 97, 98, 99); South Carolina (27a, 38, 40, 47b); Virginia (12a, 41); and military (18a, 58).

A number with an "a" appended indicates either that more than one lodge was assigned the same number or that a lodge was suspended and then revived.

The warrants of Nos. 49, 47b and 86 were not issued.

The origins of new lodges are based upon their constitution dates.

Lodges "ceased" in basically two ways: by voluntary surrender of the warrant by the members or by order of the Grand Lodge. Various terms were used to describe such warrants: "surrendered," "returned," "vacated," or "ceased."

Seventy-two lodges were in operation by the end of 1811.

Sources: "Information Pertaining to Early Freemasonry in the Western Hemisphere, Including the Warrant and Constitution Dates of the Subordinate Lodges under the Provincial and Present Grand Lodge of F. and A.M. of Pennsylvania" (unpublished list); Joshua L. Lyte, comp., *Reprint of the Minutes of the Grand Lodge of Pennsylvania* (Phila., 1895-1907), Vol. I, *1779-1801;* Vol. II, *1801-1810;* Vol. III, *1811-1816;* Charles E. Meyer, *Masonic Lodges in Pennsylvania from 1730 to 1880, "Moderns" and "Ancients"* (Phila., n.d.); Register of Members, Vol. 1, 1789-1823; Julius F. Sachse, *Old Masonic Lodges of Pennsylvania, "Moderns" and "Ancients,"* Vol. II, *1779-1800* (Phila., 1912, 1913).

TABLE 3
Geographical Distribution of Pennsylvania Lodges, 1786-1811

County	Number of new lodges (lodge numbers)	(%)	Number of ceased lodges (lodge numbers)	(%)
Allegheny	1 (113)	1.6		
Bedford	1 (48)	1.6	1 (48)	6.7
Berks	3 (47d, 62, 66)	4.9	1 (47d)	6.7
Bucks	2 (57, 94)	3.3	2 (25, 57)	11.8
Chester	3 (50, 75, 80)	4.9	1 (80)	5.9
Cumberland	2 (56, 76)	3.3	2 (56, 76)	13.3
Dauphin	1 (101)	1.6		
Delaware	1 (69)	1.6		
Erie	1 (124)	1.6		
Fayette	3 (60, 92, 110)	4.9		
Franklin	2 (74, 79)	3.3	1 (74)	6.7
Huntingdon	2 (55, 85)	3.3	1 (55)	6.7
Lancaster	3 (46, 104, 116)	4.9		
Luzerne	5 (61, 65, 70, 108, 119)	8.2	1 (65)	6.7
Lycoming	1 (106)	1.6		
Mifflin	1 (68)	1.6		
Montgomery			2 (8, 31a)	13.3
Northumberland	1 (100)	1.6		
Philadelphia	21 (19a, 51, 52, 53, 59, 67, 71, 72, 73, 81, 91, 102, 114, 115, 121, 125, 126, 127, 128, 130, 131)	34.4	3 (4, 13a, 53)	20.0
Somerset	1 (84)	1.6		
Tioga	1 (120)	1.6		
Washington	1 (54)	1.6		
Wayne	2 (82, 83)	3.3		
Westmoreland	1 (64)	1.6		
York	1 (123)	1.6		
Totals	61	100.0	15	100.0

Sources: "Information Pertaining to Early Freemasonry in the Western Hemisphere, Including the Warrant and Constitution Dates of the Subordinate Lodges under the Provincial and Present Grand Lodge of F. and A.M. of Pennsylvania" (unpublished list); Joshua L. Lyte, comp., *Reprint of the Minutes of the Grand Lodge of Pennsylvania* (Phila., 1895-1907), Vol. I, *1779-1801;* Vol. II, *1801-1810;* Vol. III, *1811-1816;* Charles E. Meyer, *Masonic Lodges in Pennsylvania from 1730 to 1880, "Moderns" and "Ancients"* (Phila., n.d.); Register of Members, Vol. 1, 1789-1823; Julius F. Sachse, *Old Masonic Lodges of Pennsylvania, "Moderns" and "Ancients,"* Vol. II, *1779-1800* (Phila., 1912, 1913).

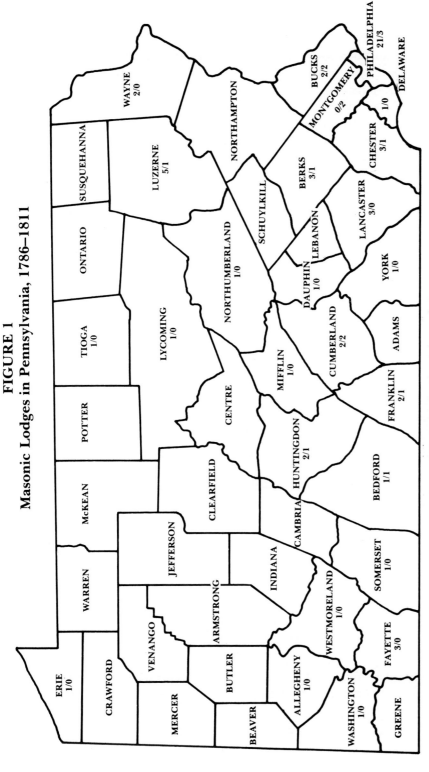

FIGURE 1
Masonic Lodges in Pennsylvania, 1786–1811

PENNSYLVANIA IN 1811 (46 counties)

Key: new/ceased lodges
Totals: 61/15   Net: +46

Sources: Information Pertaining to Early Freemasonry in the Western Hemisphere, Including the Warrant and Constitution Dates of the Subordinate Lodges under the Provincial and Present Grand Lodge of F. and A.M. of Pennsylvania" (unpublished list); Joshua L. Lyte, comp., *Reprint of the Minutes of the Grand Lodge of Pennsylvania* (Phila., 1895-1907), Vol. I, *1779-1801;* Vol. II, *1801-1810;* Vol. III, *1811-1816;* Charles E. Meyer, *Masonic Lodges in Pennsylvania from 1730 to 1880,* "Moderns" and "Ancients" (Phila., n.d.); Register of Members, Vol. I, 1789-1823; Julius F. Sachse, *Old Masonic Lodges of Pennsylvania,* "Moderns" and "Ancients," Vol. II, *1779-1800* (Phila., 1912, 1913).

Membership also increased substantially; by the end of 1811 net membership stood at a level more than five times higher than that of 1786 (see Appendix F). Most of the increase was in Philadelphia lodges (1,199 members), although a respectable percentage was associated with country lodges (986 members). A total of seven thousand men were either initiated or admitted into the Masonic Fraternity in this period, the largest number in 1811. No doubt, the favorable publicity generated by the dedication of the new hall was responsible for increased interest. Another factor was the appearance, in April 1811, of an official Masonic journal, the *Freemason's Magazine*, edited by one of the Grand Chaplains, George Richards. In addition to information pertaining to Freemasonry, this periodical contained numerous articles of general interest. Masonic leaders may have had second thoughts about this publication, however, or public interest was not as great as anticipated, because it ceased operation less than a year later.[48]

The occupational backgrounds of the men who became Masons in this period are unknown, but to judge from the size of membership fees and other expenses, they probably came at least from the middle classes. The initiation fees for most Philadelphia lodges were between $24 and $30; country lodges charged about half those amounts. In addition, the member had to make periodic contributions to the lodge's charity fund and pay Grand Lodge dues. The latter stood at a modest fifty-four cents per year in 1797, but was subsequently raised to seventy-four cents in 1799 and eighty-four cents in 1800. The fees of the city lodges exceeded a month's wages for a common laborer and about three weeks wages for a skilled artisan in Philadelphia throughout the period. This data seems to indicate that the Fraternity attracted men of secure economic status, more so in Philadelphia than in the country lodges. No doubt it was possible for men from the lower middle class to belong, as long as they met the other requirements, but membership would have entailed a greater financial sacrifice for them.[49]

The backgrounds of the six men who served as Grand Master from 1786 to 1811 are known (see Appendix C). Three were merchants, two were lawyers and one was a goldsmith. All were economically prosperous. They ranged in age at the time of their election from 32 to 65 years, on average about 48 years. In religious affiliation, they represented a variety of the Protestant denominations: three were Episcopalians, and one each was Presbyterian, Baptist and Universalist. Most of these men served three terms or less, but one, James Milnor, was in office for six years, and another, Jonathan Bayard Smith, for eleven. Two men, William Adcock and William Ball, had also served before 1786, and James Milnor continued in office after 1811.

The dedication of the Chestnut Street hall, and the growth that accompanied it, was a high point in the fortunes of Pennsylvania Freemasonry. It indicated that the Fraternity could achieve prosperity on its own without the support of its parent body, the Grand Lodge of England. These circumstances caused Grand Master Milnor to feel secure and to predict a bright future for the organization:

> It is not an unwarrantable boast of Antient [sic] Masonry, that its Foundations are laid upon a Rock, and its superstructure composed of such indestructable materials as to defy the ineffectual force of the Winds and the Waves, by whose Fury it is sometimes opposed. The Grand Architect under whose auspices it has arisen, and by whose power and goodness it has been preserved will, we Trust, continue his protection.
>
> Some who now hear me can Attest [to] the seeming Dangers of the Days of despondence that are past, and join me in the joyous Anticipation of the prosperity that we hope for in those which are to come. The strength and permanency of . . . [our Society] . . . has been proved by the alarming Trials it has undergone, and by the increased firmness as well as splendour which it now exhibits.[50]

For at least the next fifteen years, these hopes would not be disappointed, but continued expansion would be accompanied by additional challenges and by significant changes in the administrative structure of the Masonic system in Pennsylvania.

CHAPTER 5:

Growth and Reform, 1812-1825

In the years immediately following the dedication of the Masonic Hall on Chestnut Street the Fraternity lost several prominent officials by death. It gave special recognition to four of them: Jonathan Bayard Smith (d. 1812), Past Grand Master (in office, 1789-1794 and 1798-1802); Peter Le Barbier Duplessis (d. 1815), Past Deputy Grand Master (1808-1812); George A. Baker (d. 1816), Grand Secretary (1797-1816) and William Adcock (d. 1817), Past Grand Master (1782-1788).

The Grand Lodge honored Smith and Baker with elaborate funeral processions, among the largest yet held. Smith's was composed of six hundred members representing twenty subordinate lodges, whereas eight hundred Masons from twenty-two lodges participated in Baker's. Both processions assembled at the Chestnut Street hall, marched to the former residences of the deceased to receive the bodies, and then proceeded to the burial places. Smith was interred in the graveyard of the Second Presbyterian Congregation at Third and Arch Streets where the Rev. Dr. Lemuel Green gave the eulogy and the Rev. Dr. George Richards, one of the Grand Chaplains, led the Masonic funeral service. Baker was interred in the burial ground of the German Lutheran Congregation on Franklin Street between Arch and Race. An address in German was given by the pastor, the Rev. Dr. Henry Helmuth, and the Rev. Bro. George Potts, another Grand Chaplain, conducted the Masonic funeral service. Duplessis and Adcock were also buried with Masonic honors, although their ceremonies appear to have been more modest.

As an added sign of respect, the Grand Lodge resolved to drape its jewels, furniture and hangings in mourning for a period of six months for Smith and Baker and three months for Duplessis and Adcock. In the case of Baker, a committee was formed to devise plans to erect a commemorative marble monument, intended to include the names of all deceased Past Grand Masters and Deputy Grand Masters. In light of the debt incurred in building the Chestnut Street hall, the Grand Lodge considered suspending funeral processions for the future unless relatives and friends of the deceased would pay the costs, but this proposal was defeated.[1]

During the War of 1812 Masonic leaders temporarily abandoned their traditional proscription against involvement in politics. As during the Revolutionary War, the Grand Lodge openly espoused the cause of the United States. In early September 1814 the Fraternity offered the Philadelphia Committee of Public Safety the services of Pennsylvania Masons to take a tour of duty on the defenses of the city in the event of a British assault. At the same time several members of Lodge Nos. 51 and 121, then serving in various militia organizations located at Camp Bloomfield, Chester County, petitioned the Grand Lodge for a warrant to form a military lodge. The Grand Lodge responded favorably and assigned the number 140. In light of the sacrifices these men were making in the service of their country and because most were poorly paid enlisted men, the Grand Lodge, in an uncharacteristic move, exempted them from all costs and fees for the warrant. The war ended before this lodge could be constituted, however, and the warrant was returned.

No doubt, Masonic leaders justified this involvement on the grounds of national emergency; in peacetime they usually declined to participate in patriotic events. For example, in April 1804 they refused to take part in a public celebration of the acquisition of Louisiana, sponsored by the Tammany Society and the Philadelphia Legion. The Grand Lodge considered it to be ". . . incompatible with the principles of our Society to join in the procession in the Character of Masons." Masons officially maintained an attitude of political neutrality even during the tense period prior to the outbreak of the War of 1812, when British men-of-war were attacking American mercantile ships. Grand Master James Milnor recognized the heated political arguments that resulted, but forbade Masons to get involved in them. In his opinion, Freemasonry served to assuage the "spirit of heat and rancour" and to provide "an asylum of rest . . . from all the bickerings of party, and the excitement of Civil contention."[2]

In the era of the War of 1812 the Fraternity experienced repeated difficulties from illegal and unauthorized Masonic meetings. They began in the spring of 1810 when a Mason named Henry Snyder was discovered to be holding lodges in various taverns in Philadelphia and the Northern Liberties. He did so without authority of a warrant, and in his assumed role of Master, he initiated unsuspecting candidates and lectured on Masonic ideals. Synder also collected money to defray expenses and to compensate himself for his services. Snyder's example was followed by others. The Grand Lodge deprecated this practice as detrimental to the Fraternity generally and injurious to young Masons in particular. Obviously, such meetings posed a serious challenge to the jurisdiction of the Grand Lodge, which was concerned with maintaining regularity in Masonic proceedings. In a vague way, the Grand Lodge threatened to deal with the perpetrators "agreeably to the Ancient Customs and usages of

Masonry" and specifically warned the participants of certain expulsion from membership. This resolution was well publicized by printed hand-bills and otherwise; evidently the warning was sufficient to at least temporarily put a stop to this activity.[3]

Within three years however, Snyder, in cooperation with other renegade Masons, was again holding illegal Masonic meetings. The Grand Lodge vigorously investigated this renewed defiance and expelled Snyder and one of his associates, George D. Moore, in June 1813. However, it postponed the case of another participant, John Bower, who promised a defense of his conduct. In August Bower presented a letter of explanation wherein he claimed that he had been unduly pressured into joining by unscrupulous persons who repudiated the Grand Lodge. He gave a detailed description of the activities of the association, including its earlier disbanding and recent revival. Bower said that he had resigned upon the Grand Lodge's first warning and had had nothing further to do with the association. He then revealed the names of thirty-six persons involved in the illegal activity. Asking forgiveness for his acknowledged misconduct, a contrite Bower threw himself upon the mercy of the Grand Lodge, which pardoned him and formed a committee to further investigate the matter.[4]

The committee did not give its report until December of that year. It had interviewed several participants who, unlike Bower, were unrepentant in their opposition to the Grand Lodge. They asserted that since they had properly withdrawn from their own subordinate lodges, the Grand Lodge had no authority over them. They thus formed their own "independent" lodge, which they believed to be true to the principles of Freemasonry, and assumed the power of making Masons and of forming subordinate associations. By this time four such lodges were operating in Philadelphia. The Grand Lodge expelled all the participants, deprived them of all the privileges of Freemasonry and denied them any future Masonic activity in any jurisdiction.

This punishment was in accordance with a more rigorous policy, adopted two years previously, toward expelled members and rejected candidates. The Grand Lodge wished to prevent such persons from gaining Masonic affiliation within Pennsylvania, or any other jurisdiction, by printing and circulating lists of their names semi-annually. This was necessary to prevent "the Admission of improper Persons to the enjoyment of rights and Privileges to which they are not entitled [since] it lessens or may lessen the respectability of [the] Institution. . . ." By the same token, the Grand Lodge also refused to accept Masons into fellowship unless they resided within its jurisdiction and possessed a certificate of good standing from a recognized grand lodge.[5]

This treatment was enough to cause at least one participant in the unauthorized lodges to reconsider his position. Within a few months Pennel Beale, formerly of Lodge No. 67, petitioned the Grand Lodge to reinstate him, claiming that he did not fully understand the consequence of his acts or the proper method of regaining that body's good graces. He offered sufficient proof of his withdrawal from the schismatic organization and of his good intentions. The Grand Lodge, assured that "his Errors proceeded from the Misapprehension and ignorance of the Individual rather than from a Bad Heart," fraternally restored him to membership in good standing.[6]

With respect to unauthorized Masonic meetings, the Grand Lodge of Pennsylvania was challenged not only by members of its own subordinate lodges, but also by Masons from other jurisdictions. A case in point was the establishment of a "Mark" lodge in Philadelphia in December 1811 under the supposed authority of a Masonic organization headquartered in New York State. One Ezra Ames, calling himself "General Grand Scribe" of the General Grand Royal Arch Chapter of the United States of America, offered Pennsylvania Masons a degree above that of Master Mason but preparatory to the Royal Arch Degree. The Grand Lodge did not recognize this body, certainly did not approve of its operations within Pennsylvania and considered it "to destroy the respectability and Order of the Masonic system as established in this City." The Grand Lodge appealed to the "good sense and Masonic Zeal" of the Brethren and asked them to withdraw voluntarily from it.

For a time, it seems, this unauthorized Masonic activity was checked, but by July 1816, Masonic leaders had received reports of a spurious lodge under the name of "Philadelphia No. 2." Warranted by Ames, this lodge was still in operation, but it did not have the approval of either the Grand Lodge of Pennsylvania or Ames' parent body. In November 1816 the Deputy General Grand High Priest of the General Grand Royal Arch Chapter of the United States, Thomas Smith Webb, disavowed Ames' activities and recalled the warrants issued by him. He also apologized to the Grand Lodge of Pennsylvania for any offense his subordinate had committed. Although regretting that this interference had occurred in the first place, the Grand Lodge nonetheless was pleased that the foreign body had abandoned its attempt to influence Masonic affairs within Pennsylvania.[7]

Unauthorized Masonic meetings also occurred outside Pennsylvania but within the jurisdiction of the Grand Lodge. Pennsylvania-warranted lodges in Cuba, for example, faced a serious challenge by another type of Freemasonry, called "Scottish Rite." In summer 1818 the Grand Lodge was informed by Lodge No. 103, Havana, that a French "adventurer," Joseph de Glock, who had recently arrived among them, was attempting to pass himself off as a thirty-second-degree Mason under French authority and was also asserting the right to form subordinate lodges and grant degrees. Snubbed by No. 103, de Glock retaliated by charging that Ancient York Masonry took in men of lower caliber than did Scottish Rite and deliberately kept them in ignorance by not offering higher degrees. Because his fees were lower than those of "official" Freemasonry, de Glock attracted much support. He made a number of Masons and established Scottish Rite organizations including a grand consistory. Lodge No. 103 publically condemned these activities as damaging to the Fraternity and misleading to "some weak unexperienced brethren;" it warned Masons not to associate with de Glock. Except for making this statement, the "trusty and firm ancient York Masons" of the lodge did not know what to do, so they asked the Grand Lodge of Pennsylvania for guidance. They also requested a thorough explanation of the differences between the two types of Freemasonry since Scottish Rite was new to them.[8]

De Glock was known to Pennsylvania Masons because he had attempted to establish lodges in Philadelphia the previous year. Before the Grand Lodge could stop him, he had fooled at least one person into taking his false degrees. Without hesitation, the Grand Lodge condemned de Glock and his Scottish Rite as without authority and, even more important, without the same degree of antiquity as the York Rite. According to the Grand Lodge, the so-called Scottish Rite was of recent origin and was not Scottish but French. Provincial French lodges had "a great propensity to innovation [which] produced the most unwarrantable alterations upon the principles and ceremonies of the order." In contrast to French practice, the Grand Lodge of Scotland was actually a proponent of "St. John's Masonry" as practiced by the original "Ancient" Grand Lodge of England, and it had "preserved Free Masonry for Many Centuries in its original simple form."

The Grand Lodge's response to the Cuban brethren was important not so much because it silenced yet another renegade Mason, but because it illustrated the practices and beliefs of Ancient York Masonry in this period. Ancient York Masonry consisted of four degrees and no more: Entered Apprentice, Fellow Craft, Master Mason and Holy Royal Arch. Only officially warranted lodges were authorized to offer these degrees and any other body that did so was deemed spurious and unrecognized. Though it jealously guarded its prerogatives, the Grand Lodge realized that it did not have, nor could it have, control over the actions of other Masonic bodies concerning the so-called higher degrees of Freemasonry. As long as these bodies acted according to the rules of their own order, a Mason could take as many degrees as he wanted. The Grand Lodge implied that such higher degrees were of secondary importance and contributed nothing to a fuller understanding of the Craft.[9]

Continued growth of Scottish Rite Freemasonry in Cuba brought local pressure upon Lodge No. 103 to weaken its resolve to ignore unauthorized Masonic bodies. In another letter to the Grand Lodge of Pennsylvania, in November 1819, the members of Lodge No. 103 expressed the need for Masonic cooperation and unity in "a country where Masonry is severely persecuted by [the] Government." Although it officially disassociated itself from illegal Masons, No. 103 regretted doing so since "many worthy and respectable individuals, many of them our intimate friends and relations," were included in that group. Motivated by "a laudable desire to promote the prosperity of our order and [to] establish brotherly concord," Lodge No. 103 asked whether the Grand Lodge might allow fraternal communication. The Grand Lodge firmly denied this latest request and threatened unrepentant Masons with expulsion and officially established lodges with loss of warrants. Perhaps because of its attitude, but more likely because of geographical distance, the Grand Lodge of Pennsylvania soon lost control of its subordinate lodges in Cuba. In June 1821 these lodges voluntarily returned their warrants and formed the Grand Lodge of Cuba.[10]

*   *   *   *   *   *   *   *

On the evening of March 9, 1819, the Masonic Hall on Chestnut Street caught fire and was severely damaged. During a meeting of Washington Lodge No. 59 in the Grand Lodge Room on the second floor, a chimney in the ballroom below burst and the sparks resulting ignited interior stucco decorations, causing a general conflagration. The fire spread so rapidly that members of the lodge did not have time enough to close their meeting in the regular manner or even to save the lodge's books and paraphernalia. The roof and spire of the hall were destroyed and the interior gutted. No one was injured and no surrounding buildings were affected, but the Fraternity suffered the irreparable loss of an undetermined number of early documents in the archives as well as a collection of books in a recently established Masonic library.[11]

Although stunned by this tragedy, the Fraternity was not paralyzed, and acted quickly to make good its loss. On March 11 a general Masonic meeting was held at the hall of the Washington Benevolent Society on Third Street above Spruce, to take measures for reconstruction of the hall. After a prayer by Grand Chaplain Dr. William Rogers and an "eloquent and appropriate" address by Past Grand Master Samuel F. Bradford, the Masons adopted another program of raising money by subscription. A special committee was formed, consisting of three members from each subordinate lodge in the County and City of Philadelphia,

The Burning of the Masonic Hall, March 9, 1819. Painted by S. Jones. Figures by J.L. Krimmel. Engraved by J. Hill. Published by S. Kennedy & S.S. West (Historical Society of Pennsylvania).

a total of eighty-one men from twenty-seven lodges. The Trustees of the Masonic Loans reported that the Fraternity had in assets, or could raise with little difficulty, the necessary funds to rebuild the hall. For example, half the estimated cost of rebuilding, $20,000, would come from insurance. In addition, the managers of two local theaters, William Warren and William Wood of the Philadelphia and Victor Pepin of the Olympic, offered benefit performances, as did the Thespian Society of Harrisburg. A few weeks later an amateur concert (by whom is not stated) was held in Washington Hall for the benefit of the Masons.[12]

The Grand Lodge sought additional financial assistance by appealing to the Pennsylvania Assembly for tax-exempt status on the building. To this end, it urged subordinate lodges to "use their influence" on individual legislators. These lobbying efforts quickly paid off; by mid-December 1819 the Grand Lodge's petition was introduced into the House of Representatives, and a bill drawn up. This measure was accepted with little debate and without amendment. The House passed it on January 26, 1820, the Senate on Feburary 5, and it became law four days later with the governor's signature. This law exempted the Grand Lodge from all assessment and taxation for a period of twenty years, a savings estimated at $1,000 per year.[13]

Meanwhile, the Grand Lodge had to find a suitable meeting place. It arranged at once to rent the former Masonic Hall on Filbert Street, where it convened as early as March 16. A new Building Committee inspected the ruins of the building, saved what lodge property it could, and concluded that the masonry walls, which were reinforced with brick and marble, were sturdy enough to support rebuilding.

In July 1819 the Grand Lodge approved a design for the new hall. In the months since the fire a public competition for various designs for the new hall had been held but, none of these being suitable, the Building Committee devised its own plan. It incorporated several new features, such as altering the shape of the Grand Lodge Room from a circle to a square; otherwise the plan was essentially the same as that of the old hall. The lower floor included two banquet halls, one larger than the other, as well as storerooms. The second floor contained four lodge rooms: the Grand Lodge Room, the Northwest Room, the Dome Room and the Arch Room, as well as a committee room. In addition, storage space was available in the basement and attic. A separate three-story building containing a "refreshment room" and small meeting rooms was constructed at the rear of the hall and was connected to it by a passageway from the Grand Lodge Room. Both buildings had slate roofs to protect against fire. The impressive spire was not included in the new plans, however. The estimated cost of rebuilding was about $40,000.

To expedite the project the Grand Lodge employed a full-time superintendent who hired workers, kept accounts and oversaw the reconstruction. Preference was given to Masonic workers, and individual Masons were encouraged to patronize the businesses of fellow Brothers to help offset the effects of an economic depression at that time. That the Masons would even contemplate such a massive effort to reconstruct a building indicates their secure financial position, but they did try to cut down expenses wherever possible. The superintendent, a carpenter named Thomas Webb, earned $4.00 a day; the wage of other skilled carpenters was "not to exceed $1.40." Common workers received pay based on piecework at "30 percent under the Book of Prices established by the Old Carpenters' Company of Philadelphia." This standard guide spelled out fees and offered detailed illustrations of specific kinds of woodwork. Other price guides were available in this period for stonemasons, bricklayers and plasterers. Judging from these lists, the Masonic artisans and workers were slightly underpaid; the average daily wage of a master carpenter in 1820 was $1.50.[14]

The Grand Lodge took advantage of the rebuilding of the hall to modernize its facilities, especially in regard to illumination. It converted to gas as a more efficient, cheaper, safer and cleaner means of lighting. The new Masonic Hall was the first public building in Philadelphia fitted for gas. Because there was no other way to obtain the needed fuel, the Fraternity set up its own gas manufactory in the rear of the property. This operation was troubled for the first few years. For example, even though the building had a metal-covered roof, a fire broke out in the gas house in December 1820 that rendered it inoperable until repairs were made. It then had to be fireproofed at additional expense. For a time, the Fraternity considered selling or leasing the gas house, but this was not feasible because of limited demand. Problems also existed with gas leaks in the manufactory and in the main building because of faulty pipes and fixtures. Neighbors complained of noxious fumes.

Despite the costs of repairs and improvements, the gas works was running efficiently by the spring of 1822 and was even showing a profit. Thus, the Grand Lodge planned to raise additional revenue by laying underground pipes and by selling gas to other public buildings in the vicinity. It even drew up a list of prospective clients including the Philadelphia Theatre, Peale's Museum and the Atheneum, but nothing came of this scheme.[15]

By the fall of 1820 the reconstructed hall was ready for occupancy. With the exception of the spire, the outside of the new hall closely resembled the old one. In furnishing and decorating the interior the Grand Lodge spared no expense. The chief room was a large salon or ballroom on the first floor with an adjoining dining room. It was decorated with crystal chandeliers, each with several thousand pendants; floor-to-ceiling gilt mirrors were placed on the side walls. The curtains on eight large windows were made of the finest quality scarlet moreen, a heavy wool fabric, "with suitable fringe and ornaments" and the same material was used to upholster the settees and chairs. The Grand Lodge Room on the second floor, with six windows, was similarly decorated although the color scheme was purple. This room also contained four hand-carved mahogany armchairs for officers. Special cabinet work incorporating Masonic symbolism and illustrations of the ritual augmented the rooms, and all interior surfaces were finished with stucco "in a neat plain manner." Six painted wooden figures depicting Masonic virtues, carved by native American sculptor William Rush, further enhanced the beauty of the hall. These were placed in various locations throughout the building: "Silence" in a niche beside the main staircase; "Faith," "Hope" and "Charity" in the Grand Lodge Room; and two cherubs with outstretched wings in the Royal Arch Room.[16]

"Silence" by William Rush. Carved for the rebuilt Chestnut Street Hall, 1820 (Grand Lodge of Pennsylvania).

The entire cost of the rebuilding effort, including the installation of gas lines and fixtures, interior decoration, and the refitting of lodge rooms, amounted to over $63,000, which exceeded original estimates by half. This amount was adequately financed by contributions of individuals and lodges, insurance money on the old hall, leases of rooms to other societies, a new Masonic loan, and by curtailing expenses. To encourage frugality, Past Grand Masters declined to accept the traditional jewels usually given them. Also because of tight finances, the Grand Lodge Charity Fund, originally suspended in 1811, remained inoperative, although its administration was reorganized in December 1821 in preparation for a time when more money would be available. Despite optimistic expectations, systematic charitable disbursements did not resume for more than twenty years.[17]

Throughout the spring of 1820 plans were made for another lavish public procession, church service and Masonic banquet to mark the dedication of the new hall. The ceremonies were held on November 1, 1820, less than two years after the destructive fire. True to form, the Masons offered another impressive showing: "This event was celebrated by the Craft, with great pomp and splendour, and with feelings of gratitude and joy." About one thousand Brethren participated in the procession, which included three trumpeters, three military bands, members of twenty-four subordinate lodges and thirty-two designated positions of honor for Grand

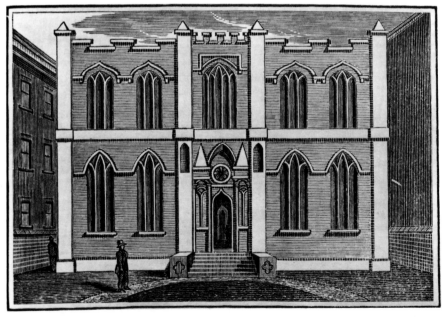

The rebuilt Masonic Hall on Chestnut Street (1820-1835). Anonymous woodcut (Historical Society of Pennsylvania).

Lodge members. They assembled at the hall of the Washington Benevolent Society and then marched to Zion Lutheran Church.

The service was attended by city officials, clergymen of various denominations, trustees of the University of Pennsylvania, directors of the Academy of Fine Arts and other guests and their wives. It included two anthems, two prayers, an oration on Masonry by Grand Master Bayse Newcomb, a hymn, an ode and a benediction. The lodge hall was dedicated in the same three-fold ceremony observed with the original hall in 1811. In the Grand Lodge Room, where forty-seven lodges were represented, two more prayers, three more odes and a canon for four voices were presented. A banquet for two hundred Masons rounded out the affair. The new Masonic Hall on Chestnut Street was the headquarters of Pennsylvania Freemasony for the next fifteen years, the longest period of service of any Masonic building to date.[18]

*   *   *   *   *   *   *   *

The reconstruction of the Chestnut Street hall enhanced the prestige of the Fraternity and gave Masons a sense of pride, but the expenses it entailed caused uneasiness. Complaints over finances combined with other issues of long standing to cause controversy in the late 1810s and early 1820s over the proper policies and functioning of the Grand Lodge. The overriding issue was the concentration of Masonic power and influence in Philadelphia to the exclusion of subordinate lodges in other parts of Pennsylvania.

As early as 1811 leaders of the Fraternity realized that a better means of communication between the head and the branches of the Masonic system was needed. Long distances caused interruptions in the payment of dues, the dissemination of Masonic knowledge, the reporting of information pertaining to members, and the representation of country lodges in the decision-making process. Periodically various suggestions for reform were made as, for example, in January 1812, when a special committee recommended Grand Visitations of country lodges, the establishment of District Deputy Grand Masters, and the appointment of Lecture Masters, but nothing came of these ideas. Five years later Grand Master Walter Kerr made similar suggestions, but still nothing was done. The extraordinary costs of building two Masonic halls within a decade served as impetus for the revival of these ideas, this time with a successful outcome.

In October 1817 the Grand Lodge received complaints from Lodge No. 21, Harrisburg, about its members' lack of knowledge of proper procedures for the granting of degrees. The lodge asked for some means of making Masonic work uniform throughout the state. This complaint was echoed six months later by Lodge No. 113, Pittsburgh, which also questioned the necessity of, and protested against, the expense of building the first Chestnut Street hall. Except for a full accounting of funds, these efforts seemed to lead nowhere until Lodge No. 43, Lancaster, took up the cause of reform. Despite firm rebuttals by the Grand Lodge, and even after losing its warrant, this lodge persisted until its aims were accomplished.[19]

In September 1819 the members of Lodge No. 43 drafted a circular letter designed to bring about the reform of Masonic administration and sent copies to every subordinate lodge in Pennsylvania. The lodge took issue with three specific practices: the different rituals permitted throughout the United States; the ineffectiveness of visitations of country lodges by Grand Lodge officers; and the ignorance and incompetence of many Masonic leaders. To correct the first abuse, the letter proposed the formation of a general grand lodge to supervise all state grand lodges according to the principle of federalism. No. 43 condemned visitations as ". . . being principally a matter of Parade and show . . . productive of but little good." The lodge was most concerned with the education of Masons on the true meaning of the ritual and symbolism and suggested the appointment of qualified individuals to offer instructional lectures. The letter deplored the expenditures involved in building the Masonic Hall in Philadelphia when only a few hundred dollars per year could have been better spent in the dissemination of Masonic knowledge.[20]

No. 43 received responses from seventeen lodges. Of these, thirteen, which were country lodges, approved the letter and endorsed its contents; however, the remaining (Philadelphia) lodges objected. No. 51, for example, reprimanded No. 43 on its unconstitutional attempt at reform from below and objected to the proposed loss of independence of the Grand Lodge. Although realizing the importance of Masonic education, the members of No. 51 thought that No. 43 was out of place in suggesting changes in the entire structure. Rather, it should concentrate on educating its own leaders to be effective Masons. In response, No. 43 condemned No. 51's lack of cooperation and rejected a reprimand from another subordinate lodge. Lodge No. 43 then personally attacked the members of No. 51 and charged the Grand Lodge with arrogance, unmasonic conduct and misappropriation of funds.[21]

The Grand Lodge showed forbearance in its response to these attacks. In December 1819 it established a committee to correspond with other grand lodges and with subordinate lodges within Pennsylvania as to the effectiveness and propriety of a supreme grand lodge for the United States. It also authorized the appointment of Lecture Masters to visit the subordinate lodges and reconfirmed its dedication to democratic principles. If subordinate lodges were dissatisfied with their leaders, it was their responsibility to elect new ones.[22]

In early 1820 other lodges became embroiled in this controversy. No. 131, Philadelphia, for example, reinforced the position taken by No. 51. It questioned the efficacy of a general grand lodge and stongly disapproved of No. 43's conduct. Concerning the building of the Masonic Hall, No. 131 argued that all subordinate lodges had had an opportunity to express themselves during the planning stages and No. 43 had chosen not to do so. It was a democratic decision of benefit to the Craft. As it had done with No. 51, Lodge No. 43 denied No. 131's right to judge its conduct; its members praised the values of democracy and republicanism in the government of the United States and wished to see these extended to the Masonic Order. They reasserted their right to comment upon the workings of the Grand Lodge and once again condemned the ignorance of many Masonic leaders.[23]

During the next few years some of the complaints of Lodge No. 43 began to bear fruit. For example, an effective system of Lecture Masters was put into operation. Ironically, the Master of No. 51, Tristam B. Freeman, who later became Grand Master, was selected to visit lodges in Lancaster and Dauphin Counties. He gave lectures at several meetings of No. 43 to the general approval of the membership, and one of his orations on the principles of Freemasonry was later published. The Grand Lodge also established Masonic Tribunals in each subordinate lodge with full power to decide cases. If dissatisfied with the tribunal's decision, members could appeal to a Grand Committee on Grievances. This reform brought about a more efficient method of settling disputes. It strengthened the administration of justice within the Fraternity and reduced the need for expensive and time-consuming lawsuits in public courts.[24]

On March 9, 1822, a general meeting of Masons was held in Washington, D.C., at which representatives of various state grand lodges were present. The question of a general grand lodge was taken up and rejected. The delegation from Pennsylvania objected to such a body on a number of grounds, the most important being that it would infringe upon the jurisdictions of existing state grand lodges. Such an institution would be too unwieldy, would be unable to make prompt decisions because of distance and weather, and would probably be composed of persons chosen for their prominence in public life rather than for their Masonic qualifications. In short, the Pennsylvanians felt that a general grand lodge "would produce the greatest confusion and disorder throughout the whole fraternity." The delegation did approve occasional Masonic conventions within the United States, however. The Pennsylvania Grand Lodge had put forward this idea since the late 1780s, but it had not been implemented.[25]

Although the general Masonic meeting was conducted in a democratic manner, its results were not satisfying to the members of Lodge No. 43, and they continued in their reforming zeal. They produced another circular letter in August 1822 in which they complained vigorously of the domination of Philadelphia and of the obstacles of distance and communication that denied country lodges much representation in the decisions of the Grand Lodge. Although all subordinate lodges paid the same dues, country lodges did not have the same opportunity to participate or to express themselves. They believed that the current practice of allowing proxies to vote for the country lodges was largely a sham since the proxies were not members of the lodges they represented. Because of location, Philadelphians controlled Pennsylvania Freemasonry. In the opinion of Lodge No. 43, the remedy for this evil was the establishment of a federal constitution for Freemasonry much like that of the United States government. In this manner ritual and correspondance of membership throughout the whole United States would be made uniform and Masonry would be strengthened. Lodge No. 43 unilaterally called for a convention of delegates of the subordinate lodges of Pennsylvania to be held at Harrisburg in the beginning of 1823. This move was without precedent in Pennsylvania Freemasonry and was against Masonic rules and regulations.[26]

At this point the Grand Lodge began to lose its customary patience. In September, after conducting a careful investigation, it expressed "decided disapprobation" of the conduct of Lodge No. 43 and gave an ultimatum for the lodge to "retrace its steps and return to its Masonic obedience and faith" within two months or lose its warrant. The Grand Lodge sent this vote of censure to Lodge No. 43 along with a detailed letter from the Grand Master, Josiah Randall, that dealt with the lodge's objections point by point. This letter provides valuable insights into the organization and structure of Pennsylvania Freemasonry in this period.[27]

Randall defended the Grand Lodge's absolute authority within Pennsylvania and its independence from all other Masonic bodies. This primary "landmark" of the institution could not be changed for any reason. No other Masonic body, whether a subordinate lodge or another Grand Lodge, had the right of review over its actions. If the members of No. 43 had understood this, they would have withdrawn their proposal for a convention. The Grand Master then used No. 43's own arguments against it. If one subordinate lodge had no right to criticise another, how then could a subordinate lodge criticize the Grand Lodge? Of all the lodges in Pennsylvania, only No. 43 had expressed real dissatisfaction. Therefore, the fault must lie with the lodge itself and not with the system.

Randall defended the organization of the Grand Lodge in which only the most experienced Masons (Past Masters and members of the Grand Lodge) had the right to vote in Masonic decisions. The proposal of No. 43, by which all officers of all subordinate lodges would have the right to vote, would contribute to a power struggle within the Fraternity and would encourage lodges to subdivide to produce more officers. The older established lodges would then vie with newer inexperienced ones, whose only purpose would be to control the institution. Freemasonry would then be cheapened and would stray from its high purposes.

The Grand Master justified the location of the Grand Lodge in Philadelphia on grounds that the majority of Masons lived there and not in Harrisburg, the political capital of the Commonwealth. The examples of other grand lodges in the United States indicated that the center of Masonry of any jurisdiction was to be located in the most populous city.

Grand Master Randall further stated that No. 43's proposal for a general grand lodge had already been duly considered and rejected; the issue should end there. The power of such a body, which sooner or later would subvert the independence of the Pennsylvania Grand Lodge, would be impossible to control. The Grand Master also rejected the analogy of the federal government, whose main purpose he said was protection from foreign powers, a matter of no concern to Freemasonry.

The Grand Master next considered the financial responsibilities of the Grand Lodge. Giving a good accounting of himself and of the organization, he laid out the finances of the Grand Lodge and proved that city lodges actually paid more than country lodges and bore a heavier burden of the debt on the new Masonic Hall in Philadelphia because they were charged to use its rooms. He reminded the dissident Brethren that the building was erected not for the glory of Philadelphia Masons but for that of the entire Masonic Fraternity within the state.

Randall then reviewed recently instituted reforms. These included the division of Pennsylvania into four separate districts, each supervised by a District Deputy Grand Master,[28] who possessed almost as much authority within his district as did the Grand Master in Philadelphia, the establishment of committees on landmarks (ritual and rules and regulations) and finance, the creation of Lecture Masters and the increase of Grand Lodge visitations, both of city and country lodges. The Grand Master concluded his letter with an earnest appeal to No. 43 to return to the fold.

The Grand Master's letter was a model of decorum and careful explanation; its tone was temperate and sincere. It is therefore difficult to explain why the members of No. 43 refused to acquiesce. They rejected Randall's arguments and his fraternal appeal. They claimed the support of a majority of the country lodges and noted that the Grand Lodge's unawareness of this was further evidence of its being out of touch. The members of No. 43 once again compared the members of the Fraternity with the citizens of the United States, who had a right to question their rulers, demand redress of grievances and propose amendments or alterations in their form of government. Masonry, which existed within such a broader society, should also be dedicated to the same principles of freedom and liberty. They ended their protest with a renewed call for the Harrisburg convention and with a challenge to the Grand Lodge that implied that if nothing was amiss, then that body had nothing to fear from scrutiny of its inner workings.[29]

Such defiance was the last straw and in November 1822 the Grand Lodge called in the warrant of No. 43. In short, the lodge had been suspended and its members as a group were cut off from all Masonic fellowship. If any other lodges conducted business or otherwise associated with No. 43, should it continue to meet without authorization, they would also be suspended.

Even this step was not enough; the members of Lodge No. 43 continued their resistence. The Grand Lodge then threatened personal suspension of each member of the lodge. The officers were required to appear before the Grand Lodge to show cause why this action should not be taken. To divide the opposition, the Grand Lodge promised to continue the rights and privileges of any members who came out publicly against the actions of No. 43. The same proscriptions were leveled against Lodge No. 152, Easton, which had composed its own circular letter agreeing with No. 43 on all points in contention.[30]

In response to the latest move by the Grand Lodge the members of No. 43 returned the warrant and called a special meeting of all Masonic lodges in Lancaster County. The first was an act of compliance, whereas the second was one of defiance. This unauthorized Masonic meeting was held on December 9, 1822, in the lodge rooms of No. 43 and was attended by the representatives of five other lodges: No. 46, Ephrata; No. 104, Leacock Township; No. 116, Elizabethtown; No. 156, Drumore Township; and No. 169, Columbia. They gave full support to No. 43's proposed Masonic convention and approved the conduct of the lodge up to that point. With this backing, a committee to represent the officers of No. 43 appeared as requested by the Grand Lodge on December 16, 1822 to answer charges. Members of No. 152 appeared at the same time.[31]

The meeting opened with a statement of procedure to be followed in hearing the case against individual members, a reading of recent communications on the issues and a presentation of credentials of representatives of the two lodges. Members of Lodge No. 43 then read two protests. The first denied the right of the Grand Lodge to decide matters of membership of the subordinate lodges, except in the event of appeal.

Only subordinate lodges had the power to regulate the conduct of their members. If the Grand Lodge could do this, the power could easily be abused by demanding that members from great distances attend meetings to answer trifling charges on pain of suspension. Masons would therefore become "slaves" of the Grand Lodge, a condition that would destroy the "wisdom, strength and beauty" of the institution. These arguments did not convince the Grand Lodge, which rejected the protest.

The second protest met with more favorable response. It demanded the right of members to be presented with specific charges against them and to be allowed to confront their accusers personally, rights upheld by the laws and courts of the United States to which, the lodge argued, Masonry should be subject. Thereby, it might appear that the accuser was more deserving of censure than the accused. The protest also demanded more time for the lodge to prepare its defense, which was to be heard in a full and fair trial at some later date. A statement from Lodge No. 152 expressed views similar to those of this second protest of No. 43.

The Grand Lodge then read the charges against the accused members. Essentially, they dealt with one point: summoning an unconstitutional convention of Masons to review the location, organization and operation of the Grand Lodge and to remedy alleged grievances against that body, thus denying its supremacy and subverting its authority. The meeting adjourned until the next day, to give all parties time to consider their responses and to allow consultation among various committees.

The tone of the Grand Lodge meeting of December 17 was substantially different from that of the previous day. Overnight, the members of Lodge No. 152 had worked out an acceptable reconciliation with a Grand Lodge committee, an impetus for the members of No. 43 to do the same. The principals in the dispute agreed to mutually rescind all proceedings relative to the matter and to restore the warrants of No. 43 and No. 152. They also agreed to establish a special Grand Committee composed of not more than three members from each subordinate lodge to investigate all grievances and to recommend appropriate changes. Each subordinate lodge had the authority to choose its members for this committee and each lodge was to have one vote. Most importantly, the committee was to operate under the jurisdiction of the Grand Lodge and not outside it.[32]

These measures, however, were not sufficient to prevent the momentum of reform among the country lodges generally. The unauthorized Masonic meeting took place as scheduled on January 7 in Harrisburg. Representatives of nineteen lodges attended and passed resolutions about the grievances mentioned throughout the controversy: control over membership, fiscal responsibility, representation of country lodges and Masonic education. Although some delegates were dissatisfied, the tone of the convention was much more moderate than that of previous communications. Nonetheless, the Grand Lodge disapproved this assemblage of Masons as a serious challenge to its supremacy. By rights, those who participated should have been expelled, but since the Grand Lodge was also reformed-minded at this time, it understood the dissidents' motivations and withheld censure from all participants.[33]

The special Grand Committee, formed the previous year, met from December 25 to 28, 1823. More appropriately, it should be called a Masonic convention since one hundred sixty delegates from eighty-nine lodges attended (86.4% of those in operation). Only twenty-nine (32.6%) of the represented lodges were located in Philadelphia. All the issues that had divided Pennsylvania Freemasonry over the last few years were thoroughly discussed. The delegates' final report reaffirmed the supreme authority of the Grand Lodge and stated that it would continue to meet at Philadelphia because the majority of lodges and members were concentrated there. It did recommend, and the Grand Lodge passed, various resolutions recognizing its greater responsibility to the needs of members. These included further correspondence on the issue of a grand convention of delegates for the United States to ensure uniformity of work, more frequent visitations of country lodges by the Grand Master and by Lecture Masters, more opportunities for country lodges to participate in the decision-making process and greater fiscal accountability by the Grand Lodge to the subordinate lodges. It also passed resolutions for the more efficient operation of the Grand Holy Royal Arch Chapter. As a final gesture of reconciliation, the Grand Lodge reaffirmed its exoneration of all Masons and lodges engaged in the reform movement.[34]

The reform movement indicated that the determination of only a few lodges could effect needed changes in the administration of Pennsylvania Freemasonry. It also showed that even serious differences of opinion among Masons eventually could be resolved in a spirit of cooperation, compromise and harmony. Most dramatically, the movement indicated that the Grand Lodge of Pennsylvania, although initially conservative and traditional, could indeed become progressive and responsive. It was not a fossilized institution that would rather cut off its members and lodges than adjust to change. The Grand Lodge made it clear that the essence of Freemasonry, its ritual, was not to be changed, however. In this and later periods, it resisted every attempt at innovation in degree work and insisted upon strict adherence to the "Ancient Landmarks." It consistently took the position that Masonic ritual had resulted from the accumulated wisdom of many centuries and thus could not be altered by any individual, lodge or grand lodge lest "our forms and ceremonies would be perverted and the noble edifice of the order would present nothing but the wreck of what it once had been; an institution venerable for its antiquity and simplicity." Unlike in many other jurisdictions, the

Grand Lodge of Pennsylvania has never permitted the ritual to be written down, even in the form of a "monitor," to prompt the memories of Masons. Such publications were popular in other northeastern states in this period.[35]

By 1824 most of the negative effects of this controversy were past and the Grand Lodge turned its attention to other matters. In that year two events were significant for Freemasons: the independence of the Grand Royal Arch Chapter and the visit of Brother General Marquis de Lafayette. The Grand Chapter was originally formed in 1795 as a sub-ordinate body supervised by the Grand Lodge, and it had adopted comprehensive rules and regulations in 1798 and 1812. During that period Ancient York Rite Freemasonry consisted of four degrees, but by the early 1820s two additional degrees, "Mark Master" and "Most Excellent Master," had been added as preparatory to the Royal Arch. Because supervision of the affairs of the Grand Chapter was becoming more complex, the Grand Lodge granted that body independence and approved a revised constitution in January 1824, giving it full powers over all degrees above the third. Symbolic of its increased authority, the organization also adopted a new name: "Most Excellent Grand Holy Royal Arch Chapter," and its leader held the title of "Most Excellent Grand High Priest." Membership in Chapter consisted of all current Grand Lodge officers as well as all Past Masters, a status obtained either through actual service as Master of a subordinate lodge or through dispensation from the Grand Master or a District Deputy Grand Master. This process was known as "passing the chair." Committees of correspondence between the two Masonic bodies were also established to ensure regular communication, especially with regard to membership information.[36]

In the summer of 1824 the Marquis de Lafayette began a year-long triumphal tour of the United States, where fifty years before he had served the American cause. When he arrived in Philadelphia in September, he was greeted with great pomp and circumstance. Pennsylvania Masons were eager to be a part of the ceremonies honoring him, but they were uncertain of his membership in the Fraternity. Despite an investigation, a Grand Lodge committee could find no reliable information, but its members were satisfied with the Masonic tradition that he was made a Mason in an American military lodge during the Revolutionary War in the presence of George Washington. Based upon Lafayette's own testimony, however, later given before the Grand Lodge of Tennessee, it appears that he had been made a Mason in France as a young man even before coming to America.

On October 2 the Grand Lodge of Pennsylvania held an extra communication to make Lafayette a full member of that body, with "all the rights, dignities and privileges pertaining thereto". Three hundred Ma-

sons then participated in a festive banquet held in the first-floor hall. The
room was lavishly decorated with festoons, a canopy, a frieze, a medallion,
sculptured columns, large mirrors, Washington's Masonic apron, and
full-length portraits of Washington and Lafayette, all displaying patriotic
and Masonic themes. The Marine Corps band, stationed at the Philadelphia Navy Yard, provided music, while Brethren toasted the American
nation and its heroic founders. They were proud to link Freemasonry
with Lafayette whose "meritorious life has, indeed, justly illustrated our
principles," as well as with Franklin and Washington. In the same spirit,
they pledged a sizable contribution toward a monument over the grave
of Washington at Mount Vernon, a project originally sponsored by the
Grand Lodge of New Hampshire. Although short of money and preoccupied with their debt, Pennsylvania Masons considered these measures
important enough to warrant incurring additional expense, but without
touching the sinking fund.[37]

In the same period as the reform movement, the Grand Lodge
thoroughly revised its rules and regulations. In January 1822 it formed
a committee to prepare an updated version of the Pennsylvania Masonic
constitution, the *Ahiman Rezon*. After numerous delays and changes in
personnel, the committee submitted its draft in April 1825 and the new
edition was ready by June.[38]

The *Ahiman Rezon* of 1825 was about a hundred pages longer than
the edition of 1783 and was easier to read than the earlier version. The
first section dealt with Masonic history, which was based less upon myth
than fact. It surveyed the theories of the origins of the Craft, but was
mostly devoted to recent developments in the United States. The second
section reprinted the traditional codes of conduct for Masons, discussed
the organization of English and Pennsylvania Freemasonry, reviewed the
various constitutions and reflected upon the changes undergone as a
result of the reform movement. The third, and longest, section dealt with
important ceremonial aspects of Pennsylvania Freemasonry. It included
the proper wording for prayers and charges to candidates for each degree
and to officers as well as the specific rituals for dedication ceremonies,
funeral services, public processions, cornerstone-laying, and the consti-
tuting of lodges. The 1825 edition was rounded out with an appendix of
twenty pages, which reprinted copies of the proper forms of Masonic
documents such as Grand Lodge certificates, warrants, deputations, commissions, dispensations, petitions, membership applications and membership returns. The usual collections of Masonic songs that had augmented
eighteenth-century constitutions were deleted. This edition of the *Ahiman
Rezon* served as the basis of Pennsylvania Masonic government and practice for over thirty years.

*   *   *   *   *   *   *   *

As measured by the number of new lodges, growth of the Masonic Fraternity between 1812 and 1825 was not so dramatic as in the preceding period. Seventy-one new lodges were founded, a respectable number, but more than half eventually ceased. Nonetheless, by the end of 1825 one hundred five lodges were still in operation, the largest number to date (Table 1). That the Grand Lodge warranted fewer lodges outside of Pennsylvania (eight) than ever before indicated a more centralized focus of activity. The large proportion of the ceased lodges (twenty or 53%) located out of state was a reflection of the development of the grand lodge system throughout the Western Hemisphere. As these new organizations were established in different areas, they took control over existing lodges, originally warranted by Pennsylvania. An example was the Grand Lodge of Cuba, which took over six lodges in 1821.

Within Pennsylvania the Fraternity had rather widespread influence (Table 2, Figure 1). By 1825 Masonic lodges were established in eighty percent (41/51) of Pennsylvania's counties. The majority of these were country lodges, but the heaviest concentration was in Philadelphia, with twenty-seven percent (28/105) of the total. Because of this uneven distribution, along with financial pressure to support the building of the Chestnut Street hall, it is understandable that the country lodges developed grievances. To offset this concentration, the Grand Lodge had tried to check the formation of new Philadelphia lodges, and for five years (1818-1823) only two were founded. In the same period, twenty-one country lodges were established.[39]

Membership statistics exist for nearly all lodges (97.9%) in operation at any time between 1812 and 1825 (see Appendix G). More than nine thousand individuals were either initiated or admitted into the Society by these lodges. Over four hundred men became members each year through 1813, and between five and eight hundred annually thereafter. In 1825 alone almost eight hundred fifty men were accepted. This growth probably resulted from favorable publicity attending the Fraternity's efforts to defend Philadelphia during the War of 1812 (1814) and to rebuild the Chestnut Street hall (1819), as well as its participation in the reception of Lafayette (1824). Cumulative membership totals were consistently higher after 1812, both among the Philadelphia and non-Philadelphia lodges, but not so much for the non-Pennsylvania lodges since they were far removed from Masonic events in Pennsylvania. In fact, by the end of 1825 these lodges had ceased to be under the jurisdiction of the Grand Lodge.

Suspensions, expulsions and voluntary withdrawals were also numerous in this period. In reponse to pressure from above, subordinate lodges urged members to pay dues promptly as well as to make additional contributions to various Masonic causes. This practice was encouraged

TABLE 1
Lodges Warranted by the Grand Lodge of Pennsylvania, 1812-1825

Years	Number of new lodges (lodge numbers)		Number of ceased lodges (lodge numbers)
1812-1819	37	(25a, 132-139, 141-163, 165-169)	17 (5, 11a, 54, 68, 77, 79, 85, 92, 93, 101, 105, 110, 117, 118, 129, 133, 137)
1820-1825	34	(164, 170-187, 189-192, 194-198, 200-205)	14 (25a, 73, 103, 107, 109, 120, 122, 124, 127, 139, 154, 157, 166, 170)
Unknown, but before 1826			7 (111, 112, 161, 167, 175, 181, 205)
Totals	71	Net: +33	38 (54.8%)

Eight of the new lodges were located outside Pennsylvania, as follows: Argentina, (205); Cuba (157, 161, 166, 167, 175, 181); Mexico (191).

Twenty of the ceased lodges were located outside Pennsylvania, as follows: Argentina (205); Cuba (103, 157, 161, 166, 167, 175, 181); Delaware (5); Indian Territory (107); Louisiana (93, 109, 111, 112, 117, 118, 122, 129); Ohio (105); Trinidad (77).

A number with an "a" appended indicates either that more than one lodge was assigned the same number or that a lodge was suspended and later revived.

Lodge No. 140 (military) was warranted but never constituted.

The origins of new lodges are based upon their constitution dates.

Lodges "ceased" in basically two ways: by voluntary surrender of the warrant by the members or by order of the Grand Lodge. Various terms were used to describe such warrants: "surrendered," "returned," "vacated," or "ceased."

The warrants of Nos. 188 and 193 were cancelled before being issued.

One hundred five lodges were in operation by the end of 1825.

Sources: "Information Pertaining to Early Freemasonry in the Western Hemisphere, Including the Warrant and Constitution Dates of the Subordinate Lodges under the Provincial and Present Grand Lodge of F. and A.M. of Pennsylvania" (unpublished list); Joshua L. Lyte, comp., *Reprint of the Minutes of the Grand Lodge of Pennsylvania* (Phila., 1895-1907), Vol. III, *1811-1816;* Vol. IV, *1817-1822;* Vol. V, *1822-1827;* Charles E. Meyer, *Masonic Lodges in Pennsylvania from 1730 to 1880, "Moderns" and "Ancients"* (Phila., n.d.); *Proceedings of the Grand Lodge of Pennsylvania for 1814, 1815, 1816, 1818, 1819, 1823, 1825,* Register of Members, Vol. 1, 1789-1823; Vol. 2-1, 1795-1855; Vol. 2-2, 1818-1855.

TABLE 2
Geographical Distribution of Pennsylvania Lodges, 1812-1825

County	Number of new lodges (lodge numbers)	(%)	Number of ceased lodges (lodge numbers)	(%)
Adams	1 (200)	1.6		
Allegheny	3 (145, 165, 173)	4.8		
Beaver	1 (133)	1.6	1 (133)	5.6
Bedford	1 (137)	1.6	1 (137)	5.6
Bradford	2 (150, 163)	3.2		
Bucks	3 (25a, 168, 195)	3.2	1 (25a)	5.6
Centre	1 (192)	1.6		
Chester	5 (132, 142, 162, 174, 183)	7.9	1 (11a)	5.6
Columbia	1 (159)	1.6		
Crawford	1 (146)	1.6		
Cumberland	2 (197, 198)	3.2		
Dauphin	1 (141)	1.6	1 (101)	5.6
Erie	1 (184)	1.6	1 (124)	5.6
Fayette			2 (92, 110)	11.1
Franklin	2 (196, 202)	3.2	1 (79)	5.6
Greene	2 (153, 180)	3.2		
Huntingdon	1 (178)	1.6	1 (85)	5.6
Lancaster	2 (156, 169)	3.2		
Lebanon	1 (172)	1.6		
Lehigh	1 (151)	1.6		
Luzerne	2 (185, 204)	3.2		
Mercer	1 (182)	1.6		
Mifflin	1 (203)	1.6	1 (68)	5.6
Montgomery	3 (136, 171, 190)	4.8		
Northampton	1 (201)	1.6		
Northumberland	3 (144, 148, 152)	4.8		
Philadelphia	9 (134, 135, 139, 154, 155, 158, 160, 186, 187)	14.3	4 (73, 127, 139, 154)	22.2
Pike	2 (177, 179)	3.2		
Schuylkill	1 (138)	1.6		
Susquehanna	1 (149)	1.6		
Tioga	1 (189)	1.6	1 (120)	5.6
Union	1 (194)	1.6		
Washington	3 (143, 164, 170)	4.8	2 (54, 170)	11.1
Wayne	1 (147)	1.6		
Westmoreland	1 (176)	1.6		
Totals	63	100.0	18	100.0

Sources: "Information Pertaining to Early Freemasonry in the Western Hemisphere, Including the Warrant and Constitution Dates of the Subordinate Lodges under the Provincial and Present Grand Lodge of F. and A.M. of Pennsylvania" (unpublished list); Joshua L. Lyte, comp., *Reprint of the Minutes of the Grand Lodge of Pennsylvania* (Phila., 1895-1907), Vol. III, *1811-1816;* Vol. IV, *1817-1822;* Vol. V, *1822-1827;* Charles E. Meyer, *Masonic Lodges in Pennsylvania from 1730 to 1880, "Moderns" and "Ancients"* (Phila., n.d.); *Proceedings of the Grand Lodge of Pennsylvania for 1814, 1815, 1816, 1818, 1819, 1823, 1825,* Register of Members, Vol. 1, 1789-1823; Vol. 2-1, 1795-1855; Vol. 2-2, 1818-1855.

FIGURE 1
Masonic Lodges in Pennsylvania, 1812–1825

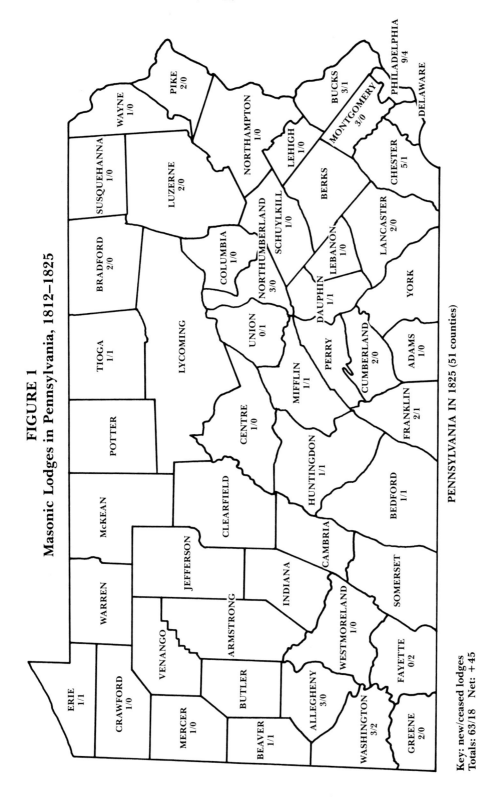

PENNSYLVANIA IN 1825 (51 counties)

Key: new/ceased lodges
Totals: 63/18   Net: +45

Sources: "Information Pertaining to Early Freemasonry in the Western Hemisphere, Including the Warrant and Constitution Dates of the Subordinate Lodges under the Provincial and Present Grand Lodge of F. and A.M. of Pennsylvania" (unpublished list); Joshua L. Lyte, comp., *Reprint of the Minutes of the Grand Lodge of Pennsylvania* (Phila., 1895-1907), Vol. III, *1811-1816;* Vol. IV, *1817-1822;* Vol. V, *1822-1827;* Charles E. Meyer, *Masonic Lodges in Pennsylvania from 1730 to 1880, "Moderns" and "Ancients"* (Phila., n.d.); *Proceedings of the Grand Lodge of Pennsylvania for 1814, 1815, 1816, 1818, 1819, 1823, 1825,* Register of Members, Vol. 1, 1789-1855; Vol. 2-1, 1795-1855; Vol. 2-2, 1818-1855.

by the Grand Lodge, which specifically advised lodges to "rid themselves of delinquent members." The costs of Masonic membership continued to remain relatively high; the initiation fees of the city lodges (about $30) were equivalent to more than a month's wages of an unskilled worker, and those of the country lodges were thirty to fifty percent less. Grand Lodge dues varied little. They were raised from eighty-four cents per year in 1812 to ninety-two cents in 1814 to a dollar in 1816. Most city lodges charged much higher annual dues, $6.00 per year or fifty cents per meeting; the dues of the country lodges were less, but varied considerably.[40]

High fees and dues alone do not account for all the ceased men, however. In this period the Grand Lodge became especially vigorous in removing from membership any men not of the highest moral character:

Intemperance, voluntary idleness, licentiousness, profaneness, willful desertion, and neglect of wives and children, with a catalogue of minor transgressions, all deserve the abhorrence of the virtuous; and if there perchance be any enrolled amongst our members, who by their irregular lives bring scandal upon Masonry, they should be held up to the world as traitors to the cause they have espoused, and as unworthy of a seat within the walls of our Temple.

Evidently nothing substantial was done about this problem; as late as June 1825, Masonic leaders were still complaining of the immoral behavior of some members. Such persons, of course, were a minority. Even if all those listed as suspended or expelled were in fact guilty of immoral conduct — and clearly they were not — they would amount to only about fifteen percent of the total membership. In an organization that prided itself on respectable principles, however, this percentage was too high. Despite its problems with recalcitrant members and uncooperative lodges, the record of Pennsylvania Freemasonry was consistently upward over time.[41]

In conformity to new regulations regarding membership, subordinate lodges began in 1824 to record the occupations and ages of men initiated or admitted. This data provides a valuable record of the backgrounds of Masons in this period (see Appendix G). Representing one hundred thirteen separate occupations, these individuals came from all walks of life. The largest single group was that of skilled craftsmen or artisans (34.0%), distantly followed by men employed in agriculture (15.0%), in professional service (14.9%) and in trade and commerce (12.2%). These percentages remained consistent among all categories of lodges: all lodges, Philadelphia lodges and non-Philadelphia lodges. This information indicates that Freemasonry was most appealing to individuals who lived in cities or small towns. Farmers were the largest single group in all lodges and in the country lodges, but merchants comprised the largest group in the city lodges. The percentages of these most numerous occupations were not high (14 to 19%), however, and confirm that Freemasonry was widespread through the community at large.

Freemasonry also attracted men of all ages, although most were young at the time of their admission. The mean age of more than nine hundred persons who became Masons in 1824 and 1825 was 29.7 years for all lodges, 28 years for Philadelphia lodges and 30.1 years for country lodges. These persons ranged in age from 21 years, the age of eligibility, to over 50 years (about two dozen men). One individual was 81 years old when he became a Mason.[42]

As a group, the leaders of Pennsylvania Freemasonry tended to be slightly older than the membership as a whole, but their occupations reflected a similar diversity. Between 1812 to 1825 eight men served as Grand Master of Pennsylvania (see Appendix C). Four were lawyers, and one each was a brickmaker, a hatmaker, a printer/bookseller and a sea captain. They ranged in age from 32 to 44 at the time of their election, with a mean of 37.4 years. Three were Episcopalians and one a Presbyterian; the religious backgrounds of the remaining four are unknown.

The most prominent Grand Master in this period, James Milnor, was in office from 1806 to 1813. A lawyer and United States congressman, Milnor led an active public life, but still found time to participate vigorously in Masonic affairs. During his term the Chestnut Street hall was built and membership increased substantially. After stepping down as Grand Master, he became an Episcopal clergyman and served as Grand Lodge Chaplain for two years. Milnor was the first Grand Master to begin systematic Grand Visitations of subordinate lodges in the county and city of Philadelphia. He was very much interested in maintaining the regularity of Masonic practices and gave frequent addresses on Masonic ideals, discipline and etiquette. He was especially concerned with preserving the reputation of the Fraternity by insisting that it accept only men of good character who behaved according to Christian principles. He also suggested various reforms of the organization, which were eventually instituted in the 1820's.

James Milnor strongly adhered to concepts of a God who was actively involved in the world, and he believed that Freemasonry's function was essentially religious. He influenced the Grand Lodge to associate itself with the Philadelphia Bible Society, of which he was also a member, by allowing collection boxes for funds to be set up in the Chestnut Street hall. He also established a school there to teach adults to read the Holy Scriptures. This Christian orientation was shared by subsequent Grand Masters, Samuel F. Bradford and Walter Kerr, who carried forward Milnor's policies. To quote from Grand Master Kerr:

While we then zealously contend for the success of our antient [sic] and honourable body, let us be careful to preserve the Spirit and copy the precepts of the religion of Christ, so shall we secure our own perpetuity and serve at the same time the best interests of man.

Freemasonry had originally been deistic in tone and spirit, but by the early nineteenth century it underwent a dramatic change in the direction of traditional Christian religious belief.[43]

*   *   *   *   *   *   *   *

By the end of 1825 Pennsylvania Freemasonry was firmly situated within American society. It enjoyed public favor, enrolled large numbers of men from all occupations over a wide area, had more lodges than ever before and was in touch with the religious and moral sentiments of the majority of Americans. Its organizational structure had recently been strengthened and any danger of division from within had been overcome. Pennsylvania's Masonic leaders were optimistic and had every reason to expect the continuance of recent prosperity:

> We believe that our Masonic Institutions are again beginning to flourish. The reign of ignorance and superstition is happily drawing to a close. The rights of man are beginning to be better understood. And all associations designed to advance the happiness and promote the welfare of the human race, will probably be better countenanced. For a long time masonry had to contend with the most formidable enemies, but now so great is the change that many of her strongest opponents have become her real friends.[44]

This statement contains more than a hint of irony since Pennsylvania Masons had no way to anticipate that they were about to experience the most serious attack upon the Order in the United States. Because of its recent reforms, the inherent value of its belief system and the efforts of a core of dedicated members, the Fraternity would ultimately withstand the Antimasonic onslaught.

CHAPTER 6:

The Antimasonic Period, 1826–1839

In 1826 a series of events harmful to Freemasonry occurred in western New York State. They were the disappearance, and probable murder, of William Morgan, an alleged Mason, who had written an exposé of the Fraternity. Masons were widely believed to have been responsible for the crime, and a strong local reaction quickly escalated into a virulent Antimasonic movement that spread throughout the northeastern states within a few years. Dedicated to the Society's extermination, Antimasonry appeared in two distinct but overlapping forms: a moral crusade and a political party. As a national organization, Antimasonry enjoyed relatively little political success, but as a reform movement it inflicted considerable damage on the Fraternity. This achievement was only temporary, however, and once Antimasonry had burned itself out, Freemasonry became stronger than before.

William Morgan, the protagonist in this drama, was born in Culpeper County, Virginia, in 1774. Although trained as a stonemason, he also followed other occupations throughout his life, including those of farmer, brewer and merchant. After living in a number of places in both the United States and Canada, he finally settled in the small rural community of Batavia in Genesee County, New York, in 1824. During the next year Morgan insinuated himself into the company of local Masons, gained admission into several lodges as a visitor, spoke at Masonic functions, and received the Royal Arch Degree. Morgan's acceptance into Masonic circles is curious since it is questionable that he was a legitimate Mason; at least no record of his taking the three basic degrees has ever been found anywhere he lived. Evidently he had learned enough of the ritual to pass himself off as a Brother, perhaps from having read various eighteenth-century exposés in circulation at that time. It also appears that New York Masons were careless in investigating potential members and did not insist upon proper proof of Masonic affiliation.

By all accounts, Morgan was not a suitable candidate for Masonic membership, although he must have possessed a certain charm and considerable wit since he was able to convince others of his qualifications. It is difficult to assess this individual accurately, but even objective sources describe him as "lazy, intemperate, quarrelsome and dishonest." He appears to have been an alcoholic who could not hold a steady job. The Masons soon realized their mistake. They struck his name from a petition to form a new lodge, cut him off from Masonic charity and probably also denied him work on a new Masonic temple being built in the area. Heavily in debt and with a wife and two children to support, Morgan was hard pressed for money. Most historians agree that this was the primary motivation for his subsequent course of action.

In March 1826 Morgan associated himself with the struggling editor and printer of the *Republican Advocate,* David C. Miller, who was also familiar with Freemasonry and had taken the first degree. Together they devised plans to publish the secrets of the Society. Although sharing Morgan's profit motive, Miller was angered by the establishment of a rival newspaper, the *Peoples' Press,* run by Masons and, perhaps because of his own lack of progress in Freemasonry, had some personal reasons for his antagonism toward the Society. The partners received financial backing for their project from two or three other persons.

News of the forthcoming book received much attention from local Masons, who enjoyed considerable prestige in the region. In this period there were lodges in sixteen of the twenty-two townships in Genesee County and half the county's officials, twelve out of twenty-four, were members of the Fraternity. Seemingly not realizing that unauthorized publication of Masonic ritual was nothing new, Masons saw Morgan's effort as a violation of a most important Masonic obligation and a threat to the integrity of their organization. These influential and important men used any means available to dissuade him. They published warnings about Morgan, "a swindler and a dangerous man," tried to buy him off, and threatened him, but to no avail. Their erstwhile colleague persisted, and in early August he delivered a manuscript to his backers in exchange for a bond of $500,000 and obtained a copyright. Ironically, Morgan received nothing for his efforts since the bond proved to be worthless and by the time his book was offered for sale in mid-December, he had disappeared.

The Masons took direct action to prevent the work's appearance. First, on September 8, and then again two nights later, they tried to destroy the manuscript by ransacking and burning Miller's printing shop, but the fire was discovered and put out before much damage had been done. The next day Masons had Morgan arrested on the charge of stealing clothes, five months before, from a tavern keeper in the town of

Canandaigua. Although released for lack of evidence, Morgan was immediately arrested again on another charge of petty theft and imprisoned. On the evening of September 12, while the jailer was absent, three Masons persuaded the jailer's wife to release Morgan by paying his fine. Shortly afterward the jailer's wife heard a commotion and then saw Morgan forced into a carriage with cries of "Murder!" After this dramatic exit Morgan disappeared from public sight.

Masons then activated their extensive network of contacts thoughout the state and various groups of them "escorted" Morgan out of the country by way of Niagara, over a hundred miles away. They worked out an arrangement with Morgan whereby he promised to keep quiet in return for money, a horse and farm in Canada, and assurances that his family might join him. This deal fell through, probably because of lack of cooperation from their Canadian Brethren, so the Masons imprisoned Morgan in Fort Niagara, an abandoned army post, while they decided what to do with him. He was last known to be alive on September 19.

What followed has never been accurately determined. According to official Masonic versions, Morgan coaxed money and a horse from his captors and rode off. Where he went is unknown, but over the next few years all manner of rumors circulated. He was reported to be living in Canada, Albany, Boston, Cuba, British Honduras and elsewhere. He was reputed to have become an Indian chief in Arizona, a Turk in Smyrna in the Ottoman Empire, and a pirate who was later hanged. Masonic historiography has pictured Morgan as an unscrupulous character who duped well-meaning but naive and trustful Masons. Even if Morgan did escape, however, Masons were guilty of several illegal acts: conspiracy, vigilantism and kidnapping, yet Masonic accounts never acknowledged this or expressed any regret. Instead, some even argued that Morgan had left Canandaigua willingly and that the whole incident was a sham designed to increase sales of his book.[1]

Antimasons asserted that Morgan was not only unlawfully apprehended, but also murdered. They alleged that when the Canadian deal fell through, the Masons panicked and murdered him in the "usual" Masonic manner ("his throat cut from ear to ear"). One version states that the Masons partially uprooted a tree, put Morgan's corpse in the opening, and then replaced the tree. A more credible explanation was that they tied weights to his body and threw it into the Niagara river.

Convenient to the Antimasons' cause, a partially decomposed corpse washed up on the shores of Lake Ontario thirteen months after Morgan had disappeared. The initial coroner's inquest found that it was an unknown person and the body was quietly buried. The Antimasons refused to let the matter rest, however, and demanded that the body be disinterred so Morgan's widow might examine it. After considerable urging and with some hesitancy, she testified that the body was her husband's, even though she admitted that it bore only a slight resemblance to him. This was enough, however, and the body, now officially Morgan's, was buried again with great Antimasonic ceremony. Meanwhile, Mrs. Timothy Monroe of Upper Canada had heard about the case and came to New York to look for her husband who had disappeared a month before. At a third inquest, after a second disinterment, she had no trouble identifying the corpse. The arrangement of the teeth, as well as the realization that the body was too well preserved to have been in the water for over a year, confirmed her testimony. Although not Morgan's after all, the corpse had nonetheless served the Antimasons' purpose.

Within a month of Morgan's disappearance, Antimasonic sentiment on the local level was beginning to increase, both publicly and privately within the lodges. Miller, who had everything to gain financially by exploiting his accomplice's abduction, encouraged this excitement by printing fifty thousand circulars calling for information on the identity of the perpetrators. He also advertised the forthcoming release of Morgan's book, entitled *Illustrations of Masonry, By One of the Fraternity Who Has Devoted Thirty Years to the Subject*, which gave detailed accounts of passwords, hand grips, secret signs and oaths and obligations. Although it purported to be accurate, little of it was original, as a comparison with earlier exposures indicates. Nonetheless, the work was so popular that five editions were published in two years.[2]

At the same time three reactions to the Morgan case occurred on a state-wide level, one religious and two political. Elder David Bernard, a Baptist minister prominent in upstate New York and a Mason, publicly renounced his membership and issued scathing denunciations of the Fraternity from the pulpit. He established the tone for a host of Antimasonic tracts that, appearing quickly, pictured Freemasonry as "murderous, vile, anti-Christian, atheistic and unpatriotic." Bernard supported his opinions by extensive research into the operations of the Society and later published them as *Light on Masonry* (Utica, 1829), subsequently the most important Antimasonic work. Another Baptist minister, John G. Stearns, reinforced Bernard's views by attacking Freemasonry as a "substitute religion." Other clergymen took up the banner of reform and called a series of meetings of various Protestant denominations in western New York State. These assemblies drew up numerous proposals, resolutions and petitions, sponsored publications, and purged church memberships of Masons. By the end of 1827 the moral crusade against the Fraternity was well under way.

News of the Morgan incident quickly reached Albany. Governor DeWitt Clinton, Past Grand Master of New York, encouraged the vigorous pursuit of the matter and offered rewards for information leading to the arrest and conviction of the offenders. Statewide, various citizen's committees also demanded justice. These efforts resulted in a Grand Jury investigation at Canandaigua in November 1826 that indicted four men, who were later tried on charges of conspiracy and kidnapping; they got off lightly since these offenses were legally only misdemeanors. Rather than calming the furor, the trial seemed to indicate that influential Masons were able to control the legal process for their own benefit. In the spring of 1827 Governor Clinton increased the size of the reward and called on the New York legislature to sponsor a more thorough investigation, which he believed to be beyond the means of local authorities. Although his proposals received support in committee, they were defeated when put to a vote. Repeated public demands for justice occasioned nineteen more Grand Jury investigations in five New York counties over the next four years, which indicted a total of fifty Masons. Although many of these men were subsequently brought to trial, only a handful were convicted, and only of minor offenses.

Ambitious politicians at this time, notably Thurlow Weed of Rochester, were looking for a "cause" around which to organize a new political party; they made political capital out of the Morgan incident. In their hands, the spontaneously formed Antimasonic societies, which were motivated by moral indignation, were transformed into the Antimasonic Party, whose aim was to win political office. Local and regional conventions in New York put forward candidates dedicated to the extirpation of Freemasonry as a means of removing from power the established Democratic Party, which identified with the Society. The political movement rapidly gained momentum and was able to influence events until the early 1840s.

William Morgan's fate has never been determined, but that is not really important. Most historians consider the "Morgan Affair," as it was called, to be a minor episode that eventually would have died down. What was significant was the successful cover-up of the particulars of the case by powerful Masons. The efforts of legal authorities to ascertain the truth were thwarted repeatedly by the refusal or inability of witnesses to present concrete evidence, although hundreds of persons were called to testify. It was this well-publicized challenge to the important republican principle of equality before the law, rather than Morgan's disappearance alone, which inspired the origins of Antimasonry and was responsible for its growth.[3]

*   *   *   *   *   *   *   *

Despite the furor the Morgan incident caused in New York State, Pennsylvania Freemasonry was not affected immediately. If Pennsylvania Masons heard about the case when it occurred, they certainly kept quiet about it. The Grand Lodge of Pennsylvania traditionally maintained a policy of silence regarding such attacks to avoid negative publicity. A case in point was an episode in February 1821. The Presbyterian Synod of Pittsburgh had condemned the Fraternity on grounds that it had "a pernicious influence on morals and religion" and urged Church leaders to discourage members of their flocks from joining Masonic lodges and to ask their parishoners who were members to withdraw. When private individuals took it upon themselves to defend the Society publicly, the Grand Lodge reprimanded them, saying that it was the exclusive prerogative of the Grand Lodge to answer charges; otherwise "much injury may be inflicted upon Freemasonry." The Grand Lodge chose not to respond, however, and the matter died quietly.[4]

In the first few years following the Morgan Affair the Grand Lodge of Pennsylvania saw no necessity to defend itself against outside attacks. Instead, it concentrated upon its daily business. Its leaders looked upon its role as a supervisory body more seriously than ever before and extended its judicial, legislative and executive functions. The Grand Lodge acted as a court of appeal for aggrieved members, supervised conduct of individual Masons, reviewed operations of subordinate lodges, received membership returns and dues, granted charity, acted upon petitions for new lodges, engaged in numerous reviews of finances and took measures to redeem the debt for the rebuilt Masonic Hall. It also kept in close touch with local lodges through the system of District Deputy Grand Masters, which proved effective. By the end of 1827 fourteen Masonic districts had been organized and the leader of each was required to make an annual report of the status of Freemasonry in his region.[5]

In 1826 the Grand Lodge created the new office of Grand Lecturer and appointed David Nathans to hold it. His duty was to conduct a "general visit of instruction to the lodges located beyond the City and County of Philadelphia" and to make sure that members "have been attentive to their Masonic duties and correct in their work." In nine months Nathans traveled nearly 2,400 miles and visited seventy-two, or about eighty percent, of the country lodges. After examining minutes and records, attending lodge meetings, inspecting meeting places, giving lectures on Masonic subjects and engaging in a general policing of lodges, Nathans offered a comprehensive report the following March. Of the visited lodges, half (thirty-six) were described as "flourishing." Their memberships were increasing, they had no financial difficulties, and some were even able to erect buildings exclusively for Masonic purposes. Although another twelve lodges had fewer members, they nonetheless were "zealous in their performance of Masonic labours." About twenty lodges were not so fortunate. They were either debt-ridden, which a more understanding policy on the part of the Grand Lodge would relieve, or they were in a state of decline. Some of these had too few members, some were improperly managed, and some lacked sufficient understanding of Masonic principles. In a few cases the situation was so serious that Nathans recommended that their warrants be recalled. He could give no reliable report on four lodges because they had not received sufficient notice of his coming.

All in all, Nathans held a positive impression of the condition of Freemasonry in Pennsylvania:

> In the aggregate, the country lodges under this jurisdiction are highly prosperous and exhibit considerable improvement . . . . A strong desire to promote the great ends of the institution very generally prevailed and it may be added that the brethren and the lodges almost without exception were well satisfied with the parental administration of the regulations of the grand lodge.

Although generally pleased with the results of his investigation, the Grand Lecturer offered a few suggestions to correct "errors of minor importance." These faults dealt with record-keeping, election and installation of officers, treatment of candidates for membership, expulsions and by-laws. Nathans recommended greater accuracy and care in record keeping, stricter adherence to rules and regulations, more propriety during Masonic functions, and a greater uniformity of Masonic practices in the state. In sum, he believed that a general tightening was in order.

The Grand Lecturer's report also hinted at difficulties with the public reception of Freemasonry in certain parts of the state. For example, it made reference to "various and powerful discouragements which have reduced Masonry in Bradford County to a low ebb," but offered no details. Since this county is on the border with New York, it is likely that Antimasonic feeling had already crossed state lines. The report also mentioned "strong prejudices against the order generally . . . arising from the unmasonic conduct of a lodge [No. 56] which met in Carlisle upwards of twenty years ago," but these appear to have been unrelated to the Morgan Affair. The effects of this hostility were limited, however, since Freemasonry had made successful comebacks in those regions by the time the report was made, or so it was claimed.[6]

The Grand Lecturer's comprehensive survey indicated that Freemasonry in Pennsylvania was basically healthy and well administered. The authority of the Grand Lodge was accepted and any uncomfortable feelings generated by the reform movement, led by Lodge No. 43 a few years earlier, had been overcome. The leadership in Philadelphia proved attentive to the needs of its membership throughout the state and felt a high degree of accountability.

In the same month Nathans made his report on the country lodges the Grand Lodge received results of a study of the condition of the city lodges. This explained why it had refused the requests of local Masons to establish two new lodges in Philadelphia. Evidently the petitioners were dissatisfied with the methods of operation or the personalities of their current lodge and wished to secede from it. The Grand Lodge would not tolerate such an action as it was "so manifestly injurious to the craft." An appropriate consideration in warranting lodges was population density, but with twenty-five Philadelphia lodges already in operation, the Grand Lodge thought that ample opportunity existed for "the diffusion of masonic light, and the establishment of ready means of intercommunion among the brethren." To form new lodges too close to existing ones would reduce the membership of a lodge "so as to render its pecuniary burdens intolerable, and a rotation of competent officers impracticable." As it was, only fourteen Philadelphia lodges were strong enough to meet these goals credibly. Moreover, the more successful lodges were established before 1810. Therefore, the committee concluded, "the Masonic welfare has not been promoted by the increase of the number of the city lodges, and . . . it is inexpedient to grant new Warrants in the city of Philadelphia." Special circumstances arose occasionally, however, and the Grand Lodge approved a petition from Masons of Kensington, which, although within Philadelphia County, was a separate village. It was too far away from the Masonic Hall on Chestnut Street for Masons to conveniently attend the lodges that met there, and so a new lodge, No. 211, was warranted.[7]

The first notice in Masonic sources of an effect of the Antimasonic movement in Pennsylvania was made in March 1828, when the Grand Lodge formed a special nine-man committee "to enquire whether any special measures be now necessary for the preservation and security of the interests of masonry within this Commonwealth." The committee reported within a month, but orally; it is, therefore, impossible to know what was said. Because Pennsylvania Masons customarily refrained from writing down any sensitive information, however, it must have been significant. Apparently no resolutions were passed nor were actions taken, and nothing further was said in Grand Lodge about the matter for over a year.

Through the remainder of 1828 and throughout 1829 the crusade against Freemasonry was carried into Pennsylvania with some force. Antimasonic newspapers circulated, local political parties were organized and petitions calling for an investigation into the Fraternity were sent to the Pennsylvania General Assembly. In March 1829 David Nathans, who once again served as Grand Lecturer, offered a cautiously optimistic report on the condition of Freemasonry in Pennsylvania, but it was not so positive as that of 1827. It tried to soften any negative effects of the movement and offered a rebuttal to the Antimasonic position. A portion of Nathans' report is worth quoting since it appears to be one of the opening assertions in the Masonic controversy in Pennsylvania:

> Masonry in this Commonwealth may be considered as flourishing in all the thickly-settled portions of the State. The lodges generally are composed of the most influential and respectable men in their respective neighbourhoods and by the strict attention to moral and masonic duties command the respect of the community. In many places where old prejudices against the order formerly existed in great force, these have either worn away entirely or have been materially diminished and it is comparatively in few places that the lodges have suffered from newly excited opposition. In the northern and thinly-settled portions of the State where the lodges are few in number and most of the members reside at great distances from the lodges they belong to and from one another, their prosperity and increase have been partially checked by the systematic opposition which had its origin in a neighbouring state. In but few other parts has this opposition been of effect.[8]

Subsequent events proved that this hope — that the effects of Antimasonry might be limited — was little more than wishful thinking.

In the course of 1829 various groups of citizens throughout the state held well-attended Antimasonic meetings, notably in Lancaster in April, Gibson (Susquehanna County) in June, and Philadelphia in September. The first meeting urged that a state convention of the Antimasonic Party be called, the second condemned Freemasonry on religious grounds, and the third issued a comprehensive public statement against the Society.

The statement of the Philadelphia Antimasons, which was based upon Bernard's recently published *Light on Masonry*, was quickly brought into print. Its basic argument was that Freemasonry was evil because it was secret; if it had nothing to hide and if its work were truly moral and good, why not open it to public inspection? Throughout history, secret societies always conspired toward sinister ends, and Freemasonry was no exception. The "natural tendency" of such organizations was to seek power and influence at the expense of legitimate authority, and Freemasons, by giving political preference to their fellows, undermined the institutions of a free society.

The "concerned citizens" of Philadelphia who supported these views also took issue with many other aspects of Freemasonry. They criticized the "ridiculously absurd and impiously pompous" titles of the Society, which, originating in Eastern despotisms, were "incompatible with republican government." They also condemned extra judicial oaths that bound

Masons to a "higher" system of justice requiring absolute obedience, even to the point of committing murder. Freemasonry was also viewed as anti-Christian. Although it used quasi-religious ceremonies and advocated seemingly Christian beliefs, its activities mocked true religion and substituted an atheistic or deistic system. The Fraternity was also wealthy and used only a small portion of its money for charitable purposes; the rest it spent on temples, paraphernalia and "senseless cermonies and exhibitions." It was true that some good men had associated with the Masons, such as George Washington, but Washington later repented and cautioned against secret societies in his Farewell Address. Finally, Freemasonry allegedly encouraged "intemperance, licentiousness and dissipation," which were repugnant to the moral sense of the whole community. In condemning the Society, the Philadelphia Antimasons used colorful language. They likened lodges to "dens of vipers . . . which have fastened their fangs on civil liberty and the Christian religion" and saw them "growing up like a poisonous fungi [sic]."[9]

The "Philadelphia Citizens' Address" called for the immediate suppression of the Fraternity and thus represented a real threat to the Masons, but it elicited no official response. The Grand Lodge offered no public statements or rebuttals, but it did curtail public processions. In March 1829 the Grand Lodge debated whether to forbid individual Masons from participating in processions of the International Order of Odd Fellows. Evidently Masonic leaders believed that association with another secret society would not help, and might even hurt, their own cause. Some Masons who were also ardent Odd Fellows claimed that the Grand Lodge had no right to interfere with their private actions which did not violate Masonic principles. They stated that the Order of Odd Fellows was "strictly a moral, charitable and beneficial institution [whose] chief end and aim [was] the relief of the distressed and the amelioration of the condition of the unfortunate." The petitioners convinced the Grand Lodge that no harm to Freemasonry could result from their participation and the resolution was not adopted. In June the Grand Lodge decreed that no subordinate lodge could hold any procession without prior permission of the appropriate District Deputy Grand Master.

By keeping silent and maintaining a low profile Masonic leaders wished to deprive the new attacks upon the Fraternity of unwarranted attention. The Grand Lodge tried to conduct business as usual, but found it impossible to do so since the Antimasonic movement intruded more and more upon the workings of the Order. Although declining to present their case before the "profane," Masonic leaders still found it necessary to prepare defenses of the Society for the instruction of members.[10]

In December 1829 a special committee offered the traditional address of appreciation to Grand Master Thomas Kittera, who was retiring after three years of service, but it was less a review of Kittera's contributions than a spirited defense of the Fraternity. It reviewed the persecutions Freemasonry had long endured in Europe. Unenlightened individuals and despotic powers, determined to crush Freemasonry, used every means at their disposal, but were unable to "extinguish the sacred fire of the order which warms the bosom of every genuine ancient mason." Masons were advised to regard current attacks in the same light. What was particularly troublesome to the authors of the address, however, was not opposition itself, to which they almost had grown accustomed, but rather the organized and systematic nature of the Antimasonic movement. They referred to Morgan's kidnapping, although not specifically by name, and considered it to be the result of "errors and crimes of ignorant and infatuated men (but no true masons)." Unfortunately for Freemasonry, "deluded fellow Citizens" were confusing these renegades "with the order of which they were unworthy members." They firmly believed that the Society should be able to withstand the test of time, with the help of the "Great Grand Master," and that Masonry "will arise invigorated to new and successful exertions in all her might and strength against this Goliath of the Philistines." In his response to the address, Kittera agreed:

> The prejudice which designing men are endeavouring to extend against us will be as short lived as it is bitter and unfounded. A Society based upon the principles of Masonry has nothing to dread from the attacks. Let us but oppose their clamour with silence and their malevolence [will cease].[11]

As late as 1829 Pennsylvania Masons either did not fully appreciate the extent of the opposition or, if they did, chose to believe it would not matter. In any case, they were about to discover the strength of its negative effects. Even as the Grand Lodge indulged in these self-congratulatory sentiments, financial reports indicated that revenues from subordinate lodges were showing a "sensible decline." The cause, the Committee of Finance recognized, was "the artificial and extraordinary excitement which has unfortunately lately sprung up against Masonry and will probably some time longer operate injuriously upon the contributions of members and the regular payment of dues." The committee recommended "a strict economy in the disbursements of the Grand Lodge" and a general, detailed attention to finances. By the spring of 1830 the operations of a few lodges were becoming unsteady. Either they fell behind in their financial obligations or they petitioned for permission to temporarily suspend operations or to hold fewer meetings per year than required. Only a handful of lodges actually failed in the late 1820s and early 1830s, but the Grand Lodge feared that more would do so. It accordingly organized a special committee to prepare an address on Antimasonry to be delivered to subordinate lodges, but there is no evidence that this was ever done.[12]

One positive event for Pennsylvania Freemasons in 1829 was the presentation, on July 3, of George Washington's Masonic apron to the Grand Lodge of Pennsylvania by the Washington Benevolent Society. Of white satin, the apron had been richly embroidered with Masonic and patriotic symbols by Madame de Lafayette. The Marquis had intended it as a tribute to his mentor, friend and fellow Mason, and had presented it to Washington at Mt. Vernon in August 1784. Washington is known to have worn it while presiding over Masonic ceremonies at the laying of the cornerstone of the United States Capitol in September 1793. This precious relic was proudly displayed in the Grand Lodge room, where it served as welcome inspiration to disheartened Masons. Three years later, in February 1832, the members of Lodge No. 51 presented the Grand Lodge with a full-length portrait of Washington, a copy of one by Gilbert Stuart.[13]

Much to the annoyance of the Pennsylvania Grand Lodge, the Antimasons chose Philadelphia as the site for their first national convention, September 11 to 17, 1830. The dates coincided with the fourth anniversary of Morgan's disappearance. Ninety-six delegates from ten states and one territory attended, but proceedings were dominated by delegates from New York (twenty-six), Pennsylvania (twenty-five) and Massachusetts (fifteen). Little of a concrete political nature was accomplished, except agreement on a platform dedicated to the destruction of Freemasonry and the establishment of a committee of correspondence. Since so few states were represented, delegates were not able to choose presidential and vice-presidential candidates; they were obliged to postpone such decisions until another convention scheduled for Baltimore the following year.

What was important, however, was that the convention's well-organized and systematic attack upon Freemasonry now captured national attention. Delegates gave detailed reports on specific subjects: the Morgan incident and the Masonic obstruction of justice connected with it; the origins and character of Freemasonry; the history of Antimasonry; Masonic oaths; and the relationship between Freemasonry and Christianity, among other topics. In addition, a group of so-called "seceding Masons" offered an exposition of Masonic ritual, including passwords and signs for the numerous degrees, and extensive debates revealed evidence of the supposed "dangers" of Freemasonry. Members of the convention charged that the Fraternity posed a serious challenge to the American system of politics, law, morality and religion and that it stifled the free exchange of ideas. For example, Thaddeus Stevens, from Pennsylvania, argued that since only one (Antimasonic) Philadelphia newspaper reported on the convention, this was clear evidence that Masons controlled the press for their own purposes. The Antimasons also criti-

Washington's Masonic Apron (Grand Lodge of Pennsylvania).

cized the integrity of Masonic ritual and belief for historical inaccuracies and inherent contradictions. Before adjourning, the delegates drafted a comprehensive "Address to the People" that summarized information obtained about Freemasonry's nature and influence. It contained much illustrative material, such as the following exchange in mock imitation of the question-and-answer technique of Masonic ritual: "Q: For what purpose was Freemasonry instituted? A: Freemasonry was instituted to dupe the simple for the benefit of the crafty." This pamphlet was immediately printed and strongly urged its readers to join together to extirpate the Society.

The charges made at the convention were not really new; they had been circulating for nearly four years, but they were significant because influential men now took them seriously. The reports and debates were of a relatively high intellectual order and their arguments were presented in a reasonable way with little trace of extremism or fanaticism. Typically, and probably to their disadvantage, Philadelphia Masons refused to respond to the many charges, even though the convention was held in their own city.[14]

In the course of 1831 one of the Pennsylvania delegates, John Clarke, a Philadelphia printer, took advantage of the growing animosity toward Freemasonry to further both the cause and his personal fortunes. He reprinted two important exposés by a leading Connecticut Antimason, Avery Allyn. The first of these, *A Ritual of Freemasonry,* gave the verbatim text of the ritual and passwords of every Masonic degree. It also included engravings of the handgrips, points of fellowship, signs of distress, and positions for initiations and other ceremonies. The second was a pocket-sized printing of nearly two hundred Masonic oaths and penalties. At the same time Clarke also issued the first edition of the *Sun Anti-Masonic Almanac,* which complemented his own Antimasonic newspaper of the same name. These crudely illustrated works were written in a popular style designed to agitate readers against Freemasonry. For example, the *Ritual* contained Allyn's testimony that he had personally heard Morgan's murderer confess his crime and explain how he had escaped justice by exploiting his Masonic contacts; the *Almanac* contained details of seven additional alleged Masonic murders. There is no way to ascertain the success of these publications, but judging from their rapid appearance and the Fraternity's subsequent problems, they must have been effective.[15]

Another boost to the Antimasonic cause occurred at this time with the political conversion of Richard Rush of York County, who had renounced his membership in Union Lodge No. 121, Philadelphia, a few years earlier. The son of the prominent Philadelphia physician Benjamin Rush, he had served in positions of national prominence including attorney general (1814-1817), secretary of state (1817), minister to Great

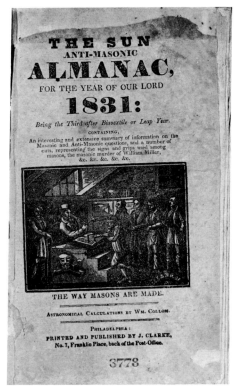

Title Page of the *Sun Antimasonic Almanac* for 1831 (Grand
Lodge of Pennsylvania).

Britain (1817-1825), comptroller (1811) and secretary of the treasury
(1825-1828) and vice-presidental candidate (1828). Between May and
November 1831 Rush wrote a series of well-publicized letters affirming
his belief that the Masons were guilty of murdering Morgan and of
obstructing justice to prevent their proper punishment. He saw the Society as evil and condemned it as a subversive force in American society.
Rush also called for all citizens "to dispell the solemn folly, and break the
tyrannical fetters of Masonry." The Antimasonic Party briefly considered
Rush as a possible presidential candidate in the 1832 election, and put
him forward shortly thereafter for the Senate. When these efforts failed,
Rush grew disillusioned with the Party and became a Jacksonian Democrat, although he remained opposed to the Society.[16]

In December 1831 Pennsylvania Masons suffered the loss of their
most prominent and wealthiest Brother. On the day after Christmas
Stephen Girard died, and his funeral was held four days later. It was well
advertised and many organizations were invited to participate, including
the Grand Lodge of Pennsylvania. Despite reluctance to draw public
attention to themselves at that time, Masonic leaders accepted, much to
their later regret.

The Masons occupied a position of honor in the funeral procession, being third in line, after city officials and the wardens of the port, and ahead of seven other societies. Consisting of three thousand participants and witnessed by an estimated twenty thousand spectators, the procession marched from Girard's residence on North Water Street to the burial ground of Holy Trinity Roman Catholic Church at the corner of Sixth and Spruce Streets, where services were scheduled. To avoid criticism members of the Fraternity refrained from wearing aprons, and the officers of the Grand Lodge wore only collars and jewels; their presence nonetheless offended the presiding clergyman, Bishop Patrick Kenrick. He assumed that the Masons were about to perform their own funeral service, without benefit of clergy, and forbade it, ordering the body deposited silently in a nearby vault without any ceremonies at all.

Following Girard's interment, the Masons remembered their deceased Brother in their own way. Four hundred members reassembled in the Grand Lodge Room, where they heard "an appropriate address" by the Grand Master and an "elegant prayer" by the Grand Chaplain. The Grand Lodge then resolved to go into mourning for a period of six months by draping the jewels, hangings and furniture of the lodge room in black, the traditional gesture of respect for deceased Past Grand Masters, and to commission a portrait of Girard by Bass Otis, to be hung in that room.

A possible explanation for Masonic willingness to participate in the public procession was that Stephen Girard had left a bequest of $20,000 to the Fraternity. This amount was not all in cash but included certificates of Girard's shares of the Masonic loans. The money was to be invested in a secure stock until it rose to $30,000, at which time its interest was to be used for charitable purposes, "in order that the real and benevolent purposes of masonic institutions may be attained." Girard cautioned that this money was to go only to "poor and respectable brethren" and he added general advice that Masonic lodges should "not admit to membership or to receive members from other lodges unless the applicants shall absolutely be men of sound and good morals." The Grand Lodge set up the Stephen Girard Charity Fund according to the provisions of the will. Masons were pleased with Girard's comments about the membership of the Fraternity since they were "in strict conformity with the principles and constitutions of our ancient order."[17]

The incident at Holy Trinity Church no doubt contributed to more negative public feeling against the Fraternity at a time when it could least afford it. As a result, the Grand Lodge absolutely refused to participate in any other public ceremonies for the remainder of the Antimasonic period. The most notable example of this new policy occurred only two months later when the Grand Lodge declined the invitation of a Philadelphia citizens' committee to take part in a large procession to commemorate the centenary of Washington's birth. This event turned out to be, in the words of one historian, "the most stupendous parade in these years." Some fifteen thousand marchers from all manner of associations, trades, and occupations, as well as city officials, participated, but no Masons. Some members of the Fraternity wanted to "illuminate the front of the Hall, provided the Public Buildings in Chestnut Street are," but even this proposal failed to be approved. Pennsylvania Masons had always been proud of Washington's Masonic connection and in earlier periods had taken advantage of every opportunity to make it widely known. That they declined to do so on this special occasion is one indication of their extreme caution and of the strength of the opposition.[18]

In the early 1830s certain aspects of the administration of Pennsylvania Freemasonry faltered and its financial difficulties increased. In November 1831 the Grand Lodge reorganized the supervision of the Masonic Hall. Previously, there had been separate Hall and Gas Committees, composed of unpaid amateurs. This practice had resulted in rapid turnover of personnel and much inefficiency. The functions of these committees were consolidated into one full-time superintendent who was responsible for all matters pertaining to the building. His first projects included much-needed renovations to the property, such as tearing down the iron fence and wall, repairing and resurfacing the pavement and installing ornamental gas lamps on the front of the hall.[19]

The Grand Secretary's office also suffered from confusion and disorganization. In June 1832 the current holder of that position, John M. Read, complained of the poor record keeping by his predecessor. Information pertaining to membership, dispensations, certificates and returns of lodges was either lost or left unrecorded, partly because clerks had been employed who had improper knowledge of Masonic procedures. All papers were "in great confusion" and the "real situation of the Grand Lodge could not be ascertained" from them. Read called for reforms in the system of record keeping and asked subordinate lodges to cooperate. His ideas were implemented gradually over the next four years.

Other officials also suggested reforms: the reorganization of individual country lodges that were falling behind in their financial obligations and in reporting membership information; more regularity of attendance by Grand Lodge officers; and tightening of policies on the admission of visitors. This last measure was designed both to acquire revenues by charging admission fees and to prevent unauthorized persons from gaining access to Masonic secrets. The Philadelphia lodges appear to have been stable in this period, however, at least according to Grand Master Michael Nisbet, who was "highly pleased . . . with the brightening prospects of the fraternity" after his annual visitation to them.[20]

Financial reports became more frequent in the early 1830s and were increasingly marked by fears of inability to meet Grand Lodge obligations. Finance Committee members were especially concerned with meeting the payments on the various Masonic loans taken out in connection with the rebuilding of the Chestnut Street hall in 1819 and 1820. In January 1833 this debt was substantial, amounting to $54,000, whereas the sinking fund had a balance of only about $5,100. In addition, the Grand Lodge had to pay the salaries of certain officials and employees, interest to shareholders of the loans and wages of workmen for repairs to the hall, expenses that amounted to another $11,000, not to mention ongoing charitable disbursements. The Grand Lodge took out another Masonic loan for $6,000 at five percent interest, but financial stability was still elusive, and at the end of the year a special twenty-one man committee was formed to find a solution.[21]

Amid these financial difficulties and against the backdrop of the Antimasonic movement, the Grand Lodge celebrated the supposed one-hundredth anniversary "of the establishment of The First Lodge in Pennsylvania of which Lodge Brother Benjamin Franklin was the First Master." More than three hundred Brethren attended an extra grand communication on June 24, 1834, where "a very beautiful and instructive masonic address" was delivered by the Deputy Grand Master, George M. Dallas. What is curious about this address is that it contained no information pertaining to the historical events it was meant to commemorate. By coincidence, Pennsylvania Masons had just received news of the death of the Marquis de Lafayette, and Dallas spent most of his time talking about the "virtues and exploits of this exalted Mason." Evidently, the historical evidence known to Masons at that time went no further back than 1734, which was at least three years later than the establishment of the first confirmed Masonic lodge in Pennsylvania.[22]

Although this celebration was strictly a Masonic affair, news of it spread beyond Masonic circles. A Philadelphia printer, John Gest, who played an important role in local Antimasonic politics, heard of it and took advantage of the occasion to print his own strongly worded tract against the Fraternity. In it Gest defended the character of St. John the Baptist "against the foul slander and wicked libel of Freemasons." The tract argued that the character of the saint was out of keeping with the practices of the Fraternity and that he would join the Antimasons if he were alive. Gest followed this clever pamphlet a year later with a similar defense of St. John the Evangelist and King Solomon, other supposed biblical Masons. This work was addressed to George M. Dallas, "lately promoted to the high (but infamous) office of Right Worshipful Grand Master, of the Grand Lodge of Pennsylvania." Gest also produced an edition of Masonic oaths and penalties. These and other contemporary attacks weakened Pennsylvania Freemasonry at a critical time in its history.[23]

In the course of 1835 the financial condition of the Grand Lodge significantly worsened. In March the regular Finance Committee, as well as the special twenty-one-man committee appointed a few months earlier, offered comprehensive financial reports. Their conclusions were not encouraging. The current debts of the Grand Lodge were so large and the prospects for improvement were so poor that both committees suggested that the Masonic Hall on Chestnut Street be sold and a smaller one purchased. They figured that the current hall and lot would bring about $120,000, which, after paying off the debt, purchasing and repairing a new hall, would leave a surplus of about $20,000.

Before recommending this, however, the committees had considered several alternatives to increase income. One was the construction of several buildings at the front of the property for shops and stores, but this measure would have necessitated considerable cash outlay and a new loan, which the Grand Lodge could ill afford. Another concern was that the tax-exempt status for the hall, granted in 1820 by the Pennsylvania Assembly, was to expire within five years and would entail additional charges of about $1,000 per year. Seeing bankruptcy and dissolution as real possibilities, these men were concerned not only with the short-term financial health of the Fraternity, but also with its very existence:

> [We] . . . have proposed an efficient remedy for existing difficulties and a prevention of Future similar troubles. The situation of the Grand Lodge is alarming to every Friend of the Order and Ruin to the Craft seems to be inevitable if no Remedy is adopted. The Plan which your Committee proposes, relinquishes none of the high Standing of the order; it frees us from Debt, furnishes us with a Beautiful Building, releases the Subordinate Lodges from existing enthralment and future heavy taxation, encourages the Craft in regular attendance, insures Prosperity by opening the door to Membership, renews the affection and fealty of the County Lodges to the Grand Lodge, Gives to each Lodge a Means of Charity and Places at the disposal of the Grand Lodge a Magnificent Sum from the Interest of which, the wants of a distressed Worthy Brother, his Widow or his Orphans may be Amply Supplied and thus the great object of our order be fully attained.

The Grand Lodge accepted this report without debate and appointed a five-man committee to solicit offers for the hall and to find suitable new quarters.[24]

The Masons chose not to advertise the sale of their property "for reasons which most of the Members will understand," but rather quietly to inquire among "Several Capitalists who expressed a desire to possess the Premises." Over the next few months the Grand Lodge received two offers. The Franklin Institute first made an offer of $75,000 cash and their building on Seventh Street, and then subsequently changed it to

$110,000 cash without the building. The Philadelphia Museum did better, with $115,000 and the provision that the Masons could still use the Grand Lodge room for a yearly rental of $1,250. Believing that their property was worth more, the Masons refused both offers. Eventually, however, they were obliged to accept $110,550 from a lawyer named William Swain, who evidently acted as an intermediary since he immediately assigned his rights to the Franklin Institute. The Institute was attracted by the favorable location of the Masonic property, and rapidly rising real estate values promised a substantial return on its investment. The necessary papers were drawn up and the sale was concluded in October. The Franklin Institute agreed to pay $15,000 on closing, $20,000 on January 1, 1836, and the balance in three equal payments due January 1, 1838, 1840 and 1842. The last four installments were to constitute a loan from the Masons at a yearly interest rate of five percent.

Meanwhile, the committee to find a new meeting place recommended the purchase of Washington Hall on Third Street above Spruce, for the modest sum of $25,000, with $9,000 down and the rest payable in unspecified installments at a annual rate of four percent interest. Accordingly, the deed and mortgage papers were executed in late August 1835.

Designed by architect Robert Mills, and completed in 1816, Washington Hall was a commodious two-story brick building with sufficient space for the Society's needs, but certain changes were necessary, such as conversion to gas lighting and alteration of existing rooms for Masonic purposes. A "grand saloon" with galleries, measuring one hundred twenty feet long, seventy feet wide and forty-five feet high, was divided into two meeting rooms, one for the Grand Lodge and the other for subordinate lodges. Minor changes were made in another lodge room of unknown dimensions, several committee rooms, each eighteen by twenty feet, and a banquet room, one hundred seventeen feet long and thirty feet wide. The building was already decorated with appropriate architectural adornments, and most of the fixtures, furniture and trappings were transferred from the old hall to the new one. The Grand Lodge estimated the cost of improvements at not more than $16,000.[25]

Masonic custom required a dedication ceremony whenever the Fraternity moved into a new hall. Accordingly, a proposal for the dedication of Washington Hall was made in October, but it sounded as though it were from an earlier era of Masonic history. It was for a public procession in full regalia to a church where a reverend Brother would deliver a sermon and say prayers, to be followed by a return to the hall. This proposal was debated for about a month. In a Grand Lodge meeting on November 2, four separate attempts were necessary to defeat the measure, and then only by a narrow margin of two votes. Instead, the Grand Lodge resolved to hold the dedication quietly within the hall without any

Masonic meeting place (1835-1855). Drawing by William Strickland. Engraving by George Strickland (Grand Lodge of Pennsylvania).

public display. The cost of alterations had exceeded the proposed limit by $3,000, but there was no time for discussion of this extra amount since the architect, Thomas U. Walter, promised that the building would be ready for the St. John's Day celebration; so the Grand Lodge came up with more money.

Although it is not known how many members attended, twenty-eight lodges were represented at this special communication, a number higher than average for this period. In the first part of the ceremony, a representative of the architect, who was not a Mason, presented the tools used in the renovations. This Grand Lodge member, Joseph R. Chandler, then gave "a very Beautiful and Impressive Speech on the Purity and Benevolence of the Order." The hall was then dedicated in the usual Masonic manner. The members of the Grand Lodge proceeded around the room three times, in turn strewing corn, pouring wine, and then pouring oil. Separate invocations were made to the "Grand Architect of the Universe," to "Virtue and Science" and to "Universal Charity." The Grand Chaplain offered prayers both before and after this ceremony and the Brethren sang three odes and a canon for four voices. The high point of the dedication was an address by Grand Master Dallas, which in a "Strain of Solemn Eloquence," reminded Masons of the necessity to adhere to their principles and to stand upright in the face of the "Embarrassing situation in which the Enemies of Free Masonry had placed the Order."[26]

By the end of 1835 the Masons of Pennsylvania had thus taken a few steps backward in order to consolidate their position. The remaining core of members earnestly hoped for the cessation of hostility toward the Society. Their struggle was not yet over, however, and even as they made arrangements to occupy their new hall, a new and more intense phase of Antimasonry was under way.

*   *   *   *   *   *   *   *

In the mid- to late 1830s the nature and effects of Freemasonry upon society became issues of heated debate in the Pennsylvania House of Representatives. The moving force in this phase of Antimasonry was Thaddeus Stevens of Adams County, who launched a barrage of attacks upon the Fraternity throughout the period. Both personally and professionally, Stevens was a frustrated individual, and this circumstance may explain his vindictive nature. Born with a clubfoot, he had an alcoholic father, who deserted his family, and a mother who lost herself to religious fanaticism. While a student at Dartmouth College, Stevens failed to be accepted into the local Phi Beta Kappa chapter, which was a scholastic and social, but also a secret, society, and because of legal technicalities, was not admitted to the Pennsylvania bar, despite being qualified. In addition, Masonic rumor had it that he had applied for admission to Good Samaritan Lodge No. 200 in Gettysburg, Pa., but was blackballed. No doubt motivated by a need for public recognition and a desire for political influence, Stevens became an active Antimason in 1829 and organized the party in his home county. Despite repeated legislative defeats, he persisted in his dedication to exterminate Freemasonry until public interest waned and his own political ambitions led him in other directions.[27]

Stevens' initial bill, brought forward on February 10, 1834, dealt with the supposed influence of Freemasonry on subverting impartial judicial proceedings. He proposed to disqualify Masonic jurors, judges and sheriffs in cases where one party was a Mason and the other was not, but this measure failed by a vote of forty-five to thirty-one. Stevens also proposed that a special committee with subpoena power be appointed "to inquire into the evils of masonry and the extent and influence of its oaths and obligations upon the community." A committee was formed, with Stevens at its head, but the House failed to give it legal authority to hear testimony or to obtain written evidence, even after Stevens had modified his original proposal several times. Determined in his course of action, Stevens next introduced a bill prohibiting the administration of Masonic and all other secret "extra judicial oaths, obligations and promises in the nature of oaths." This measure, however, was not brought to a vote. He suffered another setback at the same time when a countercommittee was formed for the purpose of investigating the "unjust and wicked operations" of Antimasonry. Throughout the spring of 1834 members of both committees presented numerous memorials from concerned citizens of Pennsylvania as evidence of public support for their respective activities.[28]

Stevens' committee issued a report which was read on March 20. It complained that its efforts properly to investigate Pennsylvania Freemasonry were hamstrung by recent House votes and by the refusal of the clerk and speaker of the House to issue the necessary subpoenas. These actions it considered to be irresponsible and unresponsive to the wishes of "a large number of highly respectable citizens" who had appealed to the legislature,

> stating their belief that the masonic fraternity is associated for purposes inconsistent with the equal rights and privileges which are the birth-right of every freeman; that they are bound together by secret obligations and oaths, illegal, immoral and blasphemous, subversive of all public law, and hostile to the pure administration of justice.

The report recommended that Governor George Wolf be called before the House to testify as to "the principles and practices of the Order of which he is so conspicuous a member," and it wanted him to yield his private papers, which "might throw much light on the question [of] how far Masonry secures political and Executive favor." The report also declared that it was the duty of the government to see "that in future none of our respectable citizens should be entrapped into such a degrading and painful thraldom [Freemasonry]."

This statement was forcefully answered in early April by the opposing committee. Its members were not Masons and had "no peculiar motive or inclination to support the Order" but they nonetheless realized the positive benefits offered by a society composed of "ten or fifteen thousand of our most useful, intelligent and eminent citizens of all parties." In their opinion, the Antimasonic movement "libels our country, its government and its constituted authorities," "calumniates the memory of the founders of our republic" and "is quite unadapted to the climate, common sense, and sober feelings of Pennsylvania." They compared Antimasonry to the Salem witchcraft trials and to the religious persecutions of "the darkest ages of arbitrary ignorance." Considering debate in the legislature on the subject of Freemasonry to be a foolish waste of time, energy and money that could be better applied to more important business, they asked to be discharged from further duties.

A few members of this committee, however, disagreed and issued a statement of minority opinion. Their report argued the Antimasonic cause and endorsed the party's platform, originally issued in 1830. Freemasonry was dangerous because it was secret and because it challenged the American way of life. The Society followed its own laws and imposed its own punishments, including the "execution" of renegade members, and it used personal connections to control government offices. The report cited numerous examples of Masonic murders, especially that of William Morgan, gave evidence of political influence and concluded with a transcript of the oaths of obligations of the first four degrees. These charges were nothing new, however, and much of the substance of the report appears to have been copied from readily available Antimasonic publications.

Although the House did nothing to implement the three reports, it did conclude that they contained information of public interest and ordered that three thousand copies of each be printed for distribution throughout Pennsylvania, one-third of them in German, as was the practice in the state at that time.[29]

When the legislative session ended in mid-April 1834, none of Stevens' Antimasonic measures had met with success, but nonetheless he had gained prominence as a leader of the anti-Jackson forces. Over the next few months he built a strong local base of support for his cause, and when the General Assembly reconvened later that year, he came back with renewed vigor. On December 10, in one of the more notable denunciations of Freemasonry of the period, Stevens condemned the Fraternity as:

> . . . injurious to the rights and dangerous to the liberties of the people; it imposes upon its members oaths and obligations unauthorized by and inconsistent with the laws of the country; it binds its members to give a preference to each other in all things over the rest of their fellow-citizens . . . to conceal the secrets and crimes of each other, not excepting even murder or treason; to espouse each other's cause, . . . whether they be right or wrong; to avenge even to death, the violation of any Masonic oaths and the revelation of any of their secrets. The rights and ceremonies of the lodges are of a degrading, immoral, and impious character.

After describing Masonic initiation practices and accusing Masons of encouraging intemperance, irreligion, and licentiousness, Stevens continued his comprehensive attack:

> [The Masonic institution] is antirepublican and an insidious and dangerous enemy to our democratic form of government; it creates and sustains secret orders of Nobility, in violation of the spirit of the constitution; it . . . assumes and secretly exercises all the prerogatives and powers of an independent kingdom; it has established a central and controlling government, extending its branches over all the civilized world . . . . it prevents the wholesome enactment and due administration of laws; it enters and corrupts our legislative halls, our executive affairs, our courts of Justice; . . . its whole tendency is to cherish a hatred of democracy and a love of aristocratic and regal forms and power . . . .

Following this emotional attack, Stevens proposed that the House judiciary committee draft a bill outlawing all "secret extrajudicial" oaths, but the motion was laid on the table. Even a measure to print Stevens' speech for the members' use was defeated. Although he introduced this and similar bills on seven separate occasions during the 1834-1835 session, Stevens' efforts produced no concrete results. As evidence of public support, his Antimasonic followers continued to introduce scores of memorials from "concerned citizens" calling for the proscription and destruction of Freemasonry, but without noticeable effect in the legislature.[30]

In the fall of 1835 an Antimason, Joseph Ritner of Washington County, was elected governor of Pennsylvania. His victory was due not to strong popular support for his candidacy, but rather to a split in the Democratic Party, which put forward two candidates. The two Democrats, former Governor George Wolf and Henry A. Muhlenberg, together polled more votes than Ritner. As a minority party, the Antimasons would be able to influence events in the Assembly only by forming a coalition with the Whigs, but even this was not possible owing to a division within their ranks.

The Pennsylvania Antimasons held a state convention at Harrisburg on December 14, 1835 to nominate candidates for the next year's national election. The meeting was dominated by the so-called "Exclusives," led by Thaddeus Stevens, who would not compromise on the destruction of Freemasonry. The moderates ("Coalitionists"), on the other hand, re- garded this issue as only one among many others, including internal improvements (especially canals), public education, the Bank of the United States, monetary policy, and waste and corruption in government. In his inaugural address delivered on December 15, Governor Ritner publicly showed himself to be a member of the moderate majority. He offered a variety of policies and only touched upon opposition to Freemasonry. He pledged to maintain "the supremacy of the laws and the equal rights of the people, whether threatened or assailed by individuals, or by secret, sworn associations" and to listen to the people who "have willed the destruction of all secret societies."[31]

Although disappointed with Ritner's lack of enthusiasm for their cause, the Exclusives nonetheless took encouragement from their party's recent electoral victories, and in the new session of the Assembly, Stevens launched another series of attacks upon the Fraternity. Already on De- cember 7, 1835, he introduced yet another bill to suppress secret societies "bound together by secret and unlawful oaths," and was soon appointed chairman of another committee. With great effort Stevens pushed through his measure, bill No. 4, which was designed to eradicate Freemasonry by outlawing extrajudicial oaths. It passed the House of Representatives on February 27, 1836, but only by a margin of five votes. It was sent to the Senate the same day, but after months of delaying, the upper house refused to approve it and the matter died.[32]

Although the Exclusives were unable to pass bills outlawing Masonic oaths and suppressing secret societies, they were strong enough in the 1835-1836 session to launch a full-scale legislative investigation of the Fraternity, something Stevens had been trying to accomplish for several years. His new committee began work on December 23 and generated much publicity throughout the Commonwealth over the next three months. The committee first drew up a list of detailed questions to be submitted to each witness. A witness was to be asked whether he was or had been a Mason, if so of what degree and with what lodge affiliation; what the oaths and obligations were and if they were in accordance with published exposés of the ritual; whether he held degrees higher than the third, and if so to reveal the ceremonies pertaining to them; whether Knights Tem- plar drank blood out of a human skull; and whether Freemasonry had the same structure everywhere; as well as many other questions. The committee then recommended that some hundred persons be subpoened, including all present and past officers of the Grand Lodge of Pennsylvania.

The House debated in early January whether that body had the legal right to compel witnesses to appear. A representative from Philadelphia, William B. Reed, argued in favor of issuing the subpoenas. The power to investigate, he said, was as important as the power to legislate, and the legal process was supreme over personal, religious or ethical considerations, including Masonic obligations. The House voted fifty-nine to twenty-six to issue the subpoenas under penalty of attaching the property of persons called. Despite this measure, only slightly more than half the witnesses summoned actually came to Harrisburg; of these, only five agreed to testify: three Masons, one Odd Fellow and one non-Mason. The first four admitted that published exposés of oaths and ritual were substantially accurate. One of the Masons, James H. Shedd of Dayton, Ohio, claimed to have played a minor role in Morgan's abduction and gave detailed, but inconclusive, evidence. The non-Mason, Jacob Mechling, a former member of the Pennsylvania Assembly, testified that members of the Grand Lodge of Pennsylvania had tried to influence legislators to obtain special financial concessions by offering to make them Masons without fee.

A number of prominent Masons refused to testify before Stevens' committee and agreed to observe a policy of passive resistance as an example to others. One of these was former Governor Wolf, who denied on constitutional grounds the committee's authority to compel persons to appear. He called the investigation an "inquisition" and refused to allow himself to be "a willing instrument to gratify an idle curiosity, or to minister to the prying inquisitiveness of prejudice and ignorance on the one hand or the designing artifices of a reckless demagogueism on the other." He then offered a strong defense of Freemasonry, declaring the Fraternity to be a lawful association, founded on moral principles, that exerted no influence over elections or judicial proceedings. Despite these sentiments, Wolf personally appeared before Stevens' committee on January 11, but refused to be sworn. Wolf's resistance frustrated Stevens, who hinted vaguely at future legal reprisals.

Past Grand Master George M. Dallas also was subpoened, but he also refused to be sworn, although he delivered a "serious and impressive" speech before the committee. He stated that he had never violated the laws of Pennsylvania, even though he had been a Mason for more than twenty years. He voluntarily took Masonic oaths, which were "perfectly compatible with the paramount obligations and duties of a citizen to his country." Reinforcing the arguments presented by Wolf, Dallas asserted that the entire investigation was illegal according to the Pennsylvania state constitution. Following the leads of Wolf and Dallas, eight other Masonic witnesses also delivered protests to the committee that explained their refusal to testify. One of these, the Rev. William T. Sprole, a Grand Deacon, accused the committee of being motivated by personal prejudice rather than a desire to obtain the truth. This charge infuriated Stevens, who abruptly interrupted and told him to sit down. When Sprole attempted to explain himself further, the chairman cut him off with a curt: "Not one word, sir!" These proceedings generated much popular interest. The "crowd of visitors" attending them was so large that the committee was obliged to meet in the spacious House Chamber instead of the smaller Supreme Court Chamber, where it had formerly met.

Frustrated by the intransigence of so many witnesses, Stevens' committee then issued a report that named twenty-four individuals who had refused to give sworn testimony. The officers of the Grand Lodge of Pennsylvania were additionally cited for refusing to produce books, records and documents as required by subpoena. The committee singled out two men for special condemnation: George M. Dallas and the Rev. Mr. Sprole, the first for his "indecorous and insolent" manner and the second for sentiments that were "disorderly and insulting, both to the committee and to the House of Representatives; charging conduct and motives to both, which the dignity of neither could tolerate." The committee then proposed that the sergeant-at-arms take the witnesses into custody and bring them to the bar of the House to answer for their contempt.

This proposal prompted considerable debate in the House on January 20. Although the Masons' supporters argued that the witnesses were legally justified in their refusal to testify and should be set free, the committee's resolution passed, but by a margin of only four votes. The twenty-four named persons, as well as one other Mason, were arrested the next day. Stevens then asked that they be forced to testify under threat of attachment, a demand rejected by the majority. The speaker then proceeded to call the witnesses one by one, beginning with George Wolf, but each refused to testify. Over the next two days numerous proposals to punish the recalcitrant witnesses were made, debated and defeated as were measures in their defense. At one point, the speaker authorized the witnesses to defend their actions, but their spokesman, Dallas, declined to do so. Finally, on January 22 a member from Philadelphia offered a resolution that the House "forbear inflicting any punishment for the contempt against the House by the witnesses . . . [and that they] be discharged from the custody of the sergeant-at-arms forthwith." This measure passed by a vote of fifty-five to thirty-seven. Before leaving Harrisburg, on January 26, the witnesses issued a public statement defending their conduct and reiterating the positive nature of Freemasonry.[33]

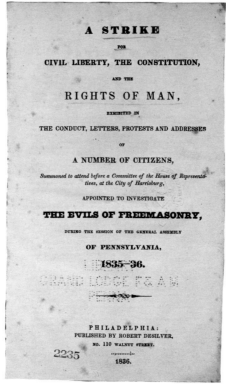

A STRIKE

FOR

CIVIL LIBERTY, THE CONSTITUTION,

AND THE

RIGHTS OF MAN,

EXHIBITED IN

THE CONDUCT, LETTERS, PROTESTS AND ADDRESSES

OF

A NUMBER OF CITIZENS,

Summoned to attend before a Committee of the House of Representatives, at the City of Harrisburg,

APPOINTED TO INVESTIGATE

THE EVILS OF FREEMASONRY,

DURING THE SESSION OF THE GENERAL ASSEMBLY

OF PENNSYLVANIA,

1835-36.

PHILADELPHIA:
PUBLISHED BY ROBERT DESILVER,
NO. 110 WALNUT STREET.
1836.

Title Page of *A Strike for Civil Liberty* (Grand Lodge of Pennsylvania).

Although the dismissal of the Masonic witnesses was a serious defeat for Stevens and his faction, he refused to recognize it as such. His committee held more public sessions on the issue of Freemasonry on January 28 and March 3 that produced additional testimony by four seceding Masons on Masonic influence on the choice of candidates for office and the administration of justice. On June 13 Stevens reviewed the progress and results of the legislative investigation in another emotional speech to the House. He asserted that the given testimony, although much less than he would have liked, was sufficient to prove the truth of all allegations against Freemasonry. Once again, he especially condemned Wolf, Dallas and Sprole: the first for allowing Masonic obligations to influence his decisions as governor, the second for "great personal rudeness and insolence," and the third for "haughty bearing and irreverent conduct." That the officers of the Grand Lodge refused to allow their papers to be examined was "undeniable evidence of . . . deep depravity." According to Stevens, these men must have been guilty: "How fearful, criminal, or disgraceful must have been the facts which truth would have disclosed, when to conceal them, they thus braved the authority of the law, incurred the risk of legal penalties, and covered themselves with the suspicion, odium and indignation of honest men!" Stevens believed that they went unpunished because of party politics; Democrats and Whigs had conspired to "protect and screen" the Masons. The people of Pennsylvania "may entertain no false hope of eradicating from the soil masonry, that curse of their country, until a majority of both branches of the legislature shall be composed of avowed political antimasons."[34]

Most members of the General Assembly and of the rank and file of the Antimasonic Party remained unconvinced, however, and no further legislative action against the Fraternity was taken during the remainder of 1836. Stevens' investigations had cost the Commonwealth at least $1,600, had caused disrupting partisan disputes within the House, and had produced no substantial evidence of the danger of the Masonic Fraternity. Public support for Stevens' actions also declined. The House heard fewer and fewer memorials against Freemasonry, and Stevens lost his seat in the fall elections.[35]

Governor Ritner, however, appears to have been swayed by Stevens' way of thinking, at least in part. In his annual message to the legislature on December 8, 1836, Ritner considered the "chief evil of the time" to be "that spirit of lawless combination, unknown to our open and equal institutions, and opposed to the genius of Republicanism, against which the Father of his Country, sent forth his last and most solemn warning." Ritner claimed that Freemasonry in Washington's day was relatively harmless but "has since assumed the dangerous character of [a] regularly organized, oath bound, secret working, wide spread and powerful society." He also called for "a full investigation of the nature of secret societies, and the passage of proper laws for their suppression or control, forever to remove this stumbling-block."

Some members of the House liked what they heard and encouraged Ritner to develop this theme. On March 8, 1837, he delivered a comprehensive "defense" of Washington's membership in the Fraternity. Essentially, Ritner argued that Washington had joined the Masonic Order only out of the indiscretion and curiosity of youth and did not return to it when mature. Ritner also believed that extant letters attesting to Washington's later association with, and reverence for, the Society were spurious. In December he once more made a brief reference to Freemasonry and recommended the passage of a law against extrajudicial oaths, but this proposal was not implemented. Opposition to the Fraternity now remained only a minor issue in Pennsylvania politics. By this time struggling for survival, the Antimasonic Party was occupied with issues of a broader appeal. By the end of 1839 the Pennsylvania Antimasonic organization had been absorbed into the Whig Party, although remnants of it were able to maintain some local influence for a few more years.[36]

*   *   *   *   *   *   *   *

Even though the Antimasons' organized attack failed to destroy Pennsylvania Freemasonry, it nonetheless inflicted serious damage. One of the seriously weakened areas was finances. In the period of the legislative investigations the Grand Lodge was preoccupied with making ends meet, and it often had to review its financial condition. The sale of the Chestnut Street hall in 1835 only temporarily alleviated these problems. Therefore, the Grand Lodge had to find other sources of revenue, such as renting portions of its meeting hall to other organizations and to private individuals. At first this was difficult because of the widespread negative publicity. Not until mid-1837 was the Grand lodge able to rent four first-floor rooms and the cellars, and then only at the low rate of $475 per year. Nonetheless, this income helped to balance the budget, and soon the Grand Lodge began to show a surplus of revenues over expenditures.[37]

One of the tenants of Washington Hall was an Episcopal clergyman, the Rev. Frederick Plummer, who used a back room for Sunday morning religious services. He was one of the most reliable tenants, from the standpoint both of regularity of payment and of length of contract. This was an ironic commentary on the Antimasonic movement, which accused Freemasonry of anti-Christian and atheistic beliefs. Throughout the Antimasonic period, as well as before and after it, the Grand Lodge of Pennsylvania appointed chaplains of various denominations to offer invocations to the "Grand Architect of the Universe" at official functions, and it frequently held special meetings to make prominent ministers Masons.[38]

Although the general financial health of the Grand Lodge began to improve, that of subordinate lodges remained insecure. Throughout 1836 and into 1837, more and more lodges defaulted on their dues and cited "the extreme Oppression they have experienced from the Enemies of the order." Showing commendable understanding, the Grand Lodge extended all possible credit to the lodges and tried to work out compromises, rather than to vacate their warrants, as was the usual practice. One such measure was the temporary reduction of dues, membership and admission fees, as well as of rental charges for use of rooms in the lodge hall. This policy "would better enable the Lodges to assist the numerous Worthy Applicants for charity, and tend . . . to place the Lodges in their former flourishing condition."[39]

Despite its attempts to aid and encourage the subordinate lodges, the Grand Lodge ultimately had to admit the seriousness of their circumstances. On February 6, 1837, it vacated the warrants of fifty-five lodges, comprising about fifty-six percent of all lodges then in operation (Table 1). This was the worst single day in Pennsylvania Masonic history. According to Masonic rules and regulations, the vacated lodges had been in arrears of dues for at least two years; probably they had actually failed on the local level some time earlier. Of these fifty-five lodges, two revived before the end of the year and thirteen others did so within ten years. Seven months later another six lodges were placed on probation. At the end of the year only forty-three lodges were "officially" functioning, and many of these were also weak; by the end of 1838 another five had ceased. Between 1826 to 1839, therefore, six and a half times as many lodges ceased as were founded, the majority of the failures occurring after 1832. No new Pennsylvania lodge had been warranted since the middle of 1831 (No. 216, Schuylkill County).

Lodge failures were widespread throughout the Commonwealth (Table 2, Figure 1). In each of thirty-eight counties at least one Masonic lodge ceased operations. Other counties had even more failures; the worst cases were Lancaster with five and Chester with seven. The influence of the Antimasonic Party was particularly strong in these areas. Rural areas generally seemed to suffer more than urban ones. Philadelphia, which had had twenty-eight functioning lodges before 1826, only lost four of them (14.3%), whereas twenty-eight other counties lost all of their lodges. Important to the fate of Masonic lodges was the prevalence of the Antimasonic press. At least fifty-nine newspapers, either wholly or partially dedicated to the diffusion of Antimasonic propaganda, were in operation in thirty-four counties throughout this period (Table 3, Figure 1). The correlation between the Antimasonic press and the failure of Masonic lodges was not exact, however; four counties had Antimasonic newspapers but no Masonic lodges, and eight counties had failed Masonic lodges but no newspapers, but the influence of such literature probably was not limited by strict geographical boundaries.

Insight into the condition of the failed lodges can be gained from a letter from two Pittsburgh lodges, Nos. 45 and 113:

> The persecution we have labored under for several years past . . . has been the cause of many of our luke warm Members withdrawing their aid and Support from us; there still is [sic] a worthy few who adhere strictly to the Good cause in this City and are determined that the Institution shall revive amongst us; but we find we are in Arrears to your honorable Body, more Dues . . . than we would be able to Pay for years to come.

Lodge No. 119, Luzerne County, survived the attack, but it was not in very good condition either:

> We have had to Combat with much opposition in this Vicinity on the Subject of Masonry. We have done no Business for some Years to increase the Funds of the lodge and our Situation at this time is quite Unpleasant.[40]

TABLE 1
Pennsylvania Freemasonry in Crisis, 1826-1839

Years	Number of new lodges (lodge numbers)	Number of ceased lodges (lodge numbers)
1826-1832	12 (199, 206-213, 215-217)	14 (73, 100, 134, 144, 145, 148, 149, 177, 183, 184, 185, 202, 210, 217)
1833-1839	0	65 (21, 46, 50, 61, 64, 66, 69, 70, 75, 82, 83, 84, 94, 104, 106, 108, 116, 123, 126, 131, 132, 136, 141, 142, 143, 146, 147, 150, 151, 156, 159, 162, 163, 164, 165, 168, 169, 171, 172, 173, 174, 176, 178, 179, 180, 182, 189, 191, 192, 194, 195, 196, 197, 198, 199, 200, 203, 204, 206, 207, 208, 209, 212, 213, 215)
Totals	12 Net: −67	79 (658%)

Lodges in Operation by the End of the Year

Year	Number of Lodges	Year	Number of Lodges
1826	104	1833	103
1827	109	1834	102
1828	108	1835	102
1829	105	1836	99
1830	104	1837	43*
1831	104	1838	38
1832	104	1839	38

*On February 6, 1837, fifty-five lodges were officially vacated and three other lodges were added later in the same year. Two of these revived by the end of 1837 and thirteen others within ten years.

Only one lodge (No. 217, Uruguay) was warranted outside Pennsylvania. Both Nos. 217 and 191 (Mexico) failed in this period. Thereafter the jurisdiction of the Grand Lodge was limited by state boundaries.

Lodges that revived within a year of their ceasing are not considered to be failed lodges; their suspension was only temporary.

Lodge No. 214 was warranted, but not constituted.

The origins of new lodges are based upon their constitution dates.

Lodges "ceased" in basically two ways: by voluntary surrender of the warrant by the members or by order of the Grand Lodge. Various terms were used to describe such warrants: "surrendered," "returned," "vacated," or "ceased."

Sources: Joshua L. Lyte, comp., *Reprint of the Minutes of the Grand Lodge of Pennsylvania* (Phila., 1895-1907), Vol. V, *1822-1827*, Vol. VI, *1828-1839;* "Information Pertaining to Early Freemasonry in the Western Hemisphere, Including the Warrant and Constitution Dates of the Subordinate Lodges under the Provincial and Present Grand Lodge of F. and A.M. of Pennsylvania" (unpublished list); Charles E. Meyer, *Masonic Lodges in Pennsylvania from 1730 to 1880, "Moderns" and "Ancients"* (Phila., n.d.); Register of Members, Vol. 2-1, 1795-1855; Vol. 2-2, 1818-1855.

TABLE 2
Geographical Distribution of Pennsylvania Lodges, 1826-1839

County	Number of new lodges (lodge numbers)	(%)	Number of ceased lodges (lodge numbers)	(%)
Adams*			1 (200)	1.3
Allegheny			3 (145, 165, 173)	3.9
Bedford*	1 (210)	10.0	1 (210)	1.3
Berks			1 (66)	1.3
Bradford*			3 (108, 150, 163)	3.9
Bucks*			3 (94, 168, 195)	3.9
Centre*			1 (192)	1.3
Chester			7 (50, 75, 132, 142, 162, 174, 183)	9.1
Columbia*			1 (159)	1.3
Crawford*			1 (146)	1.3
Cumberland*			2 (197, 198)	2.6
Dauphin*			2 (21, 141)	2.6
Delaware			1 (69)	1.3
Erie*			1 (184)	1.3
Fayette	1 (215)	10.0	1 (215)	1.3
Franklin*			2 (196, 202)	2.6
Greene			1 (180)	1.3
Huntingdon*			1 (178)	1.3
Lancaster			5 (46, 104, 116, 156, 169)	6.5
Lebanon*			1 (172)	1.3
Lehigh*			1 (151)	1.3
Luzerne			4 (61, 70, 185, 204)	5.2
Lycoming*			2 (106, 199)	2.6
Mercer*			1 (182)	1.3
Mifflin*			1 (203)	1.3
Montgomery*			2 (136, 171)	2.6
Northumberland*			3 (100, 144, 148)	3.9
Philadelphia	1 (211)	10.0	4 (73, 126, 131, 134)	5.2
Perry*	1 (208)	10.0	1 (208)	1.3
Pike*			2 (177, 179)	2.6
Schuylkill	1 (216)	10.0		
Somerset*			1 (84)	1.3
Susquehanna*	3 (206, 207, 213)	30.0	4 (149, 206, 207, 213)	5.2
Tioga*			1 (189)	1.3
Union*			1 (194)	1.3
Washington*	1 (209)	10.0	3 (143, 164, 209)	3.9
Wayne*			3 (82, 83, 147)	3.9
Westmoreland*			2 (64, 176)	2.8
York	1 (212)	10.0	2 (123, 212)	2.6
Totals	10	100.0	77	100.0

*County that lost all of its Masonic lodges.

Sources: Joshua L. Lyte, comp., *Reprint of the Minutes of the of the Grand Lodge of Pennsylvania* (Phila., 1895-1907), Vol. V, *1822-1827*, Vol. VI, *1828-1839;* "Information Pertaining to Early Freemasonry in the Western Hemisphere, Including the Warrant and Constitution Dates of the Subordinate Lodges under the Provincial and Present Grand Lodge of F. and A.M. of Pennsylvania" (unpublished list); Charles E. Meyer, *Masonic Lodges in Pennsylvania from 1730 to 1880, "Moderns" and "Ancients"* (Phila., n.d.); Register of Members, Vol. 2-1, 1795-1855; Vol. 2-2, 1818-1855.

TABLE 3
Geographical Distribution of Antimasonic Newspapers, 1828-1835

County	Number of Newspapers
Adams	2
Allegheny	1
Armstrong*	1
Bedford	1
Berks	1
Bradford	1
Bucks	2
Butler*	1
Chester	3
Crawford	2
Cumberland	2
Dauphin	5
Delaware	1
Erie	1
Fayette	1
Franklin	1
Huntingdon	2
Indiana*	1
Lancaster	7
Lebanon	2
Lehigh	2
Luzerne	1
Mercer	2
Mifflin	1
Montgomery	2
Northumberland	2
Philadelphia	1
Somerset	1
Susquehanna	1
Union	3
Warren*	1
Washington	1
Westmoreland	1
York	2
Total	59

*Counties without Masonic lodges.

Eight counties (Centre, Columbia, Greene, Lycoming, Perry, Pike, Tioga, Wayne) had Masonic lodges that failed, but no Antimasonic newspapers.

Beginning in 1826 several antimasonic newspapers printed in New York were also in circulation in Pennsylvania.

Sources: William L. Cummings, *A Bibliography of Anti-Masonry* (New York, 1963); Milton W. Hamilton, "Anti-Masonic Newspapers, 1826-1834," *Papers of the Bibliographical Society of America, XXXII* (1932); "Pennsylvania," *Union List of Newspapers, 1820-1936* (New York, 1967, reprint of 1937 ed.), 589-630.

FIGURE 1
Masonic Lodges in Pennsylvania, 1826–1839

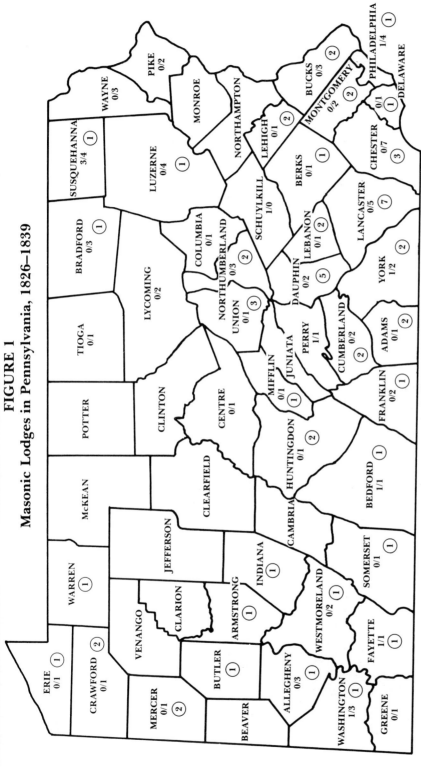

PENNSYLVANIA IN 1839 (55 counties)

Key: new/ceased lodges
Totals: 10/77   Net: − 67
Number of antimasonic newspapers circled

*County that lost all of its Masonic lodges.

Sources: Joshua L. Lyte, comp., *Reprint of the Minutes of the of the Grand Lodge of Pennsylvania* (Phila., 1895-1907), Vol. V, *1822-1827*, Vol. VI, *1828-1839*; "Information Pertaining to Early Freemasonry in the Western Hemisphere, Including the Warrant and Constitution Dates of the Subordinate Lodges under the Provincial and Present Grand Lodge of F. and A.M. of Pennsylvania" (unpublished list); Charles E. Meyer, *Masonic Lodges in Pennsylvania from 1730 to 1880, "Moderns" and "Ancients"* (Phila., n.d.); Register of Members, Vol. 2-1, 1795-1855; Vol. 2-2, 1818-1855.

As could be expected, the membership of the Masonic Fraternity in Pennsylvania also suffered severely during the Antimasonic period (see Appendix H). From 1826 to 1839 only about four thousand men were initiated or admitted, a poor record compared to the previous thirteen-year period when nine thousand men became members. Each year the number of new members consistently fell off until 1835, when fewer than one hundred fifty new men entered; thereafter, came a slight but un-steady increase. At the same time suspensions, expulsions and voluntary withdrawals increased dramatically, and most years showed a net loss in membership. The lowest point was reached in 1837, when more than fourteen hundred men were dropped from the rolls. The cumulative totals declined dramatically from about thirty-seven hundred members in 1825 to about sixteen hundred in 1837, a loss of more than half the membership. As a group, the Philadelphia lodges were healthier than the state-wide average; they only lost about twenty-five percent of their mem-bers. The country lodges, on the contrary, nearly went out of existence, losing about seventy-five percent of theirs.

The Antimasonic movement also did considerable psychological damage to the Fraternity. It instilled a lack of confidence in its leaders, who as a group maintained a rather low profile. They seldom gave ad-dresses or advised on effective countermeasures, except to counsel the Masonic virtues of steadfastness and silence. They really could do little else. No doubt, they were privately disheartened, but they allowed no evidence of this attitude to emerge in their official activities. Eight men served as Grand Master in this troubled period (see Appendix C). All were professional men or well-to-do entrepreneurs: five were lawyers, and one each was an auctioneer, a customs official and a dry goods merchant. They were men of maturity and experience—on the average about 45 years old at the time of their election—and all made contribu-tions to the broader society throughout their lives.

The most prominent of the Grand Masters during the Antimasonic era was George M. Dallas, who led the defense of the Fraternity against the Stevens committee. He was a man of impressive political attainments, who had been mayor of Philadelphia (1829), attorney general of Penn-sylvania (1829) and United States senator (1831-1833), and who was to become minister to Russia (1837) and to Great Britain (1856-1861) and, most important, vice-president of the United States under Polk (1845-1849). It was to the Fraternity's great benefit that such an individual was its official spokesman at its time of greatest need.[41]

Although a few more lodges failed and membership remained low after 1837, Pennsylvania's Masonic leaders began to see the first glimmer of recovery. In a report given in February 1838 Robert Clarke, District Deputy Grand Master of Fayette and Greene Counties, gave a brief history of the "Virulent opposition" the Fraternity suffered in his area. This had been encouraged by the publication of Antimasonic newspapers:

> abounding as they did in Misstatements, Marked by the Traits which always Characterize Vulgar Scuffles for Power with all the Rancor of Party Malevolence, of Political Persecution, they were of course offensive to the upright and intelligent portion of the Community . . . . The Masons bore all with Patience, and there are now Symptoms of a reaction in their favor.

In March the Grand Lodge lifted its previous ban on publicizing its activities and resolved to advertise its meetings in at least four local newspapers.[42]

By 1839 some local lodges were already beginning to look back at the Antimasonic period, as though it were no longer a current issue. Believing the danger to be past, they were able to speak out about their experiences. For example, Lodge No. 138, Schuylkill County, dramatically related its recent history:

> Since our last Report we have had an accession of 14 New Members, all Men of highly respectable Standing in Society, Zealous and Useful in our Order. We have also been relieved from the burden of a few of the old Members who have outlived their Usefulness. When we Compare our present prospects with the experience of a few years past we have truly Cause to rejoice. There was a period of Several Years Since 1830 when No. 138 was literally Struggling for Existence, when the Clouds of Opposition Lowered darkly around us when the Energies of nearly all the Members were prostrated before Antimasonry, a little Spartan Band of Four threw themselves into the Breach determined to Cling to the last to the Charter of their Masonic Existence and we have succeeded beyond our Sanguine Hopes.[43]

At the the same time the Grand Lodge Committee of Correspondence received reports of activities from other Masonic jurisdictions throughout the United States. These attested to the beginning of a general recovery of the Society, and they generated a positive response from the Pennsylvania Grand Lodge: "Its present prospects are now decidedly of an onward Nature and . . . your Committee cannot but congratulate the Fraternity in those States, on the bright hope of better days which now begins to dawn upon them." One District Deputy Grand Master, Joseph Kingsberry of Bradford and Tioga Counties, was confident that the severe crisis of Freemasonry was already past:

I have now the pleasure to state to you that Antimasonry in this quarter is either dead or asleep. If dead, we shall not in any violent manner, tread upon its ashes; but suffer them as time may operate, to be scattered by the winds of heaven; If asleep, we shall not by any boisterous exultation wake the Monster up to any new vituperation, but endeavor to preserve the even tenor of our way in peace and quietness.[44]

Statements such as these served an important function in the process of revitalization of Freemasonry. They offered emotional satisfaction to Masons by reconfirming the worth of their organization and by validating its policy of quiet dignity as a means of resisting opponents. The survivors of the Antimasonic furor were strengthened by the experience and became even more dedicated to the Fraternity than they had been before.

CHAPTER 7:

The Era of Recovery,
1840-1855

In the early 1840s, even before the furor of Antimasonry had completely died out, the Grand Lodge of Pennsylvania was already on its way toward recovery. The Fraternity's first concern was to increase efficiency by reorganizing its operations. Standing committees were given greater responsibilities and new ones were created. These dealt specifically with finance, correspondence, superintendence of the hall, the Grand Lodge Charity Fund, the Stephen Girard Charity Fund, publication, by-laws, and landmarks, and they reported regularly on their areas of specialization. The functions of most major officials were enhanced, and additional junior level administrators, such as Grand Deacons and Grand Stewards, were also appointed.

The Grand Secretary's office received special attention because it had been most seriously weakened during the preceding years. Inadequate record keeping had caused "much confusion, Loss and waste of time," and the Grand Lodge realized that a more professional system was necessary. The Grand Secretary was now required to report more frequently to the Grand Lodge. He variously performed some of the most important functions of the Fraternity by keeping abreast of the monthly operations of the subordinate lodges and supplying reliable information on which the Grand Lodge acted.

One of his first projects was to undertake a complete inventory of all papers possessed by the Fraternity. The number of documents was staggering, even at this early point in Pennsylvania Masonic history. Their extent is even more impressive considering the probable destruction of many documents in the fire of 1819 and the possible loss of others during the Antimasonic period. The cataloged documents included minutes, membership records, certificates, journals, correspondence, warrants, account books, seals, and "miscellaneous papers." Also listed were jewels, aprons, hangings, and other paraphernalia of defunct lodges, which were required to return all property to the Grand Lodge upon disbanding. Moreover, the Grand Secretary listed one hundred forty-eight unspecified "Boxes or Drawers containing the Archives," which were stored in his office. A special room, called a "fireproof," held the more valuable documents, such as mortgages, loan certificates, insurance policies, deeds, bonds, Stephen Girard's will, and papers relating to George Washington. The location of this special room is unknown, except that it was "attached" to Washington Hall, where Philadelphia Masons met. Obviously, the Grand Lodge took a serious interest in preserving its historical evidence in a way not done before, perhaps as a result of greater self-appreciation developed during the Antimasonic period.[1]

Not every area of Masonic administration in Pennsylvania was expanded in the early 1840s, at least not initially. A case in point was the system of Masonic districts, originally created in 1822. During the Antimasonic years, the number of districts was reduced from fourteen to eight because of the cessation of many country lodges. Rather than having District Deputy Grand Masters supervise fewer and fewer lodges, the Grand Lodge had attached weaker districts onto stronger ones. Grand Master James Page was a staunch defender of this cutback. Despite pressure from local lodges, especially from Pittsburgh where no separate district existed, Page firmly refused to allow the system to expand irresponsibly, believing that this encouraged weakness. He suggested, and the Grand Lodge concurred, that a Masonic district should be composed of no fewer than five subordinate lodges. If one District Deputy Grand Master was appointed for each county, one popular suggestion, some officials would have little to do, since several counties had no Masonic lodge and others only one. In the second case, the District Deputy Grand Master would supersede the functions and impinge upon the rights of the Master of the subordinate lodge. District Deputy Grand Masters were required to visit lodges on circuit, to inquire as to their condition and proceedings, to give Masonic advice and instruction, and to report progress to the Grand Lodge. In Page's opinion, this function could be best served by "a proper number of them."[2]

Reorganization of the central administration of the Fraternity continued into the 1850s. A number of practices allowed to die during the Antimasonic period were revived and new ones initiated. Grand Masters made more frequent Grand Visitations to city lodges; they offered more inspirational addresses; the number of Masonic districts increased to pre-1826 levels; alphabetical lists of suspended and expelled members were printed and circulated; special lodges of instruction were held; uniformity in regalia was reestablished; new rules and regulations were collected and distributed; and greater accountability of the Grand Treasurer's office was achieved.[3]

The office of Grand Lecturer, inactive since 1829, was also revived in response to frequent requests by country lodges for regular instruction in Masonic ritual. Such instruction was actually the responsibility of the District Deputy Grand Masters, but because their districts covered so large an area, they often could not visit all the lodges under their supervision. In 1852 Grand Master Bournonville appointed Charles E. Blumenthal, Master of Lodge No. 260, Carlisle, Grand Lecturer on a temporary basis. Blumenthal had volunteered to serve without pay until a permanent position could be created. In his first three months in office Blumenthal visited fifteen lodges and found most of them to be in desperate need of instruction. He saw work performed in such a "loose and careless way [that] the symmetry and beauty was completely lost." Errors had crept in not because of any deliberate attempt to corrupt Masonic ritual but through ignorance. Other lodges suffered from not having any proper meeting place. Blumenthal filled a definite need; his visits were welcomed by "apt pupils" who were eager for more Masonic learning.

Impressed by Blumenthal's accomplishment, the Grand Lodge granted him compensation and re-established the office of Grand Lecturer on a permanent basis with him as its first occupant. During the next year Blumenthal traveled over three thousand miles. He was able to visit only twenty-two lodges because he had to make repeated visits to some. His findings confirmed his report of a year earlier. Although most lodges were prosperous in terms of numbers and financial condition, they displayed a distressing lack of uniformity in their work. Blumenthal likened the variations throughout the state to a "patchwork more fanciful than a lady's quilt." He thought the problem was that too many Masons equated quantity with quality:

> . . . the permanent prosperity of a Lodge should not be sought for by increasing the numbers of its members, but rather by improving their character and guarding against the introduction of improper material. Yet there are some whose zeal for the spread of Masonry causes them to be too anxious for a numerical increase. A high Initiation fee and increased monthly contributions would serve as a salutary check to such indiscreet zeal.[4]

Blumenthal's recommendations were heeded. Grand Masters Whitney in 1850, Bournonville in 1853 and Hutchinson in 1854 all cautioned against a too-rapid increase in membership. Lowered admission standards would attract unworthy individuals, contribute to a relaxation of Masonic ideals, and bring "more discredit on our Order . . . than from all the opposition that can possibly be brought against us." Masonry gained only by the accession of members who "bring with them high moral and religious character, intelligence, and disposition to sacrifice upon its shrine every motive of selfishness and every object of self-interest." Notwithstanding these warnings, the Fraternity enjoyed tremendous growth during its recovery.[5]

One definite sign of recovery was financial. Throughout the period the Finance Committee regularly reviewed the economic health of the Fraternity and prepared detailed quarterly statements that showed continued improvement. Reacting to one such account in mid-1846, Grand Master Page remarked that the condition of the organization was "sound and imposing;" with proper care it would result in a few years in "a perfectly independent attitude." During the next decade this sanguine prediction was fulfilled as financial security was gradually but steadily achieved. Most subordinate lodges paid their dues in full and on time, most tenants paid their rent regularly, various investments flourished, and additional debts and losses were kept to a minimum. By December 1850 Grand Master William Whitney could report: "I think that I may with confidence say, that at no period, within the memory of the most aged Brother now present, has our Order, throughout the State, been so prosperous as we find it at the present time."

The Fraternity's main aim was redemption of the huge construction debt it had assumed before the Antimasonic period. Year after year, money left over after operating expenses were paid was diligently plowed into the sinking fund and then carefully invested. This policy was ultimately successful and in early March 1854 the Finance Committee reported that the old debt, amounting to more that $75,000 and including Masonic loans and mortgages, was completely paid off. This accomplishment attested to the Fraternity's skillful financial management. The Finance Committee was proud that even during the "fearful pecuniary crisis [an economic depression from 1837 to 1843] which prostrated not only individuals, but our banks and savings institutions," the Grand Lodge in over thirty years had never missed an interest payment. Amazingly, even the Antimasonic turmoil failed to disrupt this process. Not only did this debt-free situation cause relief on the part of Pennsylvania Masons, but the Grand Lodge's untarnished credit enabled it to borrow more easily for future projects.[6]

The finances of the two charity funds, kept separate from the general account, also became more secure in the 1840s and 1850s. The Stephen Girard Charity Fund was the more prosperous. According to the terms of the benefactor's will, the income was to be invested until the principal reached $30,000; thereafter, the annual income was to be disbursed to worthy persons. Thanks to wise investments in real estate, stocks and bonds, the trustees of the fund were able to report substantial interest income as early as March 1842; however, the first actual disbursement — in the amount of $300 — did not occur until 1844. Over the next few years, $1,500 to $1,800 were disbursed annually, and after 1850 the amount increased to about $2,000 (Table 1).

TABLE 1
Charitable Disbursements of the Grand Lodge of Pennsylvania, 1844-1855

Year	Stephen Girard Charity Fund			Grand Lodge Charity Fund		
	Amount ($)	Number of Persons	Average Grant ($)	Amount ($)	Number of Persons	Average Grant ($)
1844	300	21	14	100*	—	—
1845	825	43	19	150	—	—
1846	1,523	76	20	145	—	—
1847	1,524	76	20	115	23	5
1848	1,757	73	24	160	—	—
1849	1,800*	—	—	145	—	—
1850	1,945	78	25	189	—	—
1851	1,895	69	27	300*	—	—
1852	1,995	119	17	250	40	6
1853	1,745	74	24	295	42	7
1854	2,240	87	26	285	34	8
1855	2,060	94	22	445	39	11

*money appropriated, actual amount used not given.

Dashes indicate that no information is available.

The Girard Fund aided "distressed worthy brothers" and the General Fund provided for the widows, orphans and other needy female dependents of deceased Masons in good standing.

All applications for relief had to be in writing and approved by two Master Masons.

Not all recipients of charity came from Pennsylvania, although most did.

Subordinate lodges had their own separate charity funds. Information on the amounts disbursed is not generally available.

No charity was disbursed by either fund before 1844.

All figures have been rounded off to the nearest dollar.

Sources: Grand Lodge of Pennsylvania, *Abstract of tthe Proceedings for 1846*, 16; *1847*, 7; *1850*, 9; *1851*, 9; *1853*, 18; *1854*, 11f.; *1855*, 14f.; Joshua L. Lyte, comp., *Reprint of the Minutes of the Grand Lodge of Pennsylvania* (Phila., 1895-1907), Vol. VII, *1840-1848*, 240, 259, 267, 324, 387, 400, 438, 522, February 3, March 3, 1845, March 2, December 7, 27, 1846, September 6, 1847, December 27, 1848; Vol. VIII, *1849-1854*, 54, 123, 130, 187, 197, 290, 387f., 474; December 17, 1849, December 16, 27, 1850, December 15-27, 1851, December 27, 1852, December 27, 1853, December 27, 1854; Vol. IX, *1855-1858*, 355, December 27, 1855.

The trustees, composed of twenty-one members of the Grand Lodge, restricted charity to "poor and respectable brothers," whose applications were countersigned by two Past Masters. No individual was allowed to receive more than $30 at one time, although he might reapply under certain circumstances. There were no geographical restrictions ("Country, clime or jurisdiction, are alike unimportant"), but the majority of recipients were Pennsylvania residents. The trustees interpreted their responsibilities broadly, even hoping to be able to pay the funeral expenses of deceased "worthy" Brothers, but the Grand Lodge overruled this policy as being out of accord with Girard's will. In contrast to the Girard Fund, the general Grand Lodge Charity Fund, reorganized in 1840, was limited to a principal of only about $2,000, from which only $100 to $200 per year in interest might be disbursed. The exclusive purpose of this fund was to help provide for the needs of widows, orphans and other female relatives of deceased Masons. Its trustees, composed of one member from each subordinate lodge, actively sought contributions from subordinate lodges and from individuals as its basic source of income.

In the early 1850s more principal became available in the fund and the annual disbursements rose to between $300 and $400 (Table 1). The trustees were still dissatisfied, however. They were embarrassed that their resources were far exceeded by those of the Stephen Girard Charity Fund, they regretted that they had constantly to appeal for money, and they wanted to "exhibit incontestable evidence that Charity with [the Brethren] was not an unmeaning word." Even more important, they judged the current system to be run haphazardly. Donations were made in a "diffuse and careless manner" that failed to provide sufficient funds, and the available money was unevenly disbursed.

To correct this situation the trustees proposed new regulations designed both to increase the resources of the Charity Fund and to relieve pressure on the subordinate lodges. These measures were adopted in June 1855. The Grand Lodge pledged a contribution of $3,000 per year and every subordinate lodge was to subscribe $1.00 annually for each active member. This money would be invested and allowed to accumulate interest for a period of ten years until the sum of at least $50,000 had been reached. Annual interest on this amount, estimated at approximately $5,000, would then be available for disbursement. For greater efficiency, the trustees of the new fund were reduced to five, each entrusted with careful management of the money. Four other members were appointed "Almoners." Their responsibity was to review petitions and to award relief. No applicant could obtain more that $50 at one time but assistance was not necessarily monetary. The Almoners could provide certain material necessities to the poor or could obtain employment for them. The Grand Lodge thus believed that "regularity, harmony, and practicable equality in the distribution of our charitable donations" would be achieved. The new fund began operation in October when approximately $10,000 was transferred to it from the old fund. Another $1,300 had subsequently been raised. A portion of the interest was used to meet current charitable expenses, but most of it was reinvested.[7]

The improved financial health of the two Grand Lodge charity funds in the 1840s and 1850s permitted the Fraternity to get on with one of its main objectives, the relief of distress, which had been side-tracked in the recent past by more pressing concerns. In charitable disbursements the Masons were comparatively generous. The two Grand Lodge charity funds alone, exclusive of amounts given by subordinate lodges, equaled or exceeded those given by other private Philadelphia charitable organizations of the same period.[8]

The Grand Lodge encouraged charity in other forms as well, for example, in support for education. In June 1843 it urged individual Masons to send contributions to the Grand Lodge of Missouri, which had purchased land for several educational institutions, including a college, an academy and a primary school. Although most students were expected to pay for tuition and board, these institutions also offered free education to "needy, orphan children of deceased members of the Masonic Fraternity." The Pennsylvania Grand Lodge believed this work would do "incalculable good" both to the cause of education "in the Great West" and to the "honor of Masonry throughout the country." One of the Grand Chaplains, the Rev. E. Stiles Ely, acted as liaison between the two jurisdictions. In subsequent years similar institutions were established in Kentucky, Tennessee and North Carolina, and the Pennsylvania Grand Lodge also donated money to these, whenever feasible.[9]

Although the Masonic Fraternity in Pennsylvania was beginning to feel more secure in the 1840s, it nonetheless still maintained a relatively low profile. The most notable evidence of this was its avoidance of public processions on important Masonic occasions. The Saint John's Days were celebrated privately without fanfare and no lavish funeral processions were held. During these years the Fraternity lost several prominent officials: Past Grand Masters Michael Nisbet (in office 1831-1832) and T. B. Freeman (1836); Grand Chaplain James Wiltbank (d. 1842); and Grand Tyler, Charles Schnider (d. 1844), but little notice was taken, other than by eulogies at Grand Lodge meetings, draping Grand Lodge hangings and jewels in mourning, sending condolences to families and attending funerals as private individuals without regalia. It appears that no Masonic services were performed, nor was any other public Fraternal recognition offered. Even the deaths in 1845 of James Milnor, a notable early nineteenth-century Grand Master, and former President and Past Grand

Master (Tenn.) Andrew Jackson elicited no significant notice. This was in contrast to the funeral obsequies of Masonic officials of earlier generations in which hundreds of members took part.[10]

Pennsylvania Masonic leaders do not appear to have been opposed to public Masonic ceremonies in principle, at least patriotic or cultural functions, since they participated in several sponsored by other jurisdictions in this period. For example, Grand Lodge officers were present at the dedication of the Bunker Hill Monument on June 24, 1845, and the laying of the cornerstones of the Smithsonian Institution on May 1, 1847 and of the Washington Monument on July 4, 1848. Past Grand Master of Pennsylvania, George M. Dallas, then vice-president of the United States, delivered the keynote address at the Smithsonian Institution. These were major Masonic functions in which hundreds of Brethren openly participated, especially at the Washington Monument celebration: "[There were] Freemasons of every order, with their richest regalia, including the precious gavel and apron of Washington himself."

Although they were well received at these affairs by other Masons and by the general public, the Pennsylvania Grand Lodge officers could not yet countenance such openness within their own jurisdiction. For example, a resolution to hold a public Masonic festival in January 1848 in recognition of the visit to Philadelphia of two Mexican war heroes, Major General John A. Quitman and Brigadier General James Shields, also Masons, was defeated in Grand Lodge by a margin of more than two to one. In July 1850 the Fraternity declined to participate in a funeral procession and memorial service for President Zachary Taylor, although specifically invited by the Philadelphia City Councils. This meant only that the Fraternity was still hesitant about public scrutiny, not that it had become less patriotic. For example, in December 1846 a special Grand Lodge meeting was held to allow three Mexican war volunteers to take all three degrees in one night by dispensation, a practice not used since the Revolutionary War.

In another patriotic move, in 1851, the Grand Lodge ordered a block of Pennsylvania white marble to be cut in the shape of a keystone for incorporation into the Washington Monument. Measuring six feet by three, it bore an inscription commemorating the Masonic virtues of Washington and was placed on the inner face of the obelisk on the second landing.[11]

Only after mid-century did Pennsylvania Masons resume the older tradition of open participation in public processions. Coincidentally, as with its last public ceremony, held in late 1831, it related to the Fraternity's most notable benefactor, Stephen Girard. When the main building of the college for orphan boys that Girard had endowed was nearing completion in the late 1840s, the commissioners in charge of the construction arranged to disinter his remains from a vault on the grounds of Holy Trinity Church and reinter them at the college. These arrangements were controversial. Girard's heirs objected because he had clearly specified his final resting place, and the local Roman Catholic authorities objected on religious grounds, thus reawakening American nativist and anti-Roman Catholic feeling in Philadelphia. The commissioners persisted, obtaining a certificate from the Board of Health, but the parish gravedigger still refused to be part of the plan, and appealed to Bishop Kenrick. Having lost none of his earlier Antimasonic fervor, which had created an incident nearly twenty years before, the Bishop assented, saying that the body should never have been buried in consecrated ground in the first place since Girard, as a Freemason, could not have been a good Roman Catholic.

In early January 1851 Girard's remains were unearthed and deposited at the establishment of a leading Roman Catholic undertaker, Simon Gartland. They had originally been placed in a lead coffin, which was intact, within a larger wooden box, which was partly decayed. That the lead coffin remained unattended in the undertaker's yard distressed Girard's heirs. A few days later the coffin was opened in front of prominent witnesses and was found to contain very little: a skull and a few bones. Promptly sealed again, the coffin was placed within a larger cloth-covered one and then taken to the college on January 9. Having received full authority over the remains from the Philadelphia City Councils, the Board of Commissioners deposited them into a sealed cedar case in a third story room with a quiet ceremony attended by only a few teachers and orphans. The room was locked and the key given to the president of the college. This measure was intended as only temporary until more formal plans could be made to place Girard's remains in an elegant sarcophagus then nearing completion.

In July 1851 the Board of Commissioners requested Grand Master William Whitney to allow the Grand Lodge to participate in public ceremonies on September 30. On behalf of the Fraternity, Whitney accepted the invitation and called a special meeting of the Grand Lodge, which gave its approval. All subordinate lodges throughout the Commonwealth were urged to encourage their members to participate. Individual Masons were required to wear a full suit of black, along with white kid gloves, a plain blue sash and a white apron lined in blue. Officers were expected to appear in full regalia, which included purple collars and sashes and white satin aprons trimmed with purple. The Grand Lodge offered to supply the sashes and aprons so that uniformity and regularity would be maintained.

Four days before the anticipated public ceremony some of Girard's heirs filed for an injunction in the Court of Common Pleas to stop the proceedings. They pointed out that Girard in his will had specified that he wanted to be buried in consecrated ground. They also claimed that the removal of the body was illegal, and they rejected the idea of a Masonic procession. This petition raised a variety of issues: Did Girard's heirs have jurisdiction over the remains? Was the original removal illegal? Would the Masons conduct a special ceremony that would be offensive to the Roman Catholic Church? Would there be a religious ceremony at all? Should the body be returned to the churchyard, left in the upper room or placed in the intended final resting place? Or should nothing be done until the court could decide? Actually, the heirs had waited too long to intervene, and the court was forced by pressure of time and circumstances to disallow the injunction.

In addition to the Masons, Girard's relatives and numerous city officials were invited to participate. Although Girard had made gifts to a variety of causes and organizations, the Masonic Fraternity was the only organization included in the arrangements, which attests to the special regard Girard must have held toward it, or at least this was the commissioners' perception. It is perhaps significant that, the previous March, the president of the college, William Henry Allen, was made a Mason at a special communication of the Grand Lodge, receiving all three degrees in one night. In any case, the Masons were pleased to be involved. To encourage the greatest number of participants, they advertised the procession in the local papers. This public exposure was uncharacteristic of Masonic behavior in recent years.

On the morning of September 30, 1851, Masons from twenty-eight subordinate lodges, all but five in the city itself, assembled at various points and walked to the Masonic Hall on South Third Street where Grand Lodge members met them. The procession was arranged according to dates of warrants, the most recent first. The exception was No. 3, which came last, since contemporary Masons believed that Girard had been a member of that lodge. Next came the Grand Stewards of the Stephen Girard Charity Fund and finally members of the Grand Lodge. Interspersed with the lodges were six military bands that provided musical accompaniment. Following a well-publicized route along Third, Walnut and Fourth Streets, the Masonic procession marched to the front of the State House on Chestnut Street, where it was joined by various Philadelphia city officials at noon. The procession then moved up Chestnut to Twelfth, north on Twelfth to Ridge Road, and then to the college, where it arrived about one o'clock.

More than fifteen hundred Masons, as well as one hundred fifty others, participated in the procession, which occupied more than six city blocks. This was nearly double the size of any previous procession. The members of the Fraternity bore themselves in a dignified manner and generated much public interest:

"[They] formed altogether the most respectable body of men ever seen in any public parade in this City. The regalia of the subordinate lodges elicited universal admiration, it being at once simple, chaste and elegant. The lodges walked with a steadiness of carriage and precision of step that were admirable. The most exceptional order and decorum prevailed. The streets through which the [Masons] moved were thronged with thousands of spectators, and every door, balcony, and window was filled with fair gazers. As far as the eye could penetrate in the direction of the route, there was an immense multitude of human beings to be seen."

The head of the procession marched around the college grounds until the rear had entered the gates. Then ranks were opened and the Grand Lodge, city officials and the remains passed through the lines, made a full circuit of the walks and stopped at a special platform constructed on the east side of the main building. The coffin, covered with black cloth and a Masonic apron, was borne by eight Past Masters. Four Past Grand Masters served as honorary pall bearers. The commissioners of the college, along with city officials and Grand Lodge members, took their places on the platform and the other participants, including some three hundred orphans and teachers, gathered in front of it. A Masonic dirge, composed by Dr. W. P. Cunnington, the leader of the orchestra of the Walnut Street Theatre, was played by the various musical organizations present.

This dirge was followed by a lengthy eulogy by Past Grand Master and United States congressman, Joseph R. Chandler. Portraying Girard as mariner, merchant and patriot, but mostly as philanthropist, he argued that Girard's feeling for his fellow man was sincere and his generosity unselfish, not motivated by any desire for fame or recognition. The orator undertook "to connect the beauties of Brother Girard's character with the principles and practices of our Order."

Grand Master Whitney then offered a few appropriate remarks regarding the Masonic funeral service. The coffin was then carried inside and was deposited in a beautiful, but simple, sarcophagus of Italian marble placed behind a statue of Girard in the vestibule of the college. While the dirge was performed again, the procession reassembled and passed through the college, each member placing upon the coffin a sprig of evergreen, symbolizing the Masonic belief in eternal life. The whole scene generated a deep emotional effect: "[It] was a beautiful scene. The solemnities at the tomb were most imposing. The music of the dirge . . . was characterized by an indescribable sadness and grandeur."

That evening the Grand Lodge offered its members and visiting Brethren a light buffet meal at the Musical Fund Hall on Locust Street west of Eighth. Catered by Jones's Exchange Hotel on Dock Street, the menu included various cold dishes of a wide variety of fish, meat and fowl, as well as desserts, fruits and a selection of champagnes, sherries, madeiras and Rhine wines. One of the delicacies, which reflected contemporary tastes, was buffalo tongue. The activities connected with Stephen Girard's obsequies excited neither untoward incidents nor Antimasonic feeling, as some Masons had feared they might, and ultimately gained for the Fraternity the public respect it had not enjoyed for over twenty-five years.[12]

As it recovered the Grand Lodge of Pennsylvania continued to show itself as a conservative organization dedicated to the principles of its founders. It firmly resisted innovations in Masonic rules and regulations, ritual and other practices. It also opposed public exposure of Masonic principles, no matter how benign the intent. For example, in 1843, the Grand Lodge refused permission to several Masons who wished to publish a "Freemason's Monitor" of the type approved by other jurisdictions; a year later it condemned another work in wide circulation, called "The Masonic Trestle Board," produced by a Massachusetts Mason. It believed such works would do "vast injury to the Masonic Fraternity" and it thus "uniformly reprobated" them. On the contrary, the Grand Lodge asserted:

> The *Ahiman Rezon* is a sufficient text book and furnishes all that is desirous to be known out of the Lodge, as a standard it gives what is wanting with respect to the spirit and object of Masonry. As to the forms, these are for the Lodge alone, within its walls to be sacredly kept from the eyes & ears of the uninitiated, cherished by the memory and enshrined in the heart of every brother.

The Grand Lodge also protested a convention of fifteen grand lodges, held in Baltimore in May 1843, whose purpose was to agree upon a uniform system of work and to establish a general grand lodge for the United States. The Grand Lodge "positively refused" to consider these old and worn-out issues. A similar convention, held four years later, evoked an even stronger response from Pennsylvania Masons:

> From the time when this project was first started in the Year 1790 up to the present period, the Grand Lodge of Pennsylvania has uniformly disapproved of it, and so far from having faltered in her opinion upon the Subject, experience has but convinced her of the prudence of her course, and confirmed her in the resolution originally taken and faithfully adhered to. Every investigation of the proposition has resulted in a still deeper conviction that it can produce no good to the order, and must work injury to Masonry, and ought therefore at once and finally to be abandoned. The Grand Lodge of Pennsylvania can under no circumstances be induced to countenance it and this [is] her fixed determination.[13]

In the 1840s and early 1850s the Fraternity was fortunate in being led by men of unquestioned dedication. The Antimasonic period had strengthened their resolve while they served in subordinate positions, and they brought renewed enthusiasm with them when they rose to Pennsylvania's highest Masonic office. Nine men served as Grand Master in this period. As in the past, they came from many occupations, but the majority were professional men (three lawyers, one merchant, one physician); four were artisans (two carpenters, one stonemason and one house painter). Although all made contributions to Freemasonry, four in particular stand out: Joseph R. Chandler (in office 1841-1842) James Page (1846-1847), William Whitney (1850-1851) and Anthony Bournonville (1852-1853) These men were among the better-educated Pennsylvania Masonic leaders and were more actively involved in running the Fraternity than many of their predecessors. They enthusiastically conducted annual Grand Visitations of subordinate lodges, made comprehensive annual reports on the condition of the Fraternity, and offered, where needed, a sense of direction for the future.

Chandler's legacy of speeches is impressive. During his term of office he delivered twelve important addresses at various Masonic functions, notably on Grand Visitations. Unlike most other Grand Masters, who usually delivered one standarized address to each lodge, Chandler composed original addresses for each lodge he visited. They dealt with a variety of subjects: "On the Duties of Masons to Masonry;" "On the Duties of Individual Masons;" "On the Unity of Masons;" "On the Moral Qualities of Masonry;" "On the Physical Benefits of Masonry;" "On the Masonic Character of Washington;" "On Masonic Language;" "Objections to Masonry Answered;" "On the Origin and Progress of Masonry;" and "On Masonic Obedience." Later printed and distributed, these addresses influenced Masonic ideology. Even after retiring from office, Chandler continued for a number of years to give addresses on Masonic occasions, both in Pennsylvania and elsewhere. No other Pennsylvania Grand Master from any period was so prolific. Prominent at first in local and then in national politics, Chandler had access to a broader audience and took advantage of the opportunity to increase the Fraternity's standing in the public eye.

Unfortunately, these particular addresses did not contain many facts regarding the current status, practices or history of Freemasonry; of course, they revealed nothing of the ritual or "mysteries" of the Fraternity. Instead, they dealt with the ideals, inner attitudes and outward behavior of Masons. As such they had broader appeal than the typical "progress report" usually offered by other Grand Masters. They were written in the rhetorical style of the period and probably sounded better than they now read. Much of what they contained were constantly repeated time-tested truths and generalities. Nonetheless, they reveal interesting aspects of Chandler's philosophy, and presumably that of the Grand Lodge. Chandler advocated a kind of secular religion that valued private morals and public virtue, love of enemies (the Antimasons) and the giving of charity to the unfortunate, but was devoid of theology. This denotes a change in viewpoint from the days of Grand Masters James Milnor and James Kerr, when the Fraternity was doctrinally Christian in orientation. Chandler did, however, stress the compatibility of Freemasonry with traditional Christianity and said that one did not substitute for the other, but rather complemented it. The Fraternity preferred to leave the beliefs of individual Masons alone.

Chandler was also attracted by romanticized episodes exhibiting the worth of the Fraternity as a mutual benefit society, an aspect not often mentioned in earlier Masonic addresses. He gave accounts of a widow and her children about to be evicted for not paying rent; of a sailor shipwrecked on a foreign shore; and of a respectable man fallen on hard times and addicted to drink. All were saved by giving a Masonic sign recognized by another Mason in a position to help. Chandler's views may be summarized in the following characteristic phrase: "A unity of purpose in the great morals of life; a devotion to virtue . . . a close regard for the laws of the community in which we reside; an avoidance of all those excesses by which general order is violated."[14]

Chandler's approach to Masonic issues was one of gentle advice and kindly instruction; by contrast, that of Grand Master Page seems harsher. He appears to have been a stickler for detail who refused to alter even slightly past practices, which he regarded as a "sacred trust to be guarded." This quality was admirable in the leader of a Society that had a strong historical sense, but at times Page was uncompromising. He regarded the role of the Grand Master not as that of a caretaker, but as one of active involvement in the everyday affairs of the Fraternity, and he stressed the importance of respect and obedience of all Masons to the office of Grand Master. Page was among the more fluent authors of visitation addresses, and he even composed several prayers to be used at Masonic functions. Page's attitude toward traditional Christianity was similar to Chandler's. He made only discreet references to its theology, yet relied heavily upon its morality:

> Our Temple based upon Religion, is dedicated to Love & Charity. Here we bow (in humility) the knee to our God the Common father of all, the Supreme Architect above in whom is everything and without whom we are as dust & ashes . . . . Reverence for the Deity, and gratitude for the blessings of heaven, are enjoined in every degree of our ceremonies. They should pervade the Craft, and fill the soul of every Mason.

In the same manner, Masonic odes and prayers offered on festive occasions in this period borrowed Christian terminology for God, such as "Father of Mercy, Truth and Grace," the "Mighty God," and "Heaven's High King," but were careful to make no specific reference to Jesus Christ.[15]

The tone of the administrations of Whitney and Bournonville, in marked contrast to Page's, was one of quiet repose. Although equally dedicated to Masonic principles and equally interested in the Fraternity's business, these men saw their roles differently than their predecessor. They believed that the Grand Master should remain above partisan conflict and should act as a mediator. They saw the office as one of stewardship whose responsibility was to protect the ideals of Masonry as handed down from "time immemorial" and to pass them on unchanged. This approach can be best understood in light of the renewed prosperity of the Fraternity in Pennsylvania. By the early 1850s finances were secure, central administration was tightening, membership was increasing and public acceptance was more readily forthcoming. They saw no need, as Chandler and Page had, for forceful and innovative leadership. Progress was satisfactory and these men preferred to keep it that way. To quote Grand Master Whitney on his retirement from office:

> My wish has been, while I have presided over this Grand Lodge, not to lay out or establish any new channels, through which might flow, in gentle streams, the benefits of our Order; but to follow in the long and well beaten paths and to maintain the same unimpaired, which were marked out with so much wisdom and care by those who have long since gone to their eternal homes, and which have been perpetuated from generation to generation down to the present time.

Accepting Chandler's secularization of religious virtues, Whitney and Bournonville softened traditional Christian attitudes even more and deliberately left theological positions vague so as not to offend.[16]

*   *   *   *   *   *   *   *

The major preoccupation of the Grand Lodge in the period of recovery was the status of the old Masonic Hall on Chestnut Street. It had been sold in 1835 to the Franklin Institute, which had agreed to pay $110,550 over seven years according to a fixed schedule. Soon after the sale was made, however, the fortunes of the Institute declined and it was able to make only the first payment in full. After repeated Masonic pressure, some partial payments were made, but more than half the total amount was still unpaid by early 1840. This matter was pressing since the Grand Lodge was obligated to repay the holders of various issues of Masonic loans, totaling more than $15,000, and it had "no other resources" than the mortgage of the Franklin Institute. Because of the Panic of 1837 the Institute was unable to raise sufficient money and appeared near insolvency. The Masons formed a special committee and hired a lawyer to find a solution. After unsuccessfully employing a number of other measures, the Grand Lodge finally offered to negotiate a more modest repayment schedule. Even this could not be worked out, however, and in November 1841 the Fraternity took back the Chestnut Street hall at a price of $85,550.

The Franklin Institute promised to pay $9,000 in back interest, as well as interest on this amount, and gave as security a mortgage on its own building on Seventh Street. It defaulted on this obligation as well, however. The Grand Lodge obtained the mortgage and sold it to a speculator, Samuel Brolasky. It also sold $600 worth of furniture, which the Franklin Institute had also pledged and lost. These proceeds were used to repay money that it had recently borrowed to temporarily relieve the pressure of the Masonic loans and to pay back taxes. The remainder was placed in reserve to meet future obligations.[17]

The Grand Lodge took possession of the Chestnut Street hall and lot on January 1, 1842, although a deed was not executed until March. Needless to say, not only had the Franklin Institute not been able to realize its ambitious plans for the property, but it had also allowed the building to fall into disrepair. The management of the building was assigned not to the standing Hall Committee, which dealt with the current Masonic meeting place, Washington Hall, but to the Grand Treasurer, whose responsibility it was to find tenants, to hire a superindendent, to make repairs and to keep accounts. For the next four years, rooms in the Chestnut Street hall were rented on a short-term basis to a variety of organizations, such as the county commissioners, a public school, a private school, the gas company, and the Sons of Temperance. These tenants provided an annual income of $3,000 to $5,000. Although appreciated, this revenue was uncertain and thus was insufficient to meet the Fraternity's long-term financial commitments. Accordingly, the Grand Lodge again decided to sell the hall. It received several offers to assume the existing mortgage, but these were deemed unsatisfactory because they undervalued the real estate; the prospective purchasers intended to resell it at a profit.

In November 1845 the Grand Lodge received a proposal for a long-term lease from Edmund Peale, a member of the famous Philadelphia family and formerly the proprietor of the Baltimore Museum. Two years previously Peale had sold his collection to his chief rival, Phineas T. Barnum, and with new capital relocated to Philadelphia. Not coincidentally, at that time the noteworthy collection of the Philadelphia Museum was on the market. This collection had been assembled by Peale's grandfather, Charles Willson, and after his death in 1827 managed by his uncles, Franklin and Titian. The Museum failed and went out of business in 1843. According to the terms of the incorporation, the collection could not be sold or removed from Philadelphia. Edmund promised the directors, now headed by his uncle Rembrandt, that if they consented to a sale, he would buy the entire collection and keep it in the city. Accordingly, at a sheriff's sale in early November, Peale bid on every lot for a total exceeding $13,000. This prevented the dissolution of the Museum Company, saved the collection from dispersal, satisfied the creditors and gave Edmund a fresh opportunity. Obviously, he needed an appropriate place to exhibit the collection, which had been moved frequently, and he chose the Masonic Hall on Chestnut Street.

Peale offered to rent the hall for five years at the annual rate of $4,250, which was five percent of the existing mortgage ($85,000), and to pay all taxes. He also agreed to pay the cost of alterations and improvements, both to the building and to the grounds, subject to the Fraternity's approval and reimbursement. Peale's offer promised a steady income, and since he came highly recommended by the citizens of Baltimore, the Grand Lodge accepted it. Another advantage was that it allowed more time for the Fraternity to consider long-term plans for the property.[18]

Among these were various measures designed to enhance its commercial value. In September 1846 the Master of Lodge No. 130, William Schultz, a carpenter, proposed that four small stores be erected along the front facing Chestnut Street. Two were to be located on the west side and two on the east side of the lot, each eighteen feet wide and thirty-six feet deep. Schultz's plan allowed a "spacious entrance" of about thirty feet in the center, providing access to the hall, with twelve feet between the rear of the stores and the front of the main building. They would be finished in Gothic style, in accord with the design of the hall. Schultz offered to build the stores at his own expense and, after collecting the rents for the first three years, to donate them to the Fraternity. He believed that the stores would be "an ornament to the Hall and add much to its appearance" while yielding a "fine revenue" to the the Grand Lodge "without any outlay."

The Grand Lodge unanimously accepted these plans. A committee was formed to work with Schultz and to ensure that the "best Materials and Workmanship" were used. The addition of these buildings meant a change in insurance policies since the original policy did not cover improvements, but this change was not difficult and even resulted in a reduced premium. Within nine months the stores were completed "in a proper manner and in conformity with the specifications." The total cost was $4,279, and they generated an income of about $2,400 per year. Fully tenanted, they became the property of the Grand Lodge in March 1850.[19]

The Masonic Hall on Chestnut Street (1847-1855). Drawing by Frank H. Taylor. From an old photograph circa 1850 (Grand Lodge of Pennsylvania).

Meanwhile, the rental agreement for the main building with Edmund Peale, which initially had seemed so attractive, was beginning to sour. Having opened his museum in January 1846, Peale enjoyed some commerical success, but less than a year and a half into the contract, he began to withhold his rent, and owed $2,200 by March 1847. In a personal letter to Grand Master Page, Peale attributed his default to the extensive costs he had borne for improvements which, he argued, had "enhanced the value of the property five times the Sum" of the debt he owed. When he took possession, Peale had been obliged to remove a "collection of dirt of Ten Years Standing" and to paint the building. He had also had to spend $500 or $600 to repair the gas works. Peale felt aggrieved because he had been led to believe that the Grand Lodge would reimburse him for such costs. He also complained that the construction of the four stores restricted access to the museum and thus hurt his business.

Peale's complaint elicited a strong response from Page, who denied that he had given a promise of reimbursement; this could be made only by the Grand Lodge through proper petition. He then threatened Peale with legal action. This brought a small payment but it was deemed insufficient, and the Grand Lodge obtained a lien against Peale's property in preparation for a sheriff's sale. Peale then paid nearly all his debt and the Grand Lodge reviewed his claims for reimbursement, which eventually resulted in a credit of $500 toward his rent.

Despite this, Peale soon fell into arrears again. In April 1848 he appealed for extensions, promising a third of his gross receipts, giving up a contingent interest in the stores in the front of the hall, and offering several stocks as security; the value of these stocks fell far short of his debt, however. Financially desparate, Peale used all sorts of maneuvers to attract customers and became as much a theatrical manager as a museum curator. As an added feature, he had earlier converted the Grand Saloon on the first floor of the hall into a small theater, where more or less respectable performances took place. Now it offered a much wider variety of entertainments and guest appearances, including General Tom Thumb, the "Ethiopian Harmonists," "The Mystic Temple of Witchcraft," and even a exhibition of " 'vile living figures of male and female sexes' " which, reputedly, performed in the nude. Not unexpectedly, Peale's establishment began to attract customers from the "lower orders" of Philadelphia; this, combined with nonpayment of the rent, understandably alarmed the Masons.[20]

Its patience "entirely exhausted" by early June 1848, the Grand Lodge resorted to legal means to recover the rent. Initally, it had wished to avoid selling the entire contents of the hall because such a move would bring Peale to "positive ruin," and would destroy his ability to continue the lease; it would also obligate the Fraternity to repair the hall and to find a new tenant. Assured by its lawyer that all other claims against Peale would be satisfied if only a portion of his property were sold, the Grand Lodge reliquished its legal hold on the whole collection. It allowed the Trustees of the Bank of the United States, Peale's chief creditors, to take "all the pictures now in the Museum," to be sold privately to meet his indebtedness, with any excess to be refunded to Peale. The Masons reasoned that Peale would remain in business and would thus be able to pay the back rent from future revenues. Because of substantial claims of other creditors, however, neither Peale nor the Grand Lodge received any money from this sale, and the income of the museum showed no sign of increasing. Therefore, the Masons saw no alternative but to send the remainder of the collection to a public sale. To protect itself, the Grand Lodge decided to buy the "curiosities" if other bidders undervalued them, and then resell them later.

The Grand Lodge made six attempts in as many months to sell the balance of the collection. Because of the legal complexities of the claims made by other creditors, by Peale's wife and by a purchaser who defaulted on his payment, each attempt to sell was frustrated. Despite heavy advertisements, public interest and confidence in the sale were weakened by repeated postponements. The Grand Lodge was therefore obliged to purchase the collection, which it did at the low price of $3,200. The Masons then canceled Peale's lease and took possession of the hall and its contents on January 1, 1849. Peale, however, was still allowed to continue to advertise exhibitions of his collection and had the option of buying it back. He never did so. With an unwanted museum collection and a much-altered building, the Grand Lodge set out once again to find a reliable tenant, this time "with more watchfulness and care." The balance sheet showed that the Fraternity had lost over $3,500 as a result of this affair.[21]

After turning down a number of offers, the Grand Lodge sold the collection in March 1849 to John Robinson, Past Master of Lodge No. 3, on condition that it remain in the hall until the Grand Lodge was reimbursed for its losses. Robinson paid $4,500, $2,000 down and the balance with interest in five equal semi-annual installments. Even though it made a profit of $1,000 on the sale of the collection, the Grand Lodge did not fully recoup its loss. In conjunction with a fellow Mason and business partner, Andrew Stein, John Robinson agreed to rent the hall, with the intention of continuing the museum. The rental was $400 per month, with a $25 deduction for approved repairs over two years. The new lessees promised prompt payment with the provision that if they fell behind by only ten days, they would forfeit the hall with no reimbursement of money already paid. Two other Masons, Andrew Coffman and J. Smith Skinner, offered security for this agreement by pledging their own property; these men apparently acted out of friendship and fraternal feeling.

The new owners of the Philadelphia Museum held various special exhibitions, such as the "Grand Nautical Panorama," which made money, but after only three months they too had fallen into arrears. They also had violated the lease by removing some objects from the hall and selling them. Faced with the unpleasant task of resorting to legal pressure on members of the Fraternity, the Grand Lodge showed Robinson and Stein "all the lenity possible" and "held out to them every inducement" to meet their obligations. Meanwhile, it had another lien placed on the collection. This elicited a few small payments, but by July, Robinson and Stein wanted to cancel their contract. The Grand Lodge was agreeable, even though this meant taking back and reselling the collection, but only on condition that the tenants pay in full the back rent, amounting to $1,525, remit the remainder of the purchase price, $2,500, in cash, and vacate the premises.[22]

The primary reason that the Philadelphia Museum, under both Edmund Peale and Robinson and Stein, did not succeed was competition from an able and determined rival, namely, Phineas T. Barnum. In the late 1840s and early 1850s this consummate showman implemented a grandiose plan for controlling museum operations in the major cities on the East Coast. In 1843, as already noted, Barnum took over Edmund Peale's Baltimore Museum and in the same year he bought out Peale's uncle Rubens' New York Museum of Natural History and Science, which complemented Barnum's own American Museum, also in New York City. At the same time Barnum was in partnership with Moses Kimball, owner of the Boston Museum.

Barnum then turned to Philadelphia. In early 1849 he opened a museum in a five-story building on the southeast corner of Seventh and Chestnut, down the street from the Masonic Hall. From there he launched a comprehensive attack to "kill the other shop." In this he succeeded. In November the Grand Lodge was compelled to cancel the lease with Robinson and Stein without receiving the unpaid rent and to sell the collection at whatever price could be obtained and permit it to be removed from the hall. The only bidder for all the "curiosites" was Barnum, who paid only $3,500 for them. At the same time the lease and some furniture were sold to a "Mr. Brown," for what purpose is not known. Unlike his predecessors, however, this tenant punctually paid his rent.[23]

Although Robinson and Stein were gone from the Chestnut Street hall, the Grand Lodge was not yet finished with them. They still owed back rent, were obligated to pay for lighting fixtures they had removed from the building, and had left their gas bill unpaid. Before the Fraternity could bring pressure on them, they sued the Grand Lodge for failing to reimburse them for certain repairs. This suit was eventually dropped for want of proof, and the Grand Lodge pursued the erstwhile tenants, in a more or less fraternal way, for the money they owed. With little regard for his Masonic vows, Robinson reacted to these attempts with defiance. He became abusive toward Grand Lodge officers personally and even condemned them publicly, calling them "black legs and cheats and other opprobrious ephithets." When reprimanded for such conduct, he responded by threatening "to shoot the Grand Secretary should he come about the Chestnut St. Hall." Robinson was forbidden to attend Grand Lodge meetings and subsequently a move was made to expel him from the Fraternity. This case caused considerable debate for more than two years. Evidently Robinson gained sympathy among some Masons, who came to believe that the whole affair was the result of a misunderstanding. Action on his expulsion was indefinitely postponed, and ultimately the Grand Lodge was obliged to take a loss, which amounted to about $1,000.[24]

On March 1, 1851, the lease on the Chestnut Street hall expired and the Grand Lodge was faced with the important question of what to do with this troublesome property. As early as December 1849 a suggestion was made that the Masons resume meeting there and the Third Street hall be sold, but nothing was done about this proposal at that time. A year later, however, upon the recommendation of Grand Master Whitney, a special committee of thirteen was formed to investigate the feasibility of this proposal. The unusually high number of committee members indicates the importance of the issue. In a report six months later this committee presented the Fraternity with three options: (1) to move back to the Chestnut Street hall, after extensively rennovating it, and to sell the Third Street hall; (2) to sell both halls and build a new one at a different location; or (3) to tear down the Chestnut Street hall and build a new one on the same site. Each option was explored in a separate report by a special subcommittee.

The first favored moving back to Chestnut Street. Not only was this option popular, "a step which meets the approval of the Craft generally," but also it was to the Fraternity's financial advantage. Since the "strictest economy should be observed" in any new projects, the subcommittee recommended against building a new hall. At that time the Fraternity was nearing redemption of a substantial debt of long standing and another would not be in its interest. The repair of the old hall would entail little expenditure, perhaps between $4,000 and $7,000, which was easily affordable. The upper story of the renewed hall could be used for Masonic purposes and the lower one rented to generate an estimated income of more than $3,000 per year. This surplus could be used to pay off the remaining debt or, better yet, to create a new charity fund for Masonic widows and orphans, "thus extending the holy mission and work of practical Masonry." In a few years, if the Fraternity needed more meeting space or if it wanted more income-producing property, it could build an additional five-story building on the rear of the lot. Finally, there was an emotional reason for saving the old hall: " . . . the architecture of this ancient edifice, is at once imposing and appropriate, whilst its interior is venerated by and endeared to many of the Craft by the recollection of important events in the history of Masonry."

Another subcommittee disagreed. The hall needed too many repairs and the costs of renovation would not be offset by rental income. Moreover, new tenants might continue "the disgrace of such dances &c. as are found there now." The committee also rejected the second option: the Chestnut Street hall would probably bring a low price because of its poor condition, and land in any central location would cost a large sum. It was their opinion that only two choices were feasible: to remain in Third Street or to build an entirely new hall on Chestnut.

The third special subcommittee offered the most comprehensive report. Not only was the Third Street hall "inadequate to the convenient reception of the members," but it was also "becoming less and less central" as the city and its outlying districts rapidly expanded. Since these problems would only become worse with time, the building would soon have to be sold and the Fraternity removed from it. Regarding a site for another hall, the subcommittee found no lot so advantageously situated or inexpensive to maintain as that on Chestnut Street. The only viable option, therefore, was to move back to the old hall.

This building had serious problems, however. The rooms were not much larger than those of the Third Street hall and were inadequate for future needs. Therefore, it would be a waste of money to repair the old hall, which could only be "the imperfect fitness of which it is susceptible," and to add new buildings to the lot that eventually would have to be torn down. Construction of an entirely new hall would also permit the advantage of redesign. The committee recommended that such a building be set further back on the property. It would thus combine "the quietness of a country place" with the "convenience and publicity of access from the most frequented streets of the city." Important meeting rooms would be on the rear of the building, where windows could be opened in hot weather without street noises interfering with the proceedings. Less important committee rooms would face the front of the building. A larger front facing Chestnut Street would enhance the beauty and value of the property and allow more space between the the main hall and the four stores along the street which would be retained for income. Members of the subcommittee also saw an opportunity to make a more impressive entrance way into the hall: "a grand Masonic gateway of dark sand-stone, distinguished for its symmetry, its beauty, and its Masonic ornaments — at once a mark of the site of the Hall, and a grand embellishment to the city."

A strong argument in favor of a new hall entirely for Masonic purposes was the moral issue:

> The proposed plan has the inviting feature of freeing the G. L. from the odium which it endures by the many doubtful uses to which the old Hall is now put. The Sub-Committee do not contemplate any use of the new Hall, save for pure Masonic purposes, making a temple not of vice, dissipation and immorality — but of order, charity and love — traditions that descend from the grandest temple of God — of thoughts and acts that ascend to the throne of the Most High, in a temple not made by hands. We hope that the G. L., no longer pressed by a stern necessity, will refuse to suffer the wages of iniquity to darken and poison the holy stream of charity that flows from the pure well-springs of Masonic faith and love. It is high time that the desecration of a Masonic Hall should cease; and we the more

earnestly press upon the G.L. the proposed scheme, because it must necessarily restore the property of the Order to high and holy uses.

The subcommittee closed its well-reasoned argument with calcula-
tions showing the condition of the Grand Lodge to be sound and im-
proving. In its opinion "there exists no good reason for denying to the
Masons of Pennsylvania a place of resort commensurate with the dignity
of the Order, and adequate to the wants of a growing Fraternity." The
committee of thirteen endorsed this last report and then resolved to solicit
plans for rebuilding the Chestnut Street hall from leading architects of
the city. Obviously, because of the magnitude of the proposal, the Grand
Lodge could not make immediate decisions. Instead, it ordered that copies of the reports be printed and distributed to the subordinate lodges
for their consideration at least six weeks before the next quarterly communication in September, when the issues would be discussed.[25]

Although nothing significant was discussed at that meeting, perhaps
because insufficient time had been allowed for the subordinate lodges to
respond, three architectural plans were submitted. Meanwhile, the Masons tried to rent the hall but without success, "owing to the mutilated
condition in which Brother John Robinson left it." By the end of December the hall still remained empty. In his annual message Grand Master
Whitney remarked on the "lamentable condition" of the hall and expressed his opinion that it would be a "useless expenditure of money" to
repair it.

In the spring of 1852 the Grand Lodge was still unsure how to handle
the situation. In March a committee was formed to see whether the hall
could be sold, and when, in April, it reported no progress, a particularly
vocal member, Joseph S. Riley, protested that "all this real estate" should
be disposed of at once:

> [It has been] used by hireling proprietors for immoral, base and iniq-
> uitous purposes, by which this Grand Lodge has frequently been brought
> into vexations, [and] expensive and unprofitable litigation. Yea! even to the
> rending asunder the brotherly love and affection that should here always
> bind us together as a Band of Brothers.

Debate became so intense that further discussion had to be postponed in
the interest of continued harmony.

Another session concerning the Chestnut Street hall on May 3 was
equally stormy. Various resolutions were proposed and then postponed:
one to form a committee to carry out the recommendations of the committee of thirteen, made nearly a year before; one to sell the hall immediately; one to sell it only after all debts were paid; and one to sell both
halls and purchase a new one. Another intense debate occurred at the

September quarterly communication, which was better attended than most of this period, fifty-eight lodges being represented either by a member or a proxy. Former resolutions, some with amendments, were again put forward; some were passed, others were postponed and still others were defeated. Finally, it was decided to move back to Chestnut Street where an entirely new hall should be built, and a committee headed by Past Grand Master Whitney was formed to devise plans for it.[26]

The Committee on Plans acted quickly. At another special Grand Lodge meeting in November, it presented specific plans from three prominent local architects: Edward Collins, John Notman and Samuel Sloan. These had been chosen from among "many beautiful and excellent plans" that had been submitted. Each plan kept within a proposed budget of $80,000, which the committee calculated to be the amount that could be raised by another Masonic loan, and each was presented with the option of an iron, brown sandstone, marble or granite front. Although the plans were similar in design and dimensions, Notman's was rejected because it did not allow sufficient access to the stores in front, which Masons believed would diminish the revenue from them. Sloan's was also rejected because it did not budget enough money for statues to be erected on the facade. Therefore, the committee came to recommend Collins' plan.

The Collins plan projected a three-story Neo-Gothic structure. The first floor consisted of four stores or shops, each twenty-two and a half feet wide and running the whole depth of the lot (178 feet), two on either side of a twelve foot-wide entrance portal. The second floor contained nine rooms: a Grand Lodge room, a Blue Lodge room, a banquet room, a Grand Master's room, a Grand Secretary's room, a reception room and three large committee rooms, and the residence of the Grand Tyler. The third floor had two large meeting rooms, one for Chapter and the other for Encampments.

The committee recommended acceptance of a brown sandstone front, formation of a seven-man building committee, creation of trustees of a new Masonic loan, and compensation of $450 to the several architects for their plans. This report engendered more debate in the Grand Lodge, much in the same spirit as before, and the only agreement reached was to pay the architects. The choice of plan would be made after all plans were submitted to a vote of the members after they had an opportunity to study them.

A week later, after "considerable discussion" and contrary to the committee's recommendation, Notman's plan was accepted. The Grand Lodge chose the members of the Building Committee and the trustees of the new Masonic loan, but this process was not simple. On December 20, 1852, more contention arose over such issues as the number of persons to serve, how they were to be chosen, what powers they had and how much money was to be spent. Resolutions, amendments, counter-resolutions and postponements punctuated this special session. Finally, it was agreed to choose seven men from among the Grand Lodge members to consider design changes and to submit them for Grand Lodge approval. Five members were chosen as the trustees and they were authorized to raise $85,000. Thus, the year ended with a sense of accomplishment.[27]

The Fraternity's problems with the Chestnut Street hall were far from over, however. Fund-raising activities were hampered by the trustees' not knowing how to proceed initially, and the Building Committee discovered the need for design changes: sub-cellers were added; additional strength was given to some interior walls; the shape of the Grand Lodge Room was changed; and the front pavement was deepened. The architects had to be consulted again. Some of them, including John Notman, the favored architect, were asked to submit new plans and bids, and seven did so. Each estimated the cost at nearly double the Grand Lodge's limit of $85,000, even when an allowance of $5,000 to $7,000 was made for reusable material from the old hall. Notman, however, offered to do the work for only $130,000. Therefore, the Building Committee was obliged to gain the Grand Lodge's approval for this increased cost. On March 22 it requested authority to spend the estimated $130,000. At hearing this, "the R. W. Grand Master [Anthony Bournonville] being taken suddenly ill was obliged to leave the Grand Lodge Room." The Deputy Grand Master, James Hutchinson, took over the meeting, which reaffirmed the former limit of $85,000.

Bournonville soon recovered, and within two weeks called another special meeting of the Grand Lodge to deal with the Chestnut Street hall. The situation was more encouraging, as the Grand Treasurer reported sufficient funds to pay off the mortgage of the Third Street hall; he was ordered to do this. Then it was proposed that the trustees of the new loan be authorized to raise $110,000, of which $100,000 was to be set aside for the Building Committee's use. These resolutions were carried with relatively little debate.[28]

Nonetheless, difficulties continued, this time with the architect, Brother John Notman. Because his revised plan was favored by the Building Committee and because it had asked him to perform additional services, Notman believed he was actually commissioned to do the work, even though he had no contract. In April 1853 he demanded that the Grand Lodge affirm the arrangement by a contract or compensate him in full for his efforts in drawing up and modifying the plans. This he calculated at five percent of the estimate, or $6,500.

The committee reacted with "astonishment" to Notman's "extraordinary and unjust position." There was no evidence to support his contention that he had been hired, nor was it the committee's implied or expressed wish to engage him. As for compensation, at the beginning of the competition the Grand Lodge had authorized at first $25, and then $50, for each unsuccessful plan and $150 for the successful one. Therefore, Notman was only entitled to $150. Since the building could not be constructed within the announced financial limits, however, all plans, including Notman's, were inoperative.

Relations between the architect and his Masonic superiors now deteriorated. The Building Committee considered Notman's business practices to be generally "wanting in fairness and opressive," and since a fellow Mason was engaging in extortion, the action was nothing short of "reprehensible and without a precedent in the history of the Order . . . tending to the destruction of all confidence among the members of the craft." The committee then resolved to have nothing further to do with Notman and to proceed as though there were no design. Therefore, after two years of considering this issue the Fraternity had no plan, no architect and insufficient funds to continue with the new Chestnut Street hall.[29]

The Masons were nonetheless determined to have their new hall. In early 1853 they redoubled their efforts and moved with unaccustomed speed. By June a resolution to hold a public procession for the cornerstone laying ceremony was passed, the trustees opened subscriptions, and the Building Committee negotiated contracts with workmen. These agreements clearly specified compensation and thus, it was hoped, guaranteed that costs would stay within $85,000. Samuel Sloan, also a Mason, was chosen architect, but he was to follow the Building Committee's modifications of his original design. At the same time a superintendent was hired, as were carpenters, bricklayers, stonemasons, gas fitters and plumbers. An excavating firm was engaged to tear down the old hall and to dig the new foundation.

Demolition was underway by early September, but it did not proceed as rapidly as planned, owing to the strength of the old building. Unusually hot weather also hampered operations. This delay caused anxiety in the Building Committee, which seemingly wished to make up for lost time. It threatened to invoke a clause in the contracts that if work did not proceed as promised, the builders would have to hire additional workers at their own expense. The committee established a rigid schedule for the work: the cornerstone ceremonies to be held before cold weather set in; the superstructure of the building to be up by spring; and the hall to be completed by St. John's Day, December 27, 1854. The cornerstone was already in preparation.[30]

Only the first deadline was met. On Monday, November 21, 1853, the cornerstone-laying ceremonies were held. Unfortunately, "torrents of rain" fell when the proceedings began at noon, but this did not prevent "an immense crowd" from gathering to watch. Streets surrounding the property were "thronged by curious spectators" and store windows along the opposite side Chestnut Street were "filled with ladies." The ceremony took place on a special platform constructed across the open basement. On the east side were seated the Grand Lodge officers, attired in full regalia and on the west, a choir and orchestra, conducted by Brother William P. Cunnington, who had directed the music at the Girard obsequies. City officials, invited guests and the press occupied the center.

When all was ready, the Grand Lodge officers, the Building Committee and the architect arrived on the scene in procession as the orchestra played a grand march. Upon reaching the platform the Brethren opened their ranks and faced inwards as the Grand Master passed through to his place. One of the Grand Chaplains, the Rev. John Chambers, offered "an eloquent prayer," and the musicians presented a Masonic ode, written by a Grand Lodge member. The Grand Treasurer then announced the items placed inside the cornerstone: lists of officers and members of the Fraternity and of various committees responsible for the hall; names of city, state and federal officials; copies of the Holy Bible and the *Ahiman Rezon;* a picture of the old hall and the design of the new one; newspapers of the day; bronze medallions of Washington and Lafayette; and various gold and silver coins. These were placed in a metal box and laid inside a cavity of the inscribed stone, which was then set in place in Masonic manner by Grand Master Bournonville. "Solemn music" by the orchestra accompanied this ceremony. A prayer was offered by the Grand Master, and the musicians performed Handel's "Hallelujah Chorus." The architect was ceremonially introduced to the Grand Master, who gave him the implements of his work, a plumb, a level and a square, and a blessing to prosper in his work.

The keynote of the ceremony was an oration on Masonry by John K. Mitchell, the Junior Grand Warden. Although rhetorical in the manner of that era, Mitchell made some memorable points. Essentially, he explained the need for a new hall and stressed the practical value of Freemasonry to society. Mitchell expressed feelings of satisfaction and pride that, after so many years, Philadelphia Masons could return to a site important in their history. Although many memories were associated with the old hall, it had to be torn down to make room for an even greater one, "the largest and the finest building, ever erected by Masonry, in any country, for exclusive Masonic uses." According to Mitchell, the new hall would be "a monument of our taste, a proof of our vitality, and a refuge for the poor, the persecuted and the afflicted." Not only would the new hall beautify an important city thoroughfare, but the stores in the front would generate revenue. This income would reduce the debt on the hall and permit more funds to go into charitable work, thus benefiting Philadelphia at large. Mitchell also spoke of the value of Masonic virtues and lessons, such as republicanism, trustworthiness, order and discipline and, most of all, charity. The impressive ceremony ended with an anthem by the choir and a benediction by another Grand Chaplain, the Rev. H. W. Ducachet.[31]

Over the next two years the Building Committee kept a close eye on the progress of the construction and offered regular detailed reports to the Grand Lodge. In the middle of December 1853 it reported that the various contractors had proceeded in their work "with commendable zeal." The foundation was complete, the joists for the ground floor were nearly laid, the stone for the front was ready and the ironwork for the floor of the Grand Lodge room was under way. Cost over-runs were already developing, however; work estimated at $8,300 had actually cost more than $10,500. The members of the committee, though, were not overly concerned. Even in June 1854 when expenses had reached about $40,000, or nearly half the proposed limit, they remained confident that the whole could be completed within budget and on time, and they had no serious complaints about the contractors. By then, the groin arches supporting the second floor were up and all cement work was finished.

Meanwhile, the Grand Lodge formed a committee to sell the Third Street hall, made plans to remove furniture and fixtures from the current hall to the new one and drew up rules to rent the stores in front. Even though the Building Committee soon realized that an end-of-the-year occupancy was not possible, it still had no major complaints. It was, however, dissatisfied with a slowly-moving stone contractor who was responsible for facing the facade. He might have delayed the placing of the iron roof, but the committee intervened and arranged to have the roof placed before winter set in. By that time another $13,000 had been spent.[32]

Work continued at a satisfactory pace in the early part of 1855. In May the Building Committee reported that the hall would be ready by the end of August or the beginning of September, so the Grand Lodge proceeded to make plans for a public procession and dedication ceremony. It chose September 26, which was the sixty-ninth anniversary of the formation of the independent Grand Lodge. Much attention was paid to dress regulations, which were the same as for the Girard obsequies four years earlier. Subordinate lodges were required to inform the Grand Lodge before the middle of July of the numbers of members attending, so proper sashes and aprons could be provided for them. Lack of uniformity would not be tolerated.

In August the inevitable occurred. The Building Committee found that actual construction costs had exceeded the estimates by about $25,000. This was not only because of a rise in the price of labor and materials, although that was a major part, but also because of additional design and other changes. A granite pavement was substituted for stone; the stores were made fireproof with reinforced concrete foundations; glass floors were placed in areas under skylights in order to illuminate the basement; a wine cellar was built; and a corrugated iron roof was substituted for an ordinary tin one. Other expenses, not originally figured in, were insurance premiums, damage suits, party walls, additional architect's fees, and wages of a superintendent and a watchman.

At the same time the Furnishing Committee, which was separate from the Building Committee, requested an additional $28,000 to complete the interior properly. It wanted furniture and decoration to be durable and of the highest quality so as to reflect well upon the Fraternity. It also preferred to have the work all done at one time rather than over an extended period. Plans included the usual heavy woolen curtains, hand-carved oak and mahogany furniture, upholstered settees, crystal chandeliers, stained-glass windows, floor to ceiling mirrors, marble statuary, gas fixtures, coal stoves and furnaces, and fireplaces. Frescoed ceilings were to be put in the lodge rooms. The cost of furnishings would have been higher, except that many existing items were to be transferred from the Third Street hall.

Almost without debate the Grand Lodge authorized yet another Masonic loan, this one for $50,000, but raising the money was not so easy as before. The trustees of the new loan found that it was awkward to seek subscriptions again from the members of the Fraternity, upon which they had almost exclusively depended. "The whole ground has been gone over and the available means of the order swallowed up by the first loan . . . ." Nor could they obtain money through public sources since the Fraternity had no security but its good word, which, although enough for the lodges, was "not tangible to the world at large." The Chestnut Street hall was already pledged as security for the first Masonic loan. So the trustees devised a complicated scheme to achieve solvency. Any stocks and bonds held by the Grand Lodge were to be exchanged for those held by the Stephen Girard Charity Fund and by any subordinate lodges that had the same face value but a greater yield. All that remained of the first loan, $10,000, was to be subscribed immediately; a mortgage of $12,000 to $15,000 was to be taken out on the Third Street hall before it was sold; certain stocks and bonds were to be sold; and two-thirds of all future revenue of the Grand Lodge were to be set apart to pay interest or invest in a sinking fund. All these resolutions were accepted without controversy.[33]

In an unprecedented move the Grand Lodge allowed non-Masons into the hall prior to its dedication. The Building Committee found that public interest was high, and it was "convinced that great dissatisfaction will ensue unless the New Hall is thrown open to general inspection for a week or ten days before or after the dedication." To restrict admission only to persons who would do no damage to the premises, the committee charged a small fee of twenty-five cents for tickets. So as not to appear mercenary, the proceeds were to be used for charitable purposes. Each ticket admitted "one gentleman and such ladies as may accompany him." The hall was accordingly opened from 9 A.M. to 5 P.M. on September 20, 21, 22 and 24, in expectation of a turnout of perhaps several hundred visitors per day.

News of the open house was well publicized in local newspapers and the public response was overwhelming. Masonic officials received so many requests for admission that they ran out of tickets and were unable to collect the required fee from other visitors. During the four days the doors had to be shut frequently to allow the crowds inside to pass through before additional visitors were admitted. The Building Committee calculated that no fewer than fourteen thousand gentlemen were admitted, twenty-five hundred of them without tickets. If the committee's estimate of four ladies to each gentleman is correct, then fifty-six thousand persons toured the hall. In addition, more than four thousand tickets were issued to members of the Fraternity. Special arrangements were made for two non-Masonic groups. On the evening of the first day members of the Philadelphia Select and Common Councils, their clerks and newspaper reporters were given a special tour of the building and were treated to a light meal, and at the close of the final day orphans and officials of Girard College were given a similar reception. The opening of the New Masonic Hall was a public relations coup. It gained the Fraternity much respect and admiration and aroused the curiosity of many who were motivated to apply for Masonic initiation.[34]

The dedication ceremony took place as scheduled on Wednesday, September 26, 1855, the weather being "all that could be desired." It was one of the more impressive Masonic spectacles held in Philadelphia and local newspapers "seemed to vie with each other in gorgeous descriptions of the sights and scenes of the great procession." An estimated four thousand members of the Grand Lodge, sixty-two subordinate lodges and representatives of the grand lodges from nine other jurisdictions participated. Because there were too many participants to assemble at one place, they were arranged by lodges along the east side of Third Street and the south side of Pine from Third to Eleventh Streets, with the rear of the procession assembled at the hall at Third and Spruce. The youngest lodges marched ahead of the older ones and the Grand Lodge came last, as usual. Specific instructions applied: Masons not affiliated with any lodge were not allowed to take part; each lodge of fifty or more members was led by a marshal who was to ensure order; lodges with fewer than fifty members were attached to others; a space of two feet was kept between the files at all times during the march; and strict dress regulations were enforced. A new feature was the arrangement of the participants by height to give a more uniform appearance. A grand marshal led the whole procession, and the Grand Master and Grand Sword Bearer took up the rear. Twelve military bands were dispersed throughout.

Beginning at nine o'clock in the morning the Masons marched by a long and circuitous route along Pine Street from Third to Broad, then to Spruce, then to Twelfth, then to Walnut and then into Independence Square, between Fifth and Sixth Streets, where a special public ceremony took place at about noon. This included a prayer, two Masonic odes, a selection from Haydn's "Creation," Handel's "Hallelujah Chorus," an oration on Masonry, and a benediction. The oration, by Dr. James King, Past Master of Lodge No. 219, Pittsburgh, was instructive and, perhaps because of the audience, comprehensive. It offered a brief history of the Craft in Pennsylvania and its meeting places, drew patriotic allusions, defended the building of the hall, explained the complementary relationship between Freemasonry and Christianity, cautioned against the wrong kinds of members, and elucidated Masonic virtues and their benefits to society. As with other Masonic addresses of the period, it stressed charity:

> We believe that it will tend to refine the feelings, improve the manners, elevate the moral conduct, and smooth the asperities of life; that in the comforts it will impart, and the substantial blessings it will diffuse, by supplying the wants of the needy, relieving the sufferings of the distressed, and cheering the hearts of the desolate and lonely . . . .

Afterward, in the same order, the Masons marched around the square and exited by a rear gate. They then marched east on Walnut Street to Fifth, then to Arch, then to Seventeenth, then to Chestnut and on to the new hall.

Because of the distance covered—over fifty city blocks—the procession lasted several hours, and it was viewed by thousands of Philadelphians. The streets were "densely crowded, and bright eyes beamed from every window along the route." Public interest was encouraged because the day was a sort of unofficial holiday. Law courts, government offices, banks, shops and businesses were all closed: "The Masonic family . . . seemed to have enchanted the whole city, and for one day of vacation from all the common pursuits of life, to monopolize the public eye and attention." The procession was so impressive that even the Masons were at a loss for words: "It is almost impossible to give a description of the splendid appearance of the Brethren thus assembled — it was truly a magnificent sight, and worthy [of] the occasion." A non-Masonic source reported: "The scene was replete with life, gaiety and interest." Once in the hall, the regular Masonic dedication ceremony took place in the

Grand Lodge Room on the second floor. This was accompanied by three more prayers, an invocation, a grand march, two more Masonic odes, a repetition of Handel's "Hallelujah Chorus" and another choral piece by Haydn. Because Masonic regulations allowed only Past Masters to sit in Grand Lodge members of subordinate lodges did not participate. Instead, they filed through the first floor of the hall, exited by the rear door, and were dismissed. The ceremonies in the Grand Lodge Room continued until about four o'clock.

At seven o'clock in the evening a Masonic feast "of every luxury the season could afford, or refined taste array" was held in the banquet room. Because of space limitations attendance was by invitation only. Masonic officials from other jurisdictions participated, especially those from Massachusetts, the second most important American grand lodge. Even an Iroquois Mason was present, and he spoke about Freemasonry among American Indians. Many toasts were offered and responded to in extemporaneous addresses: "some excellent speeches were made, and when the windows of the soul were once opened, a flood of eloquence came down." The day ended "at a late hour."

What is significant about these ceremonies is that the Masons now felt sufficiently secure to parade through the city in public view. They also chose a prominent place, Independence Square, to present the major part of the program, the Masonic oration. This had never been done before in Pennsylvania. It was also unusual was that the address was delivered by a Pittsburgh Mason. The new temple of Freemasonry was thereby symbolized as a benefit to all Pennsylvania Masons, not just those near Philadelphia. The presence of many Masons from other states — about two hundred — is further indication of the broadened interest of the Pennsylvania Grand Lodge.[35]

The New Masonic Hall on Chestnut Street made a deep impression on both Masons and non-Masons alike. It was described as "one of the most imposing structures in the city" and "the most gorgeous Masonic Temple probably in the world — and certainly the most splendid in the Union." The facade, in Neo-Gothic brownstone, was enhanced by stained-glass windows and was higher than most other buildings on Chestnut Street; the finials of the central tower were one hundred forty feet above the pavement. The building took up the whole lot (101 by 178 ft.), except about nine feet, evenly divided between the north and south. A ninety-square-foot area between the front of the stores, which comprised the entire first floor, and the front of the second floor was covered with skylights to provide the stores with light and air. A large stairway was centered inside the main entrance. On the first landing the cornerstone of the first hall erected on that site and a stone commemorating the new hall were embedded in the wall.

The New Masonic Hall on Chestnut Street (1855-1873). Broadside (Grand Lodge of Pennsylvania).

The staircase led into a conversation room (42 by 25 ft.) from which stairs led to the third floor. To the west was the Grand Lodge Room (78 by 42 ft., with a 32-ft.-high ceiling), which had a visitor's gallery at the west end over four smaller rooms that increased its length to nearly one hundred feet. The Grand Lodge Room was richly decorated with all manner of gilding, frescoes, elaborately-carved officer's chairs, upholstered sofas, plush carpeting and crystal and bronze chandeliers. The room also contained six statues of Masonic virtues by famed Philadelphia sculptor, Joseph A. Bailly. They were entitled "Faith," "Hope," "Charity," "Wisdom," "Beauty," and "Strength." In sum, it was an apartment whose "gorgeous splendor has no equal in the city."

Grand Lodge Room of the New Chestnut Street Hall circa 1860. From an old photograph (Grand Lodge of Pennsylvania).

The Blue Lodge Room (56 by 30 ft.), on the second floor in the rear of the building was also richly decorated; the highlight was the placement of three of William Rush's statues, "Faith," "Hope" and "Charity," originally commissioned for the reconstructed hall of 1820. The second floor also contained a banquet room (76 by 33 ft.) with kitchen, a Tyler's room

(72 by 10 ft.), a Grand Master's room (31 by 21 ft.), a Grand Secretary's room (31 by 21 ft.), various anterooms and connecting rooms, and apartments for the residence of the Grand Tyler. A half-story over a portion of the second floor contained four committee rooms and a regalia room. The third story contained a Chapter room (78 by 30 ft.), an oval Encampment room (43 by 31 ft.), a regalia room (58 by 12 ft.), another Tyler's room (31 by 21 ft.) and more anterooms and connecting rooms.[36]

When the new hall was finally completed and furnished six months later, the Grand Lodge discovered that it had cost the staggering sum of $183,000. Ultimately the Fraternity was able to meet this obligation without too much difficulty because of its prospering financial position. By the end of 1855, for example, the entire first Masonic loan had been subscribed, the stores on the lower story had been rented, renewed efforts were under way to sell the Third Street hall, and a balance remained in the operating account. Some Masons were concerned that subscriptions to the new Masonic loan of $50,000 were not coming in quickly enough, but they realized that the total amount would not be required.[37]

"Charity" & "Wisdom" by Joseph A. Bailly. The first was carved for Washington Hall and the second for the New Masonic Hall on Chestnut Street (Grand Lodge of Pennsylvania).

The New Masonic Hall was a reflection of the recent fortunes of Pennsylvania Freemasonry. In only fifteen years the Fraternity had progressed from a persecuted minority to a publicly accepted institution. In the enthusiastic words of Grand Master James Hutchinson:

> The successful completion of this structure, besides being self-evident proof of the present prosperity of the Craft, demonstrates the indestructible vitality of Masonry, which through the unflinching fidelity of good men and true, and the guidance of an all-kind Providence, has been able to endure the severe trials of fanatic persecution, to silence and to survive hatred, envy and malice, and even to bring into its charitable folds, and cause to kneel at its altars, its thoughtless slanderers and repentant defamers, thus shedding its benignant rays into thousands of hearts, whose constant offerings on the shrine of Charity and brotherly love are already adding new lustre to its everlasting light and glory.[38]

*   *   *   *   *   *   *   *

In the period of recovery the Grand Lodge of Pennsylvania warranted a total of one hundred lodges, three-quarters of them after 1847 (Table 2). During the years of decline of the Antimasonic movement the subordinate lodges were still unsteady. In fact, the number of functioning lodges dipped to thirty-five in 1841, the lowest since the 1790s, and no new lodges were established until September 1843 (No. 218, Wayne Co.). A noticeable upturn did not occur until the late 1840s, and not until the early 1850s did the number of lodges in operation equal that before 1826. Most of the new organzations were country lodges, but the highest concentration, or twelve percent, was still to be found in Philadelphia (Table 3, Figure 1). Only three other counties (Allegheny, Luzerne, Schuylkill) had more than two or three new lodges. Since only ten percent of the subordinate lodges ceased, the record of this period as a whole was highly successful.

But the clearest evidence of the recovery of Pennsylvania Freemasonry can be found in the membership statistics from this period (see Appendix H). Between 1840 and 1855 a total of sixteen thousand men were either initiated or admitted into the Fraternity. In no other similar time span had so many new men joined. As with the numbers of lodges, real growth in membership did not take place until the early 1840s, and cumulative membership did not exceed that of 1826 until 1849. This data clearly indicates that it took more than twenty years for the Masonic Fraternity in Pennsylvania to recover fully from the devastating effects of the Antimasonic movement. Large numbers of new men did not join until the early 1850s, when the Fraternity once again opened itself to public view. Activities such as the reburial of Stephen Girard in 1851, the laying of the cornerstone of the new Chestnut Street hall in 1853, and

TABLE 2
Pennsylvania Freemasonry Revived, 1840-1855

Years	Number of new or revived lodges (lodge numbers)		Number of ceased lodges (lodge numbers)
1840-1847	27	(21a, 61a, 70a, 75a, 81a, 82a, 106a, 108a, 134a, 141a, 143a, 144a, 148a, 163a, 164a, 194a, 197a, 199a, 203a, 218, 219, 220-225)	8 (81, 82a, 102, 113, 119, 128, 141a, 160)
1848-1855	73	(25b, 126a, 131a, 156a, 226-256, 258-292, 294-296)	2 (148a, 201)
Totals	100	Net: +90	10 (10.0%)

Lodges in Operation by the End of the Year

Year	Number of Lodges	Year	Number of Lodges
1840	37	1848	68
1841	35*	1849	73
1842	37	1850	85
1843	40	1851	90
1844	42	1852	100
1845	45	1853	116
1846	52	1854	126
1847	57	1855	128

*This marks the low point of the period from 1826-1855.

The first new lodge warranted after the Antimasonic period was No. 218, Wayne County, on September 4, 1843.

Lodge No. 257 and No. 293 were warranted, but not constituted.

A number with an "a" appended indicates a lodge revived more than a year after suspension. Such revived lodges are treated as though they were new organizations.

Lodges that revived within a year of ceasing are not considered to be failed lodges; their suspension was only temporary.

The origins of new lodges are based upon their constitution dates.

Lodges "ceased" in basically two ways: by voluntary surrender of the warrant by the members or by order of the Grand Lodge. Various terms were used to describe such warrants: "surrendered," "returned," "vacated," or "ceased."

Sources: Joshua L. Lyte, comp., *Reprint of the Minutes of the Grand Lodge of Pennsylvania* (Phila., 1895-1907), Vol. VII, *1840-1848,* Vol. VIII, *1849-1854;* Vol. IX, *1855-1858;* "Information Pertaining to Early Freemasonry in the Western Hemisphere, Including the Warrant and Constitution Dates of the Subordinate Lodges under the Provincial and Present Grand Lodge of F. and A.M. of Pennsylvania" (unpublished list); Charles E. Meyer, *Masonic Lodges in Pennsylvania from 1730 to 1880, "Moderns" and "Ancients"* (Phila., n.d.); Register of Members, Vol. 2-1, 1795-1855; Vol. 2-2, 1818-1855; Vol. 3-1, 1854-1865; Vol. 3-2, 1854-1865.

TABLE 3
Geographical Distribution of Pennsylvania Lodges, 1840-1855

County	Number of new or revived lodges (lodge numbers)	(%)	Number of ceased lodges (lodge numbers)	(%)
Allegheny	8 (219, 221, 223, 231, 253, 269, 287, 288)	8.0	1 (113)	10.0
Armstrong	2 (239, 244)	2.0		
Beaver	2 (229, 259)	2.0		
Berks	1 (227)	1.0		
Blair	3 (220, 281, 282)	3.0		
Bradford	2 (163a, 280)	2.0		
Bucks	2 (25b, 245)	2.0		
Butler	1 (272)	1.0		
Cambria	1 (278)	1.0		
Carbon	1 (242)	1.0		
Centre	1 (268)	1.0		
Chester	1 (75a)	1.0		
Clarion	1 (277)	1.0		
Columbia	1 (265)	1.0		
Crawford	2 (234, 258)	2.0		
Cumberland	2 (197a, 260)	2.0		
Dauphin	2 (21a, 141a)	2.0	1 (141a)	10.0
Delaware	2 (236, 273)	2.0		
Erie	1 (235)	1.0		
Fayette	2 (228, 252)	2.0		
Franklin	1 (262)	1.0		
Greene	1 (279)	1.0		
Jefferson	1 (276)	1.0		
Lancaster	2 (156a, 286)	2.0		
Lawrence	1 (243)	1.0		
Lebanon	1 (226)	1.0		
Lehigh	1 (284)	1.0		
Luzerne	7 (61a, 108a, 70a, 233, 249, 261, 291)	7.0	1 (119)	10.0
Lycoming	3 (106a, 199a, 232)	3.0		
Mercer	3 (250, 251, 290)	3.0		
Mifflin	1 (203a)	1.0		
Montgomery	1 (254)	1.0		
Montour	1 (283)	1.0		
Northampton	1 (283)	1.0	1 (201)	10.0
Northumberland	4 (144a, 148a, 255, 256)	4.0	1 (148a)	10.0

(Continued on next page)

TABLE 3 *(Cont.)*

County	Number of new or revived lodges (lodge numbers)	(%)	Number of ceased lodges (lodge numbers)	(%)
Philadelphia	12 (81a, 126a, 134a, 131a, 230, 246, 271, 274, 289, 292, 295, 296)	12.0	4 (81, 102, 128, 160)	40.0
Schuylkill	6 (222, 238, 267, 270, 285, 294)	6.0		
Susquehanna	1 (240)	1.0		
Tioga	1 (247)	1.0		
Union	1 (194a)	1.0		
Warren	2 (241, 264)	2.0		
Washington	3 (143a, 164a, 237)	3.0		
Wayne	2 (82a, 218)	2.0	1 (82a)	10.0
Westmoreland	2 (225, 275)	2.0		
Wyoming	2 (248, 263)	2.0		
York	1 (266)	1.0		
Totals	100	100.0	10	100.0

Sources: Joshua L. Lyte, comp., *Reprint of the Minutes of the Grand Lodge of Pennsylvania* (Phila., 1895-1907), Vol. VII, *1840-1848*, Vol. VIII, *1849-1854;* Vol. IX, *1855-1858;* "Information Pertaining to Early Freemasonry in the Western Hemisphere, Including the Warrant and Constitution Dates of the Subordinate Lodges under the Provincial and Present Grand Lodge of F. and A.M. of Pennsylvania" (unpublished list); Charles E. Meyer, *Masonic Lodges in Pennsylvania from 1730 to 1880, "Moderns" and "Ancients"* (Phila., n.d.); Register of Members, Vol. 2-1, 1795-1855; Vol. 2-2, 1818-1855; Vol. 3-1, 1854-1865; Vol. 3-2, 1854-1865.

FIGURE 1
Masonic Lodges in Pennsylvania, 1840-1855

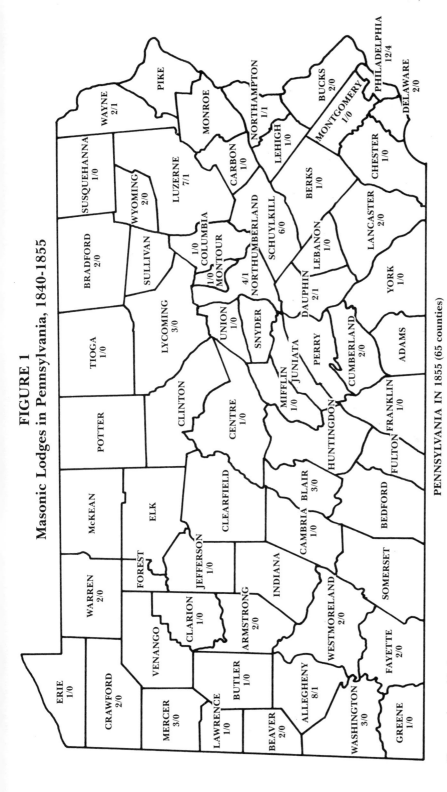

PENNSYLVANIA IN 1855 (65 counties)

Key: new/ceased lodges
Totals: 100/10   Net: +90

Sources: Joshua L. Lyte, comp., *Reprint of the Minutes of the Grand Lodge of Pennsylvania* (Phila., 1895-1907), Vol. VII, *1840-1848*, Vol. VIII, *1849-1854*; Vol. IX, *1855-1858*; "Information Pertaining to Early Freemasonry in the Western Hemisphere, Including the Warrant and Constitution Dates of the Subordinate Lodges under the Provincial and Present Grand Lodge of F. and A.M. of Pennsylvania" (unpublished list); Charles E. Meyer, *Masonic Lodges in Pennsylvania from 1730 to 1880*, "Moderns" and "Ancients" (Phila., n.d.); *Register of Members*, Vol. 2-1, 1795-1855; Vol. 2-2, 1818-1855; Vol. 3-1, 1854-1865; Vol. 3-2, 1854-1865.

the offering of public tours of the building and the dedication cermonies of 1855, substantially increased outside interest. As a whole, cumulative membership from 1826 to 1855 increased by about sixty-five percent, the growth of Philadelphia lodges being somewhat more dramatic than that of country lodges (73.7% versus 56.7%).

Occupational information is available on nearly eighteen thousand (87.9%) of the men who joined the Fraternity between 1826 and 1855 (see Appendix H). These members had more than two hundred fifty separate occupations. As in previous periods of Masonic history, no single occupational category outnumbered any others. As a whole, artisans (29.4%) represented the most numerous occupational group. They were followed by individuals engaged in trade and commerce (16.1%) and in professional service (14.6%). The most numerous single occupation was that of merchant (12.6%). These statistics are consistent among both city and country lodges. Even in rural areas most Masons were artisans of one type or another (27.8%), professionals (16.8%), or involved in trade and commerce (13.9%); only about twelve percent of them were engaged in agriculture.

Regardless of their occupation, most men who became Masons in this period probably were fairly well-to-do economically. The average entrance fee of the city lodges in the 1840s was between $25 and $30; in the 1850s they jumped to $40 to $50. Country lodges charged less, between $25 and $30 during both decades. Dues averaged about $6.00 per year for city lodges and about half that for country lodges. These fees were relatively high, considering that unskilled laborers in Philadelphia in the 1850s were paid about $1.00 per day and skilled workers about $1.50.[39]

Men who became Masons in this period were generally young at the time of their admission, but most were well beyond the minimun age of 21 years. In both city and country lodges, the average age on admission of about fifteen thousand persons from 1826 to 1855 for whom data is available, was about 32 years, although they ranged from 21 years upward. Several dozen men were older than sixty-five; one was 83 years old when he became a Mason. The average age was a few years higher than that of earlier periods, probably because of postponing applications of admission during the Antimasonic period and because of economic conditions. Establishing oneself economically was a higher priority than membership in a voluntary association.[40]

The Masons wanted men of solid backgrounds, but that was not all; in this, as in all periods, acceptance was conditioned upon an individual's possessing high moral qualities. Even at a time when the Fraternity had not yet fully recovered from a severe loss of membership, its leaders would not compromise on this point. To quote Grand Master Bournonville in 1853:

Masonry does not gain by the accession of members, unless they bring with them high moral and religious character, intelligence, and disposition to sacrifice upon its shrine every motive of selfishness and every object of self-interest. As every rude and unfinished block detracts from the symmetry, beauty and strength of the most costly structure, even so does every false or unfaithful worshipper on the altars of Masonry detract from its perfect lineaments, and endanger the harmony, stability and perpetuity of the whole. Let me therefore, my brethren, entreat of you to be cautious, judicious, circumspective and firm in permitting those from without to enter this inner temple.[41]

Even with its membership requirements of steady employment, physical perfection, and moral character, and despite residual public hostility engendered by the Antimasonic movement, Pennsylvania Freemasonry flourished in the 1840s and early 1850s. Over the next twenty years its prosperity and appeal would rise to unprecedented levels.

CHAPTER 8:

The Master Builders, 1856-1873

The Pennsylvania Masonic Fraternity entered a brief period of general tranquillity in the years immediately following the dedication of the New Masonic Hall on Chestnut Street. No major projects or pressing internal problems disrupted its steady growth or challenged the firm guidance of the Grand Lodge. Most of the innovations at this time aimed at refining the administration of the increasingly complex organization. The Grand Lodge supervised scores of new subordinate lodges, maintained stricter discipline among its members, encouraged more thorough Masonic education, carefully monitored its financial situation, and heard many appeals from aggrieved Masons, rejected candidates and expelled members. In particular, the last-mentioned function took on greater importance than ever before. So many cases arose that a new standing committee, on appeals, was established in 1856. According to the Rules and Regulations, a Brother was required to submit his complaint to arbitration within the Masonic system, no matter what it was, instead of seeking redress in the civil courts. Although hundreds of appeals were decided in this period, there is no record that any member was dissatisfied with the ultimate disposition of his case.[1]

Appeals of lodges also significantly increased, and these were handled by the Committee of Finance, if they pertained to money, by the Committee on By-Laws, if they concerned procedures, or by the Grand Lodge meeting as a committee of the whole, for other matters. Issues included disputed elections of officers, questionable practices in balloting for candidates, granting of dispensations, and proper conduct of meetings. Mostly, however, they were requests for remission of dues. Lodges were short of funds for a variety of reasons: too many charitable demands upon them; members unwilling or unable to to meet their obligations; the use of money for building new lodge halls; the destruction of records and lodge paraphernalia by floods and fires; or officers absconding with lodge funds.

Perhaps the most dramatic of these cases was that of Lodge No. 216, Pottsville, which in June 1858 could not pay its dues because of "malfeasance of certain officers. Some [money] has been recovered but the remainder will in all probability be lost, the defaulter having failed in business . . . [and is] now a confirmed and hopeless lunatic." With the exception of building new lodge halls, not considered an emergency, the Committee of Finance routinely granted temporary remission of dues or offered loans to the subordinate lodges to help them through troubled times.[2]

Because of its more extensive responsibilities the Grand Lodge needed to refine its procedures. In March 1856, upon the urging of Grand Master Peter Williamson, stricter adherence to the regulations concerning the conduct of monthly business was instituted. Meetings were now run in more orderly fashion. They opened with the reading of the minutes of earlier meetings, and this was followed by petitions and communications, reports of standing committees, reports of special committees, general returns of subordinate lodges, unfinished business and new business. Meetings were not to last beyond ten o'clock in the evening. The Grand Master reserved the right to call as many special meetings of the Grand Lodge as necessary to deal adequately with the workload. This reform did not result in an increase in the number of meetings per year, as might be expected, but rather facilitated the handling of business at the regular meetings.[3]

One of the major refinements in this period was the publication of a new edition of the *Ahiman Rezon* to replace that of 1825. For many years the Grand Lodge had distributed the older edition, but by the mid-1850s so many changes had occurred in the organization and so many questions remained unanswered that the Masons realized the need for a new version of the work. At the end of 1855, at the recommendation of Grand Master Hutchinson, a committee was formed to revise the constitution. Throughout 1856 and 1857 the committee acted in a diligent and thorough manner and frequently submitted its work for review to the Grand Lodge as a whole. In June 1857, after having heard the revision section by section, the Grand Lodge approved the new edition, and it was printed and distributed in early September. Originally two thousand copies were produced, but this number was soon increased by a thousand. Copies were offered to subordinate lodges and to Holy Royal Arch Chapters free of charge, and additional copies were sold privately to members at a modest price. Compared to the debt incurred by the Fraternity in erecting its new meeting place, the cost of the *Ahiman Rezon* was low, just over $800. The work proved to be of great benefit.[4]

The new edition of this essential Pennsylvania Masonic work was different from its predecessor of 1825. It was simplified and straightforward—the charming descriptions and rhetorical flourishes of forty years earlier were deleted—and the length of the book was reduced by more than one hundred pages. The usual sections on the composition and functions of the Grand Lodge and the subordinate lodges, the duties of officers and standing committees, the ceremonial aspects of the Fraternity and the proper forms for submitting membership information were included. Notable by its absence, however, was the informative historical survey of Freemasonry in Great Britain and the United States, which had augmented most earlier versions. An important new section was entitled "Decisions of the Grand Lodge," a compilation of legislative acts passed since 1825 on a number of issues. These issues included charity, election of officers, selection of members, process of appeals, revival of lodges, requests for remission of dues, Masonic publications, organization of Masonic districts, and relations with other jurisdictions, among others.[5]

An important new piece of legislation concerned dress and regalia, which were standardized for the first time in Pennsylvania. This measure stemmed from a committee's observation, originally made in June 1852:

> [We] find a great want of uniformity to exist among the various Lodges; there being the most marked differences in the shape, color, and materials of the collars and aprons in use, and in the form of jewels worn by Past Masters. The result of which is to produce a very motley appearance in the Grand Lodge, and greatly to enhance the price for which the same article could be procured . . . .

The new legislation standardized aprons and jewels for each rank and office with no allowance for personal preferences. Entered Apprentices were to wear a plain white lambskin apron, fourteen to sixteen inches wide and twelve to fourteen inches deep, without ornament and with white strings. Fellow Crafts wore the same, with sky-blue rosettes at the bottom and blue strings. Master Masons' aprons had a sky blue lining, one to one and a half inches deep, an additional rosette and silver tassles. Blue Lodge officers wore the symbols of their office in silver or white in the center of their aprons. The Master's apron was even more elaborate, with perpendicular and horizontal lines at the bottom, in place of the rosettes, to form three sets of two right angles each. The appropriate jewels for the various officers were as follows: Master, the square; Past Master, the square and the diagram of the forty-seventh proposition of Euclid; Senior Warden, the level; Junior Warden, the plumb; Treasurer, the cross keys; Secretary, the cross pens; Deacons, the dove; Masters of Ceremony, the cross rods; Tyler, the sword. All jewels were to be of silver and suspended from the neck by a light blue ribbon. The emblems of the sun and the five-pointed star, previously adopted by Past Masters, were strictly reserved for the use of Grand Lodge officers.[6]

An important Pennsylvania Masonic tradition initiated in the late 1850s was the commissioning of portraits of Past Grand Masters, which were to be hung in the Masonic Hall. This idea was first put forward in December 1856 by the Committee of Correspondence in its annual report of its dealings with other jurisdictions. The committee had noticed with great interest that the Grand Lodge of Massachusetts had recently secured portraits of over twenty of its Grand Masters, covering a period of eighty-five years. The committee recommended that Pennsylvania should "go and do likewise." It urged prompt action because fifteen, or half, of the Grand Masters of the "Ancient" Pennsylvania Grand Lodge were still alive. The Grand Lodge considered this a good idea and with unaccustomed speed established a special committee for that purpose.

The committee set to work immediately and had a plan within a year. This committee also considered the project to be "eminently desirable" despite the "great perseverance, large sacrifice of time and patience, and much personal toil" which it would entail and it advised prompt action. The committee suggested that all living Past Grand Masters be immediately photographed by a local Mason, Washington Lafayette Germon, who employed artists to render the photographs into oils. Likenesses of all deceased Grand Masters were believed to exist and, when located, would also be submitted to Germon's artists. The committee recommended a seated half-length pose, thirty by forty inches, which would reduce cost, but allow the wearer's collar and jewel to be shown.

The cost of hiring well-known professional artists to paint the portraits was deemed unacceptably high. The committee had in mind the notable Philadelphia portrait artist, John Neagle, who had been commissioned some years before to paint a full-length portrait of Stephen Girard. Neagle had charged $100, exclusive of the frame. Presumably this was a fair price, perhaps even low because Neagle was a Mason, but the cost of thirty such portraits would have been prohibitive. Germon's price was $60 each, a $10 discount from his usual prices, with $25 to $30 for the frame. The portraits of deceased Past Grand Masters would be more difficult to do because these men could not be referred to for certain nuances not brought out by photographs; such paintings would cost slightly more. The total cost, including frames and all contingencies, was estimated at $3,000 to $3,500. In addition to providing a high-quality product at bargain rates, another advantage was uniformity in size and execution. In order to convince the Grand Lodge, the committee had already commissioned portraits of two living Past Grand Masters, Samuel Badger and Samuel H. Perkins, as well as of Deputy Grand Master John K. Mitchell. These portraits were presented with the committee's report. Both the subjects and Grand Lodge officers were pleased with the results, and the project was approved.

Although Germon and his artists set to work promptly, progress was much slower than anticipated. Not until mid-1867 were the portraits of thirty Past Grand Masters completed. All followed the same formula of presentation: the subjects were seated with their hands and jewels positioned in the same way, and most of them had one arm resting on a table. Even the portraits of the deceased Past Grand Masters, which had been copied from surviving likenesses, were arranged in the same fashion. Thereafter, the Fraternity routinely had photographs taken and portraits painted of sitting Grand Masters. The Grand Lodge considered this to be an appropriate way to honor the memory of its leaders and to show respect for the past.[7]

The Committee of Correspondence, from which the idea of the portraits originated, became more important in the late 1850s than ever before. The number of men serving on it was increased and its duties were expanded. Its main responsibility was to receive, read, answer and file communications from other Grand Lodges, mostly from within the United States, but occasionally from other countries as well. This burdensome task involved the examination of thousands of pages of documents per year. The committee made comprehensive annual reports to the Grand Lodge that summarized the activities of other jurisdictions and cataloged the committee's reactions to them. Often going beyond objective relaying of information, these reports often provided a vehicle for issuing policy statements.

The increased activity of the Committee of Correspondence indicated that the Pennsylvania Grand Lodge was beginning to lose its traditional insularity in favor of an active interest in the affairs of the Order as a whole. The Fraternity tried to have it both ways, however, namely to become involved in the affairs of other jurisdictions when the security of Freemasonry was threatened or its landmarks were challenged, but otherwise to remain aloof and independent. Pennsylvania Masons were imbued with a strong sense of mission and regarded themselves as the guardians of truth, the opponents of innovation and the preservers of unity. These attitudes frequently led to discord between the Pennsylvania Grand Lodge and those of other states.

Shortly after midcentury numerous disputes and disagreements occurred. Some of these were minor, such as those with the Grand Lodge of New Jersey, which complained that subordinate Pennsylvania lodges were taking members from the southern and eastern part of that state, and with the Grand Lodge of Maryland, which was doing the same thing with Pennsylvania Masons. Other complaints were serious, such as the issue of periodic Masonic conventions, which the Grand Lodge of Pennsylvania had resisted consistently for eighty years. In late 1860, and again two years later, the Grand Lodge decried further attempts to organize a supervisory national Masonic body. A related proposal was the suggested establishment of a permanent system of representation between American and European grand lodges. Pennsylvania Masons found both these ideas unacceptable because, if implemented, they would seriously impinge upon the sovereignty of each grand lodge, a principle of Masonic law they considered paramount. An added objection was the great difference in methods of operation between American and European Freemasonry.

Another major issue concerned Masonic publications, which were appearing more and more frequently throughout the United States. The Grand Lodge of Pennsylvania refused to sanction the printing of any Masonic information other than its own official *Ahiman Rezon* and *Proceedings,* which were intended for the use of the Fraternity's faithful members. In the opinion of the Committee of Correspondence, other Masonic works were improperly motivated and the cause of much evil: "they are often unauthorized, crude, without much value, aimless or purposeless, as teaching Masonic knowledge, and not deserving of the prominence and importance too often attached to them . . . ."

In this period the Grand Lodge had a problem of its own with an unauthorized periodical entitled the *Masonic Mirror and Keystone,* edited and published by Leon Hyneman, Past Master of Frankford Lodge, No. 292. Appearing weekly from January 1852, this journal was "devoted to the diffusion of Masonic intelligence, literature, the fine arts, etc." It dealt with a great variety of subject matter, in both poetry and prose; discussions of Freemasonry made up only a portion of its offerings. With "more than fifteen hundred of the most intelligent Craftsmen" as subscribers, Hyneman's journal enjoyed wide appeal and contributed to a fuller understanding of the Fraternity. Despite this success, however, the *Masonic Mirror* met with strenuous resistance from the Grand Lodge. During 1859 and 1860, in an attempt to gain support for "the onward progress of an enlightened sentiment," Hyneman frequently editorialized against the organization's conservatism and "obfuscation." This did nothing to influence the Grand Lodge in his favor, and Hyneman was censured in September 1860. By the end of the year he had ceased publication of the journal. In assessing this case, the Committee on Appeals commented: ". . . the tone of the publication was offensive, derogatory to the Order and in violation of Masonic usage. No good can possibly arise from said public notice of Masonic proceedings, but much harm. [We] recommend that the Grand Lodge positively prohibit all such publications."

Such recommendations were not limited to Pennsylvania, and the Grand Lodge frequently denounced similar works appearing in other jurisdictions. Understandably, other grand lodges objected to what amounted to interference in their domestic affairs. The Grand Lodge of Vermont, for example, accused Pennsylvania Masons of deliberately choosing to labor in darkness. To this particular charge, the Committee of Correspondence responded:

. . . we need hardly be called to account, and charged with blissful ignorance and stupidity, because we are in such darkness as not to see the feeble light emanating from every individual, who catches "the infection" of writing and publishing, "dissertations" on "Masonic ethics, or literature," neither of which he may be able to comprehend nor explain.

The Grand Lodge of Texas also entered the controversy and sided with Vermont. It had some unflattering things to say about the chairman of the Pennsylvania Committee of Correspondence:

We are inclined to think that Bro. Vaux is an 'old fogey.' Now, there are two kinds of old fogies, those who have their eyes open, and those who are blind; and a blind old fogey is quite as apt to be wrong as right. He opposes everything that appears to him new, on general principles, and had Bro. Vaux, who we are inclined to regard as one of these, lived in the first part of the 18th century, and his way of thinking prevailed, we doubt if even Anderson's Constitutions would ever have seen the light. To say that [such writers and works] have injured the cause of Masonry is ridiculous.

Needless to say, Pennsylvania Masons regarded these opinions as "neither fraternal, Masonic nor respectful" and the ephithets used as "unbecoming and inexcusable." No progress was made in this period toward a resolution of differences.

The Pennsylvania Grand Lodge also incurred the displeasure of other Masonic bodies throughout the country by declining to support, for financial reasons, three important projects: the purchase of Washington's estate by the Mount Vernon Ladies Association, the completion of the Washington Monument, and the establishment of the American Masonic Home, a national institution for widows and orphans of Masons. Other jurisdictions questioned Pennsylvania's patriotism, challenged its devotion to American Freemasonry and impugned its honor. The Committee of Correspondence responded to its critics with evidence of its commitment to such causes and indignantly declared that patriotism could not be measured by money.

Another issue was the status of the Grand Lodge of Canada, which had been formed in 1856 by local lodges warranted by the several grand lodges of the British Isles. It was two years until this body was recognized by American and European grand lodges. The Grand Lodge of England was one of these, but it accepted the new organization only to a limited extent. It did not allow the Grand Lodge of Canada complete territorial jurisdiction, but reserved supervision of some lodges for itself. From the beginning the Grand Lodge of Pennsylvania considered the circumstances under which its Canadian counterpart had been formed to be revolutionary and unmasonic, and therefore refused to recognize it. Even after other grand lodges had accepted the Canadians, the Pennsylvania Grand Lodge still withheld recognition on the grounds that, according to Masonic law, there could be no shared sovereignty in one geographical area. It adhered to this position until late 1861, by which time Canadian Masons had worked out most of their differences and had established a united Masonic body.[8]

The most important issue of the 1850s was a serious Masonic schism in New York. It began in June 1849 when a dispute over membership arose within the Grand Lodge of New York which, fired by personal antagonisms, mushroomed into a full-scale revolt against the leadership that lasted nearly two decades. For a short time three grand lodges were actually operating in New York, each claiming to be the sole legitimate Masonic authority in that state.

At first the Pennsylvania Committee on Correspondence made only passing reference to the dispute, and it routinely condemned both parties for disrupting Masonic unity. In time, however, the Grand Lodge of Pennsylvania became more and more concerned about the New York situation, and it used increasingly stronger language against the New York Masons. According to the Pennsylvanians, the controversy was characterized by a "vulgarity of tone" that "inspired the Brethren throughout the whole world with grief and astonishment, if not disgust," and damaged the public image of the Fraternity. Although still officially neutral nine months after the schism began, the Pennsylvania Grand Lodge was strongly inclined to recognize as legitimate only the original Grand Lodge of New York, headed by John D. Willard, as opposed to the schismatic Grand Lodge, led by Isaac Phillips. After conducting an investigation, a special committee formed to gather information favored the so-called "Willard Grand Lodge" in April 1850. The committee's conservatism was evident in its proposed official communication to the New York Masons: ". . . the power of the Grand Master, clothed with the insignia of his high office, while sitting in open Grand Lodge is supreme, and no power can supersede him . . . . the proceedings of the dissatisfied Brethren . . . was [sic] highly improper, mistaken and reprehensible." The resolution urged and encouraged the New York Masons to heal their own wounds.

The committee was ordered to gather more information before the resolution would be considered. For the remainder of 1850 Pennsylvania Masons became increasingly more concerned about the situation in New York and its potential damage to the unity and reputation of the Fraternity. Special communications were held frequently, and Grand Lodge members began to disagree among themselves once they learned more specifics of the dispute. The resolution in favor of the Willard Grand Lodge was reconsidered and defeated, as was another that proposed the direct intervention of the Pennsylvania Grand Lodge. Meeting after meeting on this issue ended without agreement. Even Grand Master Whitney's advocacy of recognition of the Willard Grand Lodge in his annual message in December did not break the impasse among Pennsylvania Masons. Word of possible intervention reached the original New York Grand Lodge, which condemned such action as unmasonic and unauthorized.

Another issue between the two jurisdictions concerned the practice of subordinate Pennsylvania lodges admitting as visitors New York Masons who either were members of or had been expelled from one of the rival New York Grand Lodges. This practice was regarded as tacit recognition of one body or the other, depending upon the preference of the particular subordinate lodge. These disputes were too intense and too complicated to be resolved quickly, and Pennsylvania Masons seem to have given up trying, although more investigative committees were appointed and additional reports were presented. Fortunately for the harmony of Pennsylvania Freemasonry, these concerns were overshadowed by the building of the new Chestnut Street hall.[9]

The New York Masonic schism was still unhealed, however, after the Grand Lodge was firmly established in its new building, and it became a major interest of Pennsylvania Masons for the next four years. In December 1855 Grand Master Hutchinson urged the Grand Lodge to arbitrate the dispute. He believed that the organization's highly respected status within the Fraternity generally, as well as its refusal to commit itself to one side or the other, would be conducive to such a role. At the January meeting the Grand Lodge unanimously agreed with these recommendations and approved the appointment of a special five-man committee with full decision-making powers. This matter was important enough to generate a previously unknown feeling of solidarity among the members and to involve the sitting Grand Master, Peter Williamson, as well as four Past Grand Masters, who made up the committee. The original New York Grand Lodge responded both promptly and favorably, on condition that the "rebel" Grand Lodge would agree to the same terms; the latter organization ignored the offer for most of the remainder of the year, however. When it finally did respond, after repeated efforts of the committee, the rebel Grand Lodge "discourteously declined" Pennsylvania's mediation. This response was so dismissive that the committee asked to be discharged and requested that the matter be referred back to the standing Committee on Correspondence.[20]

The Committee on Correspondence accordingly resumed its supervision of the affair, along with its usual annual review of Freemasonry in other "foreign" (non-Pennsylvania) jurisdictions. In December 1856 it issued a lengthy report on the New York schism that defended the Pennsylvania Grand Lodge's actions and condemned the unmasonic and unfraternal reaction it had met with among some New York Masons. The committee felt honor-bound to respond to serious charges such as the following leveled against its parent body:

> The Grand Lodge of Pennsylvania, as a body, is insular, exclusive, and peculiar. In different respects its exterior boundaries encircle a system of Masonry that is unknown in practice to any other jurisdiction in the United States. It knows not — or if it knows, it studies not, the wants, wishes, or opinions of its sister Grand Lodges in this country. In derision and contempt of the universal opinion and practices of the Grand Lodges of this country, it continues its supervision and control over other branches of Masonry, from which, in deference to their wishes, and to preserve harmony in the Masonic fold, it should have long since separated. Its course . . . has not only created party feuds among its own members, but has caused unpleasant discussion and irritation to the body of the fraternity and to the governing Masonic bodies of the Nation.

The committee argued against each charge in turn and defended the practices of Pennsylvania Freemasonry. The major differences between Pennsylvania and other jurisdictions were the following: Pennsylvania remained true to the spirit of the founders of Freemasonry, whereas other jursidictions experimented with new ritual and beliefs; Pennsylvania encouraged charity to a greater extent than other jurisdictions and did so quietly without fanfare, unlike others; and Pennsylvania firmly believed in the separateness of individual grand lodges, which would only be damaged by cooperative ventures in Masonic government. Contrary to the accusations, the Pennsylvania Grand Lodge became involved in the New York dispute because it was concerned with the condition of Freemasonry in the country. It had deliberately remained neutral so as not to prejudice achievement of a solution by New York Masons themselves. Its actions, the Grand Lodge asserted, had been disinterested throughout.

The committee also counterattacked, accusing New York Masons of hypocrisy in pointing a finger at Pennsylvania when they had spread disruptions and dissensions within Freemasonry in their own jurisdiction. The original dispute in New York had been caused by "disgraceful" scenes within a legal and properly assembled Grand Lodge meeting, including "cries and yells and imprecations" and the seizure of a box containing the funds of the Grand Lodge. In contrast, within the Grand Lodge of Pennsylvania one might "witness the dignified decorum prevading the whole — the mild and impartial government on the part of the presiding officers, and the cheerful and willing obedience of the subordinate officers and members . . . ." The committee also excused the acceptance of New York Masons, associated with one or the other of the Grand Lodges, into fellowship with Pennsylvania Masons on grounds that Grand Lodge officers initially did not know this was taking place, and that when it became known, some of them had advised against it. They had done this personally rather than in their official capacities, however. The Grand Lodge of Pennsylvania never passed a formal resolution of non-intercourse, although many New York Masons came to believe that it had.[11]

Although the committee's strong statement was undoubtedly well intended and, in the eyes of most Pennsylvania Masonic leaders, necessary to set the record straight, it was not diplomatic and did nothing to help smooth relations between the two jurisdictions. Matters became worse throughout 1857. The original New York Grand Lodge was offended because it naturally regarded itself as legitimate; when the Grand Lodge of Pennsylvania did not openly and immediately recognize it, as did other grand lodges, it judged that Pennsylvania was deliberately snubbing it. Since it believed, erroneously, that the Pennsylvania Grand Lodge had offically forbidden its subordinate lodges from dealing with New York Masons, the Grand Lodge of New York responded in kind, not out of bitterness, but because "a sense of self-respect leaves us no other alternative." Likewise, the rebel body passed resolutions of non-correspondence with Pennsylvania Masons and issued additional denunciations of the Pennsylvania Grand Lodge. Both New York Masonic bodies were offended at not being invited to participate in the dedication of the New Masonic Hall on Chestnut Street in 1855. At that time, to show no favoritism, Pennsylvania Masonic officials had decided not to invite either group. The result was the displeasure of both.

For a time the Grand Lodge of Missouri attempted to mediate between New York and Pennsylvania. Missouri Masons fully understood the motivations of their Pennsylvania Brethren and regarded their intentions as honorable. They believed that the Pennsylvanians were justified in taking offence at the "pretty severe lecture" they had received from New York, and they also appreciated how difficult it was at that time to be a New York Mason or even a visiting Mason in that jurisdiction. Nonetheless, Missouri Masons felt that the Pennsylvania Grand Lodge probably should not have become involved in the dispute and should have openly recognized the original Grand Lodge as the best means of restoring peace.

But Pennsylvania officials did nothing. By the end of 1857 members of the Committee on Correspondence were both frustrated and embarrassed:

> In both Grand bodies are many members whom we recognize [as] brothers and friends that we honor and love, but by no act of ours must we add new complications to the difficulties already existing between the par-

ties themselves, or between either of them and us. We can, therefore, only hope that the time is not far distant when all dissensions ceasing, peace and harmony and brotherly love will be restored to the entire jurisdiction of New York, and our own feelings, motives and wishes better understood and appreciated.

During the next year the committee issued more defenses of its conduct along previous lines, but its attitude softened as it came to regard the affair as a misunderstanding, albeit a major one. The committee continued to blame the New York Masons for it, however.

At this stage the dispute centered around two essential issues. The original New York Grand Lodge wanted formal recognition from the Pennsylvania Grand Lodge, and the Pennsylvania body wanted the New York Grand Lodge to repeal its resolution of non-intercourse. The long correspondence between various officials of both jurisdictions that ensued was marked by much diplomatic maneuvering and a contest of wills. Pennsylvania argued that New York had originated the dispute when its Grand Master issued his personal edict, followed by the formal resolution of non-intercourse. Normalization of relations could be restored only when these measures were rescinded.

On the other hand, New York argued that Pennsylvania had started the controversy by forbidding Masonic correspondence with New Yorkers. Although it was made clear to the New York Grand Lodge that this had not happened, the New Yorkers charged that, even though no formal resolution of non-intercourse had been passed, a de facto exclusion of New York Masons by Pennsylvania Masons was nonetheless in effect. This claim was based on personal statements by John K. Mitchell, both as Deputy Grand Master and as Grand Master, that New York Masons believed had the force of law. This unofficial, but effective, policy was held to be only the most significant of many "unfraternal and unfriendly" acts of Pennsylvania toward New York, all of which the New Yorkers discussed in detail. New York Masons also denied that their measures had resulted from a mere misunderstanding on their part, as the Pennsylvanians condescendingly claimed. Rather, they were prompted by a thorough and careful review of the situation.

The dispute was eventually resolved and fraternal relations between New York and Pennsylvania were restored. Although it took a great deal of patience and forbearance on both sides, it was accomplished with little residual ill-feeling. Resolution of the conflict was encouraged by New York Masons' working out their differences on their own, without Pennsylvania's help, and the two Grand Lodges were reunited on November 1, 1858. The Pennsylvania Committee on Correspondence was pleased to report that it had read in the "published proceedings of the present Grand Lodge of New York" that all former difficulties had been resolved.

Therefore, in December 1858 it recommended without hesitation "that the R. W. Grand Lodge of Pennsylvania extend the right hand of fellowship to the R. W. Grand Lodge of New York, rejoicing at the same time that peace and harmony dwell within her borders . . . ." This resolution was accepted unanimously. In the words of Richard Vaux, chairman of the Committee of Correspondence: "The line of division is broken down, the obstacle removed, the inderdict has gone to the oblivion of the past, and the craft in Pennsylvania and New York are as one fold." In early February 1859 the Grand Master of New York, John L. Lewis, officallly rescinded his personal edict of non-intercourse with Pennsylvania Masons and declared the resolution of the Grand Lodge of the same intent to be "inoperative and void." Six weeks later the Pennsylvania Grand Master, Henry M. Phillips, responded with his own official proclamation removing "all obstacles to the free intercourse and communication between the Masons of [both jurisdictions]." The lengthy New York Masonic schism was finally over, interstate Masonic fellowship was once again restored, and the integrity of the Pennsylvania Grand Lodge remained intact.[12]

By the end of 1861, with the Civil War fully under way, the Grand Lodge of Pennsylvania tried to smooth the differences that had existed between itself and other jurisdictions over the course of the previous decade. In the face of a conflict that seriously threatened the vitality of Freemasonry throughout the United States, it wanted to preserve Masonic unity above all else. The Committee of Correspondence reviewed the various issues and dispassionately restated its position. The language of this communication was fraternal, however, and its tone was confident, unlike many previous ones:

> Under the influence of that conservative progress which has ever marked her proceedings, the Grand Lodge of Pennsylvania has advanced with the main body of Masonic duty, towards the goals of general usefulness. Neither dazzled by the brilliancy of light without knowledge, nor intimidated by the reproaches of zeal without faith, [the Grand Lodge], cheerful in charity, has made haste slowly on the road common to the Craft.

All the Grand Lodge wanted was to offer suggestions and opinions. It did not try to interfere with the domestic issues of other jurisdictions, but, unfortunately, its efforts were too often misunderstood. Without admitting any error, the committee left open the possibility that someone might show it had been wrong. The communication concluded with the hope that "the position, opinions, and policy of the Grand Lodge of Pennsylvania will no longer continue to be cause for anxiety to any of her sister Grand Lodges." Over the next two decades this wish was fulfilled, as other jurisdictions responded favorably to the Grand Lodge's efforts to cultivate harmonious relations with them.[13]

*   *   *   *   *   *   *   *

The Pennsylvania Masonic constitution, the *Ahiman Rezon,* specifically forbade Masons, as Masons, from participating in political activity, although, of course, they could do so as individuals. It also prohibited discussion of politics within the lodge on the grounds that this would cause division and disharmony, which were anathema to the avowed purpose of Freemasonry. Furthermore, the constitution charged each Entered Apprentice to "behave as a peaceable and dutiful subject, conforming cheerfully to the government under which he lives" and the Master of a lodge ". . . not to be concerned in plots and conspiracies against government, but patiently to submit to the decisions of the supreme legislature." In conformity to this seeming paradoxical policy of non-involvement with, but loyalty to, established authority, the leaders of Pennsylvania Freemasonry struggled, with mixed success, to avoid the political controversies surrounding the Civil War.[14]

The first effects of contemporary events upon the Fraternity in Pennsylvania occurred in late 1859, in the same month as the execution of the abolitionist John Brown. In his annual message to the Grand Lodge on December 27 Grand Master Henry M. Phillips offered a pleasing account of the "peace, concord and unity" that characterized his jurisdiction at that time, and he expressed his desire that such a spirit might also exist in "every department of life." Unfortunately, such was not the case, although Phillips encouraged Masons to work toward this end in society at large. These sentiments were not unusual; Masonic leaders had been expressing them for decades.

Phillips went further, however, by giving the members specific political advice, which had seldom been done before. He required of them "implicit obedience to the laws of the land," especially to the United States Constitution, which was designed to "regulate, preserve and perpetuate the Union of the States." He also offered a brief recapitulation of the activities and character of the Masonic "Founding Fathers" and left a clear impression of his own political views:

> I commend their work as a precious legacy to be kept and guarded by you as an inestimable jewel, and you should repress any attempt whenever made to weaken or to destroy the bond of Union that binds us together, in the brotherhood of liberty, the whole American people. I speak thus to

you, because the spirit of strife and discord is about in our country; and
your example and influence may do much to retard its progress.

Phillips urged the members to take Masonic virtues into their everyday lives and to work for the restoration of peace and harmony. He
believed that if enough men acted in concert, then perhaps catastrophe
could be avoided. A year later, when one Southern state, South Carolina,
had already seceded, Phillips even more urgently repeated his plea for
saving the Union. He praised the work of earlier Masons in creating "the
model government of the world," and called for all Masons throughout
the country to unite into one brotherhood "to aid in restoring the peace,
harmony, good will and friendly relations that should exist among the
whole American people." This policy of active involvement by individual
Masons, rather than action by Masonic bodies, became sanctioned by most
American grand lodges, both North and South, in the years immediately
preceding the Civil War; but the efforts of American Masons to maintain
peace, as well as those of politicians, were fruitless.[15]
Even after the firing on Fort Sumter had opened hostilities, some
American Masons still hoped to "appeal to the five hundred thousand
Masons of our land to step forward, and pouring the oil of peace upon
the troubled waters of civil war, roll back the raging tide, and in one
united demand make their voices heard in arresting the terrible havocs
of fraternal strife." In May 1861, when Tennessee had become the tenth
member of the Confederacy, the Pennsylvania Committee of Correspondence received a circular letter from the Grand Lodge of that state
that passionately solicited a coordinated Masonic effort for peace. It
expressed horror over the "dire calamity that seems so certainly impend-
ing over us as a people" and beseeched all Masons throughout the country
to work together, without making a judgment as to whose cause was right
and whose wrong.
The committee's response to this communication was cool, although,
like the Tennessee Masons, it deplored "the present unnatural and deeply
distressing condition of our national affairs." Pennsylvania Masons advocated complete neutrality: "Free-Masonry is a silent, unimpassioned,
abstracted observer of events. The position of the brotherhood is to stand
aloof from such evils, without partiality and without participation." Clearly,
however, they were distressed that so many of their Southern Brethren
had taken up arms against the sacred union; they thought the action
"indefensible," not only illegal, but also unmasonic. The Pennsylvanians
agreed to work toward concord, but only "among the brethren and citizens of united sovereign States in our glorious Union."[16]
Almost from the beginning of the Civil War Pennsylvania Masonic
leaders, as well as those of other jurisdictions, realized that the Fraternity

was probably "powerless to heal and unite this bleeding and distracted nation." So they refrained from further attempts to influence national affairs and turned instead to the Fraternity's true functions, to assuage suffering, to care for the sick and wounded, to provide for widows and orphans, and to show brotherly love to participants on both sides. Toward this end, a proposal was put forward in September 1862 to take up a special collection among the subordinate lodges for distressed Brethren in the military. This resulted in the formation of the Free Mason's Soldiers' Relief Association, which met monthly for the remainder of the war. The Grand Lodge also made a special grant of $2,000 to Masons in Chambersburg, who had become destitute by the Confederate burning of the town on July 30, 1864. In December 1865 it donated $1,000 to the Grand Lodge of South Carolina in response to an appeal by Masons who had suffered from the depredations of Union troops. These charitable acts were examples of the practical application of Masonic principles of non-partisanship and universality.[17]

The trustees of both standing charity funds reported an increase in the number of applications for aid during the war years, especially among soldier Masons, recently discharged from the hospital, who had no other means of paying their expenses home. Unfortunately, the trustees were limited by strict regulations and were unable to afford more than a modicum of relief. Relying almost exclusively upon interest from investments, the Girard Fund usually disbursed about $2,000 per year and the Grand Lodge Fund upwards of $1,500. Despite the extraordinary circumstances of the Civil War, there was no significant increase in these amounts; they remained rather consistent throughout the whole period between 1856 and 1865.[18]

Throughout the war the Pennsylvania Grand Lodge persisted, with remarkable restraint, in its dedication to political and military neutrality. Although its leaders praised the blessings of peace and expressed dedication to the Federal government, it did not take any definite measures either to bring about an end to hostilities or to aid in the preservation of the Union. Unlike its practice in the Revolutionary War and the War of 1812, the Pennsylvania Grand Lodge did not warrant any military lodges, despite requests from its members and the example of other jurisdictions. In the face of criticism, this strict policy was justified in late 1862 by the chairman of the Commmittee of Correspondence, Richard Vaux, on the grounds that the atmosphere of military camps and battlefields was not appropriate to the high purposes of Freemasonry. Reiterating the aims of the Fraternity, Vaux concluded: "It might be better, perhaps, that the Mason should be a soldier, than because he is a soldier, he should seek to be a Mason."

This position was reinforced two years later by Vaux's successor,

Samuel C. Perkins, who expressed his pride in Pennsylvania's "conservative course;" the Grand Lodge "has kept herself free from the difficulties, embarrassments, and entanglements which the issuing of warrants for army lodges could not but have led to." The problems, as he saw it, were many: conflicting jurisdictions because of the shifting theatres of war; armies in active service that would curtail attention to Masonic duties; and the temporary nature of the volunteer regiments. Perkins' main objection, however, was that army lodges were simply not appropriate in the current situation. The issuing of regimental warrants had originally developed in the British army, whose regular units remained in operation during times of peace; such clearly was not the case in United States during the Civil War.[19]

The Grand Lodge also refused to grant remission of dues to subordinate lodges that had exempted from payment of dues members who had volunteered for service in the United States. Although it considered this a noble and generous act on the lodges' part, the Grand Lodge could not grant such a wholesale remission of dues. Not only would such an action be against the principles of the *Ahiman Rezon,* which specified how subordinate lodges could achieve this end in certain emergency situations, but also it would not be practical in view of the need to repay the debt on the New Masonic Hall.[20]

Nor did Pennsylvania Masonic leaders follow the liberal policy of previous wars of granting dispensations to allow volunteers to receive their Masonic degrees more quickly than usual, owing to their imminent departure for the front. They feared that, because of circumstances, unqualified men would be accepted. Grand Master John Thomson (in office 1861-1862) was particularly firm on this point: "I am not willing to take the responsibility of opening so wide a door for the entrance of men into the Order, however worthy I might deem them, without the necessary and wholesome formalities which should be observed before gaining admittance." This process included a full and impartial investigation into the character of the candidate. Thomson's successor, David C. Skerrett (in office 1863-1864) occasionally granted dispensations for soldier Masons to receive the two higher degrees on the same night, but only when they had passed the entrance requirements by the usual procedures.[21]

The aloofness of the leaders of Pennsylvania Freemasonry from involvement in national affairs caused them to miss one of the most important patriotic ceremonies of the Civil War, and indeed of the entire nineteenth century, namely, the consecration of the Soldiers' National Cemetary at Gettysburg on November 19, 1863. Pennsylvania Governor Andrew G. Curtin's special agent, the Gettysburg attorney David Wills, invited the Grand Lodge to participate, and the officers of Good Samaritan Lodge No. 336, Gettysburg, urged acceptance. Wills also asked the

Grand Lodge to extend the invitation to subordinate lodges from its own and other jursidictions. Masonic leaders considered accepting, but when they learned that they would not be called upon to perform any Masonic functions, they respectfully declined. Although they appreciated:

> the praise-worthy object of consecrating [the cemetery] to the memory of the noble and lamented dead, who have offered up their lives upon the altar of their country a willing sacrifice, to sustain the Government in its efforts to quell rebellion, preserve the integrity of the Union, and maintain the supremacy of the law,

Pennsylvania Grand Lodge officers nonetheless believed that:

> it would be unusual, and contrary to the principles of our order, which seeks no popularity by public display, to appear in procession on any occasion whatever, unless called upon to perform the ancient ceremonies devolving upon us as Free and Accepted Masons.

Members of Lodge No. 336 attended nonetheless, as did various dignitaries from the Northern states and large crowds of common citizens. The most notable invited guest was, of course, Abraham Lincoln, who delivered a brief, but soon-to-be famous, address.[22]

Eighteen months later Wills once again invited the Grand Lodge of Pennsylvania to participate in another ceremony at the cemetery, this time to lay the cornerstone of the Soldiers' National Monument. Because this event was specifically Masonic in character, the Grand Officers unanimously accepted. The difference in their attitude toward the two ceremonies had nothing to do with patriotism, but concerned the degree of their involvement. As Masons they wished to be the central focus:

> Duty, honor, pride, and patriotism, and our own consistency, all united in compelling this decision. On a previous occasion we had been invited to participate in the ceremonies of consecrating the grounds upon which this monument was to be erected, and very properly declined. Now, the whole duty and responsibility would be ours—and ours alone.

On the morning of July 4, 1865, the Grand Officers joined in an "immense procession, numbering several thousands," through the town of Gettysburg. With Pennsylvania General John W. Geary as grand marshal, the procession included detachments of the Union army, navy and marines, the First City Troop of Philadelphia, veterans of the War of 1812, President Andrew Johnson, Supreme Court and other federal justices, cabinet ministers, the diplomatic corps, the governors and legislatures of several states and territories, the Senate and House of Representatives, heads of federal departments, officers of the Smithsonian Institution, members of the press, the Sanitary and Christian Commissions, the Knights Templar, the Odd Fellows, other benevolent societies, the Society of Cincinnati, clergymen, various religious, literary, scientific and industrial associations, Loyal Leagues, fire companies and private citizens. The National Union Musical Association of Baltimore provided music along the route and at the cemetery. Among the prominent military officers in attendance were Generals Meade, Grant, and Scott and Admirals Farragut and Stewart, with their respective staffs.

At the cemetery were several prayers and musical selections, short addresses by President Johnson and Governor Curtin, both of whom were Masons, a patriotic poem, and the principal address, delivered by General O. O. Howard. The traditional Masonic cornerstone-laying ceremony was conducted with the usual solemnity. Copies of important historical documents, such as the Declaration of Independence, the Articles of Confederation, the Constitution of the United States, Washington's Farewell Address and Lincoln's Gettysburg Address, along with coins and other items, were placed inside the cornerstone. Grand Master Lucius H. Scott, who presided over the ceremony, was proud of the Fratenity's role on this occasion. He believed that the cemetery and monument would serve to:

> relight the torch of liberty and freedom that has been extinguished under the foot of the proud oppressor; that there side by side, sleep the dust of thousands of gallant spirits who have offered up their lives in defense of the liberties we this day enjoy.[23]

What was admirable about Freemasonry during the Civil War is that Brethren from one side felt no malice toward those of the other, even though they disagreed over political questions. Even strongly Unionist Masons, such as Grand Master Thomson, believed that "a brother, even when engaged in rebellion against his country, is still to be considered as a Mason; his character as such being indefeasible." Masons did their duty as they saw it, yet remained loyal to a higher and deeper bond of membership in the same universal brotherhood — Freemasonry. The Civil War divided families, separating brother from brother and fathers from sons, yet it also provided examples of Masons' dedication to their ideals. Many stories, anecdotes and legends from that fratricidal conflict illustrated humane, even preferential, treatment of one Brother toward another, although they served in opposing armies.[24]

The end of the Civil War brought a sense of relief to Pennsylvania Masons. Acknowledging the preservation of the Union, the Grand Officers issued a proclamation calling on all Freemasons of the United States to restore feelings of fraternity among the Brethren and to work toward reconciliation within the country generally. The virtues and values of Freemasonry, which worked against "discord and emnity — the evil passions, revenge, distrust, hatred and malice," had emerged from the war unscathed and continued dedication to them by the members would help to heal the nation's wounds. The leaders of Pennsylvania Freemasonry welcomed the prospect of reopening fraternal communications with the Southern grand lodges, which had become alienated from their Northern counterparts during the war despite the Northerners' earnest pleas for unity in the midst of national crisis. Although they spoke in tones of peace and harmony, the Grand Officers could not help taking the opportunity to state clearly their view of the recent "deplorable contest:"

> History enthroned in the majesty of a coming judgment, with the calmness of retrospect, and the impartiality of truth will determine on whom the responsibility rests of this crime against representative government. It will award to sections and individuals their merited condemnation.[25]

*   *   *   *   *   *   *   *

During the Civil War, as in all periods, the Grand Lodge of Pennsylvania was primarily concerned with what it considered to be its proper business — the administration of the Masonic system within its jurisdiction. In so doing, it found it necessary to further reform its operations, and a number of changes were instituted. Two of these aimed at obtaining more thorough and accurate information about Freemasonry at the grassroots level. At the annual communication in December 1859 Grand Master Phillips issued two edicts, one directed to the District Deputy Grand Masters and the other to the Masters of the subordinate lodges. In the first he required his personal representatives, of which there were sixteen at the time, to keep a record book of "everything relating to Masonry occurring within your district, which you deem important or useful to be known." Phillips was particularly concerned about the condition of the subordinate lodges and the number and nature of any dispensations granted. The District Deputy Grand Masters were to report only information of which they had direct personal knowledge, and they were urged to become more actively involved in Masonic affairs. The new record books were to be reviewed annually by the Grand Secretary and, when completed, were to be filed permanently in his office. As the number of districts increased in subsequent years, the Grand Masters issued more detailed instructions and exercised an even more thorough supervision over them. In his second edict Phillips required the subordinate lodges to submit more complete information pertaining to membership.[26]

In the fall of 1863 the Committee on By-Laws introduced a measure designed not only to facilitate its own work, but also to provide more uniformity within the Masonic system. The usual function of the committee was to review the regulations of the subordinate lodges and to make changes where necessary, to ensure that they reflected the general principles of Masonic government. In recent years so many by-laws of new lodges had been submitted that the committee was beginning to find its labors "onerous." Because so many by-laws included provisions contained in the *Ahiman Rezon,* the committee suggested that extracts from that work be printed in a standarized form for use by the lodges in their own government. The lodges would be allowed to add specific information not contained therein as long as it conformed to general Masonic regulations. Notwithstanding objections from some lodges that this would infringe their independence, the Grand Lodge accepted the proposal.

One of the options left to individual lodges was that of setting their own meeting times. They could appoint whatever evening and hours for their monthly meetings that suited them. A few city lodges, however, took advantage of this flexibilty to hold sessions at unreasonable hours, even after midnight. By mid-1864 the Hall Committee felt compelled to protest: not only did "the additional cost of gas attendant on the unusually protracted labors of so many Lodges, weigh heavily on the contingent expenses of the Order," but this "most glaring abuse" also detained many heads of families from their homes and contributed to a general "demoralizing effect." The committee suggested that meetings of the subordinate lodges be conducted in the evening between the hours of six and half-past ten in the winter and seven and eleven o'clock in the summer. After many more similar complaints the Grand Lodge finally accepted this proposal in March 1867.[27]

It was also during the Civil War that Pennsylvania Masonic leaders came to realize that the magnificent New Masonic Hall on Chestnut Street, completed in 1855 at a total cost of over $180,000, was not so well constructed as they had been led to believe. Management of this building was assigned to the standing Hall Committee, composed of five members, who were to provide for the security of the hall, to make necessary repairs, to pay insurance premiums, to hire a superintendant, a janitor and other employees, and to arrange daily public tours. The committee was required to make quarterly reports and to submit detailed financial statements of its expenditures.[28]

In September 1863 the Hall Committee reported on a recurring problem with water in the sub-basements and on its futile attempts to correct it. Because they had been dug too deep the basements were continually flooded by natural underground springs. This condition damaged the foundation, made several occupants sick, and prevented the furnaces from firing properly. The previous year the committee had employed "gangs of men with pumps which were days and nights incessantly at work but without any general beneficial results." Then, at considerable expense, the furnaces were raised on platforms and the gas pipes were reworked, but the water continued to rise. The committee asked for some new machinery to heat, drain and ventilate the building. This situation prompted the Grand Lodge to inquire into the overall condition of the hall, and the committee, after a further survey, reported that at least $15,000 would be required for other, unrelated repairs. In the face of the upcoming winter, the Grand Lodge resorted to the temporary expedients of pumping the water out again and building more platforms, but it realized that major renovations were in order.[29]

Over the next six months the Hall Committee conducted a comprehensive survey of the condition of the building, and in June 1864 made its report, which included a long list of essential repairs. The previous December the Grand Lodge had allocated $21,000 to meet immediate demands, as well as ongoing expenses, but it was not prepared for the committee's final estimate of more than $45,000. This sum included not only relocating the heating system and installing a device for permanent water removal, but also altering the skylights over the stores and the central passageway, remodeling a stairway, repainting the facade, repairing interior walls, refurbishing several rooms, installing a new kitchen range in the Tyler's apartments, repainting, revarnishing and reupholstering furniture, installing fire plugs and hoses, replacing the roof, and ventilating the Grand Lodge room and other windowless meeting rooms. Even if this "heavy expense" was undertaken, the committee had no confidence that all the problems would be solved; indeed, it was convinced that "the building [has been] a gross failure both in its plan and its construction." The report concluded with a strong recommendation:

> [We] deem this occasion a fitting one to record [our] deliberate opinion, that the building is defective in every particular; that it is notoriously unsuited to the wants of the Order; that it already stands condemned by the common voice of the Fraternity and that sooner or later it will have to be disposed of and its place supplied by one better fitted for the purpose for which it was designed.

The Grand Lodge was also convinced. It promptly rescinded most of its appropriation for repairs and appointed a special nine-man committee to sell the current hall and to buy a new lot on which to build a new temple. Meanwhile, certain essential improvements, which could not wait any longer, were made at a cost of about $4,000.[30]

Over the next few years the Hall Committee continued to report the necessity for extensive emergency repairs. In 1865 and 1866, respectively, another $13,042 and $4,500 were spent above and beyond normal operating expenses. The most costly repairs were new carpeting, frescoing and painting, and structural alterations in the Chapter Room. Throughout 1865 the drainage problem in the sub-basements worsened, the water rose as high as two feet above the floor and, despite determined efforts, never dropped lower than about ten inches. The committee considered obtaining a stronger pump and filling in the basements, but concluded that the anticipated results probably would not be worth the costs. By the end of 1866, however, this problem seems finally to have been solved, not because of any action taken by the committee, but because deeper cellars were excavated for other buildings in the vicinity, and other users thereby tapped into the natural spring. Despite this, other work remained to be done, such as replastering and repainting some of the lodge rooms, due to excessive dampness, and proper ventilation.

The hall was also proving inadequate to the demands placed upon it for meeting space. In response, the Grand Lodge approved the remodeling of the interior to allow for an additional lodge room on the third floor in unused space over the main entrance. To help offset the cost of these renovations, as well as of higher utility bills, the Grand Lodge increased its rental charges to the lodges using the hall. This measure increased the revenue from this source, from about $5,250 per year to $9,000 or $10,000. Meanwhile, the Hall Committee, anticipating future "gigantic improvements," constantly repeated its recommendation for a new and better-built Masonic Temple.[31]

Understandably, when the Special Committee reported in December 1866 that it had found a suitable building lot, the members of the Grand Lodge were pleased. Located at the northeast corner of Broad and Filbert Streets, opposite the Penn Squares, the property ran one hundred fifty feet north to Cuthbert Street and two hundred fifty feet east to Juniper. It actually consisted of four individual lots. After conducting preliminary negotiations with the owners, two gentlemen named George D. Wetherill and Joseph Harrison, Jr., the committee members were confident that the lots could be obtained without difficulty for about $150,000. Agreeing that the property was "far superior to any other in this city, both in the beauty of its location and in the facility of its approach from every quarter," the Grand Lodge approved the purchase.

Although the Fraternity then held assets in excess of $600,000, the Finance Committee had reservations about the affordability of the project, so the Grand Lodge took steps to raise the necessary funds. One method was to alter the fee structure. The annual dues paid by all subordinate lodges to the Grand Lodge remained unchanged at $1 per member, but the amount paid for initiation, formerly the uniform sum of $7 each, was lowered to $2 each for the country lodges. The city lodges, on the other hand, which would receive the most benefit from the new temple, were required to pay the Grand Lodge an additional ten percent of their initiation fees. This change meant that the city lodges would pay between $10 and $12 per member. These provisions were to stay in effect until the debt was paid. The Grand Lodge also resorted to its customary method of raising money, by a Masonic loan at six percent interest, in which individual members and lodges would purchase shares for future redemption, and made plans to sell some of its real estate holdings, especially the Chestnut Street hall.[32]

In February and July 1867 the Special Committee purchased the four lots for $153,000, $2,000 under the authorized amount, but various charges and payments raised the total cost to slightly more than $158,000. The Grand Lodge then took possession of the property and ordered several buildings vacated and demolished.[33]

A number of the city's architects were then invited to furnish plans, specifications and estimates. The committee was pleased with the results: "So much skill and labor were performed by them, and the plans in such good taste and beautiful, that the Committee were somewhat embarrassed in determining what was the best, where all were very good." In December 1867 the committee chose a design by fellow Mason, James H. Windrim. Windrim's plan called for an impressive granite building in Norman style to occupy the whole lot (150 by 250 ft.), except for walkways at its base. Originally, the committee had wanted a white marble exterior, but fell back to granite when its members learned the cost of marble would be nearly $1,000,000. The new Masonic Temple was to be ninety-eight feet high, with ornamental work on the facade reaching one hundred sixty feet. A separate three-hundred-foot tower was planned for the southwest corner. The design also called for an "elegant" porch, thirty-six feet in width, over the main entrance, as well as smaller balconies over large windows on the first floor and a balustrade to run along the base of the roof.

The interior of the building was to contain three stories, as well as attics and basements. The ground floor was designed to accommodate various rooms for the Grand Officers and committees, a library, and a banquet room; the second floor was to contain most of the lodge rooms, including a Grand Lodge room, three Blue Lodge rooms and a Grand Chapter room; and the third floor was set aside for an Encampment room. Windrim's plans also provided for a number of smaller rooms on each floor and on entresol stories for various functions. The design also called for an elaborate grand staircase just inside the main entrance, about which the committee believed "a grander or more elegant stairway cannot be found in any public building in the United States." The roof was to be "perfectly fireproof, free from condensation, rust and expansion, combining permanency and durability." The new temple was to be used exclusively for Masonic purposes; it contained no apartment for the Grand Tyler, as the Chestnut Street hall did.

The committee estimated the total building costs to be in the neighborhood of $750,000 and the total time for completion to be five years. Eager for the project to be underway, the committee recommended, and the Grand Lodge approved, that the cornerstone be laid on St. John's Day next. Its initial job done, the Special Committee changed its name and function, but its composition remained the same. The Building Committee, as it was now called, would hire workmen and generally supervise the construction, and a separate body, the Trustees of the Building Fund, was to provide the necessary financing. During the next few years contributions and subscriptions came in regularly, and the Fraternity initially experienced no difficulty in raising money for the project. The financial security of the Grand Lodge was aided by the Pennsylvania legislature's granting of tax-exempt status for the new temple.[34]

The cornerstone-laying ceremonies were held as scheduled on June 24, 1868. An estimated ten thousand Masons attended, including representatives from eight other Masonic jurisdictions. Among these was A. B. Shekell, the Tyler of Potomac Lodge, Washington, D. C., who brought the gavel George Washington used to lay the cornerstone of the Federal Capitol in 1793; it was used on this occasion in Philadelphia. The procession assembled at eight o'clock in the morning at Broad and Chestnut Streets. An hour later it began to move east along Chestnut, passing the current Masonic Hall where William Rush's statue of "Silence" was displayed on the steps under a canopy of blue silk. At Seventh Street it passed under a specially constructed triumphal arch, decorated with a golden eagle, a keystone and Masonic symbols. It then moved north along Seventh to Arch, west to Broad, north to Columbia Avenue and then back down to Filbert. Numerous American flags, banners and Masonic emblems accompanied the procession, and, as usual, the participants were reported as presenting a "neat appearance." The actual cornerstone-laying ceremonies began at noon. They included three prayers, five anthems, four choruses, a grand march and an oration on King Solomon's Temple by Grand Master Richard Vaux. Vaux's theme was the consistency of Masonic ideals from ancient times to the present; he saw continuity between the nascent structure in Philadelphia and the earlier temple in Jerusalem. Although learned and literary, the oration contained the usual anachronisms and unproved assumptions common to Masonic historiography of that period.

The cornerstone (5 ft. 6½ in. long, 2 ft. 4½ in. deep and 4 ft. 9½ in. wide) was made of granite by a Masonic firm in Havre de Grace, Maryland and was covered with a white marble slab. Into it was placed a lead box containing a number of objects of Masonic significance: the Holy Bible, the *Ahiman Rezon* and other official publications, coins of the United States, pieces of wood and marble believed to be from Solomon's Temple, various Masonic medallions, newspapers, a biography of Stephen Girard and photographs of the Grand Lodge officers, among other objects. The whole event was a gratifying success for the Fraternity. In the words of Grand Master Vaux: "Never before in this jurisdiction was a more imposing and solemn ceremony performed."[35]

By the end of 1868 the foundation of the Masonic Temple had been completed, although it was several months behind schedule because of weather related delays and because of the failure of some contractors to act as promptly as promised. Loose clay and quicksand had posed a problem for the foundation of the tower, but it was dug deeper, to thirty-one feet below the pavement, and set in cement. Construction was then temporarily halted to allow the completed portions to settle. In arranging for the work the Building Committee decided to engage a series of individual contractors, rather than to hire any one particular firm. The whole project was supervised by a full-time employee, John Bolt, a member of Lodge No. 67, and watchmen were hired to prevent vandalism at the site.[36]

As the building rose, so did construction costs. By December 1868 over $209,000 had already been spent, and the committee estimated that another $190,000 was needed for 1869. These sums represented a substantial financial burden, and for the first time in its history, the Fraternity began to experience real difficulty in raising money. The first Masonic loan in the amount of $200,000 was sold out and another was underway, but even though the second loan was offered at a higher interest rate (7.3% versus 6% on the first), subscriptions lagged far behind expectations. In April 1869 the Building Committee echoed earlier reservations by expressing serious doubts as to the feasibility of the project, fearing that it would come to a sudden halt because of insufficient funds. The committee's chairman, Samuel C. Perkins, was particularly concerned:

> Has the Grand Lodge been acting blindly, unadvisedly, inconsiderately, heedlessly, without forethought, without reflection, running stupidly headlong regardless of the future, during these 3½ years? Such is the virtual, unmistakable, downright admission if we stop short, bringing the whole work to a stand-still — it is an acknowledged, open, avowed and deliberate

suicide, and not a dollar will be contributed to make the dry bones, thus heaped up, to life again.

Perkins further claimed that if the project was abandoned, the Pennsylvania Grand Lodge would become "the laughing stock of the Fraternity and of the world" and predicted the future glory of the completed Temple with Masons coming "as did the ancient Jews to the Temple of Jerusalem, three, yea, even four times a year, and strangers, yet, brethren, from all parts of this Country and of the World, will throng to its portals and offer grateful incense at its altars."

Perkins' colorful oratory prompted Grand Lodge members to put forward two schemes to remedy the situation: to mortgage the Chestnut Street hall and to open the second loan to the public. The first idea was rejected as only a means of last resort, but the second was approved, and owing to the Grand Lodge's strong credit rating, the loan was quickly sold. For the moment at least, adequate financing for the next stage of construction became available.[37]

Work progressed at a steady pace, and the Building Committee had no real cause for complaint. By December 1870 the outer shell was substantially completed, the roofing of the entire structure was imminent, the granite facade was up to the second story and expectations were that the entire exterior would be completed within a year. Final designs for the facade, which had been left more or less open in Windrim's original plans, were also drawn. Rejecting an earlier notion that the facade should reflect a variety of architectural styles, the Building Committee decided upon Norman architecture in the interest of "symmetry and harmony." A small tower was added at the northwest corner, at Broad and Cuthbert Streets, to balance the main tower at the southwest corner. There were other considerations in adopting a uniform architectural style: ". . . the entire building, as a whole, as a unit, [will be] one beautiful symbol of the massive, unchangeable, uniform, consistent harmony and stability of the fraternity. . . ." By the end of 1870 over $600,000, or eighty percent of the original estimate, had been spent, and the committee anticipated that another $500,000 was needed for completion. Although the Trustees of the Building Fund continued to express anxiety, Grand Lodge members as a whole were not overly disturbed by the uncertain financial situation, and they optimistically planned dedication ceremonies for June 24, 1873.[38]

Despite the heavy drain that the building of the Masonic Temple placed upon its resources, the Grand Lodge did not slacken in its charitable work. In fact, because of its continued wise investments of the capital of the two standing charity funds, the Fraternity was actually able to increase its disbursements in the years after the Civil War, both generally and to individuals (Table 1). In addition, the Grand Lodge made a num-

TABLE 1
Charitable Disbursements of the Grand Lodge of Pennsylvania, 1856–1873

	Stephen Girard Charity Fund			Grand Lodge Charity Fund		
Year	Amount ($)	Number of Persons	Average Grant ($)	Amount ($)	Number of Persons	Average Grant ($)
1856	1,845	78	24	1,541	96	16
1857	2,165	102	21	1,282	95	14
1858	1,904	99	19	1,355	117	12
1859	1,980	77	26	1,475	66	22
1860	2,025	80	25	1,560	78	20
1861	1,957	93	21	1,805	187	10
1862	2,007	84	24	1,500	145	10
1863	1,938	75	26	1,585	142	11
1864	1,500	45	33	1,665	118	14
1865	2,485	80	31	2,226	141	16
1866	2,970	85	35	2,540	153	17
1867	2,935	96	31	3,053	168	18
1868	2,771	105	26	2,675	153	17
1869	2,800	96	29	3,235	169	19
1870	2,845	108	26	2,956	168	18
1871	2,950	86	34	3,165	190	17
1872	2,730	96	28	2,931*	160	18
1873	3,225	111	29	2,963	170	17

*In addition to this amount, a special Destitute Widows and Orphans Fund in this year disbursed $280 to nineteen applicants.

The Girard Fund was aided "distressed worthy brothers" and the General Fund provided for the widows, orphans and other needy female dependents of deceased Masons in good standing.

All applications for relief had to be in writing and approved by two Master Masons.

Not all recipients of charity came from Pennsylvania, although most did.

Subordinate lodges had their own separate charity funds. Information on the amounts disbursed is not generally available.

All figures have been rounded off to the nearest dollar.

Sources: Grand Lodge of Pennsylvania, *Abstract of the Proceedings for 1856*, 4f., 29; *1857*, 43, 44; *1858*, 90f., 105; *1859*, 66-9; *1860*, 65f., 90f.; *1861*, 72, 78; *1862*, 19-22; *1863*, 69-71; *1864*, 18-20; *1865*, 53-55; *1866*, 27-30; *1867*, 27-29; *1868*, 156f.; *1869*, 24-26; *1870*, 41-44; *1871*, 46-50; *1872*, 69-73; *1873*, 26-29; Committee on Library, comp., *Reprint of the Minutes of the Grand Lodge of Pennsylvania* (Phila., 1895-1907), *Vol. IX, 1855-1858*, 185, 246, 262f., 314f., 327, 359f.; December 27, 1856, December 21, 28, 1857, December 20, 27, 1858; *Vol. X, 1859-1864*, 82f., 161f., 176, 255-7, 308f., 407-9, 457, 459; December 27, 1859, December 17, 27, 1860, December 27, 1861, December 27, 1862, December 28, 1863, December 27, 1864; *Vol. XI, 1865-1874*, 42, 79f., 113f., 192, 220f., 296-98, 340-43, 420-22, 457f.; December 27, 1865, December 27, 1866, December 4, 1867, December 28, 1868, December 24, 1869, December 7, 1870, December 27, 1871, December 27, 1872, December 27, 1873.

ber of special relief grants, such as $1,000 in September 1866 to Masons in Portland, Maine, who had suffered from a disastrous fire, another $1,000 in June of 1867 to "destitute Brethren in the South," and substantially larger sums beginning in October 1871 to aid victims of the famous Chicago fire. Because of the severity of the Chicago fire, a special Masonic Board of Relief was established in that city, and Grand Master Samuel C. Perkins became the president of its auditing commission. This agency raised over $90,000 from members of various grand lodges, although not all this money was actually needed.[39]

In the last three years of construction costs continued to escalate, but the Grand Lodge successfully used various strategies to meet them. It offered four more public Masonic loans, which were favorably received; it raised room rental charges to the subordinate lodges; and it increased membership dues again. As of December 1871, the city lodges had to pay annual dues of $2 per member and $10 for each initiation, in addition to the ten percent premium of its own initiation fees. Although the annual dues of the country lodges remained steady at $1 per member, the amount paid the Grand Lodge for each initiation rose to $8. These measures were intended to be temporary; it was expected that the fees would revert to 1867 levels once the debt was paid. In addition, efforts were made to sell the Chestnut Street hall, but this had not been accomplished by the end of 1873 primarily because of the economic depression of that year.[40]

The final stages of work on the Temple progressed smoothly and no major problems occurred. There were a few delays by contractors in meeting deadlines, especially in regard to the roof, and some last-minute details of the interior work required the dedication to be postponed for several months, but these matters were not serious. The Building Committee did, however, experience a shock at this time, but not because of the construction. In a special election held in October 1870 the people of Philadelphia chose the Penn Squares, to the southwest of the Temple, as the site of a new administrative center, called the "Public Buildings," and by late summer 1871 excavations were underway there. In its negotiations with Philadelphia officials, the Grand Lodge's Building Committee had been led to believe that the areas surrounding the Temple would be left as open space forever, an important consideration in selecting the location. In light of the new developments, the committee regretted that the Fraternity had put so much effort and expense into the exterior of the Temple, which would now be largely obscured; it recommended that pressure be put upon public authorities to redesign or relocate their buildings. Masonic opposition became part of a broader movement to keep the Penn Squares open. A suit against the Public Buildings Commission was carried as far as the Pennsylvania Supreme Court, but the efforts to preserve the squares failed.

One of the options considered by the Public Buildings Commission was four separate buildings, one on each of the smaller squares. This configuration would have meant that the building on the northeast corner would have been within fifty or sixty feet of the Filbert Street front of the Masonic Temple. This plan was rejected, however, perhaps because several highly placed Masons were members of the commission; instead, one building, the present City Hall, was erected at the center of the squares at Broad and Market Streets. Between it and the Filbert Street front of the Temple was a distance of two hundred five feet, a sufficient space to keep that side open to view.[41]

In most particulars, the completed Masonic Temple conformed to Windrim's original designs. The exterior was composed of two types of granite: the western and southern fronts, facing Broad and Filbert Streets, used Cape Ann syenite, which was grayish white in color; the eastern and northern fronts, facing Juniper and Cuthbert Streets, were of Fox Island granite. The deeply recessed Norman arched portal was built of Quincy granite. It was heavily decorated in floral patterns and set off by four columns on each side. Although all the granite was of good quality, a better grade was used on the fronts that would more readily be seen. The grand tower on the southwest was reduced in height from three hundred to two hundred fifty feet, and its foundation was dug deeper than planned, for greater security. Six turrets and spires decorated the main tower, and other turrets were placed around the top of the cornice.

Modeled on King Solomon's Temple in Jerusalem, the building contained three entrances: the main one on the west, another on the east and the third on the south. The grand entrance off Broad Street opened onto the grand stair hall, measuring forty by forty-five feet, which was finished in Corinthian style. Notable features of this stairway included Egyptian sphinxes symbolizing wisdom, strength and beauty at the base, a large stained-glass window on the landing and hand-rubbed marble ornamentation. The grand stairway opened onto the central hall, which ran the length of the first floor. It was finished in Doric style, with a pavement of white and black marble tiles, and measured twenty by sixty-four feet. This hall led to the central stair hall, made of cast iron with an ebony handrail and Lisbon marble wainscoting; it measured twenty-seven by forty-five feet. Beyond that, the central hall extended another seventy feet to the Juniper Street entrance. On the first floor of the Temple were offices for Masonic officials and their staffs, as well as the Library, the Banquet Hall, a lodge room called "Oriental Hall," and number of committee rooms. All the offices contained fireproof vaults for current records and valuable historic Masonic documents.

Most of the Masonic meeting rooms were located on the second or principal floor. The major rooms were "Corinthian Hall" (105 ft. long,

51 ft. wide and 50 ft. high) where the Grand Lodge met, and "Renaissance Hall" (90 ft. long, 50 ft. wide and 50 ft. high) which as used by Grand Chapter. The others were the Blue Lodge rooms: "Egyptian Hall," "Norman Hall," and "Ionic Hall," each of which measured seventy-five long, fifty feet wide and thirty feet high. The second floor also contained numerous anterooms, regalia rooms and cloak rooms. Above the smaller lodge rooms on the eastern part of the building was a third story containing "Gothic Hall" (90 ft. long, 45 ft. wide and 40 ft. high), the meeting place of the Knights Templar. Although the basic architectural styles of the meeting rooms were substantially complete in 1873, extensive interior decoration, based upon European and Middle Eastern examples, was yet to be done. An elaborate system of duct work provided ventilation and heat throughout the building, a number of well-placed skylights allowed natural light to filter into it by day and numerous gas fixtures of a variety of designs illuminated it after dark.[42]

The Grand Lodge Room in 1873. From *Frank Leslie's Illustrated Newspaper*, October 11, 1873 (Grand Lodge of Pennsylvania).

A notable feature of the Temple was the Grand Lodge Library, located on the first floor. Measuring sixty-five feet long, forty-five feet wide and thirty feet high, it was finished in Italian Renaissance style with a row of columns dividing it in half. The six Bailly statues from the Grand

Lodge Room of the Chestnut Street hall were placed here, as well as numerous bookcases and library furniture. Large windows on the south and east provided ample natural light. No room specifically designated for a library had been incorporated into the design of any previous Masonic meeting place, although a small room for that purpose had been appropriated in the original Chestnut Street hall. The library collection at that time was destroyed by the fire of 1819, and nothing had been done since then to replace it. Motivated by the constant urgings of its own members and by the examples of other grand lodges, Pennsylvania Masonic leaders of the late 1860s gradually realized the value of a central place where "legitimate and proper" works pertaining to Freemasonry could be collected and studied. With such a resource readily available, Masons could become better informed about the origins and aims of the Fraternity and, by consulting recognized authorities on various subjects, would be able to settle disputed points of Masonic belief or practice.

Toward that end, a new Committee on Library was formed in June 1871 for the express purpose of acquiring as many worthwhile publications as possible, not "the mass of trash that passes by the name of 'Masonic literature' gotten up to sell, nor . . . magazines, newspapers, or reviews devoted ostensibly to the interest of the Order; but volumes of history, biography and science, as well as Masonry." Although it periodically received small sums from the Grand Lodge, the library grew mostly by donations of material. By the time the Temple was completed one hundred fifty bound volumes of official proceedings of various grand lodges as well as three hundred Masonic reference works had been acquired. Included among these were copies of rare early publications, such as Anderson's *Constitutions* of 1723 and Benjamin Franklin's 1734 reprint. The Library Committee also planned a number of future projects, such as a commemorative volume pertaining to the new Temple and the printing of all of the minutes of the Pennsylvania Grand Lodge. Clearly the Masons of the 1870s had renewed interest in the history of their Fraternity.[43]

On September 26, 1873, the eighty-seventh anniversary of its independence, the Grand Lodge of Pennsylvania held lavish ceremonies to dedicate the new Masonic Temple. The festivities began at half-past eight in the morning with the traditional Masonic procession; the youngest lodges were first in line, and the members and officers of the Grand Lodge came at the rear. The procession contained more than thirteen thousand members from one hundred fifty-four subordinate lodges, as well as representatives of twenty-four other Masonic jurisdictions; thirty-two brass bands were interspersed throughout. Because of their great number, the marchers were divided into twenty-eight divisions, each headed by an assistant grand marshal, and the whole was presided over by a grand marshal. The procession marched on the west side of Broad Street from Chestnut to Columbia and then down the east side as far as Arch Street. When the vanguard reached the new Temple, the lines opened and faced inward, and Grand Lodge members marched through from rear to front. It was three o-clock before they were able to enter the building, and it took another three hours before all the members of the subordinate lodges could do so.[44]

Once inside the Temple, one of the bands proceeded up the left side of the main staircase to a position on the landing where it played appropriate selections as the subordinate lodges marched through the lower hall. The members of the Grand Lodge ascended the right side of the

The Dedication Procession, September 26, 1873. From the *Daily Graphic*, New York, September 30, 1873 (Grand Lodge of Pennsylvania).

staircase and proceeded to Renaissance Hall to await "vouching," an inspection of an individual's Masonic credentials by the Grand Tyler, before being allowed to enter Corinthian Hall for the dedication ceremonies. An orchestra and chorus were already in place in the room, and they provided music throughout the ceremony. This began with proclamations of the authority of the Grand Officers, followed by the architect's ritual presentation of the implements of his work. The Grand Master then dedicated the Temple in the usual Masonic manner, which consisted of nine rotations around the hall, the strewing of corn, wine and oil, and separate dedications to "Freemasonry," "Virtue and Silence" and "Universal Benevolence," all punctuated with prayers, invocations, psalms, and vocal music. Past Grand Master Robert A. Lamberton then deliverd an oration on Masonic history and principles, which was more solidly based upon fact that most speeches on this subject. The ceremony concluded with Handel's "Hallelujah Chorus" and another prayer. At eight o'clock, the members of the Grand Lodge and their invited guests, about two hundred fifty persons, participated in a banquet that lasted for most of the rest of the evening. A number of Masonic toasts were offered, and musical accompaniment added to the festive atmosphere.[45]

On September 29 and 30 two more elaborate dedication ceremonies were held in the new Masonic Temple by allied organizations. The first was by the Grand Chapter of the Holy Royal Arch, which used Renaissance Hall, and the second was by the Knights Templar, who used Gothic Hall. These festivities were accompanied by the usual prayers, orations, music, and banquets. A highlight of these ceremonies was a parade through Philadelphia of approximately twenty-four hundred Knights Templar, in full regalia; their appearance excited considerable public attention: "[it was] by far the most brilliant pageant ever seen in this city . . . there can be no hesitation in saying that, for real magnificence, the Templar parade has never been excelled."[46]

The Building Committee made its final report to the Grand Lodge and disbanded at the end of 1873. It presented a comprehensive accounting of the costs of the new Masonic Temple. Including the ground, building materials, salaries, expenses of the cornerstone-laying and dedication ceremonies, furnishings, heating apparatus and insurance, total costs amounted to the astonishing sum of $1,569,093. The largest single building expense was the granite, which alone was over $500,000; second was the ironwork at $127,000. The Grand Lodge was able to meet these costs comfortably; the building fund even had a balance of $7,000. By superior effort and unity of purpose the Freemasons of Pennsylvania had accomplished an enviable feat — the building of a magnificent new Temple. It became a source of continuing pride for the members of the Fraternity, who hoped that:

   the Temple may long stand as a monument of the strength, stability, prosperity and energy of the Craft in Pennsylvania; and that enriched, from time to time as opportunity and resources may allow, with decorative

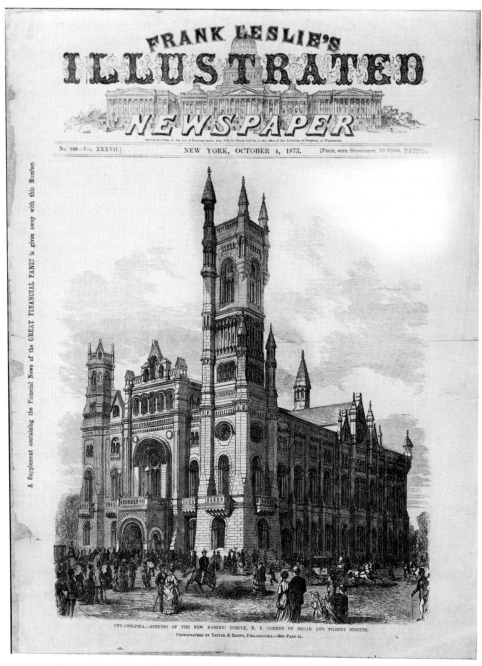

The Masonic Temple, Philadelphia, as it appeared in 1873 (Grand Lodge of Pennsylvania).

adornments and works of art, it may become more beautiful and attractive from year to year; and as a centre and home for the association of the Craft to cluster about with cheering memories of pleasure and profit had within its walls.[47]

*   *   *   *   *   *   *   *

In the eighteen years between the dedication of the New Masonic Hall on Chestnut Street and that of the Masonic Temple, the Grand Lodge of Pennsylvania was more active in warranting subordinate lodges than ever before in its history (Table 2). At the end of 1873 a total of three hundred fifty-four lodges were in operation, an increase of two hundred sixty percent since 1856. The influence of Freemasonry was more widespread than ever before; subordinate lodges were located in all but three Pennsylvania counties (Table 3, Figure 1).

Membership also increased substantially in this period; more than fifty-one thousand men entered the Fraternity either through initiation or admission (see Appendix I). This figure indicates that in this period alone twenty-five percent more men became Pennsylvania Masons than in all previous periods combined. Cumulative totals increased by seventy-five percent over those in 1855. The memberships of the Philadelphia lodges increased even more (77%), and those of the country lodges somewhat less (58%), than the averages for all lodges combined.

As in all periods, Pennsylvania Masons from 1856 to 1873 followed a wide variety of trades and professions; more than three hundred separate occupations have been identified (see Appendix I). The largest grouping were the artisans, with about twenty-two percent for all lodges combined. This percentage was slightly higher among Philadelphia lodges (28.3%) and slightly lower among country lodges (19.7%). The service fields, both non-professional and professional, were the next most numerous (14.6% and 14.4%, respectively), and men involved in trade and commerce came third (12.5%). Among the country lodges, agricultural workers were naturally a respectable percentage (13.4%), but even there the service fields were even better represented (16.1% and 14.6%), and the percentage of those in trade and commerce was nearly as high (11.8%). These occupational patterns were similar to those in previous periods of Masonic history, but the artisans were a smaller group and those in service fields slightly larger than earlier. It is clear that Freemasonry in Pennsylvania appealed mostly to independent craftsmen, professionals, and men involved with commerce, as well as others who conducted business essentially within an urban or small town environment. With their average age at admission of about 32 years, these new Masons were old enough to

TABLE 2
Lodges warranted by the Grand Lodge of Pennsylvania, 1856-1873

Years	Number of new or revived lodges (lodge numbers)	Number of ceased lodges (lodge numbers)
1856-1865	62 (297-358)	1 (235)
1866-1873	166 (359-393, 395-525)	1 (280)
Totals	228 Net: +226	2 (0.9%)

Lodges in Operation by the End of the Year

Year	Number of Lodges	Year	Number of Lodges
1856	135	1865	190
1857	144	1866	207
1858	159	1867	226
1859	167	1868	259
1860	173	1869	280
1861	174	1870	312
1862	176	1871	330
1863	176	1872	346
1864	179	1873	354

The warrant of No. 394 was never issued.

The geographical distribution of the ceased lodges is as follows: Bradford (280) and Erie (235).

By the end of 1873, Masonic lodges were located in all but three Pennsylvania counties (Forest, Fulton and Snyder).

The origins of new lodges are based upon their constitution dates.

Lodges "ceased" in basically two ways: by voluntary surrender of the warrant by the members or by order of the Grand Lodge. Various terms were used to describe such warrants: "surrendered," "returned," "vacated," or "ceased."

Sources: Committee on Library, comp., *Reprint of the Minutes of the Grand Lodge of Pennsylvania* (Phila., 1895-1907), Vol. IX, *1855-1858*, Vol. X, *1859-1864;* Vol. XI, *1865-1874;* "Information Pertaining to Early Freemasonry in the Western Hemisphere, Including the Warrant and Constitution Dates of the Subordinate Lodges under the Provincial and Present Grand Lodge of F. and A.M. of Pennsylvania" (unpublished list); Charles E. Meyer, *Masonic Lodges in Pennsylvania from 1730 to 1880, "Moderns" and "Ancients"* (Phila., n.d.); Register of Members, Vol. 3-1, 1854-1865; Vol. 3-2, 1854-1865; Vol. 4-1, 1866-1903; Vol. 4-2, 1866-1892; Vol. 4-3, 1866-1892; Vol. 4-4, 1866-1892; Vol. 5-1, 1869-1911; Vol. 5-2, 1868-1911; Vol. 5-3, 1870-1904; Vol. 5-4, 1873-1904.

TABLE 3
Geographical Distribution of Pennsylvania Lodges Founded, 1856-1873

County	Number of new lodges (lodge numbers)	%:
Adams	2 (336, 465)	0.9
Allegheny	16 (318, 321, 374, 375, 390, 430, 448, 452, 484, 489, 502, 508, 509, 510, 513, 525)	7.0
Armstrong	2 (437, 521)	0.9
Beaver	4 (411, 457, 478, 485)	1.8
Bedford	2 (320, 524)	0.9
Berks	6 (307, 367, 377, 406, 435, 479)	2.6
Blair	2 (490, 494)	0.9
Bradford	5 (306, 415, 418, 428, 471)	2.2
Bucks	2 (427, 512)	0.9
Butler	1 (429)	0.4
Cambria	1 (312)	0.4
Cameron	1 (382)	0.4
Centre	1 (391)	0.4
Chester	9 (309, 322, 340, 343, 353, 383, 405, 446, 475)	3.9
Clarion	2 (520, 522)	0.9
Clearfield	3 (314, 480, 515)	1.3
Clinton	1 (495)	0.4
Columbia	3 (349, 460, 462)	1.3
Crawford	6 (303, 372, 408, 463, 473, 498)	2.6
Cumberland	3 (302, 315, 361)	1.3
Dauphin	3 (364, 464, 486)	1.3
Delaware	2 (298, 352)	0.9
Elk	1 (379)	0.4
Erie	10 (304, 347, 362, 365, 366, 392, 399, 416, 425, 455)	4.4
Fayette	2 (346, 459)	0.9
Franklin	1 (443)	0.4
Greene	6 (329, 403, 407, 422, 497, 514)	2.6
Huntingdon	1 (300)	0.4
Indiana	3 (313, 355, 431)	1.3
Juniata	2 (324, 371)	0.9
Lancaster	4 (398, 417, 476, 496)	1.7
Lawrence	1 (433)	0.4
Lehigh	4 (326, 333, 440, 469)	1.7
Luzerne	16 (301, 323, 327, 332, 339, 345, 354, 395, 442, 466, 467, 468, 474, 499, 504, 523)	7.0
Lycoming	3 (299, 335, 397)	1.3
McKean	2 (334, 388)	1.7
Mercer	4 (389, 424, 434, 517)	1.7
Mifflin	2 (376, 492)	0.9

(Continued on next page)

TABLE 3 *(Cont.)*

County	Number of new lodges (lodge numbers)	%:
Monroe	1 (325)	0.4
Mongomery	5 (308, 310, 400, 410, 420)	2.2
Montour	1 (516)	0.4
Northampton	3 (311, 396, 413)	1.3
Northumberland	4 (378, 401, 404, 414)	1.7
Perry	3 (319, 381, 458)	1.3
Philadelphia	26 (359, 368, 369, 380, 384, 385, 386, 393, 402, 419, 432, 436, 441, 444, 449, 450, 453, 456, 481, 482, 487, 491, 493, 500, 506, 519)	11.4
Pike	1 (344)	0.4
Potter	1 (342)	0.4
Schuylkill	5 (357, 409, 426, 470, 511)	2.2
Somerset	1 (358)	0.4
Sullivan	1 (387)	0.4
Susquehanna	6 (328, 338, 360, 439, 445, 507)	2.6
Tioga	6 (317, 350, 351, 373, 421, 477)	2.6
Union	1 (370)	0.4
Venango	4 (316, 363, 483, 501)	1.7
Warren	2 (394, 412)	0.9
Washington	7 (297, 337, 356, 447, 454, 461, 488)	3.1
Wayne	3 (305, 330, 472)	1.7
Westmoreland	2 (331, 518)	0.9
Wyoming	2 (341, 438)	0.9
York	4 (348, 423, 451, 503)	1.7
Totals	228	100.0

Sources: Committee on Library, comp., *Reprint of the Minutes of the Grand Lodge of Pennsylvania* (Phila., 1895-1907), Vol. IX, *1855-1858,* Vol. X, *1859-1864;* Vol. XI, *1865-1874;* "Information Pertaining to Early Freemasonry in the Western Hemisphere, Including the Warrant and Constitution Dates of the Subordinate Lodges under the Provincial and Present Grand Lodge of F. and A.M. of Pennsylvania" (unpublished list); Charles E. Meyer, *Masonic Lodges in Pennsylvania from 1730 to 1880, "Moderns" and "Ancients"* (Phila., n.d.); Register of Members, Vol. 3-1, 1854-1865; Vol. 3-2, 1854-1865; Vol. 4-1, 1866-1903; Vol. 4-2, 1866-1892; Vol. 4-3, 1866-1892; Vol. 4-4, 1866-1892; Vol. 5-1, 1869-1911; Vol. 5-2, 1868-1911; Vol. 5-3, 1870-1904; Vol. 5-4, 1873-1904.

FIGURE 1
Masonic Lodges in Pennsylvania, 1856-1873

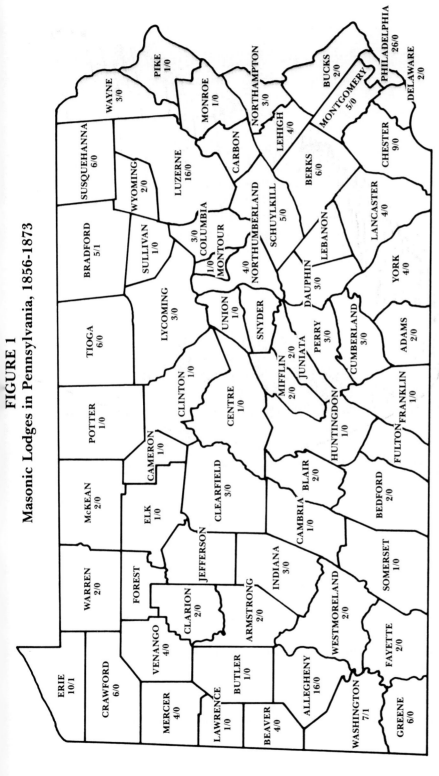

PENNSYLVANIA IN 1873 (66 Counties)

Key: new/ceased lodges
Totals: 228/2   Net: +226

Sources: Committee on Library, comp., *Reprint of the Minutes of the Grand Lodge of Pennsylvania* (Phila., 1895-1907), Vol. IX, *1855-1858*, Vol. X, *1859-1864*; Vol. XI, *1865-1874*; "Information Pertaining to Early Freemasonry in the Western Hemisphere, Including the Warrant and Constitution Dates of the Subordinate Lodges under the Provincial and Present Grand Lodge of F. and A.M. of Pennsylvania" (unpublished list); Charles E. Meyer, *Masonic Lodges in Pennsylvania from 1730 to 1880*, "Moderns" and "Ancients" (Phila., n.d.); Register of Members, Vol. 3-1, 1854-1865; Vol. 3-2, 1854-1865; Vol. 4-1, 1866-1903; Vol. 4-2, 1866-1892; Vol. 4-3, 1866-1892; Vol. 4-4, 1866-1892; Vol. 5-1, 1869-1911; Vol. 5-2, 1868-1911; Vol. 5-3, 1870-1904; Vol. 5-4, 1873-1904.

have become secure in their chosen professions, but still young enough to benefit from Masonic association in the future.[48]

These statistics are surprising, especially considering the costs of Masonic membership. Throughout most of its history the Grand Lodge had allowed subordinate lodges to set their own fees. This policy resulted in a great variation, and even abuse, because a lodge could determine the kinds of members it wanted by raising or lowering its fees accordingly. After midcentury the Grand Lodge tried to standarize fees, but this move was for a long time resisted by the lodges, which regarded it as a violation of one of their prerogatives. Nonetheless, the Grand Lodge eventually had its way. In June 1864 the city lodges were required to charge a minimum of $50 for initiation and membership and the country lodges a minimum of $30. The fees were raised again in December 1869, to $75 for the city lodges and $40 for the country lodges. The Masons made no allowance for installment payments; these fees had to be paid in full at the time of admission. Because the average daily wage of a skilled Philadelphia artisan in this period varied between $2 and $3, depending on occupation, such an individual would have had to work two or three weeks in 1864 and four to six weeks in 1869 to be able to afford the entrance fees. Common laborers would have had even more difficulty because they earned less than $1.75 a day. This data seems to indicate that the majority of the men who became Masons probably came from the higher levels of society since others could hardly afford the costs of membership.[49]

The unprecedented growth in membership during these years was not as warmly welcomed by Masonic leaders as might be expected. Although they were pleased that the Fraternity was held in high public esteem, many Grand Masters were suspicious of its gaining too much popularity. They understood why the ideals and practices of Freemasonry were so attractive, but worried that men were motivated to join because of such practical purposes as the perceived personal or professional advantages of Masonic connections. The Grand Masters repeatedly warned against admitting too many individuals and argued that making members was not necessarily equivalent to making Masons. In their annual addresses on the state of the Fraternity Grand Masters of this period insisted upon strict adherence to the moral, physical and financial requirements of membership and reaffirmed the necessity of a lodge's unanimous acceptance of a candidate.

Typical examples of this attitude can be found in the advice of Grand Master Skerrett in 1863:

> Brethren, I cannot too strongly urge upon you the necessity of exercising the strictest scrutiny into the moral character of all applicants for

admission into our Order, for admit an unworthy man into your Lodge and you know not where the evil will end.

Similar views were expressed by Grand Master Vaux in 1868:

Free Masonry never proselytizes. It seeks no strength in numbers or dignity from men. Those who are well qualified are, if found worthy, admitted; but they must come voluntarily and knock at its temple doors. Strict trial, severe tests, careful examination, thorough investigation into fitness, caution, prudence, due consideration, and above all, moral courage to do the duty which these virtues demand, are now essential in all Lodges as precedent conditions to a favorable report on those who apply for the rights and privileges of Masonry.

One obvious benefit of expanding membership, about which Masonic leaders remained strangely silent, was the economic support provided for the Fraternity's building projects and resulting long-term debts.[50]

Between 1856 and 1873 ten men held the office of Grand Master (see Appendix C). With the exception of one artisan, they came from professional backgrounds: four were lawyers, two were physicians, one each was a druggist, a merchant and an oak cooper, and one was a gentlemen of independent means. They ranged in age from 43 to 71 years at the time of their elections; the average age was 58 years. This group of Masonic leaders was about ten years older than the Grand Masters of previous periods and about twenty-five years older than most of the newly initiated or admitted members. The increased complexities of Masonic administration probably demanded greater maturity for leadership, as well as a more thorough background in Freemasonry.

Two of the Grand Masters, John K. Mitchell (in office 1858) and John L. Goddard (1867), shared the dubious distinction of dying in office. Both men were ill at the time of their elections, but neither allowed his health to deter him in pursuit of what he considered to be his duty. The deaths of these two men added to a much greater loss suffered by the Fraternity at this time. Between 1856 and 1873 no fewer than eleven Past Grand Masters departed the "earthly grand lodge" and entered the "heavenly one": Bayse Newcomb, Jr. (in office 1818-1821, d. 1856); Cornelius Stevenson (1843, d. 1860); Anthony Bournonville (1852-1853, d. 1863); George Mifflin Dallas (1835, d. 1864); William Whitney (1850-1851, d. 1865); Samuel Badger (1829-1830, d. 1866); Josiah Randall (1822-1823, d. 1866); William Barger (1844-1845, d. 1871); James Harper (1825, d. 1873); James Hutchinson (1854-1855, d. 1873); and David C. Skerrett (1863-1864, d. 1873). Each was accorded the usual public Masonic funeral service, including the delivery of an appropriate eulogy, and the Grand Lodge Room was draped in mourning for six months.[51]

Of the sitting Grand Masters the strongest leadership was shown by Richard Vaux (in office 1867-1869), who by virtue of the death of his predecessor, John Goddard, served a longer term than customary. Vaux had given extensive service to the Fraternity before his election and continued doing so until his death. He also had one of the most distinguished public records of any Pennsylvania Mason, having served as recorder of Philadelphia (1841-1847), controller of public schools (1841-1845), inspector of the Eastern State Penitentiary (1831-1892), mayor of Philadelphia (1856-1858), and member of the United States Congress (1890-1891). He served on the Board of Directors of Girard College (1859-1862), was president of the Philadelphia Club (1888-1894), and was a prominent member of the Historical Society of Pennsylvania and of the American Philosophical Society. He also wrote important works on penology.[52]

In his numerous addresses to the Fraternity Vaux was consistently conservative, refusing to consider any innovation, however slight, in Masonic principles and practices. He insisted upon the maintenance of secrecy and thus censured unofficial Masonic publications; he forbade the public display of Masonic dress and emblems except on special occasions; he insisted upon a high level of proficiency before a candidate could advance in the degree system; he was reluctant to grant any dispensations; he was against general Masonic conventions; and he was against the involvement of American grand lodges in the workings of European Freemasonry. Against all criticism Vaux staunchly defended the Pennsylvania manner of working, regarding its most notable feature as the teaching of profound spiritual truths, while at the same time remaining the model of simplicity.

Grand Master Vaux also maintained the traditional religious outlook of the Fraternity, which had so often been expressed by previous Pennsylvania Masonic leaders. For example, he advised his fellow Masons to follow God's will in all things: "We are not only the work of His hands, but the creation of His divine power, and the subjects of His providence. We submit to His decrees, in hope and faith, for God is Love and Truth, and doeth what is pleasing in His sight."[53]

The direction that Vaux set for the Fraternity was closely followed by his successors, Robert A. Lamberton (in office 1870-1871) and Samuel C. Perkins (1872-1873). This was especially true with regard to Vaux's religious views. Both men offered frequent prayers of thanksgiving to God, who they believed had blessed the Fraternity with prosperity. Lamberton, the more committed of the two officers, even closed one of his annual addresses with the traditional benediction used in many Christian churches: "The Lord bless thee and keep thee; the Lord make His face to shine upon thee, and be gracious unto thee; the Lord lift up his countenance upon thee, and give thee peace."[54]

The religious views of the Fraternity were misunderstood by the established churches in this, as in all periods, and Masonic leaders believed that a public expression of religious belief was necessary. An eloquent explanation of the relationship between Freemasonry and religion was offered by the Committee of Correspondence during Vaux's term of office:

> What institution assumes the care of the widow and the orphan with more unceasing effort than the Masonic Order, or does it more effectually? What institution inculcates purer lessons of morality to aid in keeping the members unspotted from the vices that afflict our race? But religion is not the object of the association, although it inculcates its precepts. Any one who supposes it to be an enemy of religion knows nothing of the Order — nor are those who think that Masons consider it a substitute for the Church any better informed. It has no heavenly origin, but is of the earth and of human invention. It seeks to improve the condition of mankind without regard to the religion they profess, The atheist can never enter its portals or be received into its brotherhood. Masonry makes no pretensions to be able to save a soul by its teachings, but it does profess to be able to make the rude more refined in feeling and sentiment, to make the avaricious more charitable and less fond of self; to humanize the heart and induce all within its influences to feel that as men they owe duties to their fellow-men which no human law teaches, and which nothing but the development of the principle of universal fraternity can stimulate to action, Why then should churches war against our institution? Simply because as a body they are ignorant of its aims and its obligations.[55]

As comprehensive and accurate as this statement was, it nonetheless largely fell on the deaf ears of many non-Masons. Although there would never again be such a well-organized attack as had occurred between 1826 and 1840, the Masonic Fraternity throughout its subsequent history would continue to endure an ongoing, and largely one-sided, dispute with organized religion, which felt that church functions were challenged and disesteemed by Freemasonry.

*   *   *   *   *   *   *   *

By the end of 1873 the Grand Lodge of Pennsylvania had been in existence for one hundred forty-two years, eighty seven of them as an independent institution. During that time it had grown from a small band of fifteen men in one Philadelphia lodge to thirty-eight thousand members in three hundred fifty-four lodges throughout the Commonwealth.

In the interim some ninety thousand individuals had become associated with the Fraternity. Sooner or later, most of these men had ceased being members for one reason or another: violations of Masonic rules and regulations; non-payment of dues; death; geographical relocation or simply a loss of interest. At one point in their lives, however, these men had been exposed to the high ideals and practical morality inculcated in Masonic teachings. If they were in any way affected by what they had experienced within the lodges, they must have applied at least some beneficial and humanitarian principles to their daily lives. Masonic influence within the broader society must therefore have been deep and widespread. Even after many Pennsylvania Masonic meeting places had fallen into ruin, Masonic ideals remained intact, conveyed from one generation to another through an unchanging and unchangeable method of imparting knowledge about oneself, about one's obligations to one's fellow man, and about one's God.

NOTES

Abbreviations of Frequently Cited Works

B&S Norris S. Barratt and Julius F. Sachse, comp., *Freemasonry in Pennsylvania, 1727-1907 as shown by the records of Lodge No. 2, F. and A.M. of Philadelphia from the year 1757 compiled from original sources* (Phila., 1908-1919), I, *1757-1781*, II, *1781-1813*, III, *1814-1855.*

GLM Committee on Library, *Reprint of the Minutes of the Right Worshipful Grand Lodge of the Most Ancient and Honorable Fraternity of Free and Accepted Masons of Pennsylvania* (Phila., 1895-1908). I, *1779-1801*, II, *1801-1810*, III, *1811-1816*, IV, *1817-1822*, V, *1822-1827*, VI, *1828-1839*, VII, *1840-1848*, VIII, *1849-1854*, IX, *1855-1858*, X, *1859-1864*, XI, *1865-1874.*

OML Julius F. Sachse, *Old Masonic Lodges of Pennsylvania, "Moderns" and "Ancients," 1730-1800* (Phila., 1912-1913), I, *1730-1777*, II, *1779-1791.*

PRO *Proceedings of the Grand Lodge of F. & A.M. of Pennsylvania* (by year).

240

Chapter 1

1. The most recent general histories of Freemasonry are Henry Wilson Coil, *Freemasonry Through Six Centuries* (Richmond, Va., 1967, 1968), 2 vols. and Fred L. Pick, G. Norman Knight and Frederick Smyth, *The Pocket History of Freemasonry* (London, 1969). These authors lament the poor state of previous Masonic scholarship and do not accept many traditions as factually correct. Although not exhaustive or completely unbiased, these works are helpful for basic information. For a more complete discussion of Masonic historiography, see Wayne A. Huss, "Pennsylvania Freemasonry: An Intellectual and Social Analysis, 1727-1826" (Ph.D. diss., Temple University, Phila., 1984).

2. Coil, I, 6f. has sifted through twenty-five different theories on the origins of Freemasonry, but the one discussed in the text seems to make the most sense and to be the best substantiated. Pick, et. al., 22f., agree. It was once thought that medieval French and German building societies, known respectively as the "Compagnonnage" and the "Steinmetzen," were the antecedents of modern Freemasonry, but these claims have since been proved faulty (Coil, I, 44-65; Pick, et. al, 18-21). A good summary of the medieval masonic bodies, their membership and functions, appears in Douglas Knoop and G. P. Jones, *The Medieval Mason* (Manchester, 1949).

3. Coil, I, 119-121; Pick, et. al., 25-28; *The Shorter Oxford English Dictionary* (London, 1977), I, 804.

4. The Regius MS is closely mirrored by another constitution, known as the Cooke MS, dating from about 1410. Both documents are discussed in Pick, et. al., 34-48 and Coil, I, 9, 28. See also Frederick M. Hunter, *A Study and Interpretation of the Regius Manuscript* (Portland, Oreg., 1952).

5. Coil, I, 30f. examines ninety-nine constitutions, whereas Pick, et. al. count one hundred twenty-five through the seventeenth century. These authors agree that they were almost exclusively of English origin, although a few originated in Scotland. A summary of these documents also appears in a comprehensive survey: Douglas Knoop and G. P. Jones, *A Handlist of Masonic Documents* (Manchester, 1942), which records one hundred seventy-four through the eighteenth century.

6. These and other references to seventeenth century Freemasonry are discussed in Coil, I, 85-101 and Pick, et. al., 50-59.

7. Douglas Knoop, G.P. Jones and Douglas Hamer, in *The Early Masonic Catechisms* (Manchester, 1963), reproduce these documents and provide a competent, scholarly exposition of them. Most sources were discovered in the twentieth century. Knoop, Jones and Hamer believe that these manuscripts are worthy of serious critical study, contrary to the views of such "authorities" as Robert F. Gould, *The History of Freemasonry* (New York, 1885), I, 1-30, who knew of some of them but did not appreciate their value.

8. Edinburgh Register House MS (1696); Chetwoode Crawley MS (c. 1700); Kevan MS (c. 1714); Sloane MS (c. 1700); Dumfries No. 4 MS (c. 1710); Trinity College, Dublin MS (1711); *A Mason's Examination* (1723); *The Grand Mystery of Free-Masonry Discover'd* (1724); *The Whole Institution of Masonry* (1724); *The Whole Institution of Free-Masonry Opened* (1725); among others.

9. For example, the characteristics of the Masonic handgrip, as described in the Sloane MS (c. 1700), are reproduced in Knoop, Jones and Hamer, 45f: "their gripe for fellow craftes is grasping their right hands in Each other thrusting their thumb naile close upon the third Joynt of each others first ffinger . . . their Masters gripe is grasping their right hands in each other placing their four finger's nails hard upon the Carpus or end of the other wrist and their thumb nailes thrust hard directly between the second Joynt of the thumb and the third Joynt of the first ffinger but some say the masters grip is the

same I last described only each of their middle ffingers must reach an inch or three barly cornes Length higher to touch upon a vein yt comes from the heart [sic]." Or the following: "another [sign] is taking their handkerchief by the corner with their right hand and throw it over their Left shoulder letting it hang down their back and so walk a few steps along if any mason see it they will follow and take him by the hand." Or several final examples: "Another signe some use bending their right arme in form of a Square and laying the palm of their left hand upon their heart. Another is by twisting their eyes toward the east and twisting their mouth toward ye west Another is bending their right knee holding up their hand towards the east and if it be night or dark they will give two Little haughts and a great one as if they were forceing a bone or a lump out of ther throat . . . [sic]."

10. These pillars are mentioned in 1 Kings 7:21 and 2 Chron. 3:17.

11. Other "revivers" of Freemasonry, also members of the Royal Society, were Robert Rawlinson and Martin Folkes. Brief sketches of these persons appear in Coil, I, 142f.; *Dictionary of National Biography*, I, 380, XIV, 400, XIX, 361f.; Bernard Faÿ, *Revolution and Freemasonry, 1680-1800* (Boston, 1935), 89f.; and Arthur E. Waite, *A New Encyclopedia of Freemasonry* (New York, c. 1910), 25f., 182f.

The full citation for Anderson's publication is as follows: James Anderson, *The Constitutions of the Free-Masons containing the History, Charges, Regulations, &c of that most Ancient and Right Worshipful Fraternity* (London, 1723). The second edition (London, 1738) is more complete. Anderson was criticized by later scholars for an over-indulgence in mythology in his genealogical work, a tendency continued when compiling Masonic history.

12. Although Hiram Abiff is mentioned in the Old Testament books of 1 Kings and 2 Chronicles, no factual foundation exists for the Masonic myths associated with him. For an analysis of this subject, see Henry Wilson Coil, *Coil's Masonic Encyclopedia* (New York, 1961), 306-309.

13. This designation was self-styled because the jurisdiction only applied to a small area surrounding London and Westminster. For essays on this period see Henry Carr, ed., *Grand Lodge 1717-1967* (Oxford, 1967).

14. Pick, et. al., 80-82.

15. Anderson, *Constitutions* (London, 1738), 109.

16. Philip, Duke of Wharton, was an unreliable adventurer who espoused a variety of causes for personal gain. He followed a profligate life style, was once the president of the London Hell-Fire Club, and lost a considerable fortune. The Duke of Montague was more respectable and held high military office. A man of ability, he nonetheless had a penchant for tomfoolery, so much so that his mother-in-law, the Duchess of Marlborough, considered his " 'talents [to] lie in things natural to boys of fifteen, and he is about two and fifty' " (*Dictionary of National Biography*, LX, 410f., XXXVIII, 253f).

17. Coil, I, 246, 280f.; Pick, et. al., 96, 163, 203. The overseas lodges are listed in order of their founding.

18. These works are: "The Mystery of Masonry" (c. 1725); "Night" (1738) and "The Sleeping Congregation" (1728). The last includes an unflattering portrait of Desaguliers. See Stuart Barton, *The Genius of William Hogarth* (Sussex, 1972).

19. No published Masonic sources indicate specifically what these changes were, although they are referred to briefly in Knoop, Jones and Hamer, 157-173, which includes a copy of Prichard's work, and in Pick, et. al, 97.

20. Clement XII, *IN EMINETI* (1738). Subsequent Papal condemnations along the same lines appeared in 1751, 1821, 1825, 1829, 1832, 1846, 1856, 1884 and 1917. As recently as March 1981, John Paul II reaffirmed the Vatican's proscriptions against the Fraternity because of the Italian Masonic scandal involving Licio Gelli and P-2, but the new code of Canon Law released in January 1983 apparently reverses the centuries-old tradition by permitting Roman Catholics to become Masons as long as they do not engage in activities that specifically defame the Church and its teachings (*New York Times*, March 3, 1981, May 28, 1981, January 26, 1983).

21. For a definitive listing of anti-Masonry in this period, see the following: Melvin M. Johnson, *The Beginnings of Freemasonry in America* (New York, 1924), 60, 153, 180, 190f., 206, 226, 226, 273f., 277, 286f., 294, 328; Bernard Faÿ, *Franklin, Apostle of Modern Times* (Boston, 1929), 178-184; and Alphonse Cerza, *Antimasonry* (Transactions of the Missouri Lodge of Research, XIX, Fulton, Mo., 1962).

22. "Irregular making" included the making of Masons in an unauthorized manner, the choosing of the wrong kinds of men to become Masons, or the making of Masons for the purpose of financial gain. Coil, II, 6. The Walpole quotation is from W. S. Lewis, ed., *The Yale Edition of Horace Walpole's Correspondence*, XVIII; *Correspondence with Sir Horace Mann*, May 4, 1743 (New Haven, 1954), 226.

23. The other affected colonies were Virginia, Maryland, Georgia, South Carolina and Massachusetts.

24. No competent sociological analysis of the membership of the original "Ancient" lodges has been made, but secondary sources suggest that they were composed essentially of the poorer Irish mechanics and artisans. For example, of the first hundred names on the roll of the "Ancient" Grand Lodge, seventy-two were Irish. Coil, II, 6, 14; Pick, et. al., 104. A. C. F. Jackson, "Preston's England: The Everyday Life of Masons of the Late Eighteenth Century," *Ars Quatour Coronati* (1976), LXXXVIX, 98, says the "Ancients" were drawn from the artisan classes whose lodges were benefit societies, whereas the "Moderns" were of the higher socio-economic classes with less formal and more convivial lodges.

25. Dermott knew Latin and Hebrew and possessed skill as a writer. Pick, et. al., 100 consider him to have been "the life and soul of the Ancient movement," whereas Coil, II, 21, believes that he surpassed the qualities of all other Grand Lodge officers before or since.

26. Laurence Dermott, *Ahiman Rezon: or A Help to a Brother, Showing the Excellency of Secrecy, And the first Cause, or Motive, of the Institution of Free-Masonry; The Principles of the Craft . . .* (London, 1756). Dermott based his work on the second edition of Anderson's *Constitutions* (London, 1738) and on Edward Spratt, *The New Book of Constitutions . . . For the Use of the Lodges in Ireland* (Dublin, 1751).

The *Ahiman Rezon* saw three more editions during Dermott's lifetime and another four before 1813. The later editions contained increasingly negative comments about the "Moderns." For a discussion of the meaning of the title, see Coil, II, 21 and the introduction to a reprint of it (Bloomington, Ill., 1972), vii-xii.

27. This list has been drawn from discussions in Coil, II, 17f., and Pick, et. al., 103. Dermott, 47, considered the Royal Arch Degree to be "the Root, Heart, and Marrow of Free-Masonry," which had to be administered in a proper manner.

28. Pick, et. al., 106; Coil, II, 11f, 19.

29. Coil, II, 199-204. A new book of constitutions written in 1815 incorporated modified "Ancient" practices.

Chapter 2

1. The Coxe Deputation appears in full in Henry S. Borneman, *Early Freemasonry in Pennsylvania* (Phila., 1931), 79-81. Borneman has researched the life of Coxe and provides documentary evidence, but the information is spread throughout the work.

2. *Pennsylvania Gazette*, July 2 to 9, August 6 to 13, August 13 to 20, 1730. Additional Masonic events in the British Isles are reported in this paper through 1741. Some of these references can be found in Clifford P. McCalla, comp. and ed., *Early Newspaper Accounts of Freemasonry In Pennsylvania, England, Ireland and Scotland from 1730 to 1750* (Phila., 1886).

3. *Pennsylvania Gazette,* No. 108, December 3 to 8, 1730.

4. *Ibid.* This version of the ritual is copied verbatim from "The Mystery of Free-masonry," which originally appeared in the *Daily Journal* (London), August 15, 1730. It is reproduced with commentary in Douglas Knoop, G. P. Jones and Douglas Hamer, *The Early Masonic Catechisms* (Manchester, 1963), 152-156.

5. This may have been the technique of buying out the opposition. The opinion of Bernard Faÿ, *Benjamin Franklin, Apostle of Modern Times* (Boston, 1929), 145f., is that Franklin desired to become a member for political and social reasons, and also because of a certain intellectual affinity, and therefore "blackmailed" the Society into accepting him. This position is reaffirmed by a recent student of Franklin, Ronald W. Clark, *Benjamin Franklin, A Biography* (New York, 1983), 43f.

Borneman, 46f., discounts this notion weakly with the counter-argument that it was "unthinkable" that Franklin could thus force his way into membership. Borneman further states that the editorial comment was not Franklin's, but was copied from the London paper. A comparison of Franklin's comments with those of the original article indicates that such was not the case.

6. *Pennsylvania Gazette,* May 6 to 13, 1731.

7. The most recent authors to write about this controversy are: Fred L. Pick, G. Norman Knight and Frederick Smyth, *The Pocket History of Freemasonry* (London, 1969), 299; Ronald E. Heaton, "Pennsylvania" in Lewis C. Wes. Cook, ed., *Colonial Freemasonry* (n.p., 1973-1974), 153; Henry Wilson Coil, *Freemasonry Through Six Centuries* (Richmond, Va., 1967), I, 251.; Alex Horne, "Freemasonry Comes to America," *Transactions of the American Lodge of Research* (1977), XIV, 370-399; Alphonese Cerza, "Colonial Free-masonry in the United States," *Ars Quatuor Coronati* (1977), XC, 218-230.

Borneman, 86-101, argues that the absence of evidence does not prove the negative. Coxe did have authority to institute Masonic lodges, did live in New Jersey in the specific period of its organization and may not have wished to leave any written record in the hope of avoiding outside investigation. There is also the possibility, not mentioned by Borneman, that such evidence could have been lost or burned in the fire of 1819.

8. *Pennsylvania Gazette,* April 19 to 26, 1739.

9. Borneman takes the former view, Heaton, 155, the latter. Heaton follows *OML,* I, 15; *Pennsylvania Gazette,* June 18 to 26, 1732. For the earliest evidence of a Pennsylvania Grand Lodge, see "Liber B," St. John's Lodge, 1731-1738, in the Historical Society of Pennsylvania. Presumably, there was also an earlier "Liber A," now lost.

Masonic sources also mention a letter written November 17, 1754, by Henry Bell, of Lancaster, to Dr. Thomas Cadwalader, a member of St. John's Lodge, which stated that the first Philadelphia lodge had already been meeting for some time before the members applied for and received a charter from Daniel Coxe in fall 1730. This letter, last seen by Philadelphia Masons in 1875, has disappeared (cf. *Dedication Memorial of the New Masonic Temple, Philadelphia* (Phila., 1875), 21).

10. Borneman, 80.

11. Pennsylvania's claim to primacy has been the cause of controversy among twentieth century Masonic writers. The most notable challenge came from Melvin M. Johnson, Past Grand Master of Massachusetts, who published *The Beginnings of Freemasonry in America* (New York, 1924), which argued that the Pennsylvania Grand Lodge was formed without proper authority in so far as it did not possess a written warrant. It was not "duly constituted" according to Masonic legal definitions and therefore was "irregular." He put forward the case of the Grand Lodge of Massachusetts, formed in 1733, because that body had received a document, properly signed, sealed and delivered.

For a refutation of Johnson, see Borneman and Coil, I, 252-259. Coil's is a rambling and complicated rebuttal. The Grand Lodge of Pennsylvania also possesses correspondence on this issue between the two jurisdictions in the 1920s and 1930s.

12. Because the original of Price's deputation has not survived, historians must rely upon copies that may not be reliable. For example, they do not agree on the date, which has been reported as April 13 or April 30.

13. This claim is supported by Johnson, 115, although he produces no official Masonic document to support it. The whole issue of Price's authority is taken up by Coil, I, 263-273, in painstaking detail, but the best discussion is by Horne, who says something positive about the claims of both sides.

14. This letter, destroyed by fire in 1864, is reproduced in Coil, I, 264, in Leonard W. Labaree, ed., *The Papers of Benjamin Franklin* (New Haven, 1959), I 373-375; and in Julius F. Sachse, *Franklin as a Freemason* (Phila., 1906), 39f.

15. This letter is reproduced in Coil, I, 265, in Labaree, 375f., and in Sachse, 39f.

16. *American Weekly Mercury*, March 20 to 27, 1735. Masonic scholars do not agree on the accuracy of this report [cf. note 13].

17. Anderson's *Constitutions* (London, 1723, 1738) did not offer any rules or regulations concerning the appointment of Provincial Grand Masters, so the Grand Lodge of England was probably improvising. In accepted practice, the Provincial Grand Master was appointed by the English Grand Lodge, subject to approval by the Provincial Grand Lodge. To be legitimate, the Provincial Grand Master needed the approval of his subordinates as well as his superiors. The petition of the Massachusetts Masons is dated October 7, 1751 and is reproduced in Johnson, 369.

18. James Anderson, *The Constitutions of the Free-Masons* . . . (Phila., 1734), 1; *Pennsylvania Gazette*, May 9 to 16, 1734, May 16 to 23, 1734; Constitutions of St. John's Lodge, 1727 (Thomas Carmick MS), original document in Grand Lodge Archives and reproduced in Borneman, Appendices A and B.

19. The bulk of Anderson's work (46 pages) is composed of the legendary history of Freemasonry, whereas the rules and regulations occupy about half as much space. The English Grand Lodge had originally passed this legislation on June 24, 1721.

20. Anderson, 51.

21. *Ibid.*, 76.

22. Information pertaining to the Jones-Rees incident and the ensuing controversy appears in the following: *Pennsylvania Gazette*, June 9 to 16, 1737, June 16 to 23, 1737, January 31 to February 7, 1737/8, February 7 to 15, 1737/8; *American Weekly Mercury*, February 7 to 14, 1737/8, February 14 to 21, 1737/8.

23. Benjamin Franklin to his parents, Josiah & Abiah Franklin, April 13, 1738, in Labaree, II, 202-204, in Sachse, 72-5, and Coil, I, 275. This and the Price letters are the only three references to Freemasonry in all of Franklin's private correspondence.

24. This notice appeared in *Pennsylvania Gazette*, June 9 to 16, 1737, June 16 to 23, 1737, June 23 to 30, 1737.

25. Pennsylvania Gazette, June 25, 1741.

26. For evidence as to early meeting places, see McCalla, especially 15, 27f, for proof of the existence of both a "Sun" Tavern and a "Tun" Tavern on Water Street in the same period. Earlier Masonic historians believed that they were the same, a mistake which probably resulted from a misprint (*OML*, I, 10).

These taverns are discussed in Joseph J. Kelly, Jr., *Life and Times of Colonial Philadelphia* (Harrisburg, 1973), 160-171, John F. Watson, *Annals of Philadelphia and Pennsylvania in Olden Times* . . . (Phila., 1905), III, 344-367 and Russell F. Weigley, ed. *Philadelphia: A 300-Year History* (New York, 1982), 57f., 76. Identification of owners' names and specific locations of taverns are found in the H. B. Roach File (APS).

See Appendix B for a complete list of Masonic meeting places in Philadelphia, 1731-1873.

27. The original subscription lists are in the Grand Lodge Archives. They are also reproduced in *OML*, I, 45-47, 57f.

28. This description comes from the *Pennsylvania Packet*, September 26, 1785.

29. An advertisement for the procession appeared in *Pennsylvania Gazette*, June 20, 1755, and an account of the results appeared in June 26, 1755; Smith's sermon was

advertised for sale in the issue of July 3, 1755. This sermon appears in *The Works of William Smith, D.D.* (Phila., 1803), II, 27-42.

From 1779 to 1785, the "Ancient" Grand Lodge used the Freemason's Lodge for its own meetings. The Saint Andrew's Society also met there (*Pennsylvania Gazette*, February 18, 1755).

The scriptural passage was from 1 Pet. 2:17.

30. No minutes of either Pennsylvania Grand Lodge are extant before July 29, 1779. Therefore, one must rely upon fragmentary evidence. On November 7, 1782, the "Ancient" Grand Lodge received a communication, dated October 30, from five "Modern" Masons concerning its rental of the "Modern's" meeting hall (*GLM*, I, 52; "Subscribers to the Building Now Alive, 11 March 1782" with "Members of the First Lodge that did not contribute [MS in Grand Lodge Library]). An entry in the Minutes of Lodge No. 2 dated July 22, 1766 indicated that the "Modern" Grand Lodge with William Allen as Grand Master, may still have been operating (*B&S*, I, 168).

31. Notices of the sale of Freemason's Hall appeared in *Pennsylvania Gazette*, September 26 to 30, October 1, 1785 and *Pennsylvania Packet*, September 26, 1785; *OML*, I, 49f; *B&S*, II, 54f., 98f.; *An Address to the Inhabitants of Pennsylvania by the Freemen of the City of Philadelphia who are now confined in the Masons' Lodge . . .* (Phila., 1777); *B&S*, I, 15; *Pennsylvania Packet*, October 28, 1785, February 3 & May 24, 1786; Weigley, 132.

32. The letter is reproduced in *B&S*, II, 138.

33. Extant records pertaining to early Pennsylvania lodges are as follows: "Liber B," Tun Tavern Lodge, 1731-1738; Minutes of Lodge No. 2, "Moderns," 1749-1763; Minutes of Tun Tavern Lodge, 1749-1755; Minutes of Lodge No. 4, "Moderns," 1757-1758.

34. Franklin's Daily Journal, August 32, 1734, as quoted in *OML*, I, 27. This source does not appear in Labaree's collection.

35. Anderson, 48f., 60f.; Billy Smith, "The Material Lives of Laboring Philadelphians, 1750-1800," *William and Mary Quarterly*, (1981), XXXVIII, 171-174, 183-85. Wages and prices are calculated for the year 1755.

36. For a more thorough discussion of membership, see Wayne A. Huss, "Pennsylvania Freemasonry: An Intellectual and Social Analysis, 1727-1826" (Ph.D. diss., Temple University, Phila., 1984).

37. Masonic membership exceeded that of other successful Philadelphia societies in the same period. For example, the Carpenters' Company (1724-1760), 17 members; the Library Company (1731-1760), 152 members; the Schuylkill Fishing Co. (1732-1760), 105 members; the Saint Andrew's Society (1749-1760), 143 members; the American Philosophical Society (1743-1760), 15 members. Statistics indicate the number of new members. Sources are: Carpenters' Company Membership List; *History of the Schuylkill Fishing Company of the State in Schuylkill, 1732-1888* (Phila., 1888); A Chronological Register of the Names of the Members of the Library Company of Philadelphia (MS.); *An Historical Catalogue of the St. Andrew's Society of Philadelphia, 1749-1907* (Phila., 1907); *Transactions of the American Philosophical Society* (Phila., 1771), Vol. 1.

Chapter 3

1. Petition of Lodge No. 4, "Moderns," Philadelphia, to Grand Lodge of "Ancients," London, January 10, 1758, and cover letter of John Blackwood, Master of No. 4, to Joseph Reed, Secretary of No. 2, London, January 10, 1758 (*B&S*, I, 20-26).

This source is particularly valuable because it reproduces the minutes and other original documents of early "Ancient" Freemasonry in Pennsylvania. The minutes of the Grand Lodge of Pennsylvania do not begin until July 29, 1779, so one must rely upon the records of the premier "Ancient" subordinate lodge, No. 2.

2. Same sources as above, in addition to: Minutes of Lodge No. 4, September 13, 1757; Warrant of No. 1, Pennsylvania and No. 69, England, June 7, 1758; cover letter of Lodge No. 2, England to Lodge No. 1, Pennsylvania, August 19, 1758. The charge for the warrant was £1 14s. 6d. including postage. The Grand Lodge of England also sent by-laws for the proper governing of the lodge (*B&S*, I, 18, 31-34, 54-64).

3. List of members, Lodge No. 1, Pennsylvania, June 1759; John Blackwood, Master of Lodge No. 1 to Joseph Reed, Secretary of Lodge No. 2, London, June 21, 1759 (*B&S*, I, 39-42, 52-54).

4. Minutes of Lodge No. 1, "Ancients," February 12 and 13, April 8, 1760 (*B&S*, I, 67f., 70, 117). The minutes do not indicate the actual function of the second Masonic body. Barratt and Sachse alternately believe that it was a "lodge of instruction" or that it was the genesis of Lodge No. 3. Because the division occurred so soon after the election of William Ball as Grand Master and because Ball was appointed Master of the second section, it seems clear that it was a nascent grand lodge. The second section met on different nights than the first and had different officers, except the treasurer.

5. Copy of the original Grand Lodge Warrant in the Archives of the Grand Lodge of Pennsylvania. Its cost was £7 7s. Minutes of Lodge No. 2, March 12, 1761; Laurence Dermott, Grand Secretary, to William Ball, Provincial Grand Master, February 4, 1763; Minutes of the Grand Lodge of England, "Ancients," September 5, 1759 (*B&S*, I, 76, 113, 115f). As early as March 12, 1761, the members of Lodge No. 2 knew that their request for a Grand Lodge warrant would be received favorably. On that date, the treasurer was authorized to pay London for the warrant.

6. The circumstances of the delay in the delivery of the Grand Lodge Warrant are explained in a letter of Laurence Dermott to William Ball, January 11, 1765 (*B&S*, I, 122-124).

7. Laurence Dermott to William Ball, February 4, 1763; Minutes of Lodge No. 2, December 30, 1763, February 2, 1764 (*B&S*, I, 108, 110, 115-119).

8. The officers of No. 3 were not installed until February 1, 1765, and the warrant was not issued until October 29, 1767. Because Lodge No. 3 met in the same location as No. 2, it is unlikely that the division resulted from geographical inconvenience. It is not stated which option the members exercised. Original Minutes of No. 2, January 23, 1764, February 1, 1765 (*B&S*, I, 109, 152).

9. Original Minutes of No. 2, December 28, 1772, and miscellaneous documents in *B&S*, I, 131-135; original Minutes of No. 3, June 17, 1773, June 9, November 10, 1774; original Minutes of Lodge No. 4, June 24, December 13, 27, 1774.

10. Laurence Dermott, *Ahiman Rezon, Or, A Help to A Brother* . . . (London, 1756). Evidence that this work was known in Pennsylvania is as follows: Lodge No. 2, London, to the Brethren in Philadelphia, August 19, 1758; John Blackwood, Master of Lodge No. 2, Philadelphia, to Joseph Reed, Secretary of Lodge No, 2, London, June 21, 1759; Laurence Dermott to William Ball, January 11, 1765 (*B&S*, I, 33, 41, 123).

11. Dermott, xvii.

12. Evidence of meeting places appears in original minutes of Philadelphia Lodge Nos. 2, 3 & 4. Although Videll's Alley was also called "Lodge Alley," the building where the "Ancient" Masons met should not be confused with the one constructed by the "Moderns" in 1755. This small passageway was named after Stephen Videll/Vidal (d. 1755), a schoolmaster and member of "Modern" Lodge No. 3, Tun Tavern. See Appendix B for a complete list of Masonic meeting places in Philadelphia, 1731-1873.

13. Minutes of Lodge No. 2, October 15, 1776 (*B&S*, 281). Other affected lodges were Nos. 6, 7, 8, 9, 10, 11, 12a, 13, 14, 15, 16, 17 and 18. Surviving records are presented in *OML*.

14. Original Minutes of Lodge No. 4, November 19, 1776, state: "The Grand Officers have neglected to call a Grand Lodge for more than two years past." Evidently, the Grand Lodge did not meet again until late 1778, although surviving minutes do not

begin until July 29, 1779. The Grand Lodge's circular letter is dated October 22, 1779 (*GLM,* I, 11, 14). The quotation concerning lost minutes appears in the preface to the same work.

It is estimated that the total household budget for necessities among Philadelphia families of laborers, mariners, cordwainers and tailors stood at £73 11s. 8d. in 1776 and £109 9s. 6d. in 1783. Annual wages of common laborers in the same period rose from £55 3s. 0d. to £74 2s. 6d. Statistics are not available for 1779. Billy Smith, "The Material Lives of Laboring Philadelphians, 1750-1800," *William and Mary Quarterly* (1981), XXXVIII, 163-202.

15. Original Minutes of Lodge No. 3, June 22, 1775, June 24, 1776; *Pennsylvania Evening Post,* June 17 and 21, 1777; *Pennsylvania Gazette,* June 19, 1776; *Pennsylvania Packet,* June 10, 1776; Original minutes of Lodge No. 18, February 12, 1777.

16. The memberships of these lodges are discussed in *OML,* I, 138-143, 173f., 211-249, 330-360; *B&S,* xiii, 291; Mahlon Addis, *Two Hundred Years of Ancient York Masonry in the Western World, 1758-1958* (Phila., 1958), 21. The members of the Masonic lodges have been checked against Francis B. Heitman, *Historical Register of Officers of the Continental Army During the War of the Revolution* (Balt., 1967 [reprint]).

The breakdown of officers by lodge is as follows: No. 2, 49; No. 3, 85; No. 4, 46; No. 5, 17; No. 8, 19; No. 18, 36 (total 252). All these men were not members at the same time, however. Most obtained their Masonic credentials within a few days, by dispensation, and then moved on as their orders changed. Because existing Masonic records from this period are fragmentary, it is probably safe to assume that other Masons also served in the military.

17. Minutes of Lodge No. 18, February 9, 1778 (*OML,* I, 342).

18. *OML,* I, 361-389, and *B&S,* I, 292f. Original Minutes of No. 3, October 10, 1777, February 21, 1778.

19. Lodge No. 3 had possession of the Grand Lodge Warrant as of February 22, 1778, but no record indicates exactly when the regimental warrant was conferred. It was given the number 18, previously issued (1775) to a lodge in Dover, Delaware. There was some confusion concerning this matter in the minds of contemporaries. (cf. *OML,* I, 361-389; original Minutes, Lodge No. 3, February 21, 1778). Two histories of the regiment exist, but neither mentions its Masonic activities: Richard Cannon, *Historical Record of the Seventeenth or the Leicestershire Regiment of Foot* (London, 1848); Lt. Col. E. A. H. Webb, *History of the Services of the 17th (The Leicestershire) Regiment* (London, 1912).

20. Samuel H. Parsons to officers of Lodge No. 18, July 23, 1779, reproduced in *OML,* I, 362, and in *GLM,* II, 415, October 16, 1809.

21. Officers of Lodge No. 18 to Grand Lodge of Pennsylvania, March 28, 1786, reproduced in *OML,* 387f., and mentioned in *GLM,* I, 91f., June 12, 1786. Grand Lodge of Pennsylvania to Lodge No. 18, August 11, 1786 (*OML,* I, 388). The fate of this military lodge is unknown, it is not listed as active in a general accounting of 1809 (*GLM,* II, 415).

22. St. John's Day was actually December 27, but because it was a Sunday, the Masons decided to postpone the celebration until the next day so as not to interfere with religious services. *B&S,* I, 295-307, provides copies of original documentation. See also *Pennsylvania Packet,* December 17, 21, 24, 1778; original Minutes of No. 3, December 18, 23, 1778.

23. Washington participated in other Masonic functions throughout the remainder of the war, mostly in military camps. He later became Master of a lodge in Alexandria that had originally been warranted by the Grand Lodge of Pennsylvania (No. 39, 1783). Washington had been made a Mason in Fredericksburg, Virginia, in 1752.

24. Smith was the same individual who as a "Modern" gave the sermon at the dedication of Freemason's Hall in June 1755. He had been a member of Lodge No. 2, "Ancients," since 1770, but was crafted and raised only a few days before the celebration by a special meeting of the Grand Lodge. Smith later became associated with Lodge No. 7. William Smith, *Sermon Preached in Christ-Church, Philadelphia, for the Benefit of the Poor by Appointment and Before the General Communication of Free and Accepted Masons of the State*

of Pennsylvania . . . on Monday, December 28, 1778 (Phila., 1779); *Pennsylvania Packet*, December 29, 1778 and January 2, 1779; *OML*, I, 201. The sermon also appears in *The Works of William Smith*, II, 50-67. For the relative value of the £400 raised for poor relief, see note 14.

25. *GLM*, I, 19f., 29f., January 13, 1780.

26. Open Letter to American Grand Lodges from a Committee of Army Lodges in Camp, Morristown, N. J., February 7, 1780 (*B&S*, I, 399f.); Julius F. Sachse, *Washington's Masonic Correspondence . . .* (Phila., 1915), 137.

27. Joseph Webb, Grand Master of Massachusetts, to Grand Lodge of Pennsylvania, September 4, 1780, and Grand Lodge of Pennsylvania to Joseph Webb, October 17, 1780 (*GLM*, I, 30f., 32-35).

28. Grand Lodge of Massachusetts to Grand Lodge of Pennsylvania, January 12, 1781 (*GLM*, I 40); and Grand Lodge of Massachusetts to Grand Lodge of Pennsylvania, January 17, 1781 (*B&S*, I, 410). The issue came up from time to time. For example, similar proposals from the Grand Lodges of Georgia and South Carolina were not approved by the Grand Lodge of Pennsylvania (*GLM*, I, 145, 390-395, 426, June 7, 1790, March 3 and 28, 1800).

29. *GLM*, I, 68, December 27, 1783.

30. *GLM*, I, 14, 43f., 62f.; December 20, 1779, November 22, 1781, June 24, 1783; William Smith, ed., *Ahiman Rezon, Abridged and Digested: As a Help to all that are, or would be Free and Accepted Masons* (Phila., 1783). The cost was 5d. each if a dozen were bought or 7s. 6d. each for single copies. Smith removed most of the marginalia contained in Dermott's discursive work, including over a hundred pages of Masonic songs and epi-logues, as well as an oratorio called "Solomon's Temple."

31. There is no factual support for the "Prince Edwin Legend." Not only is there no historical record of such a Masonic meeting, but King Athelstan had no son named Edwin. He did have a half-brother by that name, but these persons lived too early to coincide with the story. A King Edwin of Northumberland had lived three centuries earlier. The originators of the legend probably combined the names of these two kings. For a discussion, see Henry Wilson Coil, *Freemasonry Through Six Centuries*, (Richmond, Va., 1967), I, 31, 40, 43; Fred L. Pick, G. Norman Knight, and Frederick Smyth, *The Pocket History of Freemasonry* (London, 1969), 40, 45, 53, 93f.; and Arthur E. Waite, *A New Encyclopedia of Freemasonry* (New York, c. 1924), 217f.

32. Smith, *Ahiman Rezon*, 30, 81, 145-166.

33. Samuel Magaw, *A Sermon delivered in St. Paul's Church on Saturday, December 27, 1783 . . . for the Benefit of the Poor by Direction, and in the Presence of The Ancient and Honorable Fraternity of Free and Accepted Masons . . .* (Phila., 1784). A bill for musicians has also survived in the amount of £6 7s. 6d.; it is reproduced in *B&S*, II, 50. Notices appeared in *Pennsylvania Packet*, December 12, 18, 27, 1783; cf. *GLM*, I, 67, 69, December 25, 27, 1783. The amount of money collected was not specified.

Magaw gave other Masonic sermons in this period, for example in Christ Church, Dover, Delaware, in 1779 and 1780, at the request of the Freemasons of that state (Phila., 1779, 1781).

34. *GLM*, I, 77f., December 20, 1784; *Pennsylvania Gazette*, December 22, 1784; William White, *The Character of St. John the Evangelist in a Charity Sermon, preached in Christ Church, Philadelphia on December 27, 1784 . . . before The Ancient and Honorable Fraternity of Free and Accepted Masons* (Phila., 1785). Notices appeared in *Pennsylvania Packet*, December 18, 25, 27, 1784. The amount of money collected on this occasion was not specified.

35. *Pennsylvania Journal*, September 24, 1785; *Pennsylvania Packet*, September 23, 1785. The establishment of the Sublime Lodge marked the beginning of Scottish Rite Freemasonry in Pennsylvania. The text of the oration, or even information on who delivered it, has not survived.

36. *GLM*, I, 48, 51f., 54f, 72, 80, 84f., August 6, November 7, December 23, 1782; June 17, 1784; March 28, October 27, 1785.

37. *GLM,* I, 84f., 85f. October 27, December 6, 1785; cf. *B&S,* II, 55-58, which reproduces relevant documentation. Philadelphia County and City Deed Book D, No. 16, 29. Joseph Dean subsequently became Senior Grand Warden in 1787, 1788 and 1789. The Dean bequest was not to the advantage of the Grand Lodge, however. After a complicated history of sale and repurchase, the lot was finally sold in March 1809 without any building on it.

38. William Smith, Grand Secretary, to Joseph Webb, Grand Master of Massachusetts, August 19, 1778 , reproduced in *B&S,* I, 403.

The following are some comparative statistics of other Philadelphia societies: The Carpenters' Company (1761-1785), 55 members; the Library Company (1761-1785), 540 members; the Schulykill Fishing Co. (1761-1785), 47 members; the Saint Andrew's Society (1761-1785), 118 members; the American Philosophical Society (1769-1785), 341 (resident) members; St. George's Society (1772-1785), 145 members. Statistics indicate number of new members. Sources are as follows: Carpenters' Company Membership List; *History of the Schuylkill Fishing Company of the State in Schuylkill, 1732-1888* (Phila., 1888); A Chronological Register of the Names of the Members of the Library Company of Philadelphia (MS); *An Historical Catalogue of the St. Andrew's Society of Philadelphia, 1749-1907* (Phila., 1907); *Transactions of the American Philosophical Society* (Phila., 1771), I; Theodore C. Knauff, *A History of the Society of the Sons of Saint George* (Phila., 1923).

39. By-Laws of Lodge No. 2, adopted June 7, 1758 (*B&S,* I, 54-64); Original Minutes of Lodge No. 3, 1767-1788, especially August 30, 1781 and December 20, 1782; Donald R. Adams, Jr., "Wages Rates in the Early National Period: Philadelphia, 1785-1830," *Journal of Economic History* (1968), XXVIII, 404-426. Billy Smith, "The Material Lives of Laboring Philadelphians, 1750-1800," *William and Mary Quarterly* (1981), XXXVIII, 163-202.

Numerous reductions were made in the membership fees, such as for soldiers. Admitted members, that is men who had been made Masons in another lodge, were charged less, as long as they could produce a certificate of good Masonic standing from their former lodge. In the case of Lodge No. 2, the cost was only £1 2s. 6d.

40. Dermott, *Ahiman Rezon,* 18-21, 27f., 54-57; Smith, *Ahiman Rezon,* 13-23.

Chapter 4

1. *GLM,* I, 71f., June 17, 1784. A copy of the letter is reproduced in *OML,* I, 122f.

For a number of years, the Grand Lodge of Pennsylvania reiterated its suggestion for periodic Masonic conventions in the United States in its responses to various proposals of Georgia, South Carolina, North Carolina and Tennesee for a superintending grand lodge, but received only limited support (*GLM,* I, 145, 394, 426, June 7, 1790, March 3, 28, 1800; II, 79, 259, 334, March 7, 1803, March 2, 1807, March 21, 1808).

2. *GLM,* I, 88f., 90, February 3, March 27, 1786.

3. *Ibid.,* 97, September 25, 1786.

4. *Ibid.,* 98. The printed minutes indicate the date of September 26 but the original handwritten minutes (Vol. A, 150) show a "6" superimposed over a "5" which may indicate that the meetings of the two bodies were, in fact, one meeting that went past midnight. The new Grand Lodge, taking up where the old one left off, would technically be meeting on a different day, hence September 26th. Probably as a means of symbolizing a "new beginning," the original minutes allow several blank pages between September 25th and 26th. A public account of the proceedings appeared in *Pennsylvania Packet,* September 29, 1786.

5. Henry Wilson Coil, *Freemasonry Through Six Centuries*, (Richmond, Va., 1968), II, 97f.

6. *GLM*, I, 99f., September 28, October 16, 1786.; Grand Lodge of Pennsylvania to Grand Lodge of England, October 16, 1786 (*B&S*, II, 133f).

7. *GLM*, I, 118, November 10, 1788.

8. Grand Lodge of England, "Moderns" to Grand Lodge of Pennsylvania (n.d.), read in Grand Lodge, December 6, 1790 (*GLM*, I, 152, reproduced in B&S, II, 136f).

9. Grand Lodge of Pennsylvania to Grand Lodge of England, "Moderns," November 18, 1791, (*B&S*, II, 138f.); Grand Lodge of Pennsylvania to Grand Lodge of England, "Ancients," October 14, 1791 (*B&S*, II, 140-142, and *GLM*, I, 173).

10. Grand Lodge of England, "Ancients" to Grand Lodge of Pennsylvania, (n.d.), but read in Grand Lodge, December 3, 1792 (*GLM*, I, 190-194 and *B&S*, II, 144-147).

11. Letters were also sent to the grand lodges in the United States several months later (*GLM*, I, 99, 100, 107, September 28, October 16, 1786, March 26, 1787).

12. The only surviving on the June celebration is a copy of the ode, which is reproduced in *B&S*, II, 120f.

13. *GLM*, I, 101f., 104f., December 2, 18, 1786, January 2, 1787; *Pennsylvania Gazette*, December 20, 1786; *Pennsylvania Packet*, December 27, 1786, which includes a description of the Fraternity and its ideals; *B&S*, II, 113; Samuel Magaw, *A Prayer Delivered in St. Paul's Church Philadelphia on Wednesday, December 27, 1786 . . . to the Honorable Fraternity of the Free and Accepted Masons of Pennsylvania* (Phila., 1787); Joseph Pilmore, *A Sermon preached in St. Paul's Church, Philadelphia on Wednesday, December 27, 1786 . . . for Relief of the Poor; Before the Honourable Fraternity of the Free and Accepted Masons of Pennsylvania* (New York, 1787). Special thanks were offered to Magaw and Pilmore by the Grand Lodge on January 2, 1787.

For a fuller discussion of the ideology of Freemasonry, see Wayne A. Huss, "Pennsylvania Freemasonry: An Intellectual and Social Analysis, 1727-1826" (Ph.D. diss., Temple University, Phila., 1984).

14. A committee to revise the By-Laws was appointed in January and reported in June 1788. The new rules and regulations were adopted on December 29, 1789. One thousand copies were printed the next year by Matthew Carey, a notable Philadelphia printer and bookseller (*GLM*, I, 112, 116, 132-39, 146, January 21, June 16, 1789, December 29, 1789, June 7, 1790).

15. *GLM*, I, 108, 111, 135f., 357, 451, 455, June 18, December 17, 1787, December 29, 1789, June 3, 1799, December 15, 27, 1800; Donald R. Adams, Jr., "Wage Rates in the Early National Period: Philadelphia, 1785-1830," *Journal of Economic History* (1968), XXVIII, 404-426; Priscilla Ferguson Clement, *Welfare and the Poor in the Nineteenth Century City: Philadelphia, 1800-1854* (Cranbury, N.J., 1985), 78, 145f., 149. The median annual expenditures of nine private Philadelphia charities in 1810 (the earliest year available) were $1,296. The charities together spent $11,593 in that year, about 13% of the outlay for public poor relief.

16. An account of Franklin's funeral appeared in *Pennsylvania Gazette*, April 28, 1790. An estimated 20,000 persons attended. In contrast to the Masons, both the United States House of Representatives and the Supreme Executive Council of Pennsylvania voted to wear badges of mourning for one month.

17. *GLM*, I, 125, 138, December 14, 1789; Rules and Regulations of 1789, Art. XXV.

18. Pilmore, 5.

19. *GLM*, I, 186, 189, June 4, September 3, 1792.

20. *Ibid.*, I, 178f., 180f., December 17, 27, 1791; January 2 and March 5, 1792; Grand Lodge Officers to His Excellency George Washington, President of the United States and George Washington to The Ancient York Masons of the Jurisdiction of Pennsylvania (original document reproduced in *B&S*, II, 173-175, *GLM*, I, 181f., and Julius F. Sachse, *Washington's Masonic Correspondence . . .* (Phila., 1915), 69-75).

21. *GLM*, I, 195, 205; December 3, 1792, December 11, 13, 1793.

22. No Grand Lodge meetings were held from June 24 to December 2, 1793. Meetings were also suspended during the yellow fever epidemics of 1797, 1798, 1799 and 1802 (*GLM*, I, 201f., 279, 332, 369, II, 1801-1810, 43). Lodge No. 2 did not meet in fall 1793 (*B&S*, II, 190).

For the composition of the Citizen's Committee as well as scattered references to the Masons, see J. H. Powell, *Bring Out Your Dead, The Yellow Fever Epidemic of 1793* (Phila., 1949), 188-190, and *B&S*, II, 193.

23. Samuel Magaw, *Things Lovely and of Good Report, A Sermon delivered in St. Paul's Church on the 27th of December 1793 . . . in the presence of the Grand Lodge of Pennsylvania* (Phila., 1794). Magaw's prayer, which repeated that offered in 1786, is reproduced, along with unidentified newspaper advertisements, in *B&S*, II, 191f., and *GLM*, I, 206f., December 27, 1793. No mention is made of Washington's exact contribution or the amount of money raised generally.

24. *GLM*, I, 227-236, November 17, 23, 30, 1795. The Grand Lodge took advantage of this opportunity to reaffirm its sovereignty: "The Supreme Masonic Jurisdiction over all Lodges of Antient [sic] York Masons, held in Pennsylvania, has uniformly been and is duly and Legally vested in the Grand Lodge of Pennsylvania." The By-Laws of the Grand Royal Arch Chapter, consisting of fifteen articles, were adopted on February 24 and March 5, 1798 (*GLM*, I, 310-315).

25. "Third Masonic Sermon," in *The Works of William Smith, D.D.*, (Phila., 1804), II, 73-88. The procession was advertised in *Poulson's American Daily Advertiser,* June 24, 1795. The Grand Lodge thanked Dr. Smith on the say day (*GLM*, I, 224; cf. *B&S*, II, 207f). By comparison, the procession of June 24, 1755 had nineteen such positions and that of December 1779 had seventeen (*Pennsylvania Gazette,* June 26, 1755; William Smith, ed., *Ahiman Rezon* [Phila., 1778], 163).

26. Address of the Grand Lodge of Pennsylvania to George Washington, President of the United States and George Washington to the Grand Lodge of Pennsylvania (reproduced in *B&S*, II, 225f.; *GLM*, I, 261, 263, 266f., December 5, 27, 1796; January 2, 1797; and Sachse, 87-94).

27. *GLM*, I, 268, 273, 290, 296, 300, 344, 347; March 6, June 19, 1797; January 15, 22, 26, 1798; January 21, March 4, 1799. Some additional slight changes of wording in the By-Laws were made in 1807 (*GLM*, II, 255, 263-268, March 2, 4, 1807).

28. For accounts of the funeral procession, see *B&S*, II, 253f.; *GLM*, I, 376f., December 26, 1799, and Russell F. Weigley, ed., *Philadelphia: A 300-Year History* (New York, 1982), 203f.

29. *GLM*, I, 379-382, December 27, 1799.

30. *B&S*, II, 258-262, which reproduces an unidentified "contemporary account" of the proceedings; *GLM*, I, 402-404, 474, March 17, 1800, June 1801; Simon Chaudron, *Funeral Oration on Brother George Washington delivered January 1, 1800 before the Grand Lodge L'Aménité* (Phila., 1800); No. 73 to Grand Lodge, February 16, 1800 (cover letter of the oration); No. 73 to Grand Lodge, Feb. 20, 1800; Lodge L'Aménité No. 73, *Lettres Ecrites à . . . l'occasion de l'oraison funebre de F. George Washington* (Phila., 1801).

Copies of the oration were sent to the Grand Lodges of New Hampshire, Massachusetts, Maryland, Virginia and Kentucky as well as to lodges in France. No. 73 received letters of acknowledgment from President John Adams, Vice-President Thomas Jefferson, Theodore Sedgwick, speaker of the House, Thomas McKean, governor of Pennsylvania and the minsters of France and Spain, among others.

31. *GLM*, I, 385-387, 395f., 397-401, 409, February 3, March 3, 17, April 21, 1800; *B&S*, II, 262-270, which reproduces appropriate documents; Samuel Magaw, *An Oration Commemorating the Virtues and Greatness of General George Washington pronounced in the German Lutheran Church, Philadelphia before the Grand Lodge of Pennsylvania* (Phila., 1800).

32. *GLM*, I, 110, 124, 148, December 17, 1787, September 28, 1789; August 16, 1790. For information on the Dean property, see *GLM*, I, 113, 115, 118, 176, 180, 282,

356, 357, January 21, June 16, December 15, 1788, December 5, 1791, March 5, 1792, December 4, 1797, March 4, June 3, 1799; II, 324, 363, March 7, October 17, 1808; *B&S*, II, 56-62, reproduces relevant documents, including deeds.

33. *GLM*, I, 148, 150, 184, 250-255, 341, 361, August 16, September 6, 1790, June 4, 1792, May 31, 1796, December 27, 1798, June 3, 1799. Detailed proposals for raising revenue in this period are found in: *GLM*, I, 163, 171, 249-255, 364-367, 444, June 6, October 13, 1791, May 31, 1796, June 24, 1799, December 1, 1800.

34. Grand Lodge Officers to His Excellency, Thomas Mifflin, Governor of the Commonwealth of Pennsylvania, November 4, 1799 (*GLM*, I, 270, November 13, 1799).

35. The Legislature granted Peale permission on March 17, 1802, as noted in J. Thomas Scharf and Thompson Wescott, *History of Philadelphia* (Phila., 1884), I, 514. James Milnor, Grand Master to George A. Baker, Grand Secretary, April 3, 1802 (*B&S*, II, 295). Also see *GLM*, I, 408f., April 21, 1800; II, 48, 62f., 73, December 6, 13, 1802, January 3, 1803; *Philadelphia City Directory, 1802*, 92.

For the Masons' further dealings with Peale's Museum, see Chapter 7.

36. *GLM*, I, 466, 474. March 16, June 1, 1801; II, 9, 11, 15, 35, 39-41, 44-47, 80-83, 129f., June 24, July 27, September 21, 1801; March 1, May 3, June 7, November 15, Dec. 6, 1802, March 7, 1803, September 3, 1804. The deed to the Filbert Street property is recorded in Philadelphia County and City Deed Book EFN, No. 8, 365, May 29, 1802. Details of the renovation appear in the Building Committee Minutes for 1802 to 1806 (Ms. in Grand Lodge Library).

37. *GLM*, II, 63-69, December 27, 1802. Public notice of the ceremony appeared in *Poulson's American Daily Advertiser*, December 27, 1802; Masonic Service Association, *Pocket Encyclopedia of Masonic Symbols* (Washington, D.C., 1963), 57f.

38. *GLM*, II, 458-460., June 4, 1810.

39. *Ibid.*, II, 169, 262, 290-294, 297-299, 377, November 4, 1805, April 6, 1807, October 5, November 16, 1807, January 16, 1809. The lot was purchased on December 7, 1807, from William Waln, a merchant, at an annual ground rent of $850 with an option to buy at 16⅔ that amount (Philadelphia County and City Deed Book EF, No. 29, 330, January 1, 1808).

The Grand Lodge proposed to sell the Filbert Street hall for $5,000 to a carpenter who offered payment in work for the new hall but this deal fell through, and the hall was sold for $500 less to Daniel Carrell, a gentleman (*GLM*, II, 411, September 4, 1809; Philadelphia County and City Deed Book JC, No. 5, 267, September 9, 1809).

The Grand Lodge had tried to secure a loan of $10,000 at six percent interest from the City Dancing Academy with provisions that it would could rent rooms in the new hall, but this deal also failed (*GLM*, II, 322f., March 7, 1808).

40. Building Committee Minutes for 1808 to 1813 (MS. in Grand Lodge Library); *GLM*, II, 322-25, 339f., 369f., 386f., 390, 430, Mar. 7, June 6, November 21, 1808; March 6, 20, October 16, 1809. These sources contain detailed descriptions of the building and indicate the progress of its construction. Plans were made to erect a statue of George Washington, but a contemporary illustration does not show it, nor was mention made of it in subsequent documentation; it probably was not done (*GLM*, II, 469f., July 2, 1810).

The cornerstone of the Chestnut Street Hall is preserved in the Grand Lodge Library, and the Latin inscription is reproduced in *B&S*, II, 401, III, 50f. This source also gives an exact description of the architecture of the building.

The Masonic Hall on Chestnut Street was William Strickland's (c. 1787-1854) first independent commission. An engraving of it was later published by William Kneass. Strickland became a Mason in Lodge No. 91 in November 1809. Agnes Addison Gilchrist, *William Strickland, Architect and Engineer, 1788-1854* (Phila., 1950); Joseph Jackson, comp., *Encyclopedia of Philadelphia*, (Harrisburg, 1933), IV, 1118f., *Dictionary of American Biography*, XVII, 137f; Scharf and Westcott, II, 1068.

41. *GLM*, II, 313-321, 397-407, 481, 484-494, March 7, 1808, June 24, 1809, November 19, December 3, 1810; III, 22-28, 33-39, March 4 and April 1, 1811.

42. *Ibid.*, III, 50-83, June 24, 1811; *Freemason's Magazine* (1811), I, 161-168. At the banquet, nine special toasts were offered: (1) "The Day—The Proudest in the Annals of our Lodge—May it prove the most propitious on the Tablets of Charity;" (2) "Our New Hall—While social Harmony reigns in its courts, its secret recesses shall prove a Sanctury for Brothers, and a lodge for the Virtues;" (3) "The Memory of Brother General George Washington—May the gratitude of Masons display itself in Deeds, and rouse the slumbering sensibility of the Nation;" (4) "The Grand Lodges of the United States—Wisdom to their deliberations, Strength to their Measures, and Moral Beauty to their Conduct;" (5) "Our Country—Devotion to its Interests: One of the proudest traits in the Masonic Character;" (6) "Our Fair Sisters—Their Happiness the principal object of our Institution;" (7) "The Academy of Fine Arts and the Society of Artists—They have sown 'good Seed in good Ground;' May they be remunerated by an abundant Harvest;" (8) "The Clergy of the United States—Guardians of the First Great Light of Masonry, they display its influence by lives spent in Acts of Piety and Devotion;" (9) "The Mystic Signal—The Last Appeal; never be it given without effect!" Public notices of the ceremonies were found in *Poulson's American Daily Advertiser,* June 24, 1811 and in printed broadsides.

43. *B&S*, II, 425, Minutes of Lodge No. 2, June 8, 1812; *GLM*, III, 62, June 24, 1811; *Poulson's American Daily Advertiser,* March 10, 1819.

44. Original estimates for the building alone went from $17,000 to $22,000 to $25,000 (*GLM*, II, 322f., 361, 363f., March 7, October 3, 17, 1808). The exact costs at the time of dedication were as follows: ground: $14,166.67; construction already completed: $40,486.58; and anticipated cost of work in progress: $16,784.30 (*GLM*, III, 32-33, April 1, 1811). For documentation on the raising of money, see *GLM*, II, 342, 352, 362f., 393, 431-437, 451, 455, 470-473, 479, June 24, September 5, October 17, 1808, June 5 and November 15, 1809, March 5, April 2, September 3, October 27, 1810; III, 33-35, 84, 90f., 118, 242, 244, April 1, July 18, September 2, November 4, 1811, January 9, 18, 1813; IV, 73, Dec. 1, 1817.

45. There were additional costs estimates of $20,000 on July 18, 1811 and $5,000 on January 9, 1813, to complete and furnish the building (*GLM*, III, 84, 242). Plans for new Masonic loans were adopted on both dates. Other documentation on the means of raising money is as follows: *GLM*, III, 90, 117f., 459, September 2, November 4, 1811, September 2, 1816; Adresses of Grand Masters Milnor and Kerr, December 7, 1812 and December 27, 1815 (*GLM*, III, 211-213, 420). The Grand Lodge took out insurance for $20,000 at an annual premium of $860 (*GLM*, III, 299, December 6, 1813).

Regarding the statues, a contemporary illustration shows three of them in place: two in niches on either side of the main entrance and one in a niche on the spire. Nothing is known about them, however. They are mentioned in *GLM*, I, 255, April 19, 1813.

Information on the efforts of the Grand Lodge to gain tax-exempt status can be found in *GLM*, III, 151, November 2, 1812, 315, 348, March 7, September 7, 1814. In January 1814 a Philadelphia delegate to the Pennsylvania House of Representatives put forward a motion to exempt the property of the Grand Lodge from taxation. Although the measure reached committee and was formulated into a bill, it was laid on the table and never acted upon. *A Brief Statement of the Cost of the New Hall of the Grand Lodge of Pennsylvania* . . . (Harrisburg, 1814); *Pennsylvania House Journal* (1813-1814), 234, 243f., January 27, 1814.

46. Information on the early tenants can be found in the Building Committee Minutes, December 3, 1811, January 28, April 29, March 24, May 12, August 11, November 17, 20, 1812, January 7, 29, 1813; *GLM*, III, 441, March 4, 1816. Victor Guillou had the longest running series of leases of all the tenants, from January 1813 to March 1824 (*GLM*, III, 244, 373f., 390, 416, 444, January 18, 1813, June 19, December 18, 1815, June 3, 1816, IV, 27, 37, 103, 111f., 342, 349, 425, 432, March 17, June 2, 1817, April 20, June 1, 1818, April 2, 23, 1821, March 4, April 1, 1822, V, 205, 227, December 27, 1823, March 1, 1824).

47. For the Grand Lodge of Delaware, see *GLM*, II, 216.
The Provincial Grand Lodge of Santo Domingo was intended as an autonomous jurisdiction, not an independent one. The Pennsylvania Grand Lodge tried to supervise

this organization and expected revenue from it, but because of the political and social turmoils of the island, the Grand Lodge eventually let go its hold in 1814 (*GLM*, II, 19, 24f., 102-104, 211-213, Dec. 7, 1801, Dec. 21, 1801, Sept. 5, 1803, Sept. 15, 1806, III, 330, Apr. 4, 1814).

Article 22 of the Rules and Regulations of 1799 provided that any subordinate lodge that did not pay its dues within two years was to be notified of its deliquency. If it did not respond within six months, its warrant was to be forfeited (*GLM*, I, 353).

48. *Freemason's Magazine* (1811), I, (1812), II; *GLM*, II, 483, December 3, 1810; III, 20, 116, May 4, October 21, 1811.

49. By-Laws of city Lodge No. 9 (1790, 1800, 1811), No. 52 (1809), No. 72 (1797, 1800) and No. 115 (1810) and country Lodge No. 75 (1803) and No. 106 (1807) (MS in Grand Secretary's office); Adams, *loc. cit.*

50. Circular Address of Grand Master Milnor, September 1811 (*GLM*, III, 122).

Chapter 5

1. *GLM*, III, 164-166, 407, 412, 478, June 24, 1812, November 20, 1815, December 16, 1816, IV, 20f., 142, March 3, 1817, October 5, 1818. *PRO 1816*, 4-9, which includes a brief biography of Baker. No details are available on the funeral services for Duplessis and Adcock.

The Grand Lodge offered similar honors to Past Grand Masters Richard Tybout (d. 1821) and Israel Israel (d. 1822). In this period it became customary to drape the hangings of the Grand Lodge Room in black for six months, although not all Past Grand Masters were given a funeral procession (*GLM*, IV, 373, 428, September 3, 1821, April 1, 1822).

2. *GLM*, III, 344, 347-350, 474, September 5, 7, October 3, 1814, October 30, 1816, II, 115, April 16, 1804, 402f.; Address of Grand Master Milnor, June 24, 1809. The Grand Lodge permitted the Chestnut Street Hall to be used for other patriotic gatherings in 1814, such as those of the Washington Benevolent Society in February and July and an anti-Napoleonic association in February (*B&S*, III, 3).

3. *GLM*, II, 450, 455f., March 5, April 2, 1810.

4. *Ibid.*, III, 249, 267, 271, 279-281, March 1, June 7, 21, August 3, 1813.

5. *Ibid.*, III, 146, 149, 236f, 301f., January 6, March 2, 1812, January 4, December 20, 1813.

6. *Ibid.*, III, 388, 393, June 5, 19, 1815.

7. It is not known how many persons were involved in the unauthorized lodge, but two members of No. 139 were disciplined for visiting it (*GLM*, III, 174, 451, 480, September 7, 1812, July 1, December 16, 1816, IV, 25f., March 17, 1817).

Thomas Smith Webb (1771-1819) was important in American Freemasonry. He held a number of high offices, was instrumental in establishing Capitular Masonry in several states, and wrote an influential book, *The Freemasons' Monitor* (1797). For a brief biography of Webb, see Henry Wilson Coil, *Freemasonry Through Six Centuries* (Richmond, Va., 1968), II, 124f.

8. *Lodge No. 103, Havana, to Grand Lodge of Pennsylvania* (*GLM*, IV, 122-129, June 15, 1818).

9. *GLM*, IV, 131-135, July 6, 1818.

10. *GLM*, IV, 212-217, 220, 359, 409, November 1, December 6, 1819, June 4, Dec. 27, 1821. By the time of the difficulty with the Scottish Rite, the Grand Lodge of Pennsylvania had warranted six lodges in Cuba: 103 (1804), 157 (1818), 161 (1818), 166 (1819), 167 (1819) and 175 (1821). Nos. 103, 157 and 166 returned their warrants and

formed the Grand Lodge of Cuba in 1821, along with two lodges from other jurisdictions. The fate of the others is unknown, but they had ceased before 1825. The Grand Lodge warranted another lodge in 1822 No. 181, but it also failed.

11. *B&S*, III, 41-53, and William B. Reed, comp., *Centennial Celebration together with The History of Washington Lodge No. 59* (Phila., 1893), 60f., give interesting accounts of the events surrounding the fire, including the reproduction of relevant documents. Accounts also appeared in *Poulson's American Daily Advertiser*, March 10, 1819, and the *Freeman's Journal*, March 10, 1819.

Frequent references in official Masonic documents are made to the "Archives," although it is not known when it was established. The Masonic library, established in early 1817, occupied a small room on the second floor (?) next to the Tyler's room, and a standing committee of three members supervised its operation and procured books and documents for its collection (*GLM*, III, 464, October 7, 1816, IV, 14, 26f., January 20, March 17, 1817.

12. *GLM*, IV, 165-174, 175, 205, March 16, April 5, October 4, 1819; *Freeman's Journal*, March 11 and 12, 1819. In addition, Lodge No. 67, Philadelphia, canceled a debt of $300 owed it by the Grand Lodge and a few months later it offered a loan of $100.

13. In 1830 the House of Representatives passed a bill repealing this act as an Antimasonic measure, but the Senate did not concur. The House tried again five years later, also without success (*GLM*, IV, 204, 209, 211, October 4, November 1, 1819; *Pennsylvania House Journal* (1819-1820), 9f., 94, 365f., 371, 376f., 392f., 509, 530f., 535; December 7, 16, 1819, January 22, 24, 25, 26, February 5, 9, 1820, (1829-1830), I, 123, 152-155, 192, 387, 393, 399, 400f., December 7, 14, 19, 1829, February 5, 6, 8, 1830, (1834-35), I, 115, 821, January 6, April 8, 1835. *Pennsylvania Senate Journal*, (1819-20), 212, 258-60, 264f., 280-82, January 26, February 4, 5, 9, 1820, (1829-30), I, 244f., February 10, 1830.

14. The Grand Lodge worked out a schedule of fees for the use of these rooms by the various Masonic bodies (*GLM*, IV, 195-198, 280f., 308f., July 19, 1819, October 2, December 18, 1820; Building Committee Minutes, March 18, 1819 to May 25, 1821, 3, 7, 8, 9, 15, 17, 20, 44, 47, March 26, April 12, 15, 16, 23 & 30, May 8, July 19, August 11, 1819.

Two editions of the *Carpenter's Company Book of Prices* were available at this time, one printed in 1786 and the other in 1805. For a discussion of wages and prices, see Donald R. Adams, Jr., "Wages Rates in the Early National Period: Philadelphia, 1785-1830," *Journal of Economic History* (1968), XXVIII, 404-426, and Charles E. Peterson, ed., *The Rules of Work of the Carpenter's Company of the City and County of Philadelphia* (Princeton, 1971), ix-xxiii. The depression of 1819 may also explain why subscriptions to the special fund established in March of 1819 were "very trifling" despite Grand Lodge pressure (*GLM*, IV, 176, April 5, 1819).

15. A Gas Committee formed in February 1820 made its first report one month later. It was estimated that the use of gas would save over $800 per year over other methods of illumination. The gasworks showed a profit of $487.74 in an eighth-month period ending April 22, 1822, and the Gas Committee estimated an annual profit of $2,553 if gas were manufactured for sale, but there is no indication that it ever was.

For reports of the Gas Committee in this period, see Gas Committee Minutes, May 15, 1820 to May 25, 1821; *GLM*, IV, 244, 248-250, 306, 311, 314, 333, 351, 363, 364-368, 370-371, 393, 454, 463-465, February 7, March 6, December 18, 27, 1820, March 5, April 26, July 2, July 31, August 3, October 1, 1821, April 15 & 30, 1822, V, 18, 25, 31, 63, 154, June 17, July 1, August 1, November 4, 1822, April 7, 1823; *B&S*, III, 94, I, 643f. The Philadelphia Gas Works was not established until 1836 and was run for several years as a private firm until the city bought it in 1841. See J. Thomas Scharf and Thompson Wescott, *History of Philadelphia* (Phila., 1884), Russell F. Weigley, ed., *Philadelphia: A 300-Year History* (New York, 1982), 285, 317.

16. *GLM*, IV, 210, November 1, 1819. The description of the interior of the rooms comes from the Furnishing Committee Minutes, April 5, 1820 to May 25, 1821. This

source gives detailed descriptions of furnishings and costs. When faced with several cost estimates, the Grand Lodge always opted for the highest quality. With reference to the cabinet work, the committee requested permission to report verbally, "as the proposals are of such a nature that no written communication could be made satisfactory."

The statues by William Rush (1756-1833) are now on display in the Masonic Temple on North Broad Street. Masonic tradition states that they were originally carved for the first Chestnut Street hall, but this is incorrect. William Kneass' engraving of the hall does indicate upright statues in two niches on the facade and one on the steeple, but no information is available on them except a reference in April 1813 to niches for statues. It is unlikely that these works would have survived the devastating fire.

The Building Committee Minutes, detailing the reconstruction after the fire, give a record of the statues. Rush was paid at least $480 in several installments for six specified works: "Faith" and "Hope" ($180), "Charity" ($150), the two cherubs ($90) and "Silence" ($60) (Building Committee Minutes, 97, 100, 103, 120, 127, 129, July 26, September 20, October 18, 1820, April 25, May 25, 1821). An outstanding balance of $44 for "Faith" and "Hope" was paid in December 1822 (*GLM*, V, 49, 93f., September 20, December 24, 1822). In July 1820 two painters were paid for three coats on three unspecified carvings, possibly by Rush. The Grand Lodge also possesses another statue by Rush, "Virtue," but no documentation exists to indicate when or for what purpose it was carved. It seems likely that it was done for either the original Chestnut Street hall or the rebuilt one. These and other works by Rush are discussed and illustrated in Pennsylvania Academy of Fine Arts, *William Rush, American Sculptor* (Phila., 1982), 121-122, 159-164.

17. A breakdown of expenses and resources for the new hall appears in *GLM*, IV, 261, 264-266, 268, May 1, June 5, July 3, 1820. The Building Committee made another cost estimate in May 1810 of $55,933.05, with a debt of $13,027.90, but even this was insufficent and the total finally came to $63,277.41 (Building Committee Minutes, 122, May 25, 1821). References to additional fund-raising efforts include the following: *GLM*, IV, 190f., 204, 208, 226, 240, 271f., June 21, October 4, November 1, December 20, 1819, February 7, September 4, 1820. The reconstructed hall carried insurance of $30,000. The Grand Lodge Charity Fund only operated sporadically from 1811 to 1844 (*GLM*, IV, 398f., December 17, 1821, V, 204, December 27, 1823.

18. *GLM*, IV, 257, 261, 268, 287-301, March 20, May 1, July 3, Nov. 1, 1820.

19. *Ibid.*, III, 116, 142, 191f., 416, October 21, 1811, January 6, November 16, December 18, 1812, IV, 16, 39, 63f., 106-109, March 3, June 2, October 20, 1817, April 20, 1818.

20. Circular Letter of Lodge No. 43, September 21, 1819.

21. No. 51 to No. 43, November 19, 1819; No. 43 to No. 51, December 17, 1819.

22. *GLM*, IV, 233f. December 27, 1819.

23. No. 131 to No. 43, January 13, 1820; No. 43 to No. 131, February 15, 1820; *GLM*, IV, 243f., 275, February 7, October 2, 1820.

24. T. B. Freeman, *Address on the Principles of Masonry delivered June 22, 1821* (Phila., 1821); printed pamphlet on Masonic Tribunals, 1820; *GLM*, IV, 284, October 16, 1820.

25. The Grand Lodges of Kentucky, Maine, Massachusetts, Mississippi, New York, North Carolina and Virginia rejected ideas of both a general grand lodge and periodic convocations of Masons, but Missouri, New Jersey and Ohio went along with Pennsylvania's suggestion (*GLM*, IV, 459, 472-479, April 30, June 3, 1822, V, 32, 47, 129, 156f., 168, 240, August 1, September 20, 1822, February 17, April 7, June 16, 1823, June 7, 1824).

26. Circular Letter of Lodge No. 43, August 14, 1822.

27. *GLM*, V, 40, 47f, September 16 and 20, 1822; Grand Master (Josiah Randall) to Officers of No. 43, September 20, 1822.

28. For a discussion of the origins and functions of this office, see Richard A. Kern, *The Office of District Deputy Grand Master in the Grand Lodge of Pennsylvania* (Phila., 1947).

These officials were required to give annual reports, many of which appear in *GLM* and *PRO*, beginning in 1824.

29. Meeting of October 9, 1822, which produced another circular letter.

30. No. 43 to Grand Lodge, November 9, 1822; *GLM*, V, 64, 71f., November 4, 18, 1822. Only one member disavowed his association with No. 43 and expressed loyalty to the Grand Lodge. Philip Reitzel to Grand Lodge, December 12, 1822 (*GLM*, V, 79); Circular letter from No. 152, October 31, 1822.

31. The Grand Lodge received the warrant of No. 43 on December 2, 1822 (*GLM*, V, 74, 77f.).

32. *GLM*, V, 75-91, December 16, 1822.

33. Proceedings of the Masonic Convention held in Harrisburg on January 7, 1823; *GLM*, V, 112, 143-147, February 3, April 7, 1823.

34. *GLM*, V, 135-137, March 3, 1823. A complete transcript of the meeting appears in *Proceedings of the Grand Committee held at Philadelphia . . . February, 1823, under the sanction of the Grand Lodge of Pennsylvania* (Phila., 1823). Original documents pertaining to the reform movement are in the Grand Secretary's office. They are also reproduced in George R. Welchans and Andrew H. Hershey, *History of Lodge No. 43, F. & A.M. of Lancaster, Pennsylvania, 1785-1935* (Lancaster, Pa., 1936), 95-139.

In the fall of 1825 Lodge No. 163, Towanda, Bradford Co., tried to revive the movement to establish a Grand Lodge at Harrisburg but no other lodges were interested. For several months No. 163 persisted until the warrant was revoked and the members expelled. The lodge was finally reconciled with the Grand Lodge in December 1826 (*GLM*, V, 346f., 357, 369-372, 385, 408, 461, 473; September 5, November 7, December 27, 1825; June 5, December 18, 1826; September 3, December 17, 1827.

35. Proceedings of the Grand Committee, 15, 16. In the eighteenth century the debate over proper ritual had been a major dispute between "Moderns" and "Ancients." In 1824 and 1825 the Grand Lodge of Pennsylvania opposed the plan of the Grand Lodge of Maine to change the working of the degrees and eventually received the support of seven other jurisdictions (GLM, V, 303, 317-321, 409, 455, February 7, March 21, 1825, December 18, 1826, June 4, 1827).

The most popular Masonic aids were: Jeremy L. Cross, *True Masonic Chart and Hieroglyphic Monitor* (New Haven, 1819); James Hardie, *The New Free-Masons' Monitor; or Masonic Guide* (New York, 1818) and Thomas Smith Webb, *The Freemasons' Monitor or Illustrations of Masonry* (Boston, 1816).

36. Chapter met four times per year as of 1813 and twice a year as of 1824. Authority to establish Mark Lodges was granted in March 1822. The new constitution was adopted by Grand Chapter in June 1823, but did not meet with approval by the Grand Lodge until January 1824. (Rules and Regulations of the Grand Royal Arch Chapter, February 24, 1798 and December 26, 1812; *GLM*, I, 310-315, III, 231-235, January 4, 1813, IV, 426, March 4, 1822, V, 184, 194, 195, 196-198, 199, 214-216, 295f., 311f., August 2, October 20, 27, November 3, Decemeber 1, 1823, January 5, 17, March 7, 1824).

37. The Grand Lodge wanted to limit expenses but at the same time make an impressive showing for Lafayette. The second desire won out, and the celebration cost just over $1,700. Despite ticket sales at $5.00 each, the Grand Lodge had a debt of $266, which was still unpaid two and a half years later. New furniture and decorations had to be purchased, and rent for rooms on the ground floor, normally in use by other societies and individuals, had to be refunded.

One of the principals in the reception of Lafayette was the sculptor, William Rush, who had done some works for the Masons a few years earlier (cf. note 16). He did two figures for a triumphal arch as well as a bust of Lafayette. The Grand Lodge subscribed $1,000 of future revenues to the monument for Washington, conditional upon the raising of a total of $10,000 (*GLM*, V, 256, 259-261, 262-266, 275, 338-340, 397, 431-434, September 4, 6, 20, October 2, December 20, 1824, June 6, 1825, March 5, 1827; Pennsylvania Academy of the Fine Arts, *William Rush*, 139-142, 170f.; Julius F. Sachse,

The History of Brother General Lafayette's Fraternal Connections with the R.W. Grand Lodge, F.& A.M. of Pennsylvania (Phila., 1916); *Pennsylvania Gazette*, September 23, 29, October 4, 6, 1824; *Proceedings of the Grand Lodge of Tennessee* (Nashville, Tenn., 1825), 11, May 4, 1824).

38. The Grand Lodge had attempted to revise its constitution at least a decade earlier but nothing substantial had come of these efforts. Instead, it reprinted in 1816 the last major revision of the Rules and Regulations (1799) (*GLM*, III, 253, 384, 385, 438, 445, 451, 461f., March 20, 1813, April 3, June 5, 1815, February 5, June 3, July 1, October 7, 1816, IV, 422, January 7, 1822, V, 21, 30, 218, 294, 324., 329f., June 17, July 8, 1822, January 5, 17, April 4, 8, 1825). *The Ahiman Rezon containing a View of the History and Polity of Free Masonry* (Phila., 1825). The price of ths edition was $1.25 each in boards and $1.50 in sheepskin binding. Quantity discounts were available (*GLM*, V, 343, 351, July 16, September 19, 1825).

39. *GLM*, IV, 87, March 2, 1818. In accordance with this ruling, the Grand Lodge rejected a petition for a new Philadelphia lodge one year later. It did allow two others to form, however: No. 158 (1818) and No. 160 (1818). The reason for granting the former was that the petition was received before the ruling went into effect; for the latter because it was French speaking and thus did not conflict with existing lodges (*GLM*, IV, 80, 87, 89, 96, 158, February 2, March 2, 16, 1818, March 1, 1819). The next Philadelphia warrant was No. 187, issued on February 17, 1823 (*GLM*, V, 126).

40. Information on raising and paying dues is as follows: *GLM*, III, 270, 358, 367, 428, 433, June 21, 1813, October 3, December 27, 1814, January 15, 30, 1816; By-Laws of City Lodge No. 2 (1821), No. 3 (1816, 1820), No. 19 (1812), No. 51 (1821), No. 52 (1814, 1818, 1821), No. 59 (1813), No. 67 (1817, 1820), No. 72 (1817), No. 81 (1812), No. 155 (1818) and of country Lodge No. 21 (1815), No. 25 (1815), No. 45 (1813, 1822), No. 75 (1817), No. 82 (1821), No. 106 (1823) [MS in Grand Secretary's office]; Adams, 406.

41. *GLM*, III, 270, June 21, 1813, IV, 56, 337, 419, October 6, 1817, March 5, 1821, December 27, 1821, V, 277, 337, December 20, 1824, June 6, 1825; *Report on Masonic Tribunals, October 16, 1820* (Phila., 1820), 2.

42. Information on the ages of members is on file in the Grand Lodge Archives.

43. James Milnor gave more addresses than any other Grand Master until this time. They were repetitive, but Milnor believed that emphasis upon time-tested truths would strengthen the organization. They also made frequent references to "Our Heavenly Father" and "Our Redeemer."

These attitudes were reiterated in the shorter addresses of Samuel F. Bradford and Walter Kerr (*GLM*, II, 276-282, 313-321, 397-407, 484-494, July 6, 1807, March 7, 1808, June 24, 1809, December 3, 1810, III, 22-28, 62-83, 107-116, 120-129, 206-215, 285-297, 404-408, 419f., March 4, June 24, October 21, November 4, 1811, December 7, 1812, November 30, 1813, November 20, December 27, 1815, IV, 16, 70-72, March 3, December 1, 1817).

For information on the Bible Society and the Adult School, see *GLM*, III, 377, 388, 409, 422, 437, March 20, June 5, November 20, December 27, 1815, February 5, 1816.

For a fuller discussion of the ideology of Freemasonry, see Wayne A. Huss, "Pennsylvania Freemasonry: An Intellectual and Social Analysis, 1727-1826" (Ph.D. diss., Temple University, Phila., 1984).

44. Address of Grand Master Walter Kerr (*GLM*, IV, 72, December 1, 1817). Similar sentiments were expressed by Grand Master James Harper at the end of 1825: "The affairs of the Grand Lodge have never been in so flourishing a condition as at the present time" (*GLM*, V, 366, December 27, 1825).

Chapter 6

1. For official Masonic versions of the "Morgan affair," see Alphonese Cerza, *Anti-Masonry* (Transactions of the Missouri Lodge of Research (Fulton, Missouri, 1962), XIX, 36-42; Henry Wilson Coil, *Freemasonry Through Six Centuries* (Richmond, Va., 1968), II, 246-255; John C. Palmer, *The Morgan Affair and Anti-Masonry* (Washington, D. C., 1924); and H. V. B. Voorhis, "The Morgan Affair of 1826," *Ars Quatuor Coronati* (1963), LXXXVI, 197-203.

Throughout the text, the term "Antimasonry" refers to the organized political party of the 1820s and 1830s, and "anti-Masonry" to other sporadic episodes in other periods.

2. It is difficult to explain why western New York Masons reacted so strongly to Morgan's exposé since numerous similar publications were readily available. The most important was *Jachin and Boaz*, originally published in London in 1762. There were twenty-five London editions before 1825 as well as thirteen American ones beginning in 1797. Morgan probably copied large portions from this and other works. In fact, he even stole the title, which was previously used by William Preston (London, 1772) and Thomas Smith Webb (New York, 1797), authors of legitimate Masonic publications.

3. For a non-Masonic explanation of the Morgan affair and the origins of the Antimasonic Party, see Ronald P. Formisano and Kathleen Smith Kutolowski, "Antimasonry and Masonry: The Genesis of Protest, 1826-1827," in *American Quarterly* (1977), XXXIX, 138-165. The most recent comprehensive scholarly discussion of this subject is William Preston Vaughn, *The Antimasonic Party in the United States, 1826-1843* (Lexington, Ky., 1983), 1-20. Most non-Masonic historians believe that Morgan was murdered.

4. Extracts of the General Assembly, Synod of Pennsylvania on the subject of Masonry, 1820-21 (typed transcript in Presbyterian Historical Society); Alfred Creigh, *Masonry and Anti-Masonry: A History of Masonry as it has existed in Pennsylvania Since 1792* (Phila., 1854), 294-96.; *GLM*, 328, 329, 331 February 5, 19, 26, 1821.

5. A fifteenth district was created five years later (*GLM*, VI, 153, December 27, 1832). The annual reports of the District Deputy Grand Masters were published in *PRO*.

6. *GLM*, V, 415-431, March 5, 1827. Original detailed journals of Nathans' visitations are in the Grand Lodge Library.

7. *GLM*, V, 438-443, March 19, 1827.

8. Several New York Antimasonic newspapers were in circulation in Pennsylvania by 1828, and the first native production appeared in New Holland, Lancaster County, in June. At least fifty-nine such papers were printed throughout the state. Lancaster County's Antimasonic Party held local meetings throughout 1828, and the first countywide convention took place in April 1829. This branch of the party subsequently became the strongest in the state. See William L. Cummings, *A Bibliography of Anti-Masonry* (New York, 1967), 11-15; *Union List of Newspapers, 1820-1936*, "Pennsylvania," (New York, 1937), 589- 630; John Edward McNeal, "The Antimasonic Party of Lancaster County; 1828-1843," *Journal of the Lancaster County Historical Society* (1965), LXIX, 59f.; *Pennsylvania House Journal* (1827-1828), I, 630, March 27, 1828; *GLM*, VI, 17, 18, 44, 51; March 17, 31, 1828, March 2, 16, 1829. A Grand Lecturer was appointed every two years.

9. *Proceedings of the General County Anti-Masonic Meeting, Held in Lancaster, April 23, 1829* (Lancaster, Pa., 1829); Sella Payne, *Substance of an Address, Delivered at an Anti-Masonic Meeting, Held in the Township of Gibson, Susquehanna County, Pa., on the 2nd Day of June 1829* (n.p., n.d.); *An Address Adopted at a Meeting of Citizens of Philadelphia, Opposed to Secret Societies; Held on Monday, September 14, 1829* (Phila., 1829).

10. *GLM*, VI, 46, 53f., 55; March 2, April 20, June 1, 1829.

11. *Ibid.*, VI, 60-62, December 7, 1829.

12. *Ibid.*, VI, 64f., 71, 79f.; December 28, 1829, March 1, 1830, September 6, 1830. As time went on, more and more lodges petitioned for temporary suspension of activities, although most eventually recovered.

13. On his way to Mt. Vernon, Lafayette had stopped at Philadelphia and had associated with Masons. This visit was impromptu and no special ceremonies were held, unlike in 1824. The apron was lined in red, white and blue silk, the national colors of both the United States and France (after 1789) and contained forty-three separate Masonic symbols. The heirs of Washington donated it to the Washington Benevolent Society in 1816, and that organization donated it to the Grand Lodge of Pennsylvania. It remains one of the most prized possessions of the Grand Lodge of Pennsylvania. See F. L. Brockett, *The Lodge of Washington: A History of the Alexandria Washington Lodge, No. 22* (Alexandria, Va., 1876), 47f.; Broadside: Bro. George Washington's Apron (Masonic Temple, n.d.); *GLM*, VI, 58, 112, December 7, 1829; February 10, 1832.

14. *The Proceedings of the United States Anti-Masonic Convention Held at Philadelphia, September 11, 1830 embracing the Journal of Proceedings, The Reports, The Debates, and the Address to the People* (Phila., 1830). This work of 164 closely printed pages was simultaneously published in seven northeastern cities (Phila., Boston, Hartford, Albany, New York, Ithaca, Utica) and was available "at most . . . bookstores in the United States." An Antimasonic state convention was held eight months later to nominate delegates to the Baltimore convention, to discuss important issues and to formulate a political platform (*Proceedings of the Anti-Masonic State Convention Held at Harrisburg on the 25th of May 1831* [Harrisburg, 1831]).

15. Avery Allyn, *A Ritual of Freemasonry, Illustrated by Numerous Engravings . . . with Notes and Remarks* (Phila., 1831); Avery Allyn, *The Book of Oaths and Penalties of the Regular, Honorary, and Ineffable Degrees of Symbolic and Knighthood Masonry* (Phila., 1831); *The Sun Anti-Masonic Almanac* (Phila., 1831, 1832, 1833).
Allyn was a "seceding" Mason disillusioned with the Order after reaching the Knights Templar Degree. He then took to the lecture circuit in five northeastern states and become an author. His works were frequently reprinted. Antimasonic almanacs were also popular in the northeastern states in this period.

16. Rush wrote four public letters in 1831 (May 4, June 30, August 13, November 8) and two more in 1833 (August 10, September 11). They were frequently reprinted, such as in *A Collection of Letters on Freemasonry in Chronological Order* (Boston, 1840). For Richard Rush's political activities in this period see Vaughn, 15, 57, 95-98, 110. Rush was a member of Union Lodge No. 121, Philadelphia from 1811 to 1827, when he voluntarily renounced his association with the Fraternity. Rush lost the senatorial contest to Democrat George M. Dallas, a prominent Mason and future Grand Master.

17. The Girard funeral was the only procession the Masons participated in throughout the Antimasonic period. The Grand Lodge invited members to participate, not through the usual Masonic channels, but in city newspapers (*GLM*, VI, 115-120, 139-141, 145; February 20, September 3, December 3, 1832). Masonic sources include reproductions of public announcements. *Philadelphia Gazette*, December 27 and 28, 1831; Russell F. Weigley, ed., *Philadelphia: A 300-Year History* (New York, 1982), 290.
Stephen Girard's Masonic membership has been the subject of much controversy. He was made a Mason in South Carolina in January 1788, but as far as is known, never affiliated with any Pennsylvania Masonic body. One reason was the loss of his right eye, a violation of the physical requirements of the *Ahiman Rezon*. A "Capt. Girard" (no first name given) was made a member of Royal Arch Lodge No. 3 in 1778, but this probably was not the same person. Girard did buy shares of various Masonic loans and served on the Board of Trustees for more than twenty years (Norris S. Barratt and Julius F. Sachse, *The History of Brother Stephen Girard's Fraternal Connections with the R. W. Grand Lodge F.& A.M. of Pennsylvania* [Phila., 1919]).

18. Masonic records do not indicate a specific reason for lack of participation in the Washington centenary celebration, but it probably related to the Girard incident specifically and the Antimasonic movement generally (*GLM*, VI, 113, 121, 128, 199, 200, 210, 226; February 10, 20, March 19, 1832; September 1, 15, 1834; March 2, 16, 1835; *Philadelphia Gazette*, February 15, 18, 20, 1832; Weigley, 289f.).

19. *GLM*, VI, 95-98, 100, November 7, December 5, 1831. The improvements to the Chestnut Street hall involved an element of favorable public relations; local citizens believed they would enhance the neighborhood. Some non-Masons even offered to help pay for them.

20. *GLM*, VI, 17, 111, 129-134, 165f., 174f., 232-234, March 17, 1828; February 6, June 4, 1832, March 4, September 16, 1833, May 4, 1835.

21. Most Grand Lodge officials served without pay, but salaries and expenses were given to the Grand Secretary, the Grand Tyler and the superintendent of hall and gas. Before 1830 end-of-the-year financial statements of the operating budget showed a comfortable surplus, but the Grand Lodge operated in the red thereafter. Most quarterly accounts also show a loss. The operating budget included interest payments to stockholders and periodic contributions to the sinking fund but not money for the charity fund (*GLM*, VI, 9, 43, 136f., 155-159, 179, 187f., 220, 227f., 286; March 3, 1828; March 2, 1829; June 18, 1832; January 21, December 16, 1833, April 7, 1834; March 16, 1835, March 7, 1836).

22. Masonic sources only give extracts from the address as they pertained to Lafayette, so perhaps the unrecorded parts dealt with history. Money collected on this occasion was used to commission a portrait of Lafayette by "an Eminent Artist" to be "put up in a conspicuous place in the Grand Lodge Room" (*GLM*, VI, 190, 193f., 195-197, 279, June 2, 16, 24, 1834; December 28, 1835).

23. John Gest, *A Brief Defense of John the Baptist Against Foul Slander and Wicked Libel of Freemasons* (Phila., 1834); John Gest, *A Brief Defense of John the Evangelist, Also of Solomon, King of Israel . . .* (Phila., 1835); John Gest, *A Selection of Masonic Oaths and Penalties . . .* (Phila., 1835).

24. *GLM*, VI, 213-226, March 16, 1835.

25. *GLM*, VI, 229-231, 236, 239-242, 243f., 245-248, 249, 252- 254; April 6, May 4, 18, June 1, June 10, July 6, 16, August 25, September 7, 1835; File MT-4 (Docs. 3-4) in Grand Lodge Archives; Philadelphia County and City Deed Book AM, No. 68, 373, August 29, 1835. A detailed description of Washington Hall appears in *B&S*, III, 286- 288.

The sale of the Chestnut Street hall as seen from the perspective of the purchaser is found in Bruce Sinclair, *Philadelphia's Philosopher Mechanics: A History of the Franklin Institute, 1824-1856* (Balt., 1974), 221-223. The deed is recorded in Philadelphia County and City Deed Book SHF, No. 2, 46, October 16, 1835.

26. *GLM*, VI, 259, 261, 266f., 271; October 9, November 2, December 7, 14, 1835. The first vote resulted in a tie of five lodges to five; when taken again with more lodges present, it was seven to seven. A motion to postpone the whole matter was defeated by a vote of forty-eight to eighteen, and the final vote was thirty-two for the procession and thirty-four against. The details of the dedication of Washington Hall are found in *GLM*, VI, 275-278, December 28, 1835. Another $3,000 was spent in completing the hall the following year (*GLM*, VI, 297, March 21, 1836).

27. A character sketch and summary of Stevens' early political career appear in Vaughn, 90f. Original records of Lodge No. 200 do not list Stevens' name, even as a rejected candidate.

28. *Pennsylvania House Journal* (1833-1834), I, 369-370, 463-465, 551-553, February 10, 25, March 10, 1834. Stevens and his supporters presented sixty-three petitions against Freemasonry. In contrast, the committee to investigate Antimasonry put forward only seven (*Ibid.*, 414f., 437, 454, 476, 505, 508, 519, 520, 547f., 551, 574, 605, 672f., 738; February 17, 20, 24, 27, March 3, 6, 10, 13, 17, 24, 31, 1834).

29. *Pennsylvania House Journal* (1833-1834), I, 647, 760, 763, 814; II, 734-37, 856- 59, 861-74; March 20, April 1, 2, 5, 1834; *Report of the Committee appointed on the Subject of Free-Masonry Read in the House of Representatives, March 20, 1834* (Harrisburg, 1834).

30. *Pennsylvania House Journal* (1834-1835), I, 25, 45-7, 435-37, 484-85, 557-59, 579, 593, 829-30; December 10, 1834; March 3, 14, 18, 19, April 8, 1835. In this session, the

House heard eighty-eight petitions for an investigation into Freemasonry (*Ibid.*, 37, 42, 49, 84, 106, 114, 125, 133, 152, 167, 188, 195, 200, 227, 245, 268, 283, 284, 313, 333, 360, 378, 400, 417, 445, 470, 493, 506, 533, 560, 589, 644, 780, December 9, 10, 11, 17, 1834, January 5, 6, 8, 9, 12, 14, 16, 17, 19, 22, 26, 29, February 2, 5, 9, 13, 16, 19, 23, 26, March 2, 5, 9, 12, 16, 19, 26, April 6, 1835).

31. *Ibid.* (1835-1836), I, 84-87, December 15, 1835; Vaughn, 100-103.

32. *Ibid.* (1835-1836), I, 11, 14, 39, 409, 430, 475, 480-483, 512-514, 524f., 564f., 570, 628-630, 636, 643-644, December 2, 3, 7, 1835, January 29, February 1, 8, 9, 13, 18, 19, 25, 26 & 27, 1836; *Pennsylvania Senate Journal* (1835-1836), I, 415, 429, 501, 511, 678f., 829f., 842-844, 850-852, 880, 887f., February 27, March 1, 11, 12, 28, May 30, 31, June 2, 4, 6, 1836.

33. *Pennsylvania House Journal* (1835-1836), I, 230f., 233, 234f., 253f., 289-321, 1357-1360, 1387, June 15, 1836, II, 221, 245-248, 386f., 819-869, January 11, 12, 14, 13, 18, 19, 20, 21, 22, 23 & 28, March 8, June 13, 15, 1836. Some of this material was later published as *Testimony Taken By the House of Representatives to Investigate the Evils of Free-masonry* (Harrisburg. 1836); 5,000 copies appeared in English and 2,000 in German. See also *A Strike for Civil Liberty, the Constitution, and the Rights of Man, exhibited in the Conduct, Letters, Protests and Adresses of A Number of Citizens, Summoned to attend before a Committee of the House of Representatives, at the City of Harrisburg, Appointed to Investigate The Evils of Freemasonry, during the session of the General Assembly of Pennsylvania, 1835-36* (Phila., 1836).

34. *Pennsylvania House Journal* (1835-1836), II, 915-920, June 13, 1836; later published as *Report of the Committee Appointed to Investigate the Evils of Freemasonry and other Secret Societies* (Harrisburg, 1836).

35. The figure of $1,600 is based upon extant receipts of payments to reimburse witnesses for travel expenses (ten cents/mile) and time ($1.50/day) for coming to Harrisburg. Even witnesses who did not testify were paid. This alone comes to fifty-five persons or $1533.80. In addition, subpoenas cost seventy-five cents each and the sergeant-at-arms, or his representative, was reimbursed for delivering them (*Pennsylvania House Journal* (1835-1836), I, 242, 264, 315, 390, 427, 456, 496, 504, 606, 625, 773, 985, 1007, 1062, 1360; II, 249, 374, 393, 481, 515-17, 553, 604, 606, 696, 752, 770, 787-89 915-20; January 14, 16, 22 & 28, February 1, 5, 11, 12, 24, 25, March 11, 25, 28, 31, April 1, June 13, 1836, (1836-1837), I, 259, 328, 413, 493, 590, II, 389, 458, 483, 515, 576f., January 6, 18, 25, February 3, 13, 23, (1837-1838), I, 1182, II, 1039, March 17, April 17, 1838).

Stevens' committee received only twenty-three petitions in the 1835-1836 session, in contrast to eighty-eight in the 1834-1835 session and sixty-three in the 1833-1834 session (*Ibid.* [1835-1836], I, 13, 103, 155f., 168, 202, 221, 271, 424, 443, December 3, 18, 1835, January 4, 5, 8, 11, 18, February 1, 4, 1836).

36. *Ibid.* (1836-1837), I, 276, 751, 764f., II, 15, 692-709, December 8, 1836, January 20, March 13, 1837, (1837-1838), II, 17, December 6, 1837; Joseph Ritner, *Vindication of General Washington from the Stigma of Adherence to Secret Societies . . .* (Boston, 1841); Vaughn, 107-112. The last reference to Antimasonry in the Pennsylvania House of Representatives was made on March 3, 1838, when a member once again proposed measures against oaths by secret societies. This proposal was laid on the table and subsequently forgotten (*Ibid.*, [1837-1838], I, 639).

Ritner's claim that Washington was ashamed of, ignored or even denigrated Freemasonry was false. The Grand Lodge of Pennsylvania has original letters, as do other grand lodges, proving that Washington remained a Mason in good standing until his death. For example, Washington, attired in a Masonic apron, laid the cornerstone of the United States Capitol in 1793 according to Masonic ceremonies.

37. Comprehensive end-of-year statements reflected positive balances from 1836 through 1839. Rented rooms included the cellars (a wine merchant), two south rooms (tenants unstated), a back room (Rev. Plummer) and a front room (a lawyer) (*GLM*, VI, 282-284, 291, 318, 327, 340, 355, 392, 435, 442, 462, March 6, 16, September 5, December 5, 1836, February 6, June 5, 1837, February 5, 1838, January 1, March 4, 1839).

38. *GLM*, V, 380f, 398, April 11, November 8, 1826, VI, 170, 351, 355, April 3, 1833, April 14, June 5, 1837. From 1826 to 1842 twenty-four men served as Grand Chaplain. The denominations of these men are as follows: Episcopalian, 9; Presbyterian, Baptist and Independent, 2 each; Methodist, German Reformed, and Universalist, 1 each. Six men could not be traced (*Philadelphia City Directories;* William B. Sprague, Annals of the American Pulpit (New York, 1857-1869), 9 vols.).

39. *GLM*, VI, 291, 316-318, March 16, September 5, 1836.

40. *Ibid.*, 342-344, 349, 360f., 366, 373, 397, February 6, April 3, June 5, September 4, 1837, February 5, 1838.

41. Background information on the Grand Masters comes from a variety of sources. For Dallas in particular, see *Dictionary of American Biography*, V, 38f.

42. *GLM*, 395, 406, February 5, March 5, 1838.

43. *Ibid.*, 437, January 21, 1839.

44. *Ibid.*, 445, 497-499, March 4, December 27, 1839.

Chapter 7

1. *GLM*, VII, 14, 15, 17, 31-34, 112, March 2, December 7, 1840, June 6, 1842.

2. *Ibid.*, VII, 336-339, 348-355, 363, June 1, 1846.

3. *Ibid.*, VIII, 137, 138f., 145, 222, 237, 247, 307, 330f., 338, 351, February 3, 17, 26, March 13, 1851, April 5, June 7, 1852, March 7, June 6, September 5, 1853.

4. *Ibid.*, VIII, 148, 251, 288f., 292-97. 348, 381, December 17, 1849, September 6, December 27, 1852, September. 5, December 27, 1853.

5. *Ibid.*, VIII, 129, 472, 504, December 27, 1850, December 27, 1854, Appendix C: "Grand Visitation Address for 1853." These directives appear to have been widely abused by rank-and-file Masons. In the early 1850s, an unusually large number of men were rejected for membership and, as was their right, they appealed to the Grand Lodge for reconsideration of their status. The aggrieved persons believed that Masons had black-balled them because of "malice, hatred, or personal spite." In many cases, the Grand Lodge had to intervene to see that "worthy" individuals were initiated or admitted, and it reprimanded Masons who had acted "unmasonically" in voting against them. For this and similar reasons, the Grand Lodge also received many petitions from suspended and expelled members (*GLM*, VII, 183, October 16, 1843, VIII, 127, 147, Dec. 27, 1850, April 7, 1851, IX, 1855-1858, *passim*).

6. Financial statements, which appeared quarterly, were complex in this period and sometimes confusing (*GLM*, VII, 12, 47, 60, 99, 140, 221, 265, 340, 356, 423, 509, March 2, 1840, March 1, 1841, March 7, 1842, March 6, 1843, March 4, 1844, March 3, 1845, June 1, 1846, June 7, 1847, Dec. 4, 1848, Dec. 27, 1849, VIII, 68, 164, 256, 386f., 406, 473, March 4, 1850, June 2, 1851, September 6, December 27, 1852, December 27, 1853, March 6, 1854, December 27, 1854, IX, 333f., December 27, 1855). Address of Grand Master James Page, June 1, 1846 (*GLM*, VII, 356f.) and addresses of Grand Master William Whitney, May 6, 1850, Dec. 27, 1850 (*GLM*, VIII, 81f., 131f.; *PRO 1845*, 9f.).

7. For information on the regulations, management and history of the Stephen Girard Fund, see *GLM*, VII, 30, 49-53, 103, 217-219, 228-232, 280, 345, 420-422, 447-550, 490-492, December 7, 1840, March 1, 1841, March 7, 1842, March 4, June 3, 1844, June 2, 1845, March 2, June 1, 1846, June 7, Dec. 6, 1847, June 5, 1848, VIII, 11-13, 91-94, 128, 165-167, 245-247, 252, 277, 332f., 426-428, March 5, 1849, July 1, December 27, 1850, June 2, 1851, June 7, September 6, December 6, 1852, June 6, 1853, June 8, 1854, IX, 48, January 15, 1855, X, 1859-1864, 132, December 17, 1860.

For information on the Grand Lodge Charity Fund, see *GLM,* VII, 186f., 235, 240, 346f., 451, October 16, 1843, September 2, 1844, June 3, 1845, December 6, 1847, VIII, 53, 123, 187, 367, December 17, 1849, December 16, 1850, December 15, 1851, December 19, 1853, IX, 15, January 15, 1855. This fund received a contribution of $500 in March 1850, the proceeds of a special Masonic charity ball held at the Musical Fund Hall (VIII, 87, June 3, 1850). On the reorganization of 1855, see *GLM,* IX, 37f., 54-63, 85, 91-93, March 5, June 18, November 5, December 3, 1855.

In 1855 the Grand Lodge also donated $500 to the city's poor, regardless of Masonic connection (*PRO 1855,* 12).

8. For comparative charitable statistics, see Priscilla Ferguson Clement, *Welfare and the Poor in the Nineteenth-Century City: Philadelphia, 1800-1854* (Cranbury, N.J., 1985), 142, 161. The median annual expenditure by thirty-seven private charities in 1850 was $2,000. The total amount given in that year was $202,336, 22% more than provided by public welfare.

9. *GLM,* VII, 168, June 5, 1843; VIII, 178, 190f., September 1, December 15, 1851. The Masonic College of Missouri was located in Marion County. It opened on May 12, 1844 and was the first institution of its kind. In the 1850s it was followed by the Montgomery Masonic college, Clarkesville, Tennessee, the Masonic Seminary of North Carolina and the Orphans' Masonic University in Kentucky (Joseph Nathan Kane, comp., *Famous First Facts,* 4th ed. (New York, 1981), 183; *Catalogue of the Officers and Students of Montgomery County Masonic College* [Clarkesville, Tenn., 1854]).

10. *GLM,* VII, 106, 108, 242, 278, 285, 288, May 14, June 6, 1842, June 17, 1844, June 2, July 7, September 1, 1845. No public funerals were given to deceased Grand Lodge officials until mid-1852 (*GLM,* VII, 136, 213, 235, January 13, 1851, March 1, June 7, 1852).

11. *GLM,* VII, 283, 380f., 426, 463f., 494, 501f., July 7, 1845, December 2, 1846, June 7, 1847, January 31, June 5, September 4, 1848, VIII, 106, 109, July 22, September 2, 1850; George Washington Warren, *The History of the Bunker Hill Monument Association . . .* (Boston, 1877), 336-340 and *passim;* George M. Dallas, *Address Delivered on the Occasion of the Laying of the Cornerstone of the Smithsonian Institution,* May 1, 1847 (Washington, D.C., 1847); *Washington Monument Dedication Ceremonies in the House of Representatives, February 21, 1885* (Washington, D. C., 1885), 6.

Zachary Taylor was not a Mason although many Masons throughout the country thought he was. For example, 450 New York City Masons turned out on July 23, 1850, for public funeral honors for him, and a few days later a lodge in Troy, New York gave him a Masonic funeral service (William R. Denslow, *10,000 Famous Freemasons* [Trenton, Mo., 1961], IV, 223f.).

The white marble block cost $500 (*GLM,* VIII, 112, 116f., 143, 192, 242, September 2, December 2, 1850, March 3, December 1, 1851, June 7, 1852).

12. For information on the reburial of Girard, see *GLM,* VIII, 145, 169-171, 179-181, 479-482, March 13, August 4, September 30, 1851; *Evening Bulletin,* September 30, 1851; *Public Ledger,* October 1, 1851; and Norris S. Barratt and Julius F. Sachse, *The History of Brother Stephen Girard's Fraternal Connections* (Phila., 1919), 23-54. This last work reproduces all relevant primary sources. As early as March 1835 the Grand Lodge had considered a procession to remove Girard's remains to the college, but in light of the Antimasonic feeling had decided to await a more propitious time, such as after the buildings of the school were completed (*GLM,* VI, 210, 226, March 2 and 16, 1835.)

13. *GLM,* VII, 167f., 176, 205, 221-223, 433, June 5, September 4, 1843, January 15, March 4, 1844, September 6, 1847. When the issue of a general grand lodge came up again in 1854, Pennsylvania Masons simply ignored it (*GLM,* VIII, 455, October 2, 1854; *PRO 1845,* 3-8).

14. *GLM,* VII, 129, 150-52, 165, 233, 410, December 27, 1842, March 6, June 5, 1843, June 3, 1844, March 1, 1847, Joseph R. Chandler, *Masonic Discourses* (Phila., 1844), 61. Chandler's other Masonic addresses include: *An Address Delivered on the Occasion of the Dedication of a New Masonic Hall . . .* (Martinsburg, Va., 1847); *An Address Delivered on the*

Occasion of the Public Installation of Officers . . . (Washington, D. C., 1850); *An Oration Delivered Before Essex Lodge* (Salem, Mass., 1851); *An Address Delivered on the Inauguration and Dedication of Washington Centennial Lodge* . . . (Washington, D. C., 1853); *Washington A Freemason* . . . (Phila., 1853).

Chandler also gave a number of non-Masonic addresses: *An Oration Delivered at the Laying of the Corner-Stone of the Soldier's Monument at Ephrata* (Lancaster, Pa., 1845); "Address delivered on the Occasion of Placing the Crowning Stone, August 29, 1846," in *A Description of the Girard College for Orphans* (Phila., 1848); *The Temporal Power of the Pope Dangerous to the Religious and Civil Liberties of the American Republic* (Maysville, Ky., 1855); *An Address Delivered Before the Girard Brotherhood of the Girard College for Orphans,* (Phila., 1855)

15. Addresses of James Page are found in *GLM,* VII, 313, 315-321, 348-363, 391-401, 458f., 469, December 27, 1845, June 1, December 27, 1846, December 27, 1847, March 6, 1848; *PRO 1845,* 9-16; *PRO 1847,* 5-17, 21-48.

16. Addresses of Grand Masters Whitney and Bournonville are found in *GLM,* VIII, 125-33, 195-200, 287-290, 383-389, 504-510; December 27, 1850, December 27, 1851, December 27, 1852, December 27, 1853; *PRO* 1850 3-12; *PRO 1851,* 3-14; *PRO 1853,* 11-21, 48-61.

Grand Masters Cornelius Stevenson (in office 1843), William Barger (1844-1845), Peter Fritz (1848-1849) and James Hutchinson (1854-1855) also gave an occasional address, but they were more or less annual progress reports on the "state of the Craft," and contained nothing noteworthy (*GLM,* VII, 187-192, 215, October 16, 1843, March 4, 1844, VIII, 60, 389f., 471-475, December 27, 1849, December 27, 1853, December 27, 1854, IX, 349-356, December 27, 1855; *PRO 1847,* 2-17; *PRO 1853,* 22-24; *PRO 1854,* 6-12; *PRO 1855,* 4-17).

17. *GLM,* VII, 14, 17, 21, 28, 35, 65, 73f., 86, 101f., 104f., 110, 122, March 2, June 1, September 7, December 7, 1840., June 7, November 15, December 20, 1841, March 7, June 6, September 5, 1842; Grand Lodge Archives File No. MT-4, docs. 3-23. The lawyer's fees were $200. For the Franklin Institute's perspective, see Bruce Sinclair, *Philadelphia's Philosopher Mechanics: A History of the Franklin Institute, 1824-1865* (Balt., 1974), 223-227.

18. *GLM,* VII, 78, 123, 126, 221, 274-276, 297f., December 6, 1841, September 5, December 5, 1842, March 4, 1844, May 5, November 3, 1845; Philadelphia County and City Deed Book GS, No. 38, 173, March 7, 1842. One of the projected improvements was a wall and railing in the front of the lot even with the street.

Edmund Peale led an adventurous life (Joseph Jackson, comp., *Encyclopedia of Philadelphia* [Harrisburg, 1932], III, 914-917; Charles Coleman Sellers, *Charles Willson Peale* [New York, 1969], 401, 405f.; Sellers, *Mr. Peale's Museum: Charles Willson Peale and the First Popular Museum of National Science and Art* [New York, 1980], 304-312).

19. *GLM,* VII, 368f., 375-378, 395, 434, September 7, October 5, December 27, 1846, September 6, 1847, VIII, 63f., 65, 67, 128, March 4, December 27, 1850. Schultz presented detailed plans for architecture and materials. Internal improvements prior to issuing the lease to E. Peale included new curtains and furniture (*GLM,* VII, 296, September 1, 1845).

20. *GLM,* VII, 413f., 426f., 441, 481f., March 1, June 7, September 6, 1847, April 17, 1848, Sellers, *Mr. Peale's Museum,* 309.

21. *GLM,* VII, 488, 503, 513f., June 5, September 4, December 4., 1848, VIII, 20-22, 33-36, June 4, September 3, 1849. The popular mammoth skeleton was no longer a part of the collection because it had been sent abroad for sale sometime earlier. The deficit of the Grand Lodge included lost rent money, legal fees and the cost of a watchman over the collection.

22. *Ibid.,* VIII, 15, 22f., 26-29, 36f., 40f.; March 5, June 4, August 6, September 3, 1849, *McElroy's Phila. Directory* (1851), 361; (1852), 375; (1853), 351. John Robinson may have been related to the Peale family as evidenced by a genealogy appearing in Sellers, *Peale,* 440f.

23. *GLM,* VIII, 44, 65, December 3, 1849, March 4, 1850; Sellers, *Mr. Peale's Museum,* 304-312, Jackson, *Encyclopedia,* III, 914-917.

24. *GLM,* VIII, 44, 65f., 128, 150f., 174f., 193, 216, December 3, 1849, March 4, December 27, 1850, April 7, September 1, December 15, 1851, March 15, 1852.

25. *Ibid.,* VIII, 55, 129, 155-162, December 17, 1849, December 27, 1850, June 2, 1851.

26. *Ibid.,* VIII, 177f., 200, 217, 219-222, 231-233, 263; September 1, December 27, 1851, March 15, April 5, May 3, September 20, 1852.

27. *Ibid.,* VIII, 267-271, 280f., 283-285, November 29, December 7, 20, 1852; Minutes of the Committee on Plans, September to December, 1852 (MS in Grand Lodge Library); *Report of the Committee on Plans* (Phila., 1852). The deed to the Chestnut Street property was later officially transferred to the trustess of the Masonic loan as security for raising funds (Philadelphia County and City Deed Book, IH, No. 31, 244, June 7, 1853; the original is on file in the Grand Lodge Archives).
Collins, Notman and Sloan were among the most accomplished Philadelphia architects of this period. Brief summaries of their careers are found in Sandra Tatman and Roger W. Moss, comp., *Biographical Dictionary of Philadelphia Architects, 1700-1930* (Boston, 1985), 156-59; 577-579; 730-534.

28. *GLM,* VIII, 300f., 310-313, 314-316; March 7, 22, April 4, 1853; Building Committee Minutes, 2 vols. (MSS in Grand Lodge Library), May 22, 1853.

29. *GLM,* VIII, 318-326, April 18, 1853; Building Committee Minutes, February 2, 4, March 2, 7, 11, 14, 15, 18, April 7, 8. In fairness to Notman, it should be noted that the Building Committee imposed extra work upon him, such as having him revise plans, attend meetings and inspect the site, and he appears to have been chosen to do the work. Four years later, when the ill feeling had died down, Notman made a humble appeal to the Grand Lodge and asked for compensation but without mentioning a specific amount. One year after this request, in December 1857, the Grand Lodge offered him $1,000 (*GLM,* IX, 170, 326, December 15, 1856, December 27, 1857). For more on this architect, see Constance M. Greiff, *John Notman, Architect* (Phila., 1979), 35f, 181-185. Greiff believes that the Masonic controversy negatively affected Notman's career.

30. *GLM,* VIII, 337, 347, 349f., June 6, September. 5, 1853. Additional information on Sloan can be found in Harold Norman Cooledge, Jr., "Samuel Sloan, Architect" (Ph.D. diss., University of Pennsylvania, 1963), 82-86. Exact details of the construction can be found in *Specification of Works and Materials on the New Masonic Hall* (n.p., n.d.); Building Committee Minutes, *passim* and Furnishing Committee Minutes, 1854-1855 (MS in Grand Lodge Library).

31. *GLM,* VIII, 361, 493-503, December 5, 1853; Appendix B: "The Laying of the Corner Stone of the New Temple, Monday, November 21, 1853;" Building Committee Minutes, August 29, September 1, 26, November 19, 1853; *PRO 1853,* 25-43. The original contents of the cornerstone were recovered and are on display in the Grand Lodge Museum.

32. *GLM,* VIII, 375, 387f., 428f., 434, 439, 449-551, December 19, 27, 1853, June 5, September 4, 1854. Finances were secure by December of 1853. Almost half the amount of the new Masonic loan, $52,000, had been subscribed, and an estimated $30,000 could be realized on the sale of the Third Street hall.

33. *Ibid.,* IX, 17, 20, 21, 40f., 50, 52f., 64-68, 69-74, January 15, May 7, June 4, 18, August 13, September 3, 1855; Building Committee Minutes, July 9, 18, 1853, August 7, 17, 31, September 14, 1854, January 4, September 28, 1855; Furnishing Committee Minutes, February 9, June 9, October 1, 1855. By January 1855 more than $95,000 of the new Masonic loan had been subscribed. The Furnishing Committee had originally estimated a cost of $20,000. Insurance for both the hall and its contents had to be continually increased until it covered the actual costs of construction. Rental of rooms for Masonic purposes was expected to yield about $7,000 per year.

34. *GLM*, IX, 67, August 13, 1855; Building Committee Minutes, August 17, September 14, 19, 25, 1855; *Daily Pennsylvanian*, September 21, 1855; *Public Ledger*, September 19 to 22, 24, 25, 1855. The Building Committee's attendance figure was an exact count. The statistics can be broken down as follows (with tickets/without tickets): day 1: 1,575/400; day 2: 1,763/500; day 3: 2,898/800; day 4: 5,263/800. The Public Ledger estimated 10,000 persons on each of the first three days and 33,000 on the final day. At least some of these people may have been repeat visitors.

35. *GLM*, IX, 329-348, Appendix A: "Dedication and Consecration of the New Hall, Chestnut Street, September 26, 1855;" *PRO 1855*. 26-55; *Cummings' Evening Bulletin*, September 26, 1855; *Ballou's Pictorial Newspaper* (Boston), October 13, 1855; *Daily Pennsylvanian*, September 18, 22, 25 to 28, 1855; *Freemason's Monthly Magazine* (Boston), November 1, 1855, 4-11; *Public Ledger*, September 26 and 27, 1855. Estimates of the number of Masons participating in the procession varied from 3,500 to 5,600. Most sources indicate about 4,000, however. Estimates of the number of spectators was as high as 200,000.

36. Exact descriptions of the New Masonic Hall can be found in Building and Funishing Commmttee Minutes, *passim; Cummings' Evening Bulletin, loc. cit., Ballou's Pictorial Newspaper, loc. cit.; Freemasons Monthly Magazine, loc. cit.; Public Ledger*, September 20, 1855, and a printed handbill for the sale of the Masonic Hall, dated January 1873. An interesting note is that the plumbing in the building was advanced for the time, several water closets were located on the second and third floors.

Joseph A. Bailly (1825-1883) was born in Paris, but adopted Philadelphia as his home. Commissioned for many private as well as public works, he was named an academician of the Pennsylvania Academy of Fine Arts in 1856 and became and instructor there in 1876. Five of his statues for the New Masonic Hall were carved of wood and one ("Charity") of lead, but all were painted to resemble marble, and they cost $300 each. The figure of "Charity" was originally made for Washington Hall in 1844. These statues are on display on the second floor of the Masonic Temple on Broad Street (*GLM*, VII, 250, December 2, 1844; Fairmont Park Association, *Sculpture of a City: Philadelphia's Treasures in Bronze and Stone* [New York, 1974], 40, 42f., 63f., 68, 73f., 82f., 91, 98, 105, 119f.; *Dictionary of American Biography*, I, 592f.).

37. *GLM*, IX, 102-106, 112, 123-127, 170, 226-228, 355, 370-371, Appendix E; December 17, 27, 1855, January 7, March 3, June 15, December 27, 1856; Building Committee Minutes, February 29, 1856. Accounts of the costs incurred in building the Masonic Hall were continually recalculated in the months following its dedication, and the amounts kept increasing. In December 1855 it stood at $155,689.81; in January 1856, $156,477.05; in February, $162,890.23; and in March, $170,808.23. The final accounting was made in June 1856 by which time $183,328.03 had been spent. The building was then considered completed and the accounts closed.

Washington Hall was sold in August of 1856 to Joseph Harrison, Jr., a gentleman, for $20,000 (*GLM*, IX, 138, 141f., 180, April 7, May 5. December 15, 1856; Philadelphia County and City Deed Book RDW, No. 103, 9, August 6, 1856.

38. *GLM*, IX, 351, December 27, 1855.

39. By-Laws of city Lodge No. 2 (1844, 1852); No. 3 (1852, 1854); No. 19 (1847, 1854, 1855); No. 51 (1850, 1853); No. 71 (1841); No. 15 (1843); No. 121 (1844, 1846); No. 187 (1847); No. 155 (1850); No. 211 (1852) and country Lodge No. 25 (1852); No. 43 (1846, 1853); No. 61 (1845); No. 108 (1846); No. 115 (1852); No. 143 (1846); No. 153 (1842); No. 155 (1854); No. 194 (1847); No. 199 (1850); No. 203 (1855); Theodore Hershberg, ed., *Philadelphia: Work, Space, Family and Group Experience in the Nineteenth Century* (New York, 1981), 146

40. Compiled age statistics are on file in the Grand Lodge Archives.

41. *PRO 1853*, 48f.

Chapter 8

1. Because of their number it is impossible to list all the citations in the Grand Lodge Minutes on appeals in this period. Suffice it to say that each meeting of the Grand Lodge received five or six appeals, in contrast to meetings of earlier periods, which heard appeals less often. Most cases dealt with members expelled for immoral conduct or suspended for non-payment of dues and who wanted to be reinstated, but others concerned members who had become involved in political disputes or in personal controversies with other members or had lent money to other Masons that was not repaid. Still other cases dealt with the acceptance or rejection of questionable candidates. The standing Committee on Appeals was established in December 1856 (*GLM*, XI, 261, December 28, 1856).

2. As with the appeals from individuals, the number of lodge appeals increased over previous periods; citations are too numerous to list here. The case of Lodge No. 116 is found in *GLM*, IX, 283, June 7, 1856.

3. *GLM*, IX, 119, March 3, 1856. From 1856-1873 the average number of meetings per year was 6.9, in contrast to the period 1840-1855, when 8.7 meetings per year were held. Most meetings held after March 1856 did not go much beyond ten o'clock in the evening.

4. *Ibid.*, IX, 37f., 190, 191f., 193, 196f., 205f., 207f., 210, 211, 214f., 216, 225f., 230, 234f., 253, 274, 350, March 5, December 27, 1855, December 27, 1856, January 19, February 2, March 2, 17, 30, April 20, June 1, June 15, September 7, December 21, 1857, March 1, 1858. Revision or reprinting of the *Ahiman Rezon* was suggested as early as spring 1848, but various committees urged that the 1825 edition, of which there were still 650 copies remaining, be sold before a new one was produced (*GLM*, VII, 477, 492f., March 6, June 5, 1848).

5. *The Ahiman Rezon or Book of Constitution, Rules and Regulations of the Grand Lodge of Pennsylvania together with the Ancient Charges and Ceremonial of the Order for the Government of the Craft under this Jurisdiction* (Phila., 1857). An updated version produced in 1868 included additional decisions of the Grand Lodge.

6. *GLM*, 131-33. At about the same time, new jewels were made for the District Deputy Grand Masters, but no details are given as to their style. The only information available is that they were of gilt silver and cost $127.50 for seventeen of them (*GLM*, IX, 260, December 28, 1857).

7. *Ibid.*, IX, 188, 236f., 254-257, 381f., December 27, 1856, September 7, December 21, 1857, XI, 168, 236, December 28, 1868, December 27, 1869; *PRO 1868*, 47f. This evidence indicates that the first group of Grand Master portraits, covering the period 1779-1867, were completed at about the same time and were mass-produced. It also explains why most of the individuals are shown dressed in the costume of the late 1850s and 1860s even though some had served in earlier periods.

As of December 1868 the likenesses of six deceased Past Grand Masters were still missing; three were subsequently located and portraits were done, but portraits of the remaining three, William Adcock (in office 1783-1788); Walter Kerr (1816-1817) and Bayse Newcomb (1818-1821) were never done, despite searches for likenesses. The first group of Grand Master portraits hangs in the central stairwell of the Masonic Temple in Philadelphia,

Germon, whose shop was located at 702 Chestnut Street in the 1850s and 1860s, was a notable nineteenth-century Philadelphia photographer. He was especially skilled in the carte-de-visite format. See William C. Darrah, *Cartes-de-Visite in Nineteenth Century Photography* (Gettysburg, Pa., 1981), 115, 132; Kenneth Finkel, *Nineteenth Century Photography in Philadelphia* (Phila, 1980), 217; *Philadelphia City Directory* (1859-1864).

8. *PRO 1856*, 31-51, *1857*, 41-70, *1858*, 23f., 24-89, *1859*, 37-48, *1860*, 7-50, *1862*, 23-52; *GLM*, IX, 158f., 188, 281, 309, 372-386, 400-413, 415-470, Appendices, F, H, I, June 16, December 27, 1856, January 5, December 27, 1857, June 7, December 20, 27,

1858, X, 33, 59-66, 97, 117f., 126-48, 169f., 235-246, 317-321; June 6, December 19, 1859, March 5, September 3, December 17, 27, 1860, December 27, 1861, December 27, 1862; *Masonic Mirror and Keystone* (1852-1860), 9 vols.

Other disputes were with Texas, over reciprocal charity disbursements, with Louisiana, over members who had obtained their degrees in different jurisdictions, and generally, over the issue of Masonic education. The body that handled interstate communication was called the "Committee on Foreign Correspondence" or simply the "Committee of Correspondence."

9. *GLM*, VIII, 48f., 69-71, 74f., 77f., 81, 126f., 438, 461f., December 17, 1849, March 4, April 15, 30, May 6, December 27, 1850, June 5, October 2, 1854; IX, 54, 76, 88, June 18, September 17, November 5, 1855; *Report of the Special Committee of the Grand Lodge . . . of New York on the Riotous Proceedings . . . of June 5, 1849* (New York, 1849).

10. *GLM*, IX, 110, 112, 129, 170, 188, 350, December 27, 1855, January 7, March 17, December 15, 27, 1856.

11. *Ibid.*, IX. 372-377, Appendix F. It is not entirely clear which New York Grand Lodge issued the denunciation, but it was most likely the schismatic one.

12. *Ibid.*, IX, 289, 317, 408-410, 413, 422-470, September 6, December 20, 1858, Appendices H, I; X, 27-29, April 4, 1859. The correspondence between the representives of the respective committees ran from September 16, 1858 to March 25, 1859. Even after the matter was settled, the New York representative, Findlay M. King, made yet another effort to justify the actions of the Grand Lodge of New York. The Pennsylvania representative, Richard Vaux, responded fraternally but forcefully, eliciting an apology from King, which Vaux acknowledged. In short, the Grand Lodge of Pennsylvania had the last word and knew that its course had been proper.

13. *GLM*, X, 232-235, December 27, 1861; *PRO 1861*, 27-33, *1863*, 34-66. Throughout the 1860s and early 1870s the annual reports of the Committee of Correspondence gave evidence of more harmony among the various Masonic jurisdictions. Communications were enhanced and more knowledge of their respective activities was shared. Although closer in spirit and general interests, the American Grand Lodges still remained independent of each other.

14. *Ahmian Rezon* (Phila, 1857), 48, 60; *PRO 1863*, 61f. These basic Masonic principles were, of course, not limited to Pennsylvania, but were common throughout American Freemasonry. The positions taken by the Pennsylvania Grand Lodge during the Civil War were echoed by those of other northern jursidictions (*GLM*, X, 401-405, 496-500, December 28, 1863, December 27, 1864).

15. *GLM*, X, 75-7, 170-171, December 27, 1859, December 27, 1860; *PRO 1859*, 57f.; Allen E. Roberts, *House Undivided: The Story of Freemasonry and the Civil War* (Fulton, Mo., 1961), 10-21.

16. *GLM*, X, 246-251, December 27, 1861; *PRO 1861*, 54-62.

17. *GLM*, X, 226, 281, 342, 437; December 27, 1861, September 1, 1862, April 6, 1863, September 5, 1864, XI, 30, December 18, 1865. Because of the intervention of an unidentified Confederate officer, who was a Mason, Chambersburg's Masonic Hall was saved from destruction (Roberts, 219).

18. See Table 1 for the charitable disbursements of this period. Because of careful management, the capital of both charity funds had exceeded $45,000 each by the early 1860s, and the Grand Lodge Charity Fund reached its goal of $50,000 in December 1865 (*GLM*, IX, 152f., 234, 269, 308, 355, December 27, 1855, June 2, 1856, September 7, December 21, 1857, December 6, 1858, X, 10, 68, 98, 161f., 167, 176, 188, 224, 227, 272f., 301, 305-307, 309, 345, 405, 409, 417, 451, 464, March 7, December 19, 1859, March 5, December 17, 1860, March 4, December 27, 1861, June 2, December 15, 27, 1862, December 28, 1863, March 7, December 19, 27, 1864, XI, 14, December 18, 1865).

The amount given to any one person was conditioned by need and by the number of applicants in any given year because of a limited sum available. The substantial resources of the Fraternity and the relatively small annual charitable disbursements caused feelings of guilt among the trustees of the funds, who frequently offered proposals for reform. A few adjustments were made from time to time, but no significant changes occurred in the way charity was handled throughout the period (*GLM*, IX, 185f., 359-361, December 27, 1856, X, 82, 163f., 177, 310, December 27, 1859, December 17, 27, 1860, December 27, 1862, XI, 221f., December 1, 1869).

19. *GLM*, X, 266, 316f., 495f., March 3, December 27, 1862, December 27, 1864; *PRO 1862*, 39, *1864*, 71f. During the American Civil War twelve Northern and nine Southern grand lodges warranted a total of 251 military lodges, 98 by the former and 153 by the latter. The greatest number of military lodges were warranted by Indiana (38) and Illinois (18) in the North, and by Texas (33), Mississippi (29), and Virginia (26) in the South. See John Black Vrooman and Allen E. Roberts, comp., *Sword and Trowel: The Story of Traveling and Military Lodges* (Fulton, Mo., 1964), 42-113.

20. *GLM*, X, 292f., 299, December 1, 15, 1862.

21. *Ibid.*, X, 169, 228, 323, 410, December 27, 1860, December 27, 1861, December 27, 1862, December 28, 1863; *PRO 1860*, 18, *1862*, 56. Grand Masters Peter Williamson (in office 1856-1857) and Henry M. Phillips (1859-1860) also adhered to a strict policy in granting dispensations.

22. David Wills played a major role in selecting the site and purchasing the land for the Soldiers' National Cemetery, and President Lincoln stayed in his home while in Gettysburg. A lodge of Odd Fellows and an encampment of Knights Templar also attended the dedication (*Cummings' Evening Telegraphic Bulletin* [Phila.], November 16, 18, 19, 20, 1863; *History and Directory of the Boroughs of Adams Co.* [Gettysburg, 1880] 29, 38, 40; *Revised Report of the Select Committee relative to the Soldiers' National Cemetary* [Harrisburg, 1865]).

Correspondence pertaining to this event is reproduced in *GLM*, X, 365-367, December 21, 1863; *PRO 1863*, 15-17. Many other Grand Lodges supported Pennsylvania's decision not to participate (*GLM*, XI, 46, 48, 49, December 27, 1865).

Andrew G. Curtin (1815-1894) was known as the "Soldier's Friend" because of the great concern he showed for their welfare. He supervised their hospital care, brought their bodies back for burial, and established relief funds for their widows and orphans. He had a distinguished political career and was a member of Bellefonte Lodge No. 268 (William R. Denslow, *10,000 Famous Freemasons* [Fulton, Mo. 1957], I, 273f.; *Dictionary of American Biography*, IV, 606-608).

23. Correspondence and the Grand Master's report appear in *GLM*, XI, 32-35, December 27, 1865; See also *Order of Masonic Ceremonies for the Laying of the Foundation Stone of the Monument in the Soldier's National Cemetery at Gettysburg, Pa., July 4, 1865* (Phila., 1865) and *Daily Evening Bulletin*, July 1, 3, 5, 6, 1865.

24. *GLM*, X, 226, 401-405, December 27, 1861, December 28, 1863; Roberts, *op. cit.* This work is essentially a collection of incidents showing how Freemasonry operated in time of war. After recognizing a brother through the the use of the "Masonic sign of distress" or the "hailing-sign of a Master Mason," one Mason spared the life of, obtained better medical treatment for, provided means of escape for, or protected the property of a fellow Mason, even at the risk of his own life or situation.

25. *GLM*, X, 311-313, December 27, 1862, XI, 1865-1874, 7-10, September 11, 1865; *PRO 1862*, 25-29; *Letter . . . from the Grand Lodge of Pennsylvania . . . to the Freemasons of the United States* (Phila., 1865). Communications with the Southern grand lodges were not restored until after 1866 (*GLM*, XI, 65, 90, December 27, 1865, December 27, 1866).

26. *GLM*, X, 90-92, 168, 553f., December 27, 1859, December 27, 1860; *PRO 1859*, 83-85. The number of Masonic districts increased to 20 in 1866, 27 in 1869, and 28 in 1870 (*GLM*, XI, 86f., 111, 311f., 317, 366-68, 440f., December 27, 1866, December 4, 1867, December 27, 1870, December 27, 1871, December 27, 1872; *PRO 1870*, 70-72, 1871, 97f., 1872, 105f.)

27. *Ahiman Rezon* (Phila., 1868), 159f.; *GLM*, X, 357-360, 374-376, 433f., 455; September 7, December 21, 1863, June 6, December 19, 1864; *PRO 1863*, 26-32. A fine of

$3 per hour was levied for violations of these provisions. As of mid-1855, all subordinate lodges meeting in the Masonic Hall were officially permitted to dispense with meetings in July and August because of the heat. This practice had been followed unofficiallly long before, however (*GLM*, IX, 53, June 18, 1855).

28. Some of the more important reports of the Hall Committee from this period can be found in *GLM*, IX, 177f., December 15, 1856; X, 20f., 47, 95, 271, 283, April 4, September 5, 1859, March 5, 1860, June 2, September 1, 1862; *PRO 1859*, 10f., 24. Tours were given every day but Sunday from nine o'clock in the morning to four o'clock in the afternoon.

29. *GLM*, X, 360f., 370f., 374, September 7, December 21, 1863.

30. *Ibid.*, X, 429-433, 453-455, June 6, December 19, 1864.

31. Committee reports from this period can be found in *GLM*, XI, 18-23, 72-78, 105f., 196, December 18, 1865, December 18, 1866, December 4, 28, 1868; *PRO 1865*, 16-25, 1866, 18-25; original Grand Lodge Minutes, Vol. M, 53f., 195, March 6, September 5, 1865. Contracts for improvements in the Masonic Hall were awarded almost exclusively to fellow Masons, provided they were otherwise qualified to do the work.

In October 1866 the deed of the Chestnut Street hall was transferred from one set of trustees to another on account of the advanced age of the former (Philadelphia County and City Deed Book LRB, No. 212, 414).

The Grand Lodge also gained revenue from the rental of the Commandery room on the third floor to Scottish Rite Masons, an independent body (*GLM*, XI, 24, March 5, 1866).

32. *GLM*, XI, 78, 103, 105-107, 128f., 137, December 17, 1866, December 4, 27, 1867; *PRO 1866*, 25f., 1867, 15f; original Grand Lodge Minutes, Vol. M, 222-225, 283-286, 319-326, February 4, 1867, September 3, 1866, June 5, 1867.

33. *GLM*, XI, 107f., December 4, 1867; *PRO 1867*, 18-20. The deeds are recorded in Philadelphia County and City Deed Book, JTO, No. 26, 30-33 and No. 65, 184-189. The first, with Wetherill, is dated February 22, 1867, and the second, with Harrison, is dated July 1, 1867.

34. *GLM*, XI, 107-111, 146, 149, 166; 289-296, February 4, December 4, December 27, 1867, December 2, 28, 1868, December 7, 1870; *PRO 1867*, 20-23. Masonic sources do not state how many architects were consulted, nor do they give names other than Windrim's; however, based on the amount of money spent for the plans ($1,000 for the successful and $500 for each unsuccessful plan; and the total of $2,500), it would seem that four architects had submitted plans. The trustees of the building fund made quarterly reports of its status.

James H. Windrim (1840-1919) had a long and distinguished career in Philadelphia. A protege of John Notman, his first break came with the Masonic Temple, about which one source reported: "his fortune was made." Windrim was a member of the first graduating class of Girard College and later designed a number of buildings for that institution. He was admitted to Lodge No. 72 in April 1868 (Register of Members, Vol. 4-1, 92; Sandra Tatman and Roger W. Moss, comp., *Biographical Dictionary of Philadelphia Architects* (Boston, 1985), 871-873).

For tax-exempt status of the Masonic Temple, see original Grand Lodge Minutes, Vol. M, 407, June 3, 1868; *Pennsylvania House Journal* (1867-1868), 962, 1219, 1282; *Pennsylvania Senate Journal* (1867-1868), 795, 799, 815, 1139f., 1187f.

35. In his choice of subject, Vaux was no doubt influenced by recent archaeological excavations in Jerusalem, to which he referred in one of his annual addresses (*GLM*, XI, 163-165, 171-183, 225f., December 28, 1868, December 27, 1869; *PRO 1868*, 37-43; 53-75; *Programe of Ceremonies with the Oration delivered by Richard Vaux for Laying the Cornerstone of the New Masonic Temple, June 24, 1868* (Phila., 1868); *Evening Star* (Phila.), June 23 and 24, 1868; *Morning Post* (Phila.), June 23, 24, 25, 1868).

The original cornerstone was opened on March 4, 1986, at the beginning of the two-hundredth anniversary celebration, and its contents placed on display in the Grand Lodge Museum.

36. *GLM,* XI, 165, 197-201, December 28, 1868; *PRO 1868,* 163-168. A list of individual contractors appears in original Grand Lodge Minutes, Vol. M, 410-424, June 3, 1868.

37. *GLM,* XI, 210-12, 280, 283f., 287, 289, 296; December 1, 1869, December 7, 1870. An Act of the Pennsylvania Assembly (No. 1228) was necessary before the Grand Lodge could go public with its Masonic loans; it was passed on April 3, 1869. In the interest of fairness the Grand Lodge later converted the first series of loans from 6 to 7.3% to match the others (*GLM,* XI, 400, 411, December 4, 1872; *Pennsylvania House Journal,* (1868-1869), 807, 825, 900, 983; *Pennsylvania Senate Journal* (1868-1869), 799, 820, 929, 995; original Grand Lodge Minutes, Vol. M., 442, 492, 507-510, September 2, 1868, March 3, April 7, 1869).

38. *GLM,* XI, 216f., 275-277, 289f., 296, 343f., October 11, 1869, June 1, December 7, 1870, December 27, 1871; *PRO 1869,* 19-21, *1870,* 10-12, 31f.

39. Pennsylvania Masons made an initial contribution of $1,000 in October 1871 to the Chicago Fire victims, with additional gifts over the next year, although exact amounts are not noted. At the end of 1872 the Pennsylvania Grand Lodge received a refund of $2,150 which was about 10% of the surplus (*GLM,* XI, 43, 98f., 325f., 432, 435-438, December 18, 1865, September 3, December 27, 1866, October 12. 1871, December 27, 1872; *PRO 1871,* 19f., *1872,* 58f., 98-103; original Grand Lodge Minutes, Vol. M., 219, 328, September 3, 1866, June 5, 1867).

40. *GLM,* XI, 324, 337f., 352, 385, 395f., 401f., 411, 451; September 6, December 6, December 27, 1871, December 4, 1872, December 3, 1873. The largest individual subscriber of the Masonic loans was a non-Mason, who held $40,000. His name was not given (original Grand Lodge Minutes, Vol. M, 237f., March 5, 1873).

41. The cornerstone of City Hall was laid with Masonic ceremonies on July 4, 1874. Past Grand Master Henry M. Phillips and Deputy Grand Master Samuel C. Perkins, both members of the Public Buildings Commission, may have had some influence on the final decision (*GLM,* XI, 344-346, 415-420, December 27, 1871, December 4, 1872; *PRO 1871,* 50-58; Joseph Jackson, comp., *Encyclopedia of Philadelphia* (Harrisburg, 1931), II, 465-468; Joseph Jackson, *Market Street, Philadelphia* (Phila., 1918), 177f.; Russell F. Weigley, ed., *Philadelphia, A Three-Hundred Year History* (New York, 1982), 16, 424-426; John Russell Young, *Memorial History of Philadelphia* (New York, 1895, 1898), I, 555-557, II, 117f.).

42. Contemporary descriptions of the building appear in *GLM,* XI, 290-296, December 7, 1870 and Library Committee, *Dedication Memorial of the New Masonic Temple* (Phila., 1875), 174-184; *PRO 1870,* 32-40.

43. *GLM,* X, 490-492, December 27, 1864, XI, 322, 348-350, 403-406, 455; June 7, December 27, 1871, December 4, 1872, December 3, 1873; *PRO 1864,* 64-67, *1871,* 6, 58-62, *1872,* 40-44, *1873,* 21-23.

44. The breakdown of the participating subordinate lodges was as follows: Philadelphia, 61; Pennsylvania other than Philadelphia, 83; and other than Pennsylvania, 10. The last group came from New York, New Jersey, Delaware, Maryland and Virginia (*Dedication Memorial,* 75-99).

45. *Ibid.,* 100-125. Toasts were made to: "the memory of the Grand Master and brethren who superintended and took active part in the building of King Solomon's Temple;" "the memory of our deceased brother, George Washington;" "Freemasonry around the Globe;" "the Masonic Fraternity;" "the amity between Grand Lodges of Freemasons throughout the Globe;" "the lodge of Freemasons;" and the Grand Lodges of Massachusetts, North Carolina, Maryland, Wisconsin and Canada.

46. *Ibid.,* 126-163.

47. *GLM,* XI, 452, 454, 459-462, June 4, December 27, 1873.

48. Compiled data on members' ages is on file in the Grand Lodge Archives.

49. *GLM,* IX, 13f., January 15, 1855, X, 406, 426f., December 28, 1863, June 6, 1864, XI, 222, December 1, 1869. The Grand Lodge's attempt to raise fees in 1855 failed.

Philadelphia metal workers earned an average of $1.82 per day between 1860 and 1867, and $2.06 from 1868 to 1875. Stone cutters earned an average of $2.19 and $3.30 a day in the same periods respectively. Regional and national averages for these occupations were slightly higher. Weekly wages are calculated on the basis of a six day work week (Clarence D. Long, *Wages and Earnings in the United States, 1860-1890* [Princeton, N. J., 1960], 125-127, 135).

50. *GLM,* X, 412, 467, 500, December 27, 1863, December 27, 1864, XI, 36, 126, 159-161, 229, December 27, 1865, December 27, 1867, December 27, 1868, December 27, 1869. The problem of too-rapid an increase in membership was common in other Masonic jurisdictions as well (GLM, XI, 56-58, December 27, 1865).

51. The inaugural addresses of Mitchell and Goddard, in which they acknowledge their ill health, appear in *GLM,* IX, 394-399, December 27, 1857 and XI, 85, December 27, 1866; *PRO 1857,* 27-36, *1866,* 37f.

Announcements and accounts of funeral proceedings of the deceased Past Grand Masters are found in *GLM,* IX, 137, 275, 279f., April 7, 1856, April 13, June 7, 1858, X, 107f., 334-339, June 4, 1860, March 2, 1863, XI, 31f., 67, 81f., 111, 129, 322, 466f., December 27, 1865, December 17, 27, 1866, July 18, December 4, 27, 1867, June 7, 1871, December 27, 1873; original Grand Lodge Minutes, Vol. M, 50, 90, 333-336, March 6, June 5, 1865, September 4, 1867, Vol. N, 52, 242, June 7, 1871, March 5, 1873. These accounts include proceedings and euologies were also printed.

52. Background information on the Grand Masters comes from a variety of sources. On Vaux in particular, see *Dictionary of American Biography,* XIX, 238f.

53. The addresses of Richard Vaux can be found in *GLM, XI, 119-130,* 155-171, 223-239, December 27, 1867, December 28, 1868, December 27, 1869; *PRO 1867,* 24, 37-51, *1868,* 24-52, *1869,* 31-56. Grand Master Lucius H. Scott (in office 1865-1866) held similar religious views, recommending that "all good men and Masons should spend the Sabbath in church" (*GLM,* XI, 30-7, 80-85, December 27, 1865, December 27, 1866; *PRO 1865,* 35-44, *1866,* 30-36).

54. The addresses of Robert Lamberton and Samuel C. Perkins can be found in *GLM,* XI, 240-245, 299-310, 350-359, 361-366, 429-440, 465-468; December 27, 1869, December 27, 1870, December 27, 1871, December 27, 1872, December 27, 1873; *PRO 1869,* 60-71; *PRO 1870,* 47-68; *PRO 1871,* 63-96; *PRO 1872,* 85-97; *PRO 1873,* 37-41.

55. *GLM,* XI, 271, December 27, 1869.

APPENDICES

APPENDIX A
Genealogy of the Right Worshipful Grand Lodge
of Free and Accepted Masons of Pennsylvania

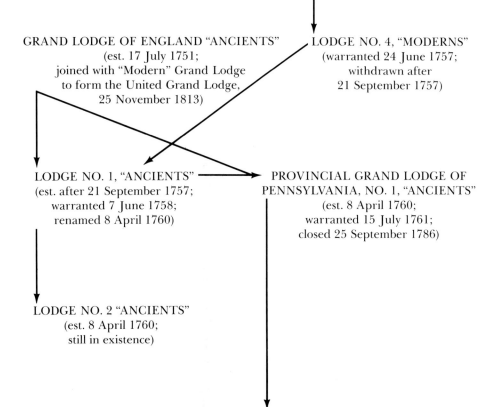

GRAND LODGE OF ENGLAND
(est. 24 June 1717;
joined with "Ancient" Grand Lodge to form
the United Grand Lodge, 25 November 1813)

PROVINCIAL GRAND LODGE OF PENNSYLVANIA
(Coxe Deputation, 5 June 1730;
Oxnard's reconfirmation of Franklin, 10 July 1749;
Lord Byron's reconfirmation of Allen, 13 March 1749/50;
ceased after 1761)

GRAND LODGE OF ENGLAND "ANCIENTS"
(est. 17 July 1751;
joined with "Modern" Grand Lodge
to form the United Grand Lodge,
25 November 1813)

LODGE NO. 4, "MODERNS"
(warranted 24 June 1757;
withdrawn after
21 September 1757)

LODGE NO. 1, "ANCIENTS"
(est. after 21 September 1757;
warranted 7 June 1758;
renamed 8 April 1760)

PROVINCIAL GRAND LODGE OF
PENNSYLVANIA, NO. 1, "ANCIENTS"
(est. 8 April 1760;
warranted 15 July 1761;
closed 25 September 1786)

LODGE NO. 2 "ANCIENTS"
(est. 8 April 1760;
still in existence)

INDEPENDENT GRAND LODGE OF PENNSYLVANIA
(est. 26 September 1786)

APPENDIX B
Masonic Meeting Places in Philadelphia, 1731–1873

Map Code	Dates	Place	Location	Lodge Name	Owner	Owner's Mbrshp
—	1731-1732	Sun Tavern	Water Street	MGL	John Hobart	MN01
A	1733-1734	Tun Tavern	SE corner Water St. & Tun Alley	MGL	Thomas Mullen	MN03
B	1735-1748	Indian King Tavern	SW corner High St. & Biddle Alley	MGL	Owen Owen	MN01
C	1749-1752	Royal Standard Tavern	High St. west of 2nd	MN02	Henry Pratt	MN01
C	1749-1755	Royal Standard Tavern	High St. west of 2nd	MGL	Henry Pratt	MN01
A	1749-1755	Tun Tavern	SE corner Water St. & Tun alley	MN03	Thomas Mullen	MN03
D	1753-1763	Fountain Inn	Market St. near London Coffee House	MN02	William Biddle	
E	1755-1761	Freemason's Lodge	Lodge Alley	MGL	Moderns	
E	1755-1763	Freemason's Lodge	Lodge Alley	MN02	Moderns	
F	1757; 1758-1759	Queen of Hungary	West side of Front above Race St.	MN04 AN02	Jeremiah Smith	
—	1762	Harp & Crown	3rd Street	AGL	Joseph Bell	AN02
G	1764	Sign of the Sugar Loaf	Corner of Market & Water Streets	AGL	John Child	AN02
—	1764-1768	Harp & Crown	3rd Street	AGL	Joseph Bell	AN02
H	1769-1772	unnamed building	Videll's Alley	AGL		
I	1770;1773	Sign of the George	SW corner 2nd & Arch Streets	AN04	Benjamin Davids	
—	1770	unnamed tavern	Walnut Street	AN03	Thomas Craig	AN03
J	1770-1773	Sign of the Buck	West side 2nd Between Race & Vine Streets	AN04	Michael Croft	
K	1772 (June)	Sign of Sir John Falstaff	NW corner 6th & Carpenter Sts.	AGL		
—	1772-1773	unnamed tavern	Walnut Street	AGL	Thomas Craig	AN03
L	1773	unnamed tavern	Water Street below the Drawbridge	AGL	Allen Moore	AN02
—	1773 (June) 1774 (June)	unnamed tavern	Upper Ferry on the Schuylkill	AGL AN03 AN04	Caleb Parry	
—	1774	unnamed tavern	Walnut Street	AN03 AN04	Ferguson Purdon	AN03
I	1775	Sign of the George	SW corner 2nd & Arch Streets	AN03	Benjamin Davids	
M	1775-1777	City Tavern	SW corner 2nd & Gold Streets	AN03	Daniel Smith	
N	1777	unnamed tavern	Corner of Elfreth's Alley & 2nd Street	AN03	Alexander Boyle	AN04
O	1777-1779	unnamed tavern	Walnut a few doors west of 2nd	AN04	Alexander Boyle	AN04
O	1778	unnamed tavern	Walnut a few doors west of 2nd	AN02 AN03	Alexander Boyle	AN04
H	1778-1787	unnamed building	Videll's Alley	AN03		
H	1779	unnamed building	Videll's Alley	AGL		
—	1779-1783	unknown tavern	unknown	AN04	Hercules Courtenay	AN04
E	1779-1785	Freemason's Lodge	Lodge Alley	AGL	Moderns	
E	1783-1785	Freemason's Lodge	Lodge Alley	AN04	Moderns	

(Continued on next page)

APPENDIX B (Cont.)

Map Code	Dates	Place	Location	Lodge Name	Owner	Owner's Mbrshp
H	1786-1790	unnamed building	Videll's Alley	AGL		
P	1787	unnamed building	Black Horse Alley	AN02		
Q	1790-1799	Free Quaker Meeting House	SW corner 5th & Arch Streets	AGL	Quakers	
R	1800-1802	Pennsylvania State House	Chestnut between 5th & 6th Streets	AGL	Commonwealth of Pennsylvania	
S	1802	dancing academy	90 N 8th Street	AGL	William Francis	AN051
T	1802-1810	Pennsylvania Freemason's Hall	South side Filbert west of 8th Street	AGL	Ancients	
U	1811-1819	Masonic Hall	North side Chestnut between 7th & 8th Streets	AGL	Ancients	
T	1819-1820	Pennsylvania Freemason's Hall	South side Filbert west of 8th Street	AGL	Ancients	
U	1820-1835	Masonic Hall	North side Chestnut between 7th & 8th Streets	AGL	Ancients	
V	1835-1855	Washington Hall	West side 3rd Street above Spruce	AGL	Ancients	
U	1855-1873	New Masonic Hall	North side Chestnut between 7th & 8th Streets	AGL	Ancients	

The prefix "M" indicates a "Modern" lodge, either grand (GL) or subordinate (by number) and "A" indicates an "Ancient" lodge.

The meeting places of the "Modern" Grand Lodge and "Modern" Lodge No. 1 were the same.

The meeting places of the "Ancient" Grand Lodge and "Ancient" Lodge No. 2 were the same from 1760-1774.

The "Ancient" Grand Lodge held no meetings from June 1774 to June 1778.

Letter codes indicate locations of meeting places on the map; meeting places without codes do not have specific enough addresses for accurate plotting on the map.

The Upper Ferry of the Schuylkill (not on map) was located just north and west of the city limits.

This data has also been arranged by place of meeting and by lodge; it is on file in the Grand Lodge Archives.

Sources: Notices in the *Pennsylvania Gazette*, 1731-1755; Treasurer's book, "Modern" Lodge No. 2, 1749-1763; Minutes of Tun Tavern Lodge, 1749-1755 [HSP]; Minutes of "Ancient" Lodges: No. 2, 1757-1787, No. 3, 1767-1786, No. 4, 1770-1786; Minutes of the Grand Lodge of Pennsylvania, 1779-1873 [all MS in Grand Lodge Library]; H. B. Roach File [APS]; John F. Watson, *Annals of Philadelphia and Pennsylvania in Olden Times* (Phila., 1905), Vol. III, 344-367.

(Continued on next page)

APPENDIX B *(Cont.)*

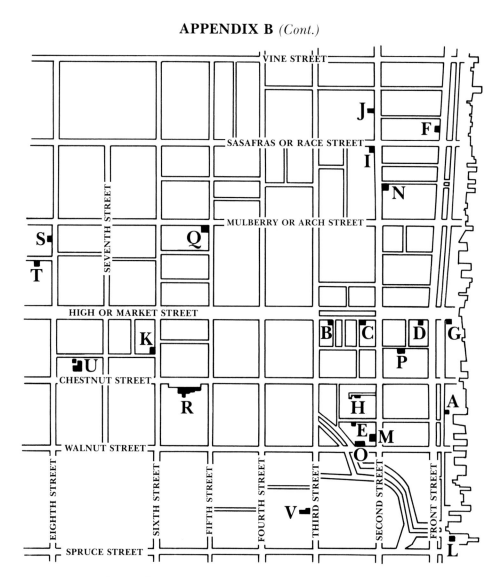

Source for Map: Benjamin Eastburn (London, 1776).

APPENDIX C
Table 1

Officers of the "Modern" Provincial Grand Lodge of Pennsylvania, 1731–1761

Year	Grand Master	Deputy Grand Master	Senior Grand Warden	Junior Grand Warden	Grand Secretary	Grand Treasurer
1731	William Allen	William Pringle	Thomas Boude	Benjamin Franklin	Thomas Boude	Thomas Boude
1732	William Allen	William Pringle	Peter Cuff	James Bingham	Thomas Boude	Thomas Boude
1733	Humphrey Murray	Thomas Hart	James Hamilton	Thomas Hopkinson		
1734	Benjamin Franklin	John Crapp	William Plumstead	Joseph Shippen		
1735	James Hamilton	Thomas Hopkinson	Joseph Shippen	Henry Pratt		
1736	Thomas Hopkinson	William Plumstead	Henry Pratt	Philip Syng		
1737	William Plumstead	Joseph Shippen	Thomas Cadwalader	Thomas Boude		
1738	Joseph Shippen	Philip Syng				
1739						
1740						
1741	Philip Syng	Thomas Boude	Lambert Emerson	Thomas Bond		
1742						
1743						
1744						
1745						
1746						
1747	William Allen					
1748	William Allen					
1749	Allen/Franklin	Thomas Bond	Joseph Shippen	Philip Syng	Daniel Byles*	William Plumstead
1750	William Allen	Benjamin Franklin	Joseph Shippen	Philip Syng	Daniel Byles*	William Plumstead
1751	William Allen					
1752	William Allen					
1753	William Allen					
1754	William Allen					
1755	William Allen	Benjamin Franklin	Thomas Bond	Joseph Shippen	William Franklin*	William Plumstead
1756	William Allen					
1757	William Allen	Benjamin Franklin	Thomas Bond	Joseph Shippen	William Franklin*	William Plumstead
1758	William Allen					
1759	William Allen					
1760	William Allen					
1761	William Allen					

*Not a member of St. John's Lodge (Masonic affiliation unknown).
Blank spaces indicate that no information is available.

Sources: Julius F. Sachse, *Old Masonic Lodges*, (Phila., 1912), Vol. 1, 20-21; Notice in *Pennsylvania Gazette* (1731-1761); "Liber B," St. John's Lodge [HSP]; Minutes of Lodge No. 4, "Moderns," June 24, 1757 [MS in Grand Lodge Library].

APPENDIX C
Table 2

Officers of the "Ancient" Provincial Grand Lodge of Pennsylvania, 1761–1785

Year	Grand Master	Deputy Grand Master	Senior Grand Warden	Junior Grand Warden	Grand Secretary	Grand Treasurer
1761	William Ball*	Blaithwaite Jones	David Hall	Hugh Lennox		
1762						
1763						
1764	William Ball	Blaithwaite Jones	David Hall	Hugh Lennox		
1765	William Ball	Blaithwaite Jones	David Hall	Hugh Lennox	John Wood	
1766						
1767	William Ball	Blaithwaite Jones	David Hall	Hugh Lennox		
1768	William Ball	Blaithwaite Jones				
1769	William Ball	Blaithwaite Jones				
1770	William Ball	Blaithwaite Jones				
1771	William Ball	John Wood				
1772	William Ball	John Wood	William Shute*	John Howard	James Fulton	
1773						
1774						
1775						
1776	William Ball	John Wood	John Howard			
1777	William Ball	John Wood	William Shute	John Howard		
1778	William Ball	John Coates	Alexander Rutherford	Jacob S. Howell	William Smith*	
1779	William Ball	John Coates	Jacob Bankson	Matthew Whitehead	William Smith	John Wood
1780	William Ball	Alexander Rutherford	William Adcock	William McIlwane	William Smith	John Wood
1781	William Ball	Alexander Rutherford	Thomas Proctor	George Ord	William Smith	Charles Young
1782	William Adcock	Alexander Rutherford	Thomas Proctor	George Ord	William Smith	Charles Young
1783	William Adcock	Alexander Rutherford	George Ord	William Tetum	Jacobs Howell	Gavin Hamilton
1784	William Adcock	Alexander Rutherford	Jonathan B. Smith	Joseph Dean	Jacobs Howell	Gavin Hamilton
1785	William Adcock	Alexander Rutherford			Assheton Humphreys	Gavin Hamilton

*Known to be former "Modern" Masons.

Elections were held in December of each year. By finding evidence of a Grand Lodge officer in the course of any one year in the sources, it is assumed that he was elected the previous December. Blank spaces indicate that no information is available.

Sources: Minutes of Lodge No. 2, Vol. I, 1758-1772, Vol. 2, 1772-1781; Minutes of Lodge No. 3; Warrant of Lodge No. 3, Oct. 20, 1767; Minutes of Lodge No. 3, Vol. I, 1767-1788 [all MS in Grand Lodge Library]; Grand Lodge Minutes, Vol. I, 9-96; Register of Members, Vol. I. 1789-1823, 120-121 [Grand Secretary's office].

APPENDIX C
Table 3

Officers of the Grand Lodge of Pennsylvania, 1786–1873

Year	Grand Master	Deputy Grand Master	Senior Grand Warden	Junior Grand Warden	Grand Secretary	Grand Treasurer
1786	William Adcock	Alexander Rutherford	Jonathan B. Smith	Joseph Dean	Gavin Hamilton	Assheton Humphreys
1787	William Adcock	Jonathan B. Smith	Joseph Dean	George Ord	Gavin Hamilton	Assheton Humphreys
1788	William Adcock	Jonathan B. Smith	Joseph Dean	George Ord	Gavin Hamilton	Assheton Humphreys
1789	Jonathan B. Smith	George Ord	Joseph Dean	Joseph Few	Gavin Hamilton	Assheton Humphreys
1790	Jonathan B. Smith	George Ord	Joseph Few	William McIlwane	Gavin Hamilton	P. Le Barbier Duplessis
1791	Jonathan B. Smith	Joseph Few	Thomas Proctor	Gavin Hamilton	Benjamin Mason	P. Le Barbier Duplessis
1792	Jonathan B. Smith	Joseph Few	Thomas Proctor	Gavin Hamilton	Benjamin Mason	P. Le Barbier Duplessis
1793	Jonathan B. Smith	John Carson	Gavin Hamilton	John McCree	Edward Fox	P. Le Barbier Duplessis
1794	Jonathan B. Smith	John Carson	John McCree	Edward Fox	Gavin Hamilton	P. Le Barbier Duplessis
1795	William Ball	William M. Smith	Thomas Town	John Poor	John McElwee	Thomas Armstrong
1796	William M. Smith	Gavin Hamilton	Thomas Town	John Poor	John McElwee	Thomas Armstrong
1797	William M. Smith	Gavin Hamilton	Thomas Town	Thomas Armstrong	John McElwee	George A. Baker
1798	Jonathan B. Smith	Gavin Hamilton	Thomas Town	David Irving	John McElwee	George A. Baker
1799	Jonathan B. Smith	Israel Israel	James Milnor	Charles Paton	John McElwee	George A. Baker
1800	Jonathan B. Smith	Israel Israel	James Milnor	Archibald Alexander	John McElwee	George A. Baker
1801	Jonathan B. Smith	Israel Israel	James Milnor	John W. Van Cleve	Gavin Hamilton	George A. Baker
1802	Jonathan B. Smith	James Milnor	John W. Van Cleve	Ebenezer Ferguson	Gavin Hamilton	George A. Baker
1803	Israel Israel	John Armantiere Monges	Ebenezer Ferguson	Robert Pullen	Gavin Hamilton	George A. Baker
1804	Israel Israel	James Milnor	Ebenezer Ferguson	Robert Pullen	Gavin Hamilton	George A. Baker
1805	Israel Israel	Frederick Wolbert	Robert Pullen	Robert Poalk	Thomas Armstrong	George A. Baker
1806	James Milnor	Frederick Wolbert	Robert Lewis	Robert Poalk	Thomas Armstrong	George A. Baker
1807	James Milnor	Frederick Wolbert	Robert Lewis	Robert Poalk	Thomas Armstrong	George A. Baker
1808	James Milnor	P. Le Barbier Duplessis	Robert Lewis	Robert Poalk	Samuel F. Bradford	George A. Baker
1809	James Milnor	P. Le Barbier Duplessis	Richard Tybout	Robert Poalk	Samuel F. Bradford	George A. Baker
1810	James Milnor	P. Le Barbier Duplessis	Richard Tybout	Joseph Burden	Samuel F. Bradford	George A. Baker
1811	James Milnor	P. Le Barbier Duplessis	Richard Tybout	Joseph Burden	Samuel F. Bradford	George A. Baker
1812	James Milnor	P. Le Barbier Duplessis	Richard Tybout	Joseph Burden	Samuel F. Bradford	George A. Baker
1813	James Milnor	Richard Tybout	Joseph Burden	Samuel F. Bradford	Walter Kerr	George A. Baker
1814	Richard Tybout	Samuel F. Bradford	Joseph Burden	Walter Kerr	Thomas Astley	George A. Baker
1815	Samuel F. Bradford	Walter Kerr	Bayse Newcomb	Richard Bache	Richard Bache	George A. Baker
1816	Walter Kerr	Bayse Newcomb	Joseph Barnes	Joseph Barnes	Joseph S. Lewis	George A. Baker
1817	Walter Kerr	Bayse Newcomb	Joseph Barnes	Thomas Elliott	Joseph S. Lewis	George A. Baker
1818	Bayse Newcomb	Joseph Barnes	Thomas Elliott	Josiah Randall	Joseph S. Lewis	George A. Baker, Jr.
1819	Bayse Newcomb	Joseph Barnes	Thomas Elliott	Josiah Randall	Joseph S. Lewis	George A. Baker, Jr.
1820	Bayse Newcomb	Thomas Elliott	Josiah Randall	William McCorkle	Joseph S. Lewis	George A. Baker, Jr.
1821	Bayse Newcomb	Thomas Elliott	Josiah Randall	James Harper	Joseph S. Lewis	George A. Baker, Jr.
1822	Josiah Randall	John Bannister Gibson	James Harper	Thomas Kittera	Joseph S. Lewis	George A. Baker, Jr.
1823	Josiah Randall	John Bannister Gibson	James Harper	Thomas Kittera	Joseph S. Lewis	George A. Baker, Jr.
1824	John Bannister Gibson	James Harper	Thomas Kittera	Samuel Badger	Joseph S. Lewis	Bernard Dahlgren
1825	James Harper	Thomas Kittera	Samuel Badger	Michael Nisbet	Joseph S. Lewis	Samuel H. Thomas

(Continued on next page)

APPENDIX C
TABLE 3 (*Cont.*)

Year	Grand Master	Deputy Grand Master	Senior Grand Warden	Junior Grand Warden	Grand Secretary	Grand Treasurer
1826	Thomas Kittera	Samuel Badger	Michael Nisbet	John Steele	Robert Toland	Samuel H. Thomas
1827	Thomas Kittera	Samuel Badger	Michael Nisbet	John Steele	Robert Toland	Samuel H. Thomas
1828	Thomas Kittera	Samuel Badger	Michael Nisbet	John Steele	Solomon Allen	Samuel H. Thomas
1829	Samuel Badger	Michael Nisbet	John Steele	George M. Dallas	Randal Hutchinson	Samuel H. Thomas
1830	Samuel Badger	Michael Nisbet	John Steele	George M. Dallas	Randal Hutchinson	Samuel H. Thomas
1831	Michael Nisbet	John Steele	George M. Dallas	Tristram B. Freeman	Samuel M. Stewart	Samuel H. Thomas
1832	Michael Nisbet	John Steele	George M. Dallas	Tristram B. Freeman	Samuel M. Stewart	Samuel H. Thomas
1833	John Steele	George M. Dallas	Tristram B. Freeman	Robert Toland	Cornelius Stevenson	John M. Read
1834	John Steele	George M. Dallas	Tristram B. Freeman	Robert Toland	Cornelius Stevenson	John M. Read
1835	George M. Dallas	Tristram B. Freeman	Robert Toland	John M. Read	Cornelius Stevenson	John M. Read
1836	Tristram B. Freeman	Robert Toland	John M. Read	Samuel H. Perkins	Robinson R. Moore	Samuel M. Stewart
1837	John M. Read	Samuel H. Perkins	William Stephens	Joseph R. Chandler	Robinson R. Moore	Samuel M. Stewart
1838	John M. Read	Samuel H. Perkins	Joseph R. Chandler	Cornelius Stevenson	Robinson R. Moore	Samuel M. Stewart
1839	Samuel H. Perkins	Joseph R. Chandler	Cornelius Stevenson	Francis Cooper	Robinson R. Moore	Samuel M. Stewart
1840	Samuel H. Perkins	Joseph R. Chandler	Cornelius Stevenson	William Barger	Robinson R. Moore	Michael Nisbet, P.G.M.
1841	Joseph R. Chandler	Cornelius Stevenson	William Barger	John W. McGrath	Robinson R. Moore	Michael Nisbet, P.G.M.
1842	Joseph R. Chandler	Cornelius Stevenson	William Barger	John W. McGrath	Robinson R. Moore	Michael Nisbet, P.G.M.
1843	Cornelius Stevenson	William Barger	James Page	Peter Fritz	John Thomson	William H. Adams
1844	William Barger	James Page	Peter Fritz	William Whitney	John Thomson	William H. Adams
1845	William Barger	James Page	Peter Fritz	William Whitney	John Thomson	William H. Adams
1846	James Page	Peter Fritz	William Whitney	Anthony Bournonville	John Thomson	William H. Adams
1847	James Page	Peter Fritz	William Whitney	Anthony Bournonville	John Thomson	William H. Adams
1848	Peter Fritz	William Whitney	Anthony Bournonville	James Hutchinson	John Thomson	William H. Adams
1849	Peter Fritz	William Whitney	Anthony Bournonville	James Hutchinson	John Thomson	William H. Adams
1850	William Whitney	Anthony Bournonville	James Hutchinson	Alexander Diamond	John Thomson	William H. Adams
1851	William Whitney	Anthony Bournonville	James Hutchinson	Alexander Diamond	John Thomson	William H. Adams
1852	Anthony Bournonville	James Hutchinson	Peter Williamson	John K. Mitchell	John Thomson	William H. Adams
1853	Anthony Bournonville	James Hutchinson	Peter Williamson	John K. Mitchell	John Thomson	William H. Adams
1854	James Hutchinson	Peter Williamson	John K. Mitchell	Henry M. Phillips	Thomas E. Baxter	William H. Adams
1855	James Hutchinson	Peter Williamson	John K. Mitchell	Henry M. Phillips	Thomas E. Baxter	William H. Adams
1856	Peter Williamson	John K. Mitchell	Henry M. Phillips	John Thomson	Thomas E. Baxter	William H. Adams
1857	Peter Williamson	John K. Mitchell	Henry M. Phillips	John Thomson	James Shields	William H. Adams
1858	John K. Mitchell	Henry M. Phillips	John Thomson	David C. Skerrett	Peter Williamson, P.G.M.	William H. Adams
1859	Henry M. Phillips	John Thomson	David C. Skerrett	Lucius H. Scott	Peter Williamson, P.G.M.	William H. Adams
1860	Henry M. Phillips	John Thomson	David C. Skerrett	Lucius H. Scott	Peter Williamson, P.G.M.	William H. Adams
1861	John Thomson	David C. Skerrett	Lucius H. Scott	John L. Goddard	Peter Williamson, P.G.M.	William H. Adams
1862	John Thomson	David C. Skerrett	Lucius H. Scott	John L. Goddard	Peter Williamson, P.G.M.	William H. Adams
1863	David C. Skerrett	Lucius H. Scott	John L. Goddard	Richard Vaux	Peter Williamson, P.G.M.	William H. Adams
1864	David C. Skerrett	Lucius H. Scott	John L. Goddard	Richard Vaux	Peter Williamson, P.G.M.	William H. Adams
1865	Lucius H. Scott	John L. Goddard	Richard Vaux	Robert A. Lamberton	Peter Williamson, P.G.M.	William H. Adams

APPENDIX C
TABLE 3 *(Cont.)*

Year	Grand Master	Deputy Grand Master	Senior Grand Warden	Junior Grand Warden	Grand Secretary	Grand Treasurer
1866	Lucius H. Scott	John L. Goddard	Richard Vaux	Robert A. Lamberton	Peter Williamson, P.G.M.	William H. Adams
1867	John L. Goddard	Richard Vaux	Robert A. Lamberton	Samuel C. Perkins	Peter Williamson, P.G.M.	John Thomson, P.G.M.
1868	Richard Vaux	Robert A. Lamberton	Samuel C. Perkins	Alfred R. Potter	Peter Williamson, P.G.M.	John Thomson, P.G.M.
1869	Richard Vaux	Robert A. Lamberton	Samuel C. Perkins	Alfred R. Potter	Peter Williamson, P.G.M.	John Thomson, P.G.M.
1870	Robert A. Lamberton	Samuel C. Perkins	Alfred R. Potter	Robert Clark	Peter Williamson, P.G.M.	John Thomson, P.G.M.
1871	Robert A. Lamberton	Samuel C. Perkins	Alfred R. Potter	Robert Clark	Peter Williamson, P.G.M.	John Thomson, P.G.M.
1872	Samuel C. Perkins	Alfred R. Potter	Robert Clark	James Madison Porter	Thomas Brown	John Thomson, P.G.M.
1873	Samuel C. Perkins	Alfred R. Potter	Robert Clark	James Madison Porter	Thomas Brown	John Thomson, P.G.M.

Sources: Joshua L. Lyte, comp., *Reprint of the Minutes of the Grand Lodge of Pennsylvania* (Phila., 1895-1907), 11 vols.

APPENDIX D
Table 1
Membership Statistics:
"Modern" Pennsylvania Freemasonry, 1731-1763

		Subordinate Lodge				
Year	No. 1	No. 2	No. 3	No. 4	Unknown	Total
1731	15	—	—	—	—	15
1732	7	—	—	—	—	7
1733	9	—	—	—	—	9
1734	12	—	—	—	—	12
1735	—	—	—	—	—	—
1736	—	—	—	—	—	—
1737	7	—	—	—	—	7
1738-1748	—	—	—	—	—	—
1749	—	4	45	—	—	49
1750	—	10	33	—	—	43
1751	—	10	24	—	—	34
1752	—	5	14	—	142	161
1753	—	7	8	—	—	15
1754	—	17	5	—	31	53
1755	—	18	2	—	—	20
1756	—	17	—	—	—	17
1757	—	39	—	15*	—	54
1758	—	15	—	19*	—	34
1759	—	23	—	1*	—	24
1760	—	35	—	—	—	35
1761	—	32	—	—	—	32
1762	—	24	—	—	—	24
1763	—	37	—	—	—	37
unknown	—	13	—	—	14	27
Totals	50	306	131	35	187	709

*Most of these men may have been "Ancient" Masons.

This table reflects the number of new names appearing on various membership lists for a given year. It does not indicate suspensions, expulsions, withdrawals or deaths, which are unknown. Therefore, cumulative totals cannot be calculated.

Although the sources give a total of 725 names, a lesser figure has been used because of duplication.

Five men were members of both Lodge No. 2 and Tun Tavern Lodge, but at different dates, and eleven members of St. John's Lodge appear on later lists. Because surviving records from this period are fragmentary, actual membership was probably higher than indicated.

Sources: "Liber B," St. John's Lodge, 1731-1738 [HSP]; List of Debts Due the Lodge, 10 October 1752; List of Subscribers for a New Lodge Building, 12 March 1752; Minutes of Lodge No. 2, "Moderns," 1749-1763; Minutes of Tun Tavern Lodge, 1749-1755 [HSP]; Minutes of Lodge No. 4, "Moderns," 1757-1758; Quarterage Account, June 1752; Subscribers to the Building Now Alive, 11 March 1782 with Members of the First Lodge That Did Not Contribute; Subscription List for the Erection of Freemason's Hall, 13 March 1754. [Unless otherwise specified, all documents are MS in Grand Lodge Library.]

APPENDIX D
Table 2
Membership Occupations:
Two "Modern" Lodges, 1731-1763

GOVERNMENT   1   (0.7%)

State/Federal
    military/naval officer   1

NON-PROFESSIONAL
SERVICE   7   (5.1%)

actor/comedian/showman   1
clerk (law/govt)   5
laborer   1

PROFESSIONAL SERVICE   21 (15.4%)

Arts/Education
    clergyman/minister   3
    dancing master   1
    schoolmaster/teacher   1
Health Care
    chemist/druggist   1
    physician/surgeon   5
Other
    lawyer (attorney,
      conveyancer, counselor,
      will-writer)   10

ARTISANS   26 (19.1%)

BUILDING TRADES   7   (5.1%)

bricklayer   5
carpenter/joiner   2

WOODWORKING   2   (1.4%)

carver   1
cooper/barrel maker   1

MISCELLANEOUS
CRAFTS   4   (2.9%)

brushmaker   1
printer/typesetter   2
upholsterer   1

RETAILERS   5   (3.6%)

store/shopkeeper   4
tobacconist/cigar maker/
    snuff maker   1

METAL CRAFTS   5   (3.6%)

blacksmith   1
goldsmith/jeweller   2
silversmith   2

CLOTHING TRADES   8   (5.8%)

bleacher/dyer   1
hatter   1
shoemaker/cordwainer   2
tanner/currier/skinner   4

FOOD PREPARATION/
SALE   4   (2.9%)

baker/confectioner/
    pastry cook   2
brewer/malter   1
distiller   1

(Continued on next page)

APPENDIX D
Table 2 *(Cont.)*

TRADE/COMMERCE	53 (38.9%)		TRAVEL & TRANSPORTATION	9	(6.6%)
boat builder	1		hotel/inn/tavernkeeper	6	
mariner/seaman	2		saddler/harness mender	3	
merchant (unspecified)[a]	10				
sailmaker	1		AGRICULTURE	2	(1.4%)
sea captain	38		farmer/yeoman	2	
supercargo	1				
			OTHER	8	(5.8%)
			transient gentleman[b]	8	

TOTAL TRACEABLE	136
PERCENTAGE TRACEABLE	75.1
TOTAL UNTRACEABLE	45
PERCENTAGE UNTRACEABLE	24.9
TOTAL	181

---

[a]These men were actually listed as "merchant/gentleman."

[b]Masonic usage indicates that these men may also have been sea captains.

This table, a sampling of 25.5% of the total known "Modern" membership, indicates the occupations of members at the time of their admission.

Masonic records seldom give occupational information in this period. This data has been obtained through research in non-Masonic sources.

Sources: Notices in the *Pennsylvania Gazette* (1727-1748); H. B. Roach File [APS]; Philadelphia Tax Lists, 1754-1756; Minutes of Tun Tavern Lodge, 1749-1755 [HSP].

APPENDIX D
Table 3
Membership Occupations: Comparative Statistics,
Two "Modern" Lodges, 1731-1763

Profession	Combined	(%)	St. John's	(%)	Tun Tavern	(%)
Government	1	0.7	0	0.0	1	1.1
Professional Service	21	15.4	13	28.2	8	8.8
Non-Professional Service	7	5.1	1	2.1	6	6.6
Artisans						
Building Trades	7	5.1	7	15.2	0	0.0
Metal Crafts	5	3.6	3	6.5	2	2.2
Woodworking	2	1.4	0	0.0	2	2.2
Clothing Trades	8	5.8	3	6.5	5	5.5
Miscellaneous	4	2.9	2	4.3	2	2.2
Retailers	5	3.6	1	2.1	4	4.4
Food Preparation/Sale	4	2.9	2	4.3	2	2.2
Trade/Commerce	53	38.9	6	13.0	47	52.3
Travel & Transportation	9	6.6	6	13.0	3	3.3
Agriculture	2	1.4	2	4.3	0	0.0
Other	8	5.8	0	0.0	8	8.9
Number Traceable	136		46		90	
% of total membership		75.1		92.0		68.7
None Listed	45		4		41	
% of total membership		24.9		8.0		31.3
Totals	181		50		131	

Sources: Notices in the *Pennsylvania Gazette* (1727-1748); H. B. Roach File [APS];
Philadelphia Tax Lists, 1754-1756; Minutes of Tun Tavern Lodge, 1749-1755 [HSP].

APPENDIX D
Figure 1
Membership Occupations:
Two "Modern" Lodges, 1731-1761

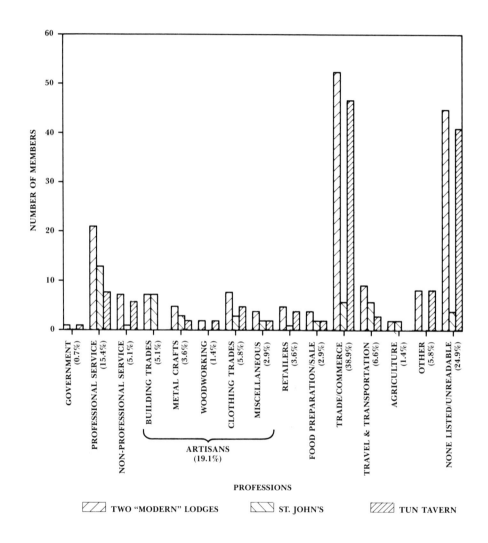

Sources: Notices in the *Pennsylvania Gazette* (1727-1748); H. B. Roach File [APS]; Philadelphia Tax Lists, 1754-1756; Minutes of Tun Tavern Lodge, 1749-1755 [HSP].

APPENDIX E
Membership Statistics:
"Ancient" Pennsylvania Freemasonry, 1758–1785

Year	All Lodges	Philadelphia	Pennsylvania Non-Phila.	Non-Pa.	Military and Traveling
1758	36	36	—	—	—
1759	19	19	—	—	—
1760	20	20	—	—	—
1761	16	16	—	—	—
1762	6	6	—	—	—
1763	7	7	—	—	—
1764	6	6	—	—	—
1765	6	3	—	3	—
1766	7	7	—	—	—
1767	22	22	—	—	—
1768	33	33	—	—	—
1769	17	17	—	—	—
1770	43	36	—	7	—
1771	18	18	—	—	—
1772	30	24	—	6	—
1773	36	16	—	20	—
1774	42	17	—	25	—
1775	49	11	—	27	11
1776	61	19	—	27	15
1777	121	96	—	22	3
1778	106	82	—	19	5
1779	245	150	7	59	29
1780	351	74	75	122	80
1781	99	48	15	25	11
1782	210	87	20	70	33
1783	149	44	18	81	6
1784	83	46	2	30	5
1785	72	29	3	35	5
Totals	1,910	989	140	578	203

This table reflects the known memberships of thirty-seven lodges (71.2% of those in operation) and shows the numbers of new men only.

Existing records seldon distinguish between initiated (men new to Freemasonry) and admitted (men already made Masons in other lodges), so these statistics are presented together.

Information pertaining to suspensions, expulsions, withdrawals and deaths for this period is insufficient, so net and cumulative totals cannot be calculated.

This data has also been arranged by individual lodges and is on file in the Grand Lodge Archives.

Background information on the members, such as occupations and ages, is not generally available for this period. It can be obtained only by further research into non-Masonic sources.

Sources: Original Minutes of Lodges No. 2 (1757-1787), No. 3 (1767-1788), No. 4 (1770-1786), No. 5 (1770-1787), No. 18 (1775-1782); original documents of Lodges No. 9 (1782-1784), No. 25 (1781, 1782, 1785) [all MS in Grand Lodge Library]; original documents of other lodges reproduced in Joshua L. Lyte, comp., *Reprint of the Minutes of the Grand Lodge of Free and Accepted Masons of Pennsylvania*, Vol. I, *1779-1801*, (Phila., 1895) and in Julius F. Sachse, *Old Masonic Lodges of Pennsylvania, "Moderns" and "Ancients," 1730-1800* (Phila., 1912, 1913), 2 vols.; Register of Members, Vol. 1, 1789-1823 (includes some data for the period before 1786) [Grand Secretary's office].

APPENDIX F
Table 1
Membership Statistics, 1786-1811

					Membership in 1785		518
Year	I	A	Sus/Exp	W/D	D	Net	Cumulative
1786	82	71	30	166	10	(53)	465
1787	29	27		78		(22)	443
1788	26	3		33	2	(6)	437
1789	35	83		19	1	98	535
1790	24	51	1	119	16	(61)	474
1791	64	58	7	125	5	(15)	459
1792	71	66	4	77	5	51	510
1793	97	54	2	70	26	53	563
1794	184	49	8	94	6	125	688
1795	249	91	7	101	20	212	900
1796	314	83	9	160	10	218	1,118
1797	257	117	22	191	13	148	1,266
1798	239	127	18	169	51	128	1,394
1799	204	57	32	146	9	74	1,468
1800	208	62	26	222	21	1	1,469
1801	207	120	37	184	19	87	1,556
1802	207	47	19	129	16	90	1,646
1803	180	37	37	164	21	(5)	1,641
1804	200	76	26	162	21	67	1,708
1805	255	68	19	148	25	131	1,839
1806	255	47	40	522	30	(290)	1,549
1807	230	78	16	208	22	62	1,611
1808	213	74	18	146	17	106	1,717
1809	277	85	18	201	23	120	1,837
1810	304	165	38	170	27	234	2,071
1811	523	260	34	260	46	443	2,514
Totals	4,934	2,056	468	4,064	462	1,996	

Key: I, initiated (men new to Freemasonry); A, admitted (men made Masons in other lodges); Sus/Exp, suspended/expelled; W/D, withdrawals; D, deceased.

This table reflects the known memberships of 100 lodges (80% of those in operation). Membership information prior to 1789 is fragmentary.

Specific breakdowns of membership statistics for all individual lodges are on file in the Grand Lodge Archives.

Background information on the members, such as occupations and ages, is not generally available for this period. It can only be obtained by further research into non-Masonic sources.

Sources: Original membership lists as follows: Lodge No. 2, April 11, 1785, December 27, 1795; No. 3, 24 June 1786; No. 4: 24 July 1786; No. 5, December 1797, December 1799; No. 9a, December 1791, December 1792, December 1793, December 1794, December 1795, December 1798; No. 11a, December 1790, December 1797, June 1800, 12a, December 1786, December 1787; No. 21: June 1797, December 1799; No. 25, January 1785, December 1800; No. 33, June 1799, No. 44, December 1791 [all MS in Grand Lodge Library]; original records of other lodges are reproduced in Joshua L. Lyte, comp., *Reprint of the Minutes of the Grand Lodge of Free and Accepted Masons of Pennsylvania*, Vol. I, *1779-1801* (Phila., 1895), 94f., 158, 175, 316, 359, 374, 406, 448, and in Julius F. Sachse, *Old Masonic Lodges, "Moderns" and "Ancients," 1730-1800* (Phila., 1912, 1913), 2 Vols.; Register of Members, Vol. I, 1789-1823 [Grand Secretary's office].

APPENDIX F
Table 2
Membership Statistics, 1786-1811:
Comparative Cumulative Totals

Year	All Lodges	Philadelphia	Pennsylvania Non-Phila.	Non-Pennsylvania
1786	465	142	145	178
1787	443	128	167	48
1788	437	107	173	157
1789	535	115	197	223
1790	474	119	122	233
1791	459	137	169	153
1792	510	170	216	124
1793	563	146	288	129
1794	688	187	364	137
1795	900	307	456	137
1796	1,118	425	550	143
1797	1,266	510	589	167
1798	1,394	463	722	209
1799	1,468	483	745	240
1800	1,469	504	708	257
1801	1,556	489	751	316
1802	1,646	528	802	316
1803	1,641	504	797	340
1804	1,708	534	785	389
1805	1,839	574	826	439
1806	1,549	580	723	246
1807	1,611	647	782	182
1808	1,717	706	790	221
1809	1,837	781	848	208
1810	2,071	936	889	246
1811	2,514	1,199	986	329

Sources: Original membership lists as follows: Lodge No. 2, April 11, 1785, December 27, 1795; No. 3, 24 June 1786; No. 4: 24 July 1786; No. 5, December 1797, December 1799; No. 9a, December 1791, December 1792, December 1793, December 1794, December 1795, December 1798; No. 11a, December 1790, December 1797, June 1800, 12a, December 1786, December 1787; No. 21: June 1797, December 1799; No. 25, January 1785, December 1800; No. 33, June 1799, No. 44, December 1791 [all MS in Grand Lodge Library]; original records of other lodges are reproduced in Joshua L. Lyte, comp., *Reprint of the Minutes of the Grand Lodge of Free and Accepted Masons of Pennsylvania*, Vol. I, *1779-1801* (Phila., 1895), 94f., 158, 175, 316, 359, 374, 406, 448, and in Julius F. Sachse, *Old Masonic Lodges, "Moderns" and "Ancients," 1730-1800* (Phila., 1912, 1913), 2 Vols.; Register of Members, Vol. I, 1789-1823 [Grand Secretary's office].

APPENDIX F
Figure 1
Membership Statistics, 1786–1811

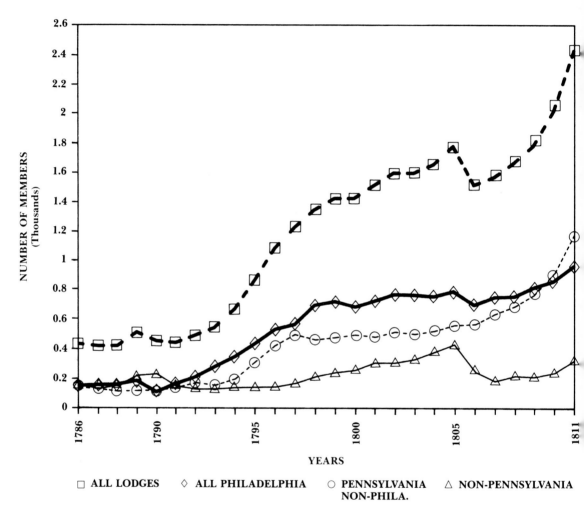

NUMBER OF MEMBERS (Thousands)

YEARS

□ ALL LODGES   ◇ ALL PHILADELPHIA   ○ PENNSYLVANIA   △ NON-PENNSYLVANIA
NON-PHILA.

CUMULATIVE TOTALS

Sources: Original membership lists as follows: Lodge No. 2, April 11, 1785, December 27, 1795; No. 3, 24 June 1786; No. 4: 24 July 1786; No. 5, December 1797, December 1799; No. 9a, December 1791, December 1792, December 1793, December 1794, December 1795, December 1798; No. 11a, December 1790, December 1797, June 1800, 12a, December 1786, December 1787; No. 21: June 1797, December 1799; No. 25, January 1785, December 1800; No. 33, June 1799, No. 44, December 1791 [all MS in Grand Lodge Library]; original records of other lodges are reproduced in Joshua L. Lyte, comp., *Reprint of the Minutes of the Grand Lodge of Free and Accepted Masons of Pennsylvania*, Vol. I, *1779-1801* (Phila., 1895), 94f., 158, 175, 316, 359, 374, 406, 448, and in Julius F. Sachse, *Old Masonic Lodges, "Moderns" and "Ancients," 1730-1800* (Phila., 1912, 1913), 2 Vols.; Register of Members, Vol. I, 1789-1823 [Grand Secretary's office].

APPENDIX G
Table 1
Membership Statistics, 1812-1825

					Membership in 1811			2,514

Year	I	A	Sus/Exp	W/D	D	Net	Cumulative
1812	372	98	49	256	46	119	2,633
1813	374	111	71	321	41	52	2,685
1814	433	151	71	465	37	11	2,696
1815	381	85	52	373	38	3	2,699
1816	468	161	84	311	38	196	2,895
1817	455	143	96	340	44	118	3,013
1818	635	182	57	391	35	334	3,347
1819	578	225	80	519	54	150	3,497
1820	595	226	115	464	60	182	3,679
1821	444	135	158	630	56	(265)	3,414
1822	535	173	75	424	46	163	3,577
1823	466	151	100	314	51	152	3,729
1824	437	157	139	625	45	(215)	3,514
1825	635	206	163	637	35	6	3,520
Totals	6,808	2,204	1,310	6,070	626	1,006	

Key: I, initiated (men new to Freemasonry); A, admitted (men made Masons in other lodges); Sus/Exp, suspended/expelled; W/D, withdrawals; D, deceased.

This table reflects the known memberships of 139 lodges (97.9% of those in operation).

Specific breakdowns of membership statistics for all individual lodges are on file in the Grand Lodge Archives.

Sources: Joshua L. Lyte, comp., *Reprint of the Minutes of the Grand Lodge of Pennsylvania,* Vol. V, *1822-1827,* 392f.; Register of Members, Vol. 1, 1789-1823, Vol. 2-1, 1818-1855, Vol. 2-2, 1818-1855 [Grand Secretary's office].

APPENDIX G
Table 2
Membership Statistics, 1812-1825:
Comparative Cumulative Totals

Year	All Lodges	Philadelphia	Pennsylvania Non-Phila.	Non-Pennsylvania
1812	2,633	1,252	1,053	328
1813	2,685	1,312	1,123	250
1814	2,696	1,339	1,090	267
1815	2,699	1,365	1,132	202
1816	2,895	1,366	1,341	188
1817	3,013	1,342	1,459	212
1818	3,347	1,447	1,553	347
1819	3,497	1,450	1,621	426
1820	3,679	1,412	1,802	465
1821	3,414	1,307	1,906	201
1822	3,577	1,285	2,039	253
1823	3,729	1,302	2,178	249
1824	3,514	1,265	2,157	92
1825	3,520	1,302	2,218	0

Sources: Joshua L. Lyte, comp., *Reprint of the Minutes of the Grand Lodge of Pennsylvania*, Vol. V, *1822-1827*, 392f.; Register of Members, Vol. 1, 1789-1823, Vol. 2-1, 1818-1855, Vol. 2-2, 1818-1855 [Grand Secretary's office.].

APPENDIX G
Table 3
Membership Occupations, 1824-1825

GOVERNMENT	38	(3.0%)	PROFESSIONAL SERVICE	191	(14.9%)
City/County/Township			Arts/Education		
alderman/mayor/ commissioner	1		author/writer	2	
constable/sheriff/ marshal	12		clergyman/minister	20	
			musician/composer	3	
judge/justice/ magistrate	10		professor/lecturer	1	
recorder/registrar	8		schoolmaster/teacher	33	
State/Federal			Health Care		
military/naval officer	2		chemist/druggist	5	
			dentists	1	
sailor/soldier	5		physician/surgeon	77	
			Other		
			engineer (var.)	3	
			lawyer (attorney, conveyancer, counselor, will-writer)	46	

NON-PROFESSIONAL SERVICE   59 (4.6%)

accountant/ bookkeeper	13	clerk (unspecified)	26
bottler	1	gardener/seedsman	2
clerk (law/govt)	2	laborer	10
		surveyor/rodman	5

ARTISANS   436 (34.0%)

BUILDING TRADES	107	(8.4%)	METAL CRAFTS	77	(6.0%)
builder/contractor	5		armorer/gunsmith	2	
bricklayer	11		blacksmith	27	
brickmaker	1		clock/watchmaker	5	
carpenter/joiner	59		coppersmith	3	
glassblower/maker	1		foundryman/ molder (var.)	6	
glass cutter/carver	2		goldsmith/jeweller	2	
mason	13		ironmonger/iron- worker	9	
painter/gilder/ decorator (var.)	5		silversmith	2	
plasterer	4		smith (unspecified)	9	
plumber	1		stove maker	1	
stone/marble cutter	4		tinplate worker	2	
wharf builder	1		tinsmith/whitesmith	9	

WOODWORKING	39	(3.0%)	CLOTHING TRADES	165	(12.9%)
cabinet/case maker	18		bleacher/dyer (var.)	2	
chair/furniture maker/ turner	2		clothier/mercer	9	
			fuller	7	
coach/wagon maker	5		furrier	1	
cooper/barrel maker	5		hatter	16	
reed maker	1		shoemaker/cordwainer	33	
wheelwright	8		spinner (cotton/wool)	3	
			tailor/pattern maker	61	
			tanner/currier/skinner	25	
			umbrella maker	1	
			weaver	7	

(Continued on next page)

APPENDIX G
Table 3 *(Cont.)*

MISCELLANEOUS CRAFTS   48 (3.7%)

bookbinder	1	papermaker	12
brushmaker	4	potter	1
comb maker	2	printer/typesetter	28

RETAILERS	20 (1.6%)	FOOD PREPARATION/ SALE	54 (4.2%)
dealer/trader	3		
perfumer	1	brewer/malter	4
peddler/salesman	2	butcher	4
store/shopkeeper	12	distiller	9
tobacconist/cigar maker/		cook	1
snuff maker	2	grocer	15
		miller/mill employee	19
		vitualler/provisioner	2

TRADE/COMMERCE	156 (12.2%)	TRAVEL & TRANSPORTATION	96 (7.5%)
broker/import/exporter	4		
mariner/seaman	17	boatman/riverman/	
merchant	122	waterman	1
pilot	5	coachman	3
sailmaker	2	hotel/inn/tavernkeeper	72
sea captain	1	liveryman	1
ship smith/shipwright	4	saddler/harness mender	17
stevedore	1	stage coach driver/	
		proprietor	1
		steward	1

INDUSTRIAL TRADES	26 (2.0%)	AGRICULTURE	192 (15.0%)
foreman/supervisor/		drover/herder	5
manager/overseer	3	farmer/yeoman	187
furnace operator/maker	1		
gauger	1	OTHER	13 (1.0%)
manufacturer (unspec.)	10	equestrian	3
manufacturer (cotton)	1	fancy business (?)	1
machinist/mechanic	2	fisherman/oysterman	1
millwright	6	gentleman	4
miner/collier	2	student	4

TOTAL TRACEABLE	1,281	
PERCENTAGE TRACEABLE	89.3	
TOTAL UNTRACEABLE	154	
PERCENTAGE UNTRACEABLE	10.7	
TOTAL	1,435	

This table reflects the known occupations of the members of 98 lodges (89.1% of those in operation) at the time of their initiations or admissions.

No occupations were listed for non-Pennsylvania lodges.

Occupational information on the period before 1824 is not generally available. It can only be obtained by further research into non-Masonic sources.

Sources: Register of Members, Vol. 1, 1789-1823, Vol. 2-1, 1818-1855, Vol. 2-2, 1818-1855, [Grand Secretary's office].

APPENDIX G
Table 4
Membership Occupations: Comparative Statistics, 1824–1825

	All Lodges	(%)	Phila.	(%)	Non-Phila.	(%)
Government	38	3.0	10	3.1	28	2.9
Professional Service	191	14.9	33	10.2	158	16.5
Non-Professional Service	59	4.6	19	5.8	40	4.2
Artisans						
Building Trades	107	8.4	29	8.9	78	8.2
Metal Crafts	77	6.0	18	5.5	59	6.2
Woodworking	39	3.0	9	2.8	30	3.1
Clothing Trades	165	12.9	44	13.5	121	12.7
Miscellaneous	48	3.7	13	4.0	35	3.7
Retailers	20	1.6	8	2.5	12	1.3
Food Preparation/Sale	54	4.2	25	7.7	29	3.0
Trade/Commerce	156	12.2	73	22.5	83	8.7
Travel & Transportation	96	7.5	22	6.8	74	7.7
Industrial Trades	26	2.0	8	2.5	18	1.9
Agriculture	192	15.0	7	2.2	185	19.4
Other	13	1.0	7	2.2	6	0.6
Number Traceable	1,281		325		956	
% of total membership		89.3		77.8		94.0
None Listed/Unreadable	154		93		61	
% of total membership		10.7		22.2		6.0
Totals	1,435		418		1,017	

Sources: Register of Members, Vol. 1, 1789-1823, Vol. 2-1, 1818-1855, Vol. 2-2, 1818-1855 [Grand Secretary's office].

APPENDIX G
Figure 1
Membership Statistics, 1812–1825

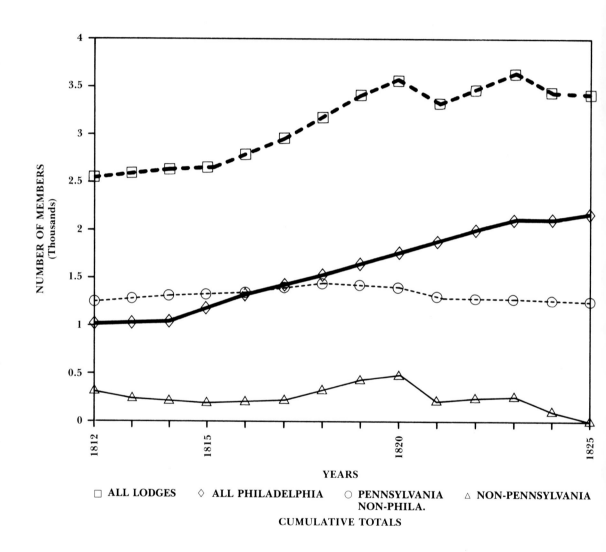

□ ALL LODGES   ◇ ALL PHILADELPHIA   ○ PENNSYLVANIA   △ NON-PENNSYLVANIA
NON-PHILA.
CUMULATIVE TOTALS

Sources: Joshua L. Lyte, comp., *Reprint of the Minutes of the Grand Lodge of Pennsylvania*, Vol. V, *1822-1827*, 392f.; Register of Members, Vol. 1, 1789-1823, Vol. 2-1, 1818-1855, Vol. 2-2, 1818-1855 [Grand Secretary's office].

APPENDIX G
Figure 2
Membership Occupations, 1824–1825

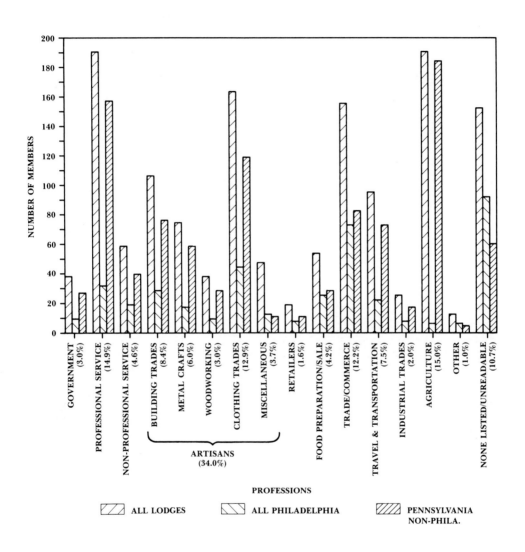

Sources: Register of Members, Vol. 1, 1789-1823, Vol. 2-1, 1818-1855, Vol. 2-2, 1818-1855 [Grand Secretary's office].

APPENDIX H
Table 1
Membership Statistics, 1826–1855

| | | | | Membership in 1825 | | | 3,520 |
Year	I	A	Sus/Exp	W/D	D	Net	Cumulative
1826	618	203	88	473	56	204	3,724
1827	489	157	132	500	42	(28)	3,696
1828	292	103	140	387	30	(162)	3,534
1829	176	80	134	297	31	(206)	3,328
1830	163	49	89	199	19	(95)	3,233
1831	123	69	60	181	31	(80)	3,153
1832	161	97	66	102	27	63	3,216
1833	120	41	79	162	24	(104)	3,112
1834	83	44	124	130	30	(157)	2,955
1835	99	43	63	97	23	(41)	2,914
1836	104	78	57	101	11	13	2,927
1837	132	64	70	1,423	27	(1,324)	1,603
1838	239	55	69	171	18	36	1,639
1839	269	75	118	81	23	122	1,761
1840	186	68	96	132	24	2	1,763
1841	179	51	82	103	16	29	1,792
1842	176	67	105	95	26	17	1,809
1843	127	80	181	126	27	(127)	1,682
1844	211	124	65	110	15	145	1,827
1845	255	143	97	152	21	128	1,955
1846	492	215	70	233	16	388	2,343
1847	548	197	61	193	26	465	2,808
1848	739	272	148	178	44	641	3,449
1849	740	231	153	280	48	490	3,939
1850	891	265	180	263	54	659	4,598
1851	1,234	274	146	293	55	1,014	5,612
1852	1,208	281	249	365	78	797	6,409
1853	1,555	380	291	428	88	1,128	7,537
1854	2,094	382	394	436	132	1,514	9,051
1855	2,040	294	341	411	89	1,493	10,544
Totals	15,743	4,482	3,948	8,102	1,151	7,024	

Key: I, initiated (men new to Freemasonry); A, admitted (men made Masons in other lodges); Sus/Exp, suspended/expelled; W/D, withdrawals; D, deceased.

This table reflects the known memberships of 215 lodges (100% of those in operation).

Specific breakdowns of membership statistics for all individual lodges are on file in the Grand Lodge Archives.

Sources: Register of Members, Vol. 2-1, 1795-1865, Vol. 2-2, 1818-1855, Vol. 3-1, 1854-1865, Vol. 3-2, 1854-1865 [Grand Secretary's office].

APPENDIX H
Table 2
Membership Statistics, 1826–1855:
Comparative Cumulative Totals

Year	All Lodges	Philadelphia	Pennsylvania Non-Phila.
1826	3,724	1,311	2,413
1827	3,696	1,297	2,399
1828	3,534	1,296	2,238
1829	3,328	1,257	2,071
1830	3,233	1,210	2,023
1831	3,153	1,157	1,996
1832	3,216	1,180	2,009
1833	3,112	1,111	2,001
1834	2,955	1,012	1,943
1835	2,914	995	1,919
1836	2,927	1,010	1,917
1837	1,603	983	620
1838	1,639	1,028	611
1839	1,761	1,140	621
1840	1,763	1,096	667
1841	1,792	1,088	704
1842	1,809	1,036	773
1843	1,682	916	766
1844	1,827	987	840
1845	1,955	1,040	915
1846	2,343	1,236	1,107
1847	2,808	1,410	1,398
1848	3,449	1,589	1,860
1849	3,939	1,701	2,238
1850	4,598	1,937	2,661
1851	5,612	2,422	3,190
1852	6,409	2,778	3,631
1853	7,537	3,380	4,157
1854	9,051	4,203	4,848
1855	10,544	4,978	5,566

Only one lodge (No. 217, Uruguay) was located outside Pennsylvania. It had 30 members not included in the above.

Sources: Register of Members, Vol. 2-1, 1795-1855, Vol. 2-2, 1818-1855, Vol. 3-1, 1854-1865, Vol. 3-2, 1854-1865 [Grand Secretary's office].

APPENDIX H
Table 3
Membership Occupations, 1826–1855

GOVERNMENT	365	(2.1%)
City/County/Township		
alderman/mayor/ commissioner	25	
constable/sheriff/ marshal	54	
judge/justice/ magistrate	57	
fire/police	26	
recorder/registrar	20	
treasurer	4	
State/Federal		
executive official	6	
congressman/senator	2	
customs official	11	
diplomat	2	
military/naval officer	64	
mint worker	1	
postal/master-worker	29	
sailor/soldier	18	
Other		
collector (tax, toll)	43	
prison keeper/warden	3	

PROFESSIONAL SERVICE	2,594	(14.6%)
Arts/Education		
artist/sculptor	51	
author/writer	3	
clergyman/minister	289	
dancing master	2	
editor/publisher	42	
librarian	1	
musician/composer	55	
professor/lecturer	32	
schoolmaster/teacher	213	
Health Care		
chemist/druggist	187	
dentist	84	
physician/surgeon	724	
Other		
architect	24	
banker	5	
engineer (var.)	265	
lawyer (attorney, conveyancer, counselor, will-writer)	617	

NON-PROFESSIONAL SERVICE   1,804   (10.1%)

accountant/bookkeeper	199	insurance agent/broker	7
actor/comedian/ showman	25	journalist/reporter	11
agent (var.)	103	laborer	79
appraiser	1	lumberman/jack	75
auctioneer	18	measurer (var.)	14
barber/hairdresser	32	messenger	2
bottler	14	notary	1
carter	18	operator	1
cashier	5	optician	4
chauffeur	1	paver	4
clerk (bank)	3	real estate agent	6
clerk (law/govt)	11	superintendant	28
clerk (unspecified)	1,040	surveyor/rodman	28
dresser	7	telegrapher	17
dispatcher	5	undertaker	12
gardener/seedsman	13	warehouseman	1
guard	2	wood corder	4
inspector (var.)	10	zookeeper	3

(Continued on next page)

APPENDIX H
Table 3 *(Cont.)*

ARTISANS   5,221   (29.4%)

BUILDING TRADES	1,825 (10.3%)		METAL CRAFTS	1,074 (6.0%)
builder/contractor	187		armorer/gunsmith	18
bricklayer	123		blacksmith	273
brickmaker	31		clock/watchmaker	103
carpenter/joiner	804		coppersmith	27
caulker	1		foundryman/molder (var.)	182
glassblower/maker	46		gold beater	4
glass cutter/carver	13		goldsmith/jeweller	86
limeburner	4		instrument maker	
mason	153		(musical/surgical)	19
nailor	8		ironmonger/ironworker	72
painter/gilder/			locksmith	9
decorator (var.)	191		silversmith	32
paperhanger	21		smith (unspecified)	46
plasterer	84		spike cutter	4
plumber	44		tinplate worker	21
roofer/slater	14		tinsmith/whitesmith	80
sash maker	3		various makers	98
saw mill owner	1		(axe, auger, bit, chain,	
sawyer	11		rod, nail, pipe, plane,	
stone/marble cutter	79		plow, pump & block,	
wharf builder	7		saw, scale, shovel, sickle,	
			spring, stove, wire)	

WOODWORKING	491 (2.8%)		CLOTHING TRADES	1,336 (7.5%)
blind maker	7		bleacher/dyer (var.)	21
box maker	8		bootmaker	37
cabinet/case maker	185		button maker	1
carver	14		calico printer	3
chair/furniture maker/			clothier/mercer	34
turner	50		fuller	19
coach/wagon maker	124		furrier	7
cooper/barrel maker	57		hatter	209
reed maker	1		lace maker	1
wheelwright	45		needle maker	1
			oilcloth maker	2
			shoemaker/cordwainer	323
			starch maker	1
			suspender maker	2
			spinner (cotton/wool)	11
			tailor/pattern maker	488
			tanner/currier/skinner	133
			umbrella maker	5
			weaver	34
			wool carder/sorter	4

MISCELLANEOUS CRAFTS   495   (2.8%)

bookbinder	57		papermaker	30
brushmaker	18		photographer	10
colourman	1		pianomaker	5
comb maker	8		potter	17
cork cutter	1		printer/typesetter	254
engraver/lithographer	44		soap boiler/maker	16
inkmaker	4		taxidermist	1
japanner/varnisher	4		upholsterer	25

(Continued on next page)

APPENDIX H
Table 3 *(Cont.)*

RETAILERS	659	(3.7%)
bookseller/stationer	63	
cutler	1	
dealer/trader (unspec.)	95	
dealer/trader	184	
(carpets, coal, milk/		
butter/eggs, ice, stoves,		
leather, wool)		
florist	1	
news agent	1	
paperseller	1	
perfumer	2	
peddler/salesman	142	
store/shopkeeper	78	
tobacconist/cigar maker/		
snuff maker	91	

FOOD PREPARATION/ SALE	710	(4.0%)
baker/confectioner/		
pastry cook	138	
bartender	11	
brewer/malter	48	
butcher	90	
coffee roaster	2	
cook	1	
distiller	36	
grocer	188	
miller/mill employee	124	
mineral water maker	2	
restaurateur	6	
sugar refiner	2	
vitualler/provisioner	61	
vinegar maker	1	

TRADE/COMMERCE	2,863	(16.1%)
boatswain	4	
boatbuilder	44	
broker/import/exporter	93	
mariner/seaman	170	
merchant (unspec.)	2,126	
merchant	113	
(china, corn, commission,		
copper, dry goods, flour,		
hardware, liquor, lumber,		
powder, salt/grain, shoes,		
wine, wooden ware)		
pilot	59	
rigger/ropemaker	33	
sailmaker	25	
sea captain	94	
shipping/docking master	12	
ship chandler	12	
ship smith/shipwright	70	
stevedore	8	

TRAVEL & TRANSPORTATION	1,133	(6.4%)
boatman/riverman/		
waterman	38	
canaller/canal supervr.	28	
coachman	4	
ferry operator	3	
hotel/inn/tavernkeeper	697	
liveryman	23	
omnibus driver	5	
porter	5	
railroad employee	76	
(agent, baggage master,		
brakeman, conductor/		
trainman, insptr.,		
suprvr., worker)		
saddler/harness mender	131	
stage coach driver/		
proprietor	20	
steamboat captain	57	
steward	4	
teamster/drayman/driver	34	
transporter	4	
travel agent	2	
trunk maker	2	

(Continued on next page)

APPENDIX H
Table 2 *(Cont.)*

INDUSTRIAL/ UTILITIES	966 (5.4%)		AGRICULTURE	1,275 (7.2%)
engine maker	17		agriculturalist	2
foreman/supervisor/			drover/herder	28
manager/overseer	48		farmer/yeoman	1,244
furnace operator/maker	8		rancher	1
gas works employee	27			
(gas fitter, gas maker, gas supervisor)				
gauger	2		OTHER	189 (1.1%)
glue boiler/maker	3			
heater/steamer	6		equestrian	7
manufacturer (unspec.)	192		fisherman/oysterman	19
manufacturer (cotton)	54		gentleman	82
(fringe, hardware, safe, salt, yarn)			landlord	19
			linguist	1
machinist/mechanic	433		student	61
millwright	72			
miner/collier	80			
oil company employee	1			
roller	16			
water works employee	7			

TOTAL TRACEABLE	17,779
PERCENT TRACEABLE	87.9
TOTAL UNTRACEABLE	2,446
PERCENT UNTRACEABLE	12.1
TOTAL	20,225

This table reflects the known occupations of the members of 215 lodges (100% of those in operation) at the time of their initiations or admissions.

Sources: Register of Members, Vol. 2-1, 1795-1855, Vol. 2-2, 1818-1855, Vol. 3-1, 1854-1865, Vol. 3-2, 1854-1865 [Grand Secretary's office].

APPENDIX H
Table 4
Membership Occupations: Comparative Statistics, 1826–1855

	All Lodges	(%)	Phila.	(%)	Non-Phila.	(%)
Government	365	2.1	153	2.0	212	2.1
Professional Service	2,594	14.6	884	11.6	1,710	16.8
Non-Professional Service	1,804	10.1	895	11.8	909	8.9
Artisans						
Building Trades	1,825	10.3	865	11.4	960	9.4
Metal Crafts	1,074	6.0	404	5.3	670	6.6
Woodworking	491	2.8	188	2.5	303	3.0
Clothing Trades	1,336	7.5	642	8.5	694	6.8
Miscellaneous	495	2.8	291	3.8	204	2.0
Retailers	659	3.7	434	5.7	225	2.2
Food Preparation/Sale	710	4.0	365	4.8	345	3.4
Trade/Commerce	2,863	16.1	1,451	19.1	1,412	13.9
Travel & Transportation	1,133	6.4	441	5.8	692	6.8
Industrial/Utilities	966	5.4	414	5.5	552	5.4
Agriculture	1,275	7.2	94	1.2	1,181	11.6
Other	189	1.1	69	0.9	120	1.2
Number Traceable	17,779		7,590		10,189	
% of total membership		87.9		90.0		86.9
None Listed/Unreadable	2,446*		878		1,538	
% of total membership		12.1		10.0		13.1
Totals	20,225		8,468		11,727	

*Includes 30 members from Lodge No. 217, Uruguay, for whom no occupations are listed.

Sources: Register of Members, Vol. 2-1, 1795-1855, Vol. 2-2, 1818-1855, Vol. 3-1, 1854-1865, Vol. 3-2, 1854-1865 [Grand Secretary's office].

APPENDIX H
Figure 1
Membership Statistics, 1826–1855

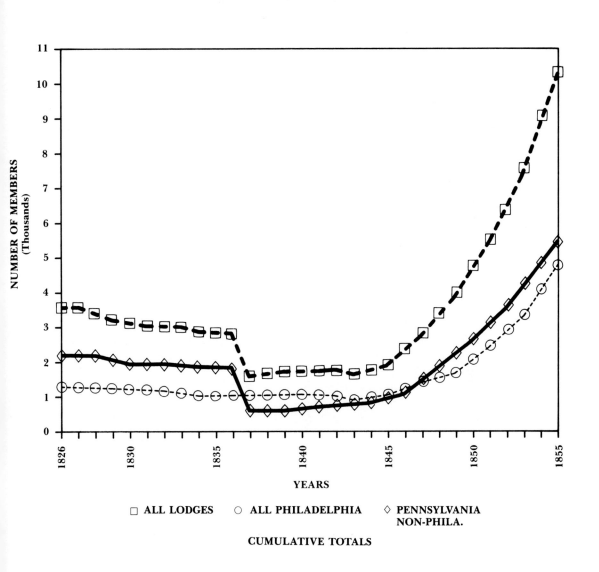

NUMBER OF MEMBERS
(Thousands)

YEARS

□ ALL LODGES   ○ ALL PHILADELPHIA   ◇ PENNSYLVANIA
NON-PHILA.

CUMULATIVE TOTALS

Sources: Register of Members, Vol. 2-1, 1795-1855, Vol. 2-2, 1818-1855, Vol. 3-1, 1854-1865, Vol. 3-2, 1854-1865 [Grand Secretary's office].

APPENDIX H
Figure 2
Membership Occupations, 1826–1855

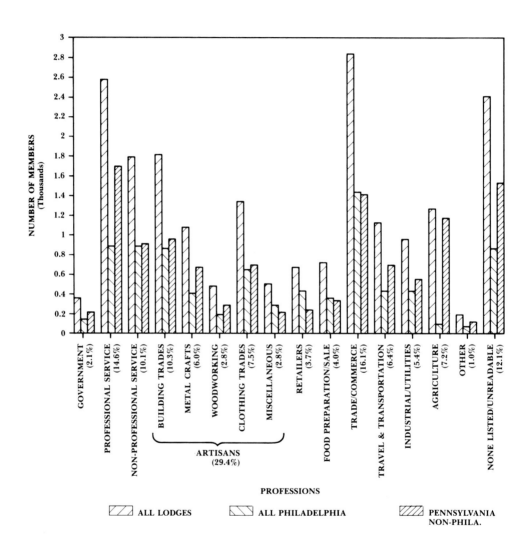

Sources: Register of Members, Vol. 2-1, 1795-1855, Vol. 2-2, 1818-1855, Vol. 3-1, 1854-1865, Vol. 3-2, 1854-1865 [Grand Secretary's office].

APPENDIX I
Table 1
Membership Statistics, 1856–1873

Year	I	A	Sus/Exp	W/D	D	Net	Membership in 1855 9,944 Cumulative
1856	1,528	358	322	467	127	970	10,914
1857	1,441	360	464	468	125	744	11,658
1858	1,246	479	519	443	153	610	12,268
1859	1,508	340	524	415	151	758	13,026
1860	1,361	273	574	316	162	582	13,608
1861	875	176	594	241	133	83	13,691
1862	1,030	208	418	256	243	321	14,012
1863	2,127	259	272	250	238	1,626	15,638
1864	2,948	376	285	379	282	2,387	18,016
1865	3,085	514	301	495	273	2,530	20,546
1866	3,148	828	343	689	324	2,620	23,166
1867	3,682	875	344	888	268	3,057	26,223
1868	3,694	955	389	829	265	3,166	29,389
1869	3,127	792	558	936	292	2,133	31,522
1870	2,759	1,033	610	943	370	1,869	33,391
1871	2,586	1,020	678	859	388	1,681	35,072
1872	2,365	770	696	637	441	1,361	36,433
1873	2,661	701	749	666	426	1,521	37,954
Totals	41,171	10,317	8,640	10,177	4,661	28,010	

Key: I, initiated (men new to Freemasonry); A, admitted (men made Masons in other lodges); Sus/Exp, suspended/expelled; W/D, withdrawals; D, deceased.

This table reflects the known memberships of 357 lodges (100% of those in operation).

Specific breakdowns of membership statistics for all individual lodges are on file in the Grand Lodge Archives.

Sources: Register of Members, Vol. 3-1, 1854-1865, Vol. 3-2, 1854-1865, Vol. 4-1, 1866-1903, Vol. 4-2, 1866-1892, Vol. 4-3, 1866-1892, Vol. 4-4, 1866-1892, Vol. 5-1, 1869-1911, Vol. 5-2, 1868-1911, Vol. 5-3, 1870-1904, Vol. 5-4, 1873-1904 [Grand Secretary's office].

APPENDIX I
Table 2
Membership Statistics, 1856–1873:
Comparative Cumulative Totals

Year	All Lodges	Philadelphia	Pennsylvania Non-Phila.
1856	10,914	5,075	5,839
1857	11,658	5,187	6,471
1858	12,268	5,114	7,154
1859	13,026	5,268	7,758
1860	13,608	5,390	8,218
1861	13,691	5,302	8,389
1862	14,012	5,298	8,714
1863	15,638	5,764	9,874
1864	18,016	6,740	11,276
1865	20,546	7,406	13,140
1866	23,166	7,918	15,248
1867	26,223	8,723	17,500
1868	29,389	9,553	19,836
1869	31,522	10,159	21,363
1870	33,391	10,711	22,680
1871	35,072	11,042	24,030
1872	36,433	11,406	25,027
1873	37,954	12,152	25,802

Sources: Register of Members, Vol. 3-1, 1854-1865, Vol. 3-2, 1854-1865, Vol. 4-1, 1866-1903, Vol. 4-2, 1866-1892, Vol. 4-3, 1866-1892, Vol. 4-4, 1866-1892, Vol. 5-1, 1869-1911, Vol. 5-2, 1868-1911, Vol. 5-3, 1870-1904, Vol. 5-4, 1873-1904 [Grand Secretary's office].

APPENDIX I
Table 3
Membership Occupations, 1856–1873

GOVERNMENT	1,110 (2.4%)	PROFESSIONAL SERVICE	6,719 (14.4%)
City/County/Township		Arts/Education	
alderman/mayor/ commissioner	22	artist/sculptor	88
constable/sheriff/ marshal	69	author/writer	7
judge/justice/ magistrate	53	clergyman/minister	1,017
fire/policeman	192	dancing master	1
recorder/registrar	37	editor/publisher	116
treasurer	20	musician/composer	120
State/Federal		professor/lecturer	10
executive official	5	schoolmaster/teacher	595
congressman/senator	4	Health Care	213
customs official	18	chemist/druggist	555
military/naval officer	225	dentist	224
mint worker	6	physician/surgeon	1,542
postal/master-worker	156	veterinarian	15
sailor/soldier	225	Other	
Other	29	architect	39
collector (tax, toll)	70	banker	105
foreign consul	2	businessman	11
prison keeper/warden	2	engineer (var.)	1,318
poor relief official	4	lawyer (attorney, conveyancer, counselor, solicitor, will-writer)	955
		scientist/inventor	1

NON-PROFESSIONAL SERVICE   6,854 (14.6%)

accountant/bookkeeper	818	inspector (var.)	47
actor/comedian/ showman	24	insurance agent/broker	144
agent (var.)	361	journalist/reporter	24
appraiser	5	laborer	333
auctioneer	25	lumberman/jack	617
barber/hairdresser	104	measurer (var.)	9
bottler	14	messenger	12
butler/valet	4	notary	4
carter/carrier	21	operator	23
cashier	50	optician	4
clerk (bank)	39	real estate agent	43
clerk (law/govt.)	34	superintendant	217
clerk (unspecified)	3,410	surveyor/rodman	50
cupper & leecher	4	telegrapher	160
dresser	7	undertaker	45
director	5	warehouseman	6
dispatcher/forwarder	65	other:	18
draftsman	10	(billiard saloon, catcher,	
gardener/seedsman	76	flagman, gatekeeper,	
guard	18	laundryman, paper carrier,	
hospital steward	4	paver, timekeeper,	
		wood corder)	

(Continued on next page)

APPENDIX I
Table 3 *(Cont.)*

ARTISANS   10,385 (22.3%)

BUILDING TRADES	4,387	(9.4%)	METAL CRAFTS	2,429	(5.2%)
builder/contractor	278		armorer/gunsmith	20	
bricklayer	228		blacksmith	803	
brickmaker	96		clock/watchmaker	169	
brickyard owner	9		coppersmith	20	
carpenter/joiner	2,077		foundryman/molder (var.)	466	
caulker	5		gold beater	9	
electrician	1		goldsmith/jeweller	196	
glassblower/maker	90		instrument maker (musical/		
glass cutter/carver	27		surgical)	21	
limeburner	12		ironmonger/ironworker	152	
mason	233		locksmith	14	
nailor/tacker	57		silversmith	38	
painter/gilder/			smith (unspecified)	21	
decorator (var.)	525		tinplate worker	45	
paperhanger	67		tinsmith/whitesmith	257	
plasterer	156		tool & die maker	12	
plumber	154		various makers	143	
roofer/slater	58		(axe, auger, bit, chain,		
sash maker	15		rod, nail, pipe, plane,		
saw mill owner	5		plow, pump & block,		
sawyer	70		saw, scale, shovel, sickle,		
stone/marble cutter	216		spring, stove, wire)		
wharf builder	8		misc. metal workers	43	

WOODWORKING	970	(2.1%)	CLOTHING TRADES	1,728	(3.7%)
blind maker	5		bleacher/dyer (var.)	53	
box maker	12		bootmaker	27	
cabinet/case maker	242		calico printer	2	
carver	24		cloth cutter	1	
chair/furniture maker/			clothier/mercer	77	
turner	117		fuller	6	
coach/wagon maker	323		furrier	15	
cooper/barrel maker	152		hatter	150	
last maker	7		hose/stocking finisher	2	
planer	3		shoemaker/cordwainer	511	
post board maker	2		spinner (cotton/wool)	52	
sign maker	6		tailor/pattern maker	482	
wheelwright	74		tanner/currier/skinner	258	
wood molder	3		weaver	41	
			wool carder/sorter	34	
			various makers	17	
			(belt, button, lace,		
			needle, suspender, oil		
			cloth, umbrella)		

MISCELLANEOUS CRAFTS   872 (1.9%)

bookbinder	66		potter	35
brushmaker	14		printer/typesetter	403
colourmixer	1		soap boiler/maker	19
cork cutter	1		upholsterer	50
engraver/lithographer	79		various makers	28
japanner/varnisher	13		(basket, candle, comb, ink,	
papermaker	31		looking glass, piano, powder,	
photographer (var.)	132		quill, whip)	

(Continued on next page)

APPENDIX I
Table 3 *(Cont.)*

RETAILERS	2,064 (4.4%)
bookseller/stationer	66
cutler	12
dealer/trader (unspec.)	148
dealer/trader	571
(carpets, coal, milk/	
butter/eggs, ice,	
stoves, leather, wool)	
florist	11
news agent	12
perfumer	4
peddler/salesman	800
store/shopkeeper	111
tobacconist/cigar maker/	
snuff maker	329

FOOD PREPARATION/ SALE	1,892 (4.0%)
baker/confectioner/	
pastry cook	252
bartender/waiter	19
brewer/malter	146
butcher	356
coffee roaster	9
cook	4
distiller	27
grocer	385
miller/mill employee	462
restaurateur/caterer	61
sugar refiner	13
victualer/provisioner	145
vintner	4
various makers	9
(butter, cheese, mineral	
water, vinegar)	

TRADE/COMMERCE	5,836 (12.5%)
boatbuilder	80
broker/import/exporter	142
mariner/seaman	193
merchant (unspec.)	4,801
merchant	295
(china, corn, commission,	
copper, dry goods, flour,	
hardware, liquor, lumber,	
powder, salt/grain, shoes,	
wine, wooden ware)	
pilot	69
rigger/ropemaker	16
sailmaker	46
sea captain	41
shipping/dock master	21
ship chandler	13
ship smith/shipwright	115
stevedore/packer	4

TRAVEL & TRANSPORTATION	2,569 (5.4%)
boatman/riverman/	
waterman	112
canaller/canal supervr.	9
coachman/omnibus driver	5
ferry operator	3
hotel/inn/tavernkeeper	827
liveryman/hostler	84
porter	8
railroad employee	1,115
(agent, baggage master,	
brakeman, conductor/	
trainman, insptr.,	
suprvr., worker)	
saddler/harness mender	201
stage coach driver/prop.	21
steamboat captain	58
steward	22
teamster/drayman/driver	69
transporter	6
travel agent	12
trunk maker	17

(Continued on next page)

APPENDIX I
Table 3 *(Cont.)*

INDUSTRIAL/ UTILITIES	4,165 (8.9%)	AGRICULTURE	4,617 (9.9%)
coal operator	28	agriculturalist	4
driller	8	beekeeper	2
engine maker	71	drover/herder	92
factory worker	41	farmer/yeoman	4,517
foreman/supervisor/ overseer	254	rancher/planter	2
furnace operator/maker	105		
gas works employee (gas fitter, gas maker, gas supervisor)	52	OTHER	579 (1.2%)
gauger	9	aeronaut/balloonist	1
glue boiler/maker	5	equestrian	8
heater/steamer	150	exhibiter	1
manufacturer (unspec.)	664	fancy business	2
manufacturer (cotton) (fringe, hardware, safe, salt, yarn)	229	fisherman/oysterman	8
		gentleman	158
machinist/mechanic	1,599	grand secretary	1
millwright	133	gymnast	2
miner/collier	470	landlord	67
oil company employee	225	linguist	1
pipefitter	2	mineralogist	1
roller	84	student	318
rubber worker	1	speculator	10
steel worker	19	standing stone	1
tile cutter	2		
water works employee	11		
welder	3		

TOTAL TRACEABLE	46,791	
PERCENT TRACEABLE	90.9	
TOTAL UNTRACEABLE	4,697	
PERCENT UNTRACEABLE	9.1	
TOTAL	51,488	

Sources: Register of Members, Vol. 3-1, 1854-1865, Vol. 3-2, 1854-1865, Vol. 4-1, 1866-1903, Vol. 4-2, 1866-1892, Vol. 4-3, 1866-1892, Vol. 4-4, 1866-1892, Vol. 5-1, 1869-1911, Vol. 5-2, 1868-1911, Vol. 5-3, 1870-1904, Vol. 5-4, 1872-1904 [Grand Secretary's office].

APPENDIX I
Table 4
Membership Occupations: Comparative Statistics, 1856–1873

	All Lodges	(%)	Phila.	(%)	Non-Phila.	(%)
Government	1,110	2.4	347	2.7	763	2.3
Professional Service	6,719	14.4	1,286	9.9	5,433	16.1
Non-Professional Service	6,854	14.6	1,914	14.7	4,941	14.6
Artisans						
Building Trades	4,387	9.4	1,435	11.0	2,952	8.7
Metal Crafts	2,429	5.2	770	5.9	1,658	4.9
Woodworking	970	2.1	328	2.5	642	1.9
Clothing Trades	1,728	3.7	701	5.4	1,027	3.0
Miscellaneous	872	1.9	455	3.5	417	1.2
Retailers	2,064	4.4	1,195	9.2	869	2.6
Food Preparation/Sale	1,892	4.0	725	5.6	1,167	3.5
Trade/Commerce	5,836	12.5	1,842	14.2	3,994	11.8
Travel & Transportation	2,569	5.5	553	4.2	2,016	5.9
Industrial/Utilities	4,165	8.9	1,281	9.8	2,885	8.5
Agriculture	4,617	9.9	96	0.7	4,521	13.4
Other	579	1.2	86	0.6	493	1.5
Number Traceable	46,791		13,013		33,778	
% of total membership		90.9		92.2		90.4
None Listed/Unreadable	4,697		1,097		3,600	
% of total membership		9.1		0.8		9.6
Totals	51,488		14,110		37,378	

Sources: Register of Members, Vol. 3-1, 1854-1865, Vol. 3-2, 1854-1865, Vol. 4-1, 1866-1903, Vol. 4-2, 1866-1892, Vol. 4-3, 1866-1892, Vol. 4-4, 1866-1892, Vol. 5-1, 1869-1911, Vol. 5-2, 1868-1911, Vol. 5-3, 1870-1904, Vol. 5-4, 1873-1904 [Grand Secretary's office].

APPENDIX I
Figure 1
Membership Statistics, 1856–1873

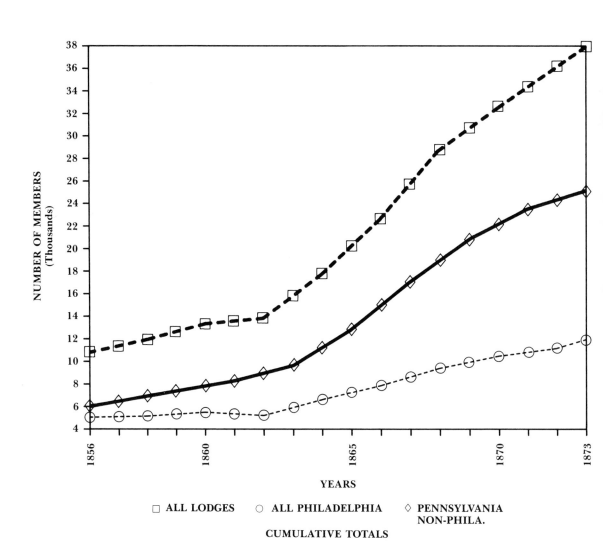

□ ALL LODGES   ○ ALL PHILADELPHIA   ◇ PENNSYLVANIA
                                                  NON-PHILA.

CUMULATIVE TOTALS

Sources: Register of Members, Vol. 3-1, 1854-1865, Vol. 3-2, 1854-1865, Vol. 4-1, 1866-1903, Vol. 4-2, 1866-1892, Vol. 4-3, 1866-1892, Vol. 4-4, 1866-1892, Vol. 5-1, 1869-1911, Vol. 5-2, 1868-1911, Vol. 5-3, 1870-1904, Vol. 5-4, 1873-1904 [Grand Secretary's office].

APPENDIX I
Figure 2
Membership Occupations, 1856–1873

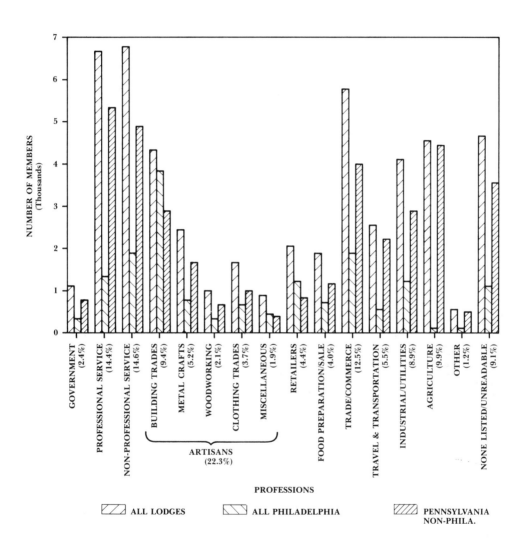

Sources: Register of Members, Vol. 3-1, 1854-1865, Vol. 3-2, 1854-1865, Vol. 4-1, 1866-1903, Vol. 4-2, 1866-1892, Vol. 4-3, 1866-1892, Vol. 4-4, 1866-1892, Vol. 5-1, 1869-1911, Vol. 5-2, 1868-1911, Vol. 5-3, 1870-1904, Vol. 5-4, 1873-1904 [Grand Secretary's office].

INDEX

Numbers in _italics_ refer to illustrations